The Relational Economy

The Relational Economy

Geographies of Knowing and Learning

Harald Bathelt

and

Johannes Glückler

OXFORD
UNIVERSITY PRESS

OXFORD

UNIVERSITY PRESS

Great Clarendon Street, Oxford OX2 6DP

Oxford University Press is a department of the University of Oxford.
It furthers the University's objective of excellence in research, scholarship,
and education by publishing worldwide in

Oxford New York

Auckland Cape Town Dar es Salaam Hong Kong Karachi
Kuala Lumpur Madrid Melbourne Mexico City Nairobi
New Delhi Shanghai Taipei Toronto

With offices in

Argentina Austria Brazil Chile Czech Republic France Greece
Guatemala Hungary Italy Japan Poland Portugal Singapore
South Korea Switzerland Thailand Turkey Ukraine Vietnam

Oxford is a registered trade mark of Oxford University Press
in the UK and in certain other countries

Published in the United States
by Oxford University Press Inc., New York

© Harald Bathelt and Johannes Glückler, 2011

The moral rights of the authors have been asserted
Database right Oxford University Press (maker)

First published 2011

British Library Cataloguing in Publication Data
Data available

Library of Congress Cataloging in Publication Data
Data available

Typeset by SPI Publisher Services, Pondicherry, India
Printed in Great Britain
on acid-free paper by
MPG Books Group, Bodmin and King's Lynn

ISBN 978–0–19–958738–4 (Hbk)
      978–0–19–958739–1 (Pbk)

1 3 5 7 9 10 8 6 4 2

For Clare, Emma, Fiona, Greta, and Katrin
without whose love and support this book would have been an impossibility

■ PREFACE

This book discusses interdisciplinary views of understanding and conceptualizing the changing global economy, by emphasizing a specific spatial perspective that mirrors unequal economic development, and selective specialization and growth processes. Recent economic developments that require further attention include the restructuring activities of existing economic cores, the rise of new industrial clusters with complex knowledge ecologies, the rapid spread of global production and innovation networks, as well as new geographies of knowledge creation and circulation, such as temporary clusters during international trade fairs or trans-local corporate knowledge networks at a global scale. This book aims to develop a coherent perspective on the changing relationship between territory and the organization and evolution of economic action. It draws on a relational framework that is used to answer specific questions related to the geography of the firm, within the context of a growing global knowledge economy. This leads to the formulation of many research questions which will be subsequently explored: How, for example, are firms, networks of firms, and production systems organized in the global economy, and why does this organization vary from place to place? What are the new geographies emerging from the need to create, access, and share economic knowledge, and sustain competitiveness? How, and in what ways, are local clusters and global production chains/networks intertwined and co-constituted? What are the impacts of global changes in technology, demand, and competition on the organization of production, and how does this vary between communities, regions, and nations?

The book develops an analytical framework that conceptualizes economic action as relational action. This relational understanding of human interaction aims to overcome the restrictions of an atomistic perspective, which views individuals as primarily driven by profit-maximization or other external behavioural imperatives. In contrast, a relational approach recognizes that values, interpretative frameworks, and decision-making practices are subject to the contextuality of the social institutions that characterize the relationships between human agents. The book applies this view to an analysis of economic action and interaction in a spatial perspective. Compared to conventional wisdom, this allows for alternative interpretations of why industrial agglomerations are successful, how local clustering and global interactions are interrelated, and why some places prosper while others do not.

A relational approach requires an investigation of the institutional context in which firms operate, be it related to a firm's value chain or to regional and national regulations. It also involves an analysis of how firms are shaped by past decisions and how these decisions limit and/or enable present-day actions. Of course, this does not mean that economic decisions are predetermined and easily predictable. They can always take off in different or new directions. Within the context of an industrial agglomeration, for example, it becomes clear that firms are dependent both on cost considerations and non-cost-related factors, such as inter-firm relations and conventions. This book will discuss these issues systematically and apply them to processes of knowledge creation and innovation. Space is often at the heart of geographical analyses. However, rather than treating space as the main object of enquiry, a relational approach focuses on the evolutionary and institutional dimensions of economic interaction in a *spatial perspective*. In this conceptualization, neither space nor regions but economic relations within and across different geographies at different scales are central to the analysis.

The book's main points of departure are the conceptual and empirical findings from studies on relational economic action in spatial perspective. This re-conceptualization aims to capture diverse conceptual debates in the social sciences and develop a coherent analytical framework for studying new geographies of economic relations. Moreover, a relational economic geography seeks to overcome some of the structural problems associated with traditional accounts in regional science. On the one hand, some of this work tends to focus on regions and other spatial representations, and the identification of their economic attributes. Regions are sometimes treated as if they were actors, while the real agents – for instance, the people who act and interact within firms and other organizations to produce economic value – are neglected. On the other hand, traditional approaches often use spatial variables related to distance as an explanatory factor in order to explain location decisions and the spatial distribution of economic activities. Such research has neglected the role of agents who actively shape their environment by involving local partners in production, by training workers, by putting pressure on policymakers to implement support policies, or by mobilizing extra-local support.

The relational approach takes such criticisms seriously and develops an alternative research design that is applicable to a variety of different research fields in economic geography, urban economics, and economic sociology. This research builds upon prior conceptual and empirical work on the changing knowledge economy, cluster conceptions, intra- and inter-firm linkages, and the development of global networks. Empirically, our focus is to explore the development of new and renewed 'geographies of economies', be it related to knowledge-based clusters, temporary face-to-face interaction, or international production networks and virtual knowledge flows. This book aims to develop this approach into a coherent conceptualization that attracts interest and a broad readership from within the field of geography, as well as economics, management studies, sociology, and political science. The goal is to contribute to contemporary debates about the role of economic, social, cultural, and political forces in spatial perspective. The book intends to contribute to and stimulate discussions about 'spatial turns' across different disciplines, and is situated within the context of debates about how best to conceptualize and structure future research in the social sciences.

The overarching agenda of this book is, thus, to demonstrate the value-added of a relational approach, and to lay out how it differs from conventional approaches in economic geography and related disciplines. We aim to illustrate how such an approach can be fruitfully applied to investigate pressing contemporary questions in a spatially varied knowledge-based economy. This involves a discussion of conceptual, methodological, and policy-related questions. In contrast to other work, this book develops a consistent framework from the bottom up and applies it systematically to empirical case studies in different local, regional, national, and cross-local contexts. The case studies reveal how a diverse mixture of methods can be used in a relational framework, spanning from qualitative interview-based work to quantitative network analysis.

This book has benefited enormously from ongoing collaborations and regular exchanges with friends and colleagues who have had a major impact on our understanding, and who continue to challenge our thinking in many ways. The ideas and conceptualizations presented in this book could not have evolved without these critical inputs. It should be clear, however, that the limitations and imperfections in this book are solely our responsibility. We have particularly benefited from intensive collaborations with Thomas Armbrüster, Christian Berndt, Jeff Boggs, Ron Boschma, Gordon Clark, Heiner Depner, Uli Dewald, Meric Gertler, Armin Gräf, Katrin Kappes (formerly Griebel), Anders Malmberg, Peter Maskell, Nina Schuldt, Mike Taylor, Caroline von Bernuth (formerly Jentsch), Guido Zakrzewski, and Gang Zeng. We are also very much indebted to Pengfei Li, Andrew Munro, Ben Spigel, Phil Turi, and Clare Wiseman for providing us with critical comments on previous book drafts, or parts thereof, and to Patrick Cohendet, Gilles Duranton, Rod Haddow, Gerald Romsa, Eike Schamp, Allen Scott, Michael Storper, and Peter Wood for valuable discussions at various stages of the project. Furthermore, we would like to thank Alexandra Kaiser for editing the visual content and Heike Dennhard, Kristina König, and Anna Mateja Schmidt for technical support in preparing the manuscript. We are especially grateful to Rachael Gibson for her superb editing job of the manuscript. Finally, we are indebted to the Oxford

University Press team, especially David Musson and Emma Lambert, for their fantastic support, and the anonymous advisors for very helpful and constructive suggestions that have significantly helped to shape the final version of this book, and enforced consistency in our argument.

Harald Bathelt and Johannes Glückler
Toronto and Heidelberg, September 2010

■ TABLE OF CONTENTS

■ LIST OF FIGURES

■ LIST OF TABLES

■ PERMISSIONS

The arguments put forward in this book are based on ideas that have developed and were published in the form of journal articles, book chapters, and working papers over the past decade. Although the book does not reproduce any of these sources, it draws on the ideas developed there in the sense that it is part of an ongoing academic project, and is an expression of the evolution in our conceptual and empirical academic activities. Acknowledgements to the original sources are as follows:

Some of the ideas presented in Chapters 1–3 draw from work published in *Journal of Economic Geography* 3 (2003): 117–144 and *Progress in Human Geography* 30 (2006): 223–236. Chapter 4 is based on ideas published in *Environment and Planning A* 37 (2005): 1545–1563. The conceptual and empirical arguments of Chapter 5 draw from studies published in *European Planning Studies* 10 (2002): 583–611 and *GeoJournal* 60 (2010). Parts of Chapter 6 are based on a publication in *Regional Studies* 41 (2007): 949–962. Chapter 7 draws on work originally published in *Progress in Human Geography* 28 (2004): 31–56, *Regional Studies* 39 (2005): 105–127, and *Environment and Planning A* 40 (2008): 1944–1965. Chapter 8 is developed from material published in *Environment and Planning A* 37 (2005): 1727–1750 and *Journal of Economic Geography* 6 (2006): 369–393. The material presented in Chapter 9 has been developed from ideas and empirical material published in *SPACES online* 6, 2008-04 and *Regional Studies* 42 (2008): 853–868. Chapter 10 draws from material published in *Geographische Zeitschrift* 96 (2008): 125–139, and Chapter 11 is based on an analysis published in *Zeitschrift für Wirtschaftsgeographie* 52 (2008): 163–179.

Permissions to draw on ideas from other publications are gratefully acknowledged from the following: We wish to thank Oxford University Press and Sage Publications, London, Los Angeles (http://online.sagepub.com) with respect to Chapters 1–3; Pion Limited, London with respect to Chapter 4; *European Planning Studies*, Taylor and Francis Group (http://www.informaworld.com), and Springer Science+Business Media with respect to Chapter 5; Taylor and Francis Group (http://www.informaworld.com) with respect to Chapter 6; Pion Limited, London, Sage Publications, London, Los Angeles (http://online.sagepub.com), and Taylor and Francis Group (http://www.informaworld.com) with respect to Chapter 7; Pion Limited, London and Oxford University Press with respect to Chapter 8; Taylor and Francis Group (http://www.informaworld.com) and *SPACES online* (http://www.

spaces-online.com) with respect to Chapter 9; Franz Steiner Verlag (http://www.steiner-verlag.de) with respect to Chapter 10; and *Zeitschrift für Wirtschaftsgeographie* with respect to Chapter 11.

Permissions to reproduce figures were kindly granted by Oxford University Press for Figure 2.1 (*Journal of Economic Geography* 3: 132), Taylor and Francis Group (http://www.informaworld.com) for Figure 5.1 (Power and Scott, eds., 2004: *Cultural Industries and the Production of Culture*: 151), Springer Science+Business Media for Figure 5.2 (*GeoJournal* 60), Taylor and Francis Group (http://www.informaworld.com) for Figure 6.1 (*Regional Studies* 41: 954), Geography Compass and Blackwell Publishing for Figure 7.1 (*Geography Compass* 1: 1292), Armin Gräf and Pion Limited, London for Figure 7.2 (*Environment and Planning A* 40: 1956), Oxford University Press for Figure 8.1 (*Journal of Economic Geography* 6: 381), Nina Schuldt and Taylor and Francis Group (http://www.informaworld.com) for Figure 9.1 (*Regional Studies* 42: 856), and Franz Steiner Verlag for Figures 10.1 and 10.2 (*Geographische Zeitschrift* 96: 134, 135).

1 Introduction

Since the 1990s, we have witnessed a growing importance of knowledge in processes of producing and servicing goods, and distributing them to markets. We have also observed the rise of a knowledge-based economy that is characterized by a number of specific developments, some of which deserve closer attention. First, knowledge has become an integral part of the development of modern technology-based industries, such as biotechnology and nanotechnology, as well as producer-related services, such as finance and consulting. Second, processes of knowledge generation and innovation have become central even to firms in traditional industries in order to stay ahead of international competitors, occupy markets niches, and maintain a competitive advantage. Third, knowledge has developed into a key resource of economic production, aside from material resources. Fourth, it appears that the processes by which knowledge is acquired and transformed into economic value have become deeply embedded in economic practices. These processes seem to steadily accelerate and have become critical drivers of economic change. In this sense, the increased circulation and production of knowledge contributes in important ways to the radicalization of modernity (Giddens 1990). This book takes these dynamic changes as a starting point to develop a relational conceptualization that aims to better understand the evolving knowledge economy.

In this context, we emphasize two aspects in particular that suggest the need for such a conceptualization. On the one hand, it is difficult to determine the price of knowledge because its demand and supply are uncertain and, therefore, hard to quantify. As a consequence, conceptions that are based on conventional market mechanisms of supply and demand have difficulty understanding specific outcomes in knowledge-based interactions. On the other hand, knowledge is not a homogenous product that is readily available across different places. It is highly contextual in nature and parts of the knowledge basis are not easily transferred between contexts and/or places. Furthermore, processes of knowledge creation are evolutionary and cumulative in nature. This leads to different development paths and specialization processes between regions and national states. A relational view of economic action and interaction takes these aspects into account. Although it is assumed that economic agents generally strive for individual economic well-being, their actions do not follow a simple optimization logic. First, decisions are shaped by the networks of social and institutional relations within which individuals and firms as collective agents operate. They are therefore highly contextual. Second, economic actions depend on prior action and past decisions. As such, they are path-dependent. Third, this does not imply that economic actors stick slavishly to existing structures and follow established technological trajectories. In fact, agents can, for instance, decide to establish new strategies and deviate from given trajectories to gain a unique competitive advantage. As a consequence, economic action and interaction are contingent.

In this introduction, we establish the contextual background for the development of a relational conceptualization. Although our primary interest and focus of enquiry relate to processes of knowledge creation and innovation, the relational conceptualization can be applied more broadly to processes of economic action and interaction. This perspective is derived from various debates and trends in the social sciences and, in particular, economic geography. What these debates all have in common is a recognition of the limited explanatory power of conventional explanations regarding the dynamics of the knowledge economy. In this chapter, we draw on these debates and intellectual turns before identifying some of the commonalities and origins of relational thinking that have arisen over time. Without providing an exhaustive review of this literature, we highlight three complementary conceptions that have developed parallel to our approach and have informed our thinking. These are the milieu school, which focuses on the social foundations of regional innovation, conceptions of global value chains and production networks, and ideas of geographies of practices. From this vantage point, we emphasize the importance of a spatial perspective in analysing the knowledge economy. In light of these issues, this chapter will outline the structure of the book, and its attempt to provide a consistent relational conceptualization of economic action and interaction in spatial perspective.

1.1 Geographic Turns in the Social Sciences

Since the 1990s, the basic foundations of economic geography have become the focus of increased scrutiny. Beyond the more fundamental critique of traditional approaches, several intellectual turns have been proposed with a view to rejuvenating, reorienting, or radically restructuring the field. This has ignited a controversial debate in the field of economic geography and other social science disciplines, such as economics and sociology, which centres on the question of what a novel economic geography should look like in terms of its research programme, key focus, and methodology (Perrons 2001). This is, partially, a reaction to the work of Krugman (1991), Fujita et al. (2001), and others who claimed to have developed a 'new economic geography' from outside the discipline. This work has been interpreted as an 'economic turn' which offers an interesting economic perspective on conventional problems of spatial distribution and equilibrium, based on an analysis of increasing returns, transportation costs, and other traded interdependencies (Martin and Sunley 1996). The corresponding approaches would, however, be better classified as 'geographical economics', because they are primarily directed towards the field of economics. They do not provide a widely applicable basis for all research in economic geography and focus primarily on quantifiable factors, while neglecting the complex social realities of economic life (Martin and Sunley 1996; Bathelt 2001*b*). This 'turn' does not provide a comprehensive research programme for economic geography because '. . . the new economic geography ignores almost as much of the reality they study as old trade theory did' (Krugman 2000: 50). Although recognizing important progress in the work of geographical economists (e.g. Duranton and Puga 2001; Glaeser 2005; Duranton 2007), economic geographers, such as Scott (2004), do not view this as a comprehensive long-term perspective of the discipline.[1]

While this literature brings economic geography closer to the core ideas of neoclassical economics,[2] others have claimed that there is a need for an 'institutional turn' (Amin 1999, 2002) or a 'cultural turn' (Crang 1997; Thrift 2000*b*; Berndt and Boeckler 2009). In this vein, Amin and Thrift (2000) suggest a fundamentally different direction, capitalizing on concepts and theories from other social sciences. Amin and Thrift (2000: 4) provocatively claim that economic geography is no longer able to 'fire the imagination' of researchers. They ask for a critical reflection and renewal of the field's basic goals, concepts, and methods. Diverse reactions to their contribution have stimulated a debate, which has unfortunately been dominated by discipline-specific political arguments, opinions, and claims. In essence, it focuses on the question of whether economic geography should be closely associated with economics or lean more towards social, political, and cultural studies. Thrift (2000*a*), for instance, identifies a growing interest in the cultural dimension of economic relations, as well as the role of economic issues in cultural studies.

While Amin and Thrift (2000) propose a cultural turn away from neoclassical economics, their critics emphasize the importance of and existing linkages with economic theories as a foundation of economic geography (Martin and Sunley 2001; Rodríguez-Pose 2001). We agree with Martin and Sunley (2001) that this debate is partly based on false dualisms, such as economic versus sociological/cultural theory and quantitative versus qualitative methodology. In our view, the discussion is unclear because it mixes normative accounts of the discipline's policy implications with epistemological and methodological arguments. The problem of diverse turns is that they are guided by political arguments and opinions which lead to conflict between the fields. They are based on a strong critique of existing approaches, yet introduce new rigidities. In principle, the question is raised as to which discipline is best suited to understanding the contemporary economic world. Each turn favours some aspects of the current social and economic reality while neglecting others.

The debate is also somewhat misdirected in that it aims to separate economic and social influences. In our view, the decisive question is not about whether economic geography should be 'economized' or 'culturalized' but about how to understand the complex interplay between the two. The economic and the social are fundamentally intertwined; they are dimensions of the same empirical reality. As such, they should be studied in the context of a dialogue between perspectives, rather than in mutual exclusion and reductionist prioritization (Stark 2000). This is what we emphasize in the relational conceptualization developed in this book.

The goal of our enquiry is to demonstrate the utility of a relational conception of economic action and interaction in conducting research on the dynamics of localized and cross-local economic processes, particularly when such processes relate to the generation and distribution of knowledge and innovation. In emphasizing the role of socio-institutional relations in economic processes and their outcomes, this book aims to provide a spatial perspective and sensitivity to spatial variation in the developing global knowledge economy. Our call for a relational conceptualization responds to the growing scholarly dissatisfaction with existing approaches that appear too deterministic and narrow-minded. Yet, we do not view this as another turn, because we do not try to isolate aspects of human life which are inseparable (see also Hudson 2004). As emphasized in Chapter 2, this conceptualization integrates economic, social, cultural, institutional, and political aspects of human agency (Bathelt and Glückler 2003*b*; Glückler and Bathelt 2003*a*). Complementing earlier work, this conceptualization pays explicit attention to the roles of institutions, economic agents and their strategies, as well as the connection between the micro- and macro-level, as suggested by Schamp (2003), Zeller and Messerli (2004), Sunley (2008), and Jones (2009).

By recognizing the structural problems in traditional approaches, which serve as a barrier to adequately understanding economic processes, relational conceptions have developed based on a micro-level perspective. Such conceptions focus on the actors in economic and social processes that result in agglomeration, economic specialization, uneven development, etc.[3] We argue that a relational perspective is particularly well suited to conceptualizing economic action and policy in spatial perspective. It also allows us to analyse the consequences of global interdependencies and their relation to processes of local concentration and specialization.

1.2 **Origins of Relational Thinking**

In tracing the roots of relational thinking, we are immediately struck by the number of individuals and research groups that have developed ideas which run parallel to the views and attitudes expressed in this book. Although it is impossible to engage in a comprehensive discussion of these different bodies of research, the following sketch highlights those streams that have been at the core of the relational conceptualization developed here.

Since the early 1980s, there has been a growing recognition that economic action is strongly shaped by the particular context in which it takes place and that firms operating, for instance, in a setting of industrial restructuring may successfully employ different strategies to overcome crises. One voice, Gordon Clark, used such ideas to reject the notion of spatial determinism in such a setting (e.g. Clark 1983). These ideas have been subsequently developed into an agency-centred approach in economic geography (Clark and Tracey 2004), and a broader scepticism towards the problem of overgeneralization in abstract theorizing (Clark 2005). From a different perspective, Andrew Sayer has been a key voice through his work on contingency in economic action and critical realism (e.g. Sayer 1992, 2000).

Around the same time, Doreen Massey, Nigel Thrift, and, later, Ash Amin, and others in the United Kingdom separately or jointly rejected the idea of conceptualizing economic geography as a spatial science which neglects the economic and social realities of economic action (e.g. Massey 1985; Amin 1994). This work has since developed to include sophisticated actor–network conceptions, de-territorialized views of knowledge creation, and a relational construction of spatial identity (e.g. Thrift 2000a; Allen 2003; Amin and Cohendet 2004; Massey 2004). This work has emphasized the increasing complexity of networks and power relationships that develop across spatial entities (Allen et al. 1998). Some of this work has become the basis of the 'cultural turn' in economic geography (e.g. Amin and Thrift 2003; Lee 2002; Thrift 2000b).[4]

Parallel to these developments, a Californian school of economic geography developed around Allen Scott, Michael Storper, and Richard Walker in the early 1980s. In this work, the space-creating forces of economic agents and windows of locational opportunity are the focus of attention, fundamentally breaking with the deterministic spatial logic of traditional approaches (e.g. Walker and Storper 1981; Scott 1988; Storper and Walker 1989). Later, the concept of untraded interdependencies was introduced to further explain the genesis and growth of industrial agglomerations (see also Storper and Venables 2004), as opposed to the traded interdependencies which have been the focus of traditional approaches. Emphasizing the role of context, Storper's conceptualization (1997c) of the 'holy trinity' defines technology, organization, and territory as three overlapping constituent pillars that create and shape regional worlds of production, and their contexts (Storper 2009).

These and other studies have influenced the Manchester school around Peter Dicken, Neil Coe, Martin Hess, Henry Yeung, and others in their work on global production networks, particularly since the 2000s. This work fundamentally builds upon a network conception of economic action (Yeung 1998) which emphasizes global connectivities (e.g. Dicken and Malmberg 2001; Dicken et al. 2001; Henderson et al. 2002). It suggests a spatial perspective in the analysis of global production networks and criticizes the narrowly conceived implications of many regional and cluster studies. Furthermore, this work emphasizes aspects of socio-institutional and cultural embeddedness in international economic interaction (Coe and Bunnell 2003; Dicken 2005).

Parallel to these developments, we have formulated a relational approach that originates in the context of German research traditions (e.g. Bathelt and Glückler 2003a, 2003b; Glückler and Bathelt 2003b). This approach is based on evolutionary and institutional conceptions and focuses on a relational understanding of economic action which is analysed in spatial perspective. The core categories of analysis revolve around interactive learning and organizational, evolutionary, and innovation processes. These ideas were based on a critique of the state of German economic geography[5] at that time, inspired by the work of the Californian school.[6] This conceptualization was also inspired by the innovative work of other economic geographers, during the 1990s, who had already identified some of the limitations and fallacies of traditional approaches (e.g. Gertler 1993, 1995; Grabher 1993a, 2002a; Maskell and Malmberg 1999b; Malmberg and Maskell 2002).

Although the different relational perspectives reflect a variety of disciplinary traditions,[7] they represent a decisive reorientation away from traditional conceptualizations of economic geography. This body of research – although not always under the umbrella of a relational conception – is united by some or all of the following characteristics (Bathelt and Glückler 2002, 2003c, 2003b; Boggs and Rantisi 2003; Ettlinger 2003; Glückler and Bathelt 2003a; Hudson 2004; Yeung 2005; Lee 2006):

1. *Focus on agents instead of space.* This work rejects the development of a spatial ontology that treats territories as if they were agents. Instead of primarily dealing with spatial representations, such as regions and national states, it stresses the opportunities and constraints of economic action and interaction within and across territorial boundaries (Bahrenberg 2002).
2. *Micro-level focus.* As a consequence, these approaches rely on a micro-level perspective that aims to understand the reasons and strategies behind economic decisions in order to explain economic processes in spatial context. The emphasis is on understanding individual and collective economic action

within macro-level contexts. This, in turn, leads to research designs that often make use of qualitative methodologies and mixed-method approaches.

3. *Economic action as social action.* This body of work criticizes the conventional assumption that economic agents possess a perfect understanding of the world and are capable of making optimal decisions to maximize their individual welfare. It focuses, instead, on the role of social context in shaping and pre-structuring economic decisions. Within such contexts, agents are motivated by goals that do not necessarily lead towards an absolute optimum, as this outcome might be neither feasible nor visible under the existing socio-institutional conditions.

4. *Institutional analysis.* As such, institutional arrangements are at the core of studies that try to understand patterns of economic behaviour or the stabilization of economic relations in space. Stable patterns do not necessarily constrain economic action or create barriers to future action; they also establish decisive conditions that enable economic interaction within and between territories, and provide the foundation for knowledge creation and innovation.

5. *Process focus.* Many studies are also characterized by a strong tendency to move beyond spatial description or static structural analysis. They aim to provide a deeper understanding of social and economic *processes*. In terms of methodology, qualitative methods, such as interview techniques, field observations, and ethnographic approaches, become more important in this work.

6. *Global–local relationships.* Instead of focussing on a specific spatial scale of analysis, such as the local or regional level, studies increasingly view the local level in relation to, and as shaped by, trans-local, trans-regional, trans-national, and global relationships. Within local/regional contexts, this work emphasizes the effects of globalization on economic organization and investigates the resulting global–local tensions.

7. *Proactive regional policy.* Such studies are consistent with a shift from a problem-solving policy mode to the design of proactive regional policy perspectives (e.g. Cooke and Morgan 1998; Asheim and Herstad 2003). This sometimes relies on explicit actor–network frameworks.

1.3 **Related Conceptions**

Especially since the 1990s, a number of conceptions have emerged from the fields of economic geography, regional economics, and international business that share a common scepticism about the explanatory power of conventional neoclassical economic conceptions in understanding the interrelated nature of social and economic processes within and across spatial contexts. We briefly introduce three conceptions that are related to the relational approach developed in this book. These are the milieu school, with its focus on exploring the social foundations of regional innovation, conceptions of global value chains and production networks, and ideas of geographies of practices.[8]

1.3.1 REGIONAL INNOVATION IN THE MILIEU SCHOOL

The research approach of the milieu school shares a great affinity with the relational approach developed here. This is particularly apparent in the work of Crevoisier (2001, 2004). The milieu school of the *Groupe de Recherche Européen sur les Milieux Innovateurs (GREMI)* is interested in understanding the reasons why some regions are characterized by a high degree of innovativeness (e.g. Fromhold-Eisebith 1995; Crevoisier 2001). Based on a critique of neoclassical economics, this approach develops a wider social perspective in explaining the mechanisms that foster regional innovation, particularly in networks of small- and medium-sized firms (Camagni 1991*b*; Ratti et al. 1997). It emphasizes economic and social practices and the role of institutions in innovation. As such, the milieu school conceptualizes influences that go beyond conventional cost factors. This view takes the role of context seriously and investigates how socio-institutional conditions shape the social division of labour between the firms in a region (Crevoisier and Maillat 1991).

Through this work, it has become clear that successful regional innovation is not just a result of the individual endeavours of firms. Instead, innovation performance is closely related to the firms' local environment and socio-institutional setting, or their milieu (Crevoisier and Maillat 1991). A milieu is viewed as a territorial production system consisting of a multitude of material, labour market, technology, and information linkages which develop within a particular commodity chain (Maillat 1998). Due to spatial proximity, firms almost automatically know about the quality and capabilities of potential partners and suppliers. This allows them to form regional partnerships at a low cost. The resulting networks of social relations form an integral component of the regional socio-institutional structure. Affiliation to the same production system and its technological traditions stimulates cooperation between the firms and promotes interactive learning and joint problem-solving (Bramanti and Ratti 1997). This is because norms, routines, shared trust, and a unique technology culture evolve over time and are largely accepted by the local agents, thus creating a particular order that is conducive to collective action.

By focussing on the regional agents, their socio-institutional contexts, and resulting networks of information flows, transactions, and problem-solving activities, the milieu approach overcomes some of the problems of regional multiplier models. As opposed to the latter approaches, it analyses regional innovation and growth based on the division of labour and interdependencies between the firms in a region. At the same time, however, the milieu school tends to overemphasize the importance of internal networks while downplaying the significance of external relationships. Although Camagni (Camagni 1991*b*: 140) rightly suggests that 'the "milieu" has to open up to external energy in order to avoid "entropic death" and a decline in its own innovative capability', not much is said about the nature of social relations with agents from outside the milieu.

In more recent work, the milieu school has become more aware of the importance of linkages with extra-local agents to secure access to information about markets, competitors, and technologies in other regions and national states (Ratti et al. 1997; Crevoisier 2001). Maillat (1998) raises some important questions about what distinguishes a stagnant from a creative innovative milieu and what forces enable a milieu to grow. To answer these questions, he makes a distinction between the internal and external relations needed to secure a milieu's success. According to this perspective, the potential of actors to advance innovation processes relies on their capability to acquire specialized information and resources from external sources and apply them in the internal divisions of labour. Such transfers are necessary if the milieu's actors are to reproduce their competencies and extend their competitiveness (Maillat et al. 1997).

A good example of the relation between internal and external structures is the development of the Swiss watch industry and its crisis. The regional crisis, which occurred in the 1970s and 1980s, was due to a collective underestimation of the new technological trajectories (i.e. quartz and digital technologies) developed in other countries, which were creating new market opportunities for the producers in these countries (Glasmeier 2000). Research results indicate that it was the opening of the Swiss production system, the integration of external partners into regional networks, and the development of new institutional settings related to new research agendas and training facilities that enabled many producers to collectively overcome the crisis (Maillat et al. 1997). In general, however, the milieu school has paid more attention to processes that take place inside the milieu than to those occurring outside of it.

1.3.2 GLOBAL VALUE CHAINS AND PRODUCTION NETWORKS

As opposed to the milieu school, the literature on global commodity/value chains and global production networks is not based on a territorial view. It focuses, instead, on the international production and marketing linkages that have increasingly developed around certain types of products, industries, or technology fields. Through processes of economic globalization, value-chain relationships have become more complex and spread-out to include a growing number of firms in different stages of the production process, located in an increasing number of countries throughout the world. The focus of this work addresses the changing nature of production and marketing linkages within the value chain. The spatiality of such dynamics is, however, often secondary in these analyses.

This is clearly visible in Gereffi's work (1994, 1999) on global commodity chains, originally analysing the apparel/clothing industry. This work recognizes that changes in fashion markets and in the organization of the retail sector have had a tremendous impact on the organization and social division of labour between US retailers and brand producers, on the one hand, and overseas factories and buyers associated with global sourcing strategies, on the other. As a consequence of this, Gereffi (1994) distinguishes two forms of governance that have developed: producer-driven versus buyer-driven commodity chains. These forms of governance are characterized by specific types of relationships and forms of power relations/control that have evolved in value-chain linkages. The first form is driven by backward linkages and production networks of large multinational manufacturers (e.g. in the automobile and computer industry); the second is dominated by large brand-name buyers (e.g. in the garment and toy industry).

Whereas the nature of power relationships and the spatial expressions of these networks have been somewhat neglected in this work, Humphrey and Schmitz (2002) are particularly interested in how the regionally concentrated producers of such value chains in developing countries could become involved in upgrading processes that reduce their dependency on the control centres and enable them to engage in the development of skills, knowledge, and competencies that potentially stimulate regional development. Their original distinction of different network forms of governance has developed further in the collaborative work of Gereffi et al. (2005). In combining different strands of the literature, they identify three variables that impact the type of governance form present in global value chains: (*a*) the degree of complexity, (*b*) the degree of codification, and (*c*) the capability of the supplier base. According to these variables, five different types of value chains can be distinguished. Aside from market-based value chains, there are modular and relational chains, both of which are characterized by a high level of complexity and a high level of supplier capability. Beyond this are captive and hierarchical chains, which are, in turn, characterized by a high level of complexity and a low level of supplier capability (Gereffi et al. 2005).

Although this work is characterized by functionalist arguments, is less concerned with agency, and tends to employ a linear understanding of power relationships (see also Henderson et al. 2002), it clearly goes beyond more deterministic conceptions of international production configurations and trade. Inspired by a reflection of these approaches, Dicken et al. (2001) suggest an actor–network-based understanding of global production networks. This perspective draws on the complex interrelationships of economic networks across different scales and emphasizes the tensions between networks and territories and the role of power relations, paying particular attention to the large transnational firms that control these networks (Henderson et al. 2002; Coe et al. 2003). This line of enquiry opens up possibilities for analysing production networks that span widely across countries by focussing on the role of the dominant agents in these networks (i.e. firms and states), and how they impact production conditions in different territories and at different levels of the production network. This first includes an analysis of how economic value is created, enhanced, and captured within these production contexts (e.g. Depner 2006; Dörry 2008; Sandmüller 2008). Second, it involves an examination of the nature and dynamics of power relationships. And, third, it investigates the embeddedness of value-creation and power relationships in social, cultural, and spatial contexts. The objective, here, is to provide a better understanding of the complex territorial and cross-territorial dynamics of economic organization in the sense of Allen et al. (1998).

Although the milieu school and the global value-chain literature develop a complex understanding of economic action in spatial perspective, they are both often viewed as extreme, competing conceptualizations. This is due to the tendency to explain economic success by drawing on the internal structure of social relations between local and regional firms in the milieu school, while emphasizing the advantages of international production organization and governance structures in cross-territorial perspective in the global value-chain literature.

1.3.3 GEOGRAPHIES OF PRACTICE

More recently, a so-called practice perspective has been established drawing on an explicit relational understanding of economic processes (Faulconbridge 2006; Ibert 2007; Jones 2007). In many ways, this perspective aims to overcome the binary distinction between local and global scales of analysis by focussing on the practices of firms, and, within these firms, on organizing and connecting production. This is done through an investigation of performative geographies (Lee 2006). Faulconbridge (2007), for instance, proposes a relational analysis of internationalization processes and their differing outcomes through an approach that differs from neoclassical approaches. By focussing on transnational law firms, Faulconbridge (2006) argues that firms are embedded in networks that cut across national systems. A micro-perspective is developed that helps to identify how management practices are socially constructed. It is argued that the internationalization processes of firms can vary significantly, even within a specific capitalist system (Jones 2007, 2008). While we do not argue in this book that the variation in the strategies and practices of multinational firms contradicts macro-conceptions, such as the varieties-of-capitalism approach (Hall and Soskice 2001*a*) or the conception of divergent business systems (Whitley 1999), the practice perspective convincingly demonstrates that firm behaviour does not follow a functional logic. The relational conceptualization suggested is very much in line with an emphasis on business practices in the context of processes of economic action and interaction.

The practice perspective emphasizes the role of firm-level analyses and qualitative methodologies (Yeung 2003). Important claims are also made regarding traditional understandings of knowledge bases in regional economies (Ibert 2007). In accordance with a relational conceptualization (Bathelt and Glückler 2005), Ibert (2007) criticizes the conventional treatment of knowledge as an object that can easily be appropriated, stored, and accumulated. In contrast, the practice perspective recognizes that knowing is situated in ongoing social practices of interaction. As such, knowledge is not exclusively produced in local networks. It results from the systematic circulation and exchange of ideas between local and non-local agents that are part of joint communities, or socially embedded in producer–user networks (Grabher et al. 2008), characterized by what could be termed 'relational proximity' (Amin and Cohendet 2004; Bouba-Olga and Grossetti 2008).

1.4 **Knowledge Flows in Spatial Perspective**

Recent approaches that deviate from conventional studies of industrial location and regional economic growth clearly demonstrate that the production, circulation, and transmission of knowledge is at the core of understanding the spatial distribution of industries and resulting geographical disparities. Regional specialization processes (Storper 1997*c*) are associated with knowledge flows that are unequal; they are spatially differentiated and produce different worlds of production and innovation. Knowledge cannot be easily or completely codified to be distributed electronically. As a consequence, it does not receive the status of a ubiquity that is available worldwide at a similar cost. In contrast, knowledge is often highly localized and selective in establishing cross-territorial linkages. It is associated with and produces different local, regional, or national development paths (Bathelt and Glückler 2005).

Questions related to how economic action and interaction take place in different locations and between agents in different places are a primary focus of the relational conceptualization (Bathelt and Glückler 2003*a*, 2003*b*). One important proposition is that it is not possible to analyse a regional or national economy independent from the economic and social relations between individual and collective agents. This does not imply, however, that spatial proximity automatically leads to the establishment of strong regional networks or self-sustaining local growth processes. Instead, it is 'relational proximity' which enables close social interaction and becomes a source of competitiveness (Amin and Cohendet 2004). Relational affinity may be influenced by, but is not restricted to, close geographical proximity. It can also develop between agents located in different regions, or even in different parts of the world, through the support of modern technological and institutional developments (Allen 2004; Bathelt and Schuldt 2008a; Bathelt and Turi 2011). This does not, of course, imply that analyses of the knowledge economy exclusively focus on relations. Firms are constantly confronted with and mobilize physical assets through individual or collective action. Economic action and decision-making processes are thus necessarily impacted by material resources and classical location conditions. Similarly, the intended and unintended results of economic action affect the structure of these resources (Werlen 1995; Crevoisier 2004). This creates a reflexive process through which resources are constantly shaped and reshaped. They are constituted in a relational way in that they rely on collective processes of resource generation and application (Glückler and Bathelt 2003b; Bathelt and Glückler 2005).

This requires that our view of the role of space in economic context be altered. First, due to the selective nature of knowledge flows and material linkages, a spatial perspective is of utmost importance in understanding the differences within and between regional and national economies. Second, instead of using space as an explanatory factor or research object, it is necessary to apply what we refer to as a spatial perspective, or geographical lens (Glückler 1999). This perspective acknowledges that economic action and interaction are always shaped by particular places and the relations between them. Through this, fundamental interdependencies between economic, social, and cultural processes within and between different places, regions, or national states are created. Economic activities necessarily interact with other economic and social processes that exist in the same places. The same agents participate in various processes simultaneously. In turn, different processes, in part, involve the same group of agents. Processes are necessarily interdependent, either because they take place within a region – involving ongoing knowledge flows among a group of agents – or between a group of regions – involving long-distance knowledge flows (Bathelt and Glückler 2003b; Glückler 2008). Interdependence can, of course, also result from the lack of direct relationships, resulting in different territorial development paths. Based on these and similar propositions, a relational agency-centred approach to economic geography (Clark and Tracey 2004; van Wezemael 2004) emphasizes processes of economic action and interaction that need to be analysed in spatial perspective. In the context of the geography of the firm, which is the central focus of this book, such an analysis would include the following:

- organizational forms that enable a more or less efficient division and integration of labour, including the variation of such forms from place to place (Sayer and Walker 1992; Maskell 2001*a*)
- the evolution of economic and social processes in different contexts (Storper and Walker 1989; Nelson 1995*a*)
- localized processes of innovation and knowledge creation (Dosi 1988; Storper 1997*c*; Maskell 2001*b*).
- the effects of communication and interaction between economic actors in the same or in different places (Gertler 1993, 1995; Lundvall and Johnson 1994).

Some of these aspects have been neglected or, at least, underexplored in traditional approaches, even though they are situated at the core of understanding localized growth and globalization tendencies in the knowledge-based economy (see also Hayter 2004).

1.5 **Structure of the Book**

This book is organized in four parts and consists of twelve chapters. Part I conceptualizes the foundations of relational thinking and lays out the main conceptual arguments that link an action-based understanding with a spatial perspective. Having revisited recent 'turns' in geographical, economic, and social thought, this chapter argues that a relational approach encourages an integrated perspective on economic processes. It also explores related conceptions of the approach.

Chapter 2 establishes the basic propositions of a relational analysis in spatial perspective. It develops the key concepts of contextuality, contingency, and path-dependence within a framework of relational action. The sources of these concepts are traced and the development of our conceptualization – from atomistic to relational behaviour, from universal to contextual action, and from reversible time to evolution – is emphasized. Chapter 2 also discusses the theoretical implications of such a perspective for the study of economic action. It combines the concept of space as a perspective with the notion of relational action.

Chapter 3 develops a conception that integrates structure and agency through the role of institutions. This chapter acknowledges the tensions between micro-level perspectives, which focus on the role of agency, and macro-level approaches, which emphasize the importance of structure. By reconciling these perspectives with an account of structuration theory, the concepts of institutions and evolution are introduced as sources of contextuality and hysteresis in spatial and temporal development. The relational perspective emphasizes the analysis of institutions and institutionalization at the micro-level. This is particularly helpful in understanding the construction and performative character of markets as institutional forms. The chapter discusses concepts and practices of market-making, and pays special attention to the contextuality of markets. The structure and dynamics of institutions establish conditions both for localized economic development and for internationalization.

Chapter 4 acknowledges that economic processes fundamentally depend on the transformation of resources into goods and services. It applies the relational perspective to the conventional notion of resources as discrete materials with well-defined use – values, and re-conceptualizes them as relational intangibles. This logic is applied to knowledge, as well as other important resources such as power and social capital. In using Penrose's theory (1959) of the growth of the firm as a starting point, the chapter introduces a new perspective on how agents create and use resources through the application of knowledge in social relations. The contextuality and contingency of this relational process of resource creation and consumption is situated within the context of a spatial perspective. Through this, the chapter develops an explicit relational conception of knowledge that is applied to different economic and geographical contexts in subsequent parts of the book.

Part II on relational clusters of knowledge applies the relational approach to the analysis of knowledge generation and innovation in spatial perspective. Empirical applications address local processes of clustering, global processes of internationalization, and the mitigating processes of local–global interdependencies.[9] This is applied to empirical examples in different industries in various regional and national contexts.

Chapter 5 develops a knowledge-based understanding of industrial clusters. It analyses the association between knowledge creation, clustering, and geographical proximity, which has been an important focus of research in the social sciences. While traditional explanations of industrial clustering assume that local networks have a positive effect on regional economic performance and well-being based on cost advantages, we argue that it is necessary to develop a knowledge-based understanding of clusters. Through this, it is possible to explain why some industrial clusters exist and continue to grow even though internal transaction networks are weak. We develop a multidimensional conceptualization of clusters, building upon the horizontal, vertical, and institutional dimensions. Particular attention is paid to the external dimension as it relates to cluster-external linkages, as well as the power relations between economic actors in the cluster. This conception is applied to an analysis of the growth of the chemical industry in the larger Yangtze Delta region in China. Our contribution highlights the role of institutional arrangements at the regional level and demonstrates how such arrangements can shape different cluster configurations. This analysis connects relational action with existing regional business models/structures.

In a similar fashion, Chapter 6 raises the question of how to conceptualize service clusters. It combines traditional conceptions such as urbanization advantages with conceptions such as reputation and economies of overview to investigate the positive externalities of service industry clustering in large cities–regions. The conceptual analysis demonstrates that conventional arguments of clustering, related to manufacturing industries, are ill-equipped to explain clustering processes in knowledge-intensive service industries. Instead, a relational account of mediated reputation effects adds to our understanding of urbanization advantages for advanced business services. This is applied to the case of consulting clusters in Germany.

Chapter 7 uses the conception of local buzz and global (i.e. trans-local) pipelines to explain how reflexive regional dynamics are generated. It transcends the traditional local–global dichotomy of the geography of knowledge and discusses the interconnection of local and non-local learning processes. The chapter highlights the conditions under which both tacit and codified knowledge can be exchanged locally and globally. A distinction is made between the learning processes that take place among actors embedded in a community by just being there (i.e. dubbed buzz) and the knowledge attained by investing in building channels of communication (called pipelines) to selected providers, especially those that are located outside the local milieu. It is argued that the coexistence of high levels of buzz and many pipelines may provide firms located in outward-looking and lively clusters with a set of particular advantages not available to outsiders. We use the case of the post-World War II growth of the Munich film and TV industry cluster, and its seemingly unexpected crisis in the early 2000s, to demonstrate the systemic weaknesses in the cluster's structure of social relations.

Part III of our book transfers these conceptions and findings to a wider perspective which analyses knowledge circulation across territories, that is, between regions and nations, and within global value chains. This part also introduces and discusses the role of new forms of virtual Internet-based interaction and temporary face-to-face interaction in complementing or replacing traditional forms of permanent face-to-face interaction.

Chapter 8 begins by analysing the processes through which knowledge-intensive services internationalize and create permanent dispersed locations in relative proximity to their clients. Since services based on specific and rare expertise are credential goods, clients buy these services on the basis of trust and reputation. This chapter revisits theories of the internationalization of the firm and criticizes conventional approaches for their implicit atomism. Instead, a relational theory of internationalization is developed, which builds on social institutions of trust and reputation, and promotes a network approach to internationalization. This is applied to the internationalization process of professional business services.

Chapter 9 conceptualizes international trade fairs as temporary clusters and suggests that temporary knowledge circulation during these events serves to initiate networks between permanent clusters, enabling the establishment of global or trans-local knowledge pipelines. This chapter claims that international trade fairs are important events which support economic processes of interactive learning and knowledge creation. Within a specific institutional setting, participants not only acquire knowledge through face-to-face communication with other agents, they also obtain information by observing and systematically monitoring other participants. This enables actors from different countries to exchange information about markets, products, and innovations. The variety of planned and unplanned meetings, and the rich ecology of information flows and different forms of interaction, creates what is referred to as global buzz. Firms use such events to consciously establish pipelines with new business partners worldwide. Using the example of two major flagship fairs in Germany, the chapter claims that these events have become important expressions of new geographies of circulation through which knowledge is created at a distance.

Chapter 10 transfers the relational conception to the analysis of global knowledge flows in corporate networks. This chapter opens the black box of intra-firm knowledge flows across distant geographies. The analysis refreshes the tradition of corporate geography and links it with research in organization studies to disentangle a relational view of the knowledge organization. The chapter uses the results obtained from detailed empirical network research in a global technology service firm to investigate the dimensions of global intra-firm knowledge flows and their vulnerability. The importance of the spatial perspective and the diversity of knowledge networks are discussed using the example of a corporate knowledge network.

Part IV discusses general ideas regarding a transfer of the relational approach to issues of economic policy in territorial context and shifts attention to possible challenges to economic action and interaction in the knowledge economy in the future.

Chapter 11 on relational policy consequences summarizes the key arguments and findings of the book and draws conclusions regarding the implications for a relational economic support policy; that is, a policy which focuses on economic agency and conceptualizes extra-regional linkages that connect territories with global resource and knowledge pools. To illustrate this, the chapter advances the foundations of a relational cluster policy.

Chapter 12 summarizes the main arguments of the relational conceptualization emphasizing differences compared with other approaches. It argues that relational thinking is particularly useful in analysing the global knowledge economy and its dynamic geographies. In the form of an outlook, it discusses conceptual and empirical challenges in the future.

Part I

Foundations of Relational Thinking

2 Relational Action in a Spatial Perspective

2.1 **Introduction**

In this chapter, we draw on the previous discussion about the various 'turns' in the social sciences to develop a conceptualization of the ways in which individuals, groups of individuals, firms, and other organizations exchange goods, services, and knowledge in order to satisfy their individual and collective economic goals. We develop this conceptualization of economic action and interaction using a micro-perspective that will be later extended to include broader macroeconomic and social structural conditions (Chapters 3 and 4). While our argument is interdisciplinary in nature, our discussion starts from the vantage point of shifting conceptualizations in the field of economic geography. This is a logical point of departure given our general emphasis on the importance of a spatial perspective in understanding variation in the organization and outcomes of economic structures and processes in different places.

Our discussion begins by identifying similar shifts in economic geography in different national contexts. We illustrate this through a comparison of recent academic practices in the form of a stylized description of regional-science-informed approaches. More generally, we describe a shift from a conventional neoclassical economic perspective towards a broader social-science-based perspective. In identifying the basic propositions of a relational perspective, our overarching goal is to develop a consistent interdisciplinary conceptualization that can be utilized in structuring investigations of economic action in different spatial contexts. This approach is integrative rather than divisive as it combines key insights from existing work in a variety of fields. Drawing on Storper's conceptualization (1997*b*, 1997*c*) of the so-called holy trinity, we introduce four fundamental dimensions of analysis in economic geography, that is, organization, evolution, innovation, and interaction (Bathelt and Glückler 2003*a*, 2003*b*). These four 'ions' represent central analytical categories in the study of economic structures and processes, and have been applied in different ways in many investigations across various disciplines. Although we view this primarily as a heuristic in analysing problems related to the geography of the firm and the organization of economic production in spatial perspective, we believe that this conceptualization can be adjusted to fit other areas of research in the social sciences.

2.2 **Transitions in Economic Geography**

As indicated in the work of Amin and Thrift (2000*b*), Scott (2000*b*), Barnes (2001), and others, a broad discussion has led to new debates about research programmes in economic geography, bringing attention to past and present transitions in the field. Without intending to oversimplify the complex and differentiated approaches within social science disciplines, we believe that the current changes in economic geography do not unfold incrementally to the extent that existing concepts are simply being improved or updated. Since the late 1980s, a wealth of new perspectives, methods, and conceptions has suggested compelling ideas to reconceptualize economic geography. In viewing the implications of this transition as paradigmatic, we interpret them in terms of a shift towards a relational economic geography (Bathelt and Glückler 2000, 2002, 2003*b*; Glückler and Bathelt 2003*a*). This evolves in phases of intense dialogue between different perspectives, yielding new arguments that may gain acceptance based on consensus and 'good reason' (Toulmin 1972).

In the context of post-World War II Anglo-American economic geography, Barnes (2001) identifies a shift from first-wave theory (i.e. the quantitative and theoretical revolution) towards new-wave theory (associated with the *cultural turn* and new economic geography). While the first approach aims to objectively formalize an independent reality, the latter describes an interpretative mode of theorizing that is open, critical, and reflexive. While such broad categorizations do not justify other disciplinary streams, such as Marxist or Feminist economic geography, they aim to describe a fundamental reorientation of the field. Interestingly, similar transitions have taken place in other national academic contexts. In Germany, for instance, economic geography witnessed a shift from a tradition based on *Länderkunde* (i.e. the science of regional description and synthesis) to *Raumwirtschaftslehre* (Schätzl 1998) or regional science, followed by what we conceptualize as a transition towards relational economic geography since the late 1990s. Although largely absent from the key debates featured in leading academic journals, other countries, such as Spain, have also witnessed a similar transition in recent years (Sánchez Hernández 2003).

We use the term 'regional science', or spatial analysis, to refer to those views of economic geography that are associated with the quantitative and theoretical revolution, which took place in the late 1950s and 1960s in American geography, when Isard (1956, 1960) established regional science as the science of the spatial order and organization of the economy (Böventer 1962). In this conceptualization, neoclassical economic theories and models were incorporated into economic geography through the integration of spatial variables, that is, the cost of transit and transport over distance. It was the objective of regional science to develop general theories and models of the spatial order of the economy. Location patterns, trade relations, and processes of agglomeration were typically explained using spatial parameters, such as distance, catchments areas, and their economic equivalents.

Since the late 1980s, a new set of ideas, conceptualizations, and models have been featured in academic publications; they have come to represent a counterweight to and critique of the regional science approach in economic geography. This body of work is characterized by multiple and often competing perspectives, as well as increased complexity in terms of the analysis of economic and social processes. Much of the critique expressed in this work can be illustrated through the simplified examples discussed below (for further examples, see Sayer 2000). This somewhat stylized discussion is not meant to deny the historical importance of the regional science tradition or its path-breaking findings. Rather, the paradigmatic reconstruction is used to identify a common set of problems and dimensions that are in need of re-conceptualization (see Scott 2000*b*).

2.2.1 EXAMPLE 1: SPATIAL CHARACTERISTICS AND THE ACTING REGION

A classical research focus of regional science is to explain why some regions grow faster than others. In order to provide an answer to this question, a number of consecutive stages of analysis are conducted in a spatial analysis. In the first stage, spatial characteristics are identified, including indicators of the regional infrastructure, labour force, other resources, and factor costs such as wage levels. In the second stage, statistical analyses (e.g. correlation and regression analyses) are conducted to uncover the typical features of both growing and shrinking regions. In many cases, causal mechanisms are derived from such analyses. It is argued, for instance, that low regional costs stimulate high regional growth. A major problem with this approach is that regions are treated as if they were the economic actors themselves having their own particular characteristics. One policy conclusion that may result from this view is that regions should lower their costs in order to stimulate growth.

Such an argument, however, neglects the fact that regions are not real actors. They are socially constructed entities, dependent upon the particular economic, social, cultural, and political settings in which people in firms and other organizations act and interact (e.g. Maskell 2001*a*). Sometimes, even one large dominant firm might cause regional growth or decline simply through its linkages with other regional agents (Romo and Schwartz 1995). This might be due to a change in the firm's overall global market strategy or a result of its integration into a global production network (Dicken et al. 2001). In other words, regional growth or decline may not be determined by the actual locational characteristics identified in a region (e.g. Schamp 2000*a*).

The limitations of this science of the spatial are nicely summarized in the following critique by Massey (1985: 11): 'There was an obsession with the identification of spatial regularities and an urge to explain them by spatial factors. The explanation of geographical patterns, it was argued, lay within the spatial. There was no need to look further.... This is an untenable position.... There are no such things as purely spatial processes; there are only particular social processes operating over space.'

2.2.2 EXAMPLE 2: LOCATION ANALYSIS AND SPATIAL INCENTIVES

Another major focus of regional science is the analysis of spatial distributions and location decisions (Isard 1956; Bartels 1988). The location analysis of a sector involves a particular methodology. In the first stage, the locational requirements of firms in a specific sector are listed. In the next stage, location factors and the particular features of individual regions and locations are identified. Finally, the locational requirements of firms and the locational characteristics of regions are systematically compared in order to find the best match. The underlying assumption of this approach is that firms seek to maximize their profits and, thus, choose the location that best satisfies their requirements, based on the region's inherent characteristics.

In this example, spatial attributes are again used as explanatory variables in analyses of location decisions and spatial distributions. In the context of quantitative regional science, Barnes (2001: 550) refers to such practices as fetishization because 'the social processes that actually produce such figures are hidden'. Critical aspects of social power underlying quantitative representations also remain concealed. In contrast, recent work in economic geography has come to realize that firms do not just act according to spatial attributes but that they actually create such spatial attributes in the first place (Scott 1988). Storper and Walker's model (1989) of geographical industrialization looks at how industries create their respective regions through the regular training of employees, recruitment of expertise from outside, support of newly established suppliers, outsourcing to other local suppliers and services, and learning processes with nearby customers. In this model, spatial structures are seen as being socially constructed. They are shaped by the complex interactions between regional actors and groups of actors, such as firms. Through a process of reflexive knowledge creation, these localized structures, in turn, influence economic decision-makers, their respective actions, and policies (Storper 1997c).

The work of economic geographers, such as Amin (1994), Lee and Wills (1997), Barnes and Gertler (1999), Bryson et al. (1999), Sheppard and Barnes (2000), Clark et al. (2000), and Coe et al. (2007), has led to new approaches and new ways of thinking that challenge the traditional regional science view.

As argued in Chapter 1, these new approaches have not yet established a fully coherent theoretical framework (e.g. Barnes 2001). What these studies share, however, is a critique of the traditional approach and its methodology, and a strong interest in understanding localized economic and social processes from an action perspective. In addition to economic theory, social theories and conceptualizations are also applied in these approaches to explain localized economic phenomena as an expression of both the economic and the social. From these trends, we recognize a comprehensive transition in economic geography towards a relational conceptualization which we characterize subsequently (for alternative characterizations, see Webber and Rigby 1996; Sheppard and Barnes 2000).

2.3 **Research Design for a Relational Perspective**

The following section draws on the above discussion to identify the core characteristics of a relational framework for the analysis of economic action and interaction in spatial perspective (Bathelt and Glückler 2000, 2003a, 2003b; Glückler and Bathelt 2003a). In suggesting this framework, our intention is *not* to proclaim a new, relational *turn* in economic geography that privileges certain aspects of human agency while neglecting others. In contrast, our conceptualization acknowledges the complex interdependencies among factors by aiming to integrate the economic and social dimensions of human action in spatial context (see Lee 2002). To this end, we identify important discrepancies between relational economic geography and regional science along five dimensions of the research design. These dimensions include the conception of space, object of knowledge, conception of action, epistemological perspective, and research goal. From this, we develop a relational framework for analysis that systematically focuses on the action and interaction of economic actors. The remainder of this chapter discusses the basic propositions of this framework (Table 2.1).

2.3.1 SPACE

A relational view of economic geography is based on the relationship between space and economy, which is contrary to that in regional science.[1] Specifically, regional science views space as a container that confines and determines economic action. From this perspective, space is treated as a separate entity that can be described and theorized independently from economic action. In contrast, a relational approach assumes that economic action transforms the localized material and institutional conditions of

Table 2.1. Changing research designs in economic geography

Dimensions of the research design	Regional science (or spatial analysis)	Relational economic geography
Conception of space	Space as object and causal factor	Space as perspective (geographical lens)
Object of knowledge	Spatially manifested consequences of action (structure)	Contextual economic relations (social practice, process)
Conception of action	Atomistic: methodological individualism	Relational: network theory/embeddedness perspective
Epistemological perspective	Neo-positivism/critical rationalism	Critical realism/evolutionary perspective
Research goal	Discovery of spatial laws of economic behaviour	Decontextualization of principles of socio-economic exchange in spatial perspective

Source: Adapted from Bathelt and Glückler (2003*b*: 124).

future economic action. Similar to Storper and Walker (1989), this approach suggests that economic actors are actively involved in the production of their own regional environments. Understanding the ways in which spatial categories and regional artefacts influence economic action thus requires an analysis of the particular economic and social contexts in which such action is embedded (Bahrenberg 1987, 2002). From both a social and an economic vantage point, spatial structures and processes have been largely under-conceptualized in regional science. In our view, space cannot be usefully employed as an explanatory factor in analyses of economic action; nor can it be treated as a separate research objective, isolated from economic and social structures and relations. Consequently, as space is not an object of causal power to explain social or economic action, it cannot be theorized (Hard 1993; Saunders 1989; Sayer 1985).[2] Of course, economic processes also have material outcomes (e.g. the material infrastructure) that are geographically localized and exist over long time periods. Since such structures clearly affect economic action and interaction in these localities, we will examine this issue further in Chapter 4.

Nonetheless, we believe that the action and interaction of economic actors should represent the core of a theoretical framework of economic geography, rather than space and spatial categories. Spatial scientists (see, for instance, Bunge 1973), however, treat spatiality as the object of knowledge in economic geography. They focus on the spatial laws governing human action, but neglect the actors themselves. Instead of treating space as a container, we provide a conceptualization of space as a *perspective* (Glückler 1999). In other words, we use space as a starting point for the development of particular questions about localized economic phenomena, but space, itself, is not our primary object of knowledge. We refer to this conception as the geographical lens. In such a conception, economic exchange, rather than space, becomes the main focus of analysis. Similarly, we do not seek to identify spatial laws but, instead, look for explanations of localized economic processes and their consequences. This is not to suggest that all economic action is locally or regionally bound; it simply implies that such action physically materializes in place. Indeed, economic action and interaction must take place somewhere, whether it is within particular places, regions, nations, or trading blocks or between them. It is precisely this spatial overlap of different social and economic processes that our geographical lens focuses on.

It is through the application of a distinct perspective to the study of an object of knowledge that discipline-specific research problems can be formulated. The spatial perspective thus encourages economic geographers to pose research questions about economic phenomena that are different from those typically asked by economists or sociologists. The brief example below illustrates this idea.

Depending on the particular disciplinary perspective used, observable changes in a firm's division of labour due to a structural crisis may lead researchers to formulate different sets of questions: A conventional sociologist might, for instance, focus on the consequences of this crisis in terms of the distribution of responsibilities and competencies within the work organization. An economist, on the other hand, may analyse the effects of this crisis on the firm's strategy, production programme, or new market opportunities. An economic geographer would employ an explicitly spatial perspective to investigate the different aspects and consequences of this crisis. Through a geographical lens, economic geographers might, for example, focus on how such a crisis impacts the local labour market, supplier relations, or the division of labour between different locations.

Without denying that such an example simplifies the problem, the point of emphasis here is that each perspective sheds light on some parts of the phenomenon while necessarily neglecting other issues. Any research findings that result from the use of a particular perspective can, however, be re-employed for new research purposes by applying a different perspective. Thus, a sociologist might use the results from a geographer's study on the localized consequences of the labour market to develop additional research questions regarding social inclusion or exclusion. An economist, in turn, might investigate it in terms of welfare and efficiency effects, and so forth. This demonstrates that space is not, in and of itself, the object of knowledge in economic geography. By using a spatial perspective, however, analyses in different disciplines might converge, generating more opportunities for constructive cross-disciplinary exchange.

2.3.2 OBJECT OF KNOWLEDGE

In contrast to regional science, a relational approach does not accept the space – economy, spatial systems, or spatial categories – as the core focus of a research programme. Instead, economic action and interaction are the central objects of knowledge in the analysis. Thrift (2000b: 698) has criticized the lack of explanation in traditional economic geography and insists that '... economic geographers cannot just be tied to the locational dimension as under-labourers for economists, noting down the "wheres" whilst economists do the "whys"'. Consequently, analyses in relational economic geography are based on a deeper understanding of the intentions and strategies of economic actors and ensembles of actors, and the patterns of how and why they behave the way they do. Economic action is viewed as being embedded in structures of social (and economic) relations; it is thus conceptualized as a highly context-specific process. Studies employing a relational approach thus focus on processes, such as institutional learning, creative interaction, economic innovation, and inter-organizational communication, and investigate these through a geographical lens, rather than simply uncovering spatial regularities and structures. Since economic processes and relations, broadly defined, are at the heart of this approach, it integrates (and requires) both economic and social theory. As such, the approach requires to relate to and to stimulate interdisciplinary debates.

2.3.3 ACTION

Similar to neoclassical economics, regional science employs an atomistic view of economic agents (Sheppard and Barnes 2000). In conventional analyses, the actions of economic agents are often seen in isolation from other agents and their institutional environments according to the rationale of a homo economicus. A relational framework, in contrast, emphasizes the importance of contextualizing human action. In other words, it views economic action as embedded in structures of ongoing social relations (Granovetter 1985; Grabher 1993a).

From an organizational perspective of economic production, this means that firms are not independent entities; rather, they are closely interconnected in communication and adjustment processes with their suppliers, customers, and institutions, and must be analysed accordingly.[3] An atomistic view of economic agents leads to a limited understanding of their activities as the role of context is neglected (Granovetter 1992b). The socio-institutional context creates opportunities for economic action and interaction that would otherwise not exist. From these opportunities, agents develop new goals and strategies for action. A relational approach in economic geography thus systematically includes context in its research programme.

This conception is particularly important when analysing the growing importance of knowledge within the economy (Lundvall and Johnson 1994). Production processes and technologies have become more complex over time, and depend on an increasing social division of labour that stretches over large distances. The competitiveness of firms also increasingly depends on systematic learning processes, critical reflections of economic practices, and ongoing incremental improvements. As such, knowledge has become a key advantage in the so-called knowledge-economy. Whereas our conceptualization of relational action allows for broader applicability, much of our discussion in this book focuses on aspects of knowledge creation and circulation in socio-economic context. Knowledge, itself, is context-specific and bound to people. And new knowledge is continuously being created through interactive processes of interpreting, integrating, and transforming existing knowledge within specific contexts. Thus, in order to understand processes of knowledge creation, it is necessary to understand how people act and interact with one another (Bathelt and Glückler 2000).

This perspective consequently pays particular attention to economic action as a social process, the structure of relations between agents, and the creation of formal and informal institutions. The role of institutions in shaping the context of economic agents has been recognized in much of the recent literature on innovations. Institutional contexts that are largely determined at the level of the nation-state, such as educational and research infrastructure, work rules, and organizational standards related to the social division of labour, have a substantial influence on the nature of economic problems and shortages identified, and the learning processes applied. The development of particular national systems of innovation is an important outcome of this (Lundvall 1992; Nelson 1993). In such systems, institutions have a strong impact on processes of interaction and innovation and, thus, shape the national production structure. The production structure, in turn, serves to strengthen, reshape, and further develop existing institutions, thus driving national specialization patterns (Lundvall and Maskell 2000).[4] In sum, the relational perspective views economic action as a process that is situated in time and place, and thus necessarily draws on institutional conceptions (Philo 1989; Giddens 1990; Martin 1994; Sunley 1996; Glückler 2001b; Bathelt and Glückler 2003a). The centrality of institutions to our conceptualization of human action is further developed in Chapter 3.

2.3.4 EPISTEMOLOGY

If we allow that human action is contextually embedded, universal laws offer limited explanatory leverage. Action in open systems is not fully predictable and, thus, cannot be adequately conceptualized through deterministic mechanisms or theories (see Peck 1996). This, however, is exactly what approaches in regional science aim to do when they apply existing, or even new, spatial laws and regularities to studies of economic action. Critical realism, in contrast, offers a fundamentally different epistemological perspective in that it systematically accounts for context-specificity in explanations of human action (Archer et al. 1998). This approach, which forms the basis for our subsequent argument, was originally developed by the British philosopher Bhaskar (1975) and propagated in the social sciences by Sayer (1992, 2000). It serves as a pragmatic epistemological alternative that attempts to avoid problems of both deductive-nomological determinism in logical empiricism and relativism in postmodern theory (Lovering 1989; Thrift 1990; Sayer 2000). Unlike postmodern approaches, critical realism does not deny the possibility of an objective reality that is independent from the individual. While the relationship between reality and human knowledge is recognized as asymmetrical, the fact that empirical observations must be necessarily mediated through concepts does not imply that they are merely a product of such concepts. Instead, empirical observations are also dependent on the structural properties of real objects (Sayer 2000: 41). Critical realism also aims to develop causal explanations for general mechanisms. In contrast to positivist approaches, however, causality is no longer implied from their universal co-occurrence.

Conventional causal analysis, as employed in regional science, is based on Hume's principle (1900) of regularity. According to this principle, an event is the cause of another subsequent event if its occurrence is always associated with the occurrence of the latter event. Constant conjunction is, in this view, used as an associative principle of causality (Sayer 2000). This explanation claims to be universal for it assumes that an event has particular consequences that occur at any time and any place in association with this event. In contrast, critical realism establishes a contextual explanation based on the principle of contingency that we apply in our approach. This approach distinguishes two types of relations between events (Sayer 1985):

1. *Necessary relations.* Relations are necessary if two events always occur in association with one another, independent from a specific context. Such non-contextual relations or universal laws are, however, extremely rare in social and economic processes (Fleetwood 2002).
2. *Contingent relations.* Relations are contingent if two events occur in conjunction with one another only under specific circumstances. Such relations are quite typical in the analysis of economic action in spatial perspective.

The principle of contingency suggests that one event does not necessarily cause another particular event. Therefore, identical preconditions for human action do not necessarily have the same consequences at any time and place. This provides an epistemological basis for a context-specific conceptualization of the intentions and consequences of human action. At the same time, it is recognized that future actions and developments are fundamentally open-ended. Contingency, however, does not result from human action alone, but also arises from differences in localized material structures, as well as from variations between places in terms of their institutional architecture.[5] This creates deviations between cities, regions, nations, etc., and results in different sets of opportunities and restrictions for economic action. Overall, this leads to particular structure–agency dynamics. Contingent action reproduces or transforms specific contextual structures which, in turn, shape the preconditions for future action. In this respect, context is related to structure and contingency associated with agency or, as Jessop (1992) would likely say, strategy. The resulting interdependence between contextual structure and contingent action corresponds with the reflexive mechanisms that lie at the heart of structuration theories, as developed by Bourdieu (1977) and Giddens (1984) – a topic that will be discussed in more detail in Chapter 3.

The application of the contingency principle does not mean, however, that research ends with a contextual explanation of particular events in particular locations at particular times. Instead, another important step of realist analysis is to go beyond individual events and their specific contexts in order to identify common factors that affect economic action. This involves the identification of causal mechanisms, as opposed to the formulation of spatial laws. This methodology aims to uncover the basic conditions underlying specific contexts, and relate them to others. In this way, decontextualization provides a methodology to identify trans-contextual structures from contextualized events.

2.3.5 RESEARCH GOAL

Instead of focusing on the description of spatial categories, processes, and regularities, relational economic geography draws explicit attention to the importance of economic agents and how they act and interact in space. It does so by applying the following changes to the research design: First, by inverting the causality between space and economy, and adopting a conception of space as perspective; second, by viewing economic action as a relational process that is situated within structures of relations; and, third, by incorporating the principle of contingency into the analysis of causal relations in order to construct an epistemological basis for studying contextual action and development. The objective of relational economic geography is thus to employ a geographical perspective to formulate research questions that are associated with the analysis of increasingly complex economic relations and processes (Bathelt and Glückler 2003a).

The transition from regional science towards a relational approach, illustrated in this section, has fundamental consequences for analyses in economic geography. It rests on three propositions regarding the notions of contextuality, path-dependence, and contingency:[6]

1. *Contextuality.* From a structural perspective, economic agents are situated within contexts of social and institutional relations (Granovetter 1985, 1992*a*, 1992*b*). Since this conceptualization views action as contextually embedded, action cannot be usefully explained through the application of universal spatial laws.
2. *Path-dependence.* From a dynamic perspective, contextuality leads to path-dependent development because past economic decisions, actions, and inter-actions enable and constrain current actions. They also direct future intentions and actions to some extent (Nelson and Winter 1982; Nelson 1995*b*).
3. *Contingency.* Economic processes are, at the same time, contingent in the sense that the agents' strategies and actions may deviate from existing development paths. Economic action in open systems is not fully determined and cannot be predicted through universal spatial laws. Despite its path-dependent development, which is shaped by a particular history, economic action is subject to unforeseeable changes and is therefore fundamentally open-ended (Sayer 1992, 2000).

Relational economic geography enables a complex understanding of economic action and its localized consequences. It integrates the importance of context without remaining at the level of describing individual structures and events (see also Storper 2009). As such, it focuses on the people, firms, and other organizations that are involved in economic decision-making, as well as on the individuals and environments that are subject to the consequences of economic action. This relational perspective does not intend to identify spatial regularities, and avoids treating regions and other spatial configurations as actors. Instead, it suggests an empirical research project that focuses on identifying social relations among agents, including the associated restrictions, practices, and key influences shaping economic processes over time. This has much in common with recent practice approaches that also base their arguments on a relational conceptuali-zation (e.g. Faulconbridge 2008). A contextual, path-dependent, and contingent perspective is quite different from theoretical programmes that view economic geography in terms of universal laws, linear developments, and closed systems. Therefore, a transition from neoclassical economic conceptions and regional science to a relational perspective of economic action requires a reformulation of the concepts used to understand economic structures and processes.

2.4 **Why a Spatial Perspective?**

One of the key characteristics of economic agency is that it varies across space. This is because business contexts differ from place to place; firms are integrated into different global value chains and face different requirements and challenges from their network partners; and institutional conditions and historical patterns of specialization also differ. All of this creates distinct conditions under which individuals and firms make decisions. And even the exact same conditions can lead to different outcomes because of the funda- mental contingency of economic action (e.g. Bahrenberg 2002). Managers in different firms, for instance, would likely interpret information from their business environment differently or draw different conclusions according to their own specific strategic choices. In short, there are fundamental spatial disparities in the distribution of economic activity, resources, industries, and growth dynamics that require the application of a spatial perspective. In addition, globalization processes result in continuous flows of information back and forth between distant agents and places, resulting in economic decisions that influence local/regional structures, as well as the globalization process itself.

Questions related to how economic action and interaction take place in different locations and between agents in different places are central to the relational conceptualization outlined above. The consequence of the above propositions is that it is not possible to analyse a region independently of the economic and social relations between its people and firms. This does not imply, however, that spatial proximity automatically leads to the establish- ment of strong local networks; rather, it is relational proximity that enables close social interaction and becomes the source of competitiveness (Amin and Cohendet 2004). Such affinity can also develop between actors located in different parts of the world, supported through modern technological and institutional developments (Allen 2003; Bathelt and Glückler 2003*a*).

This framework allows us to understand the complex realities of economic action and interaction, in ways that differ from traditional approaches. It requires, however, that our view of the role of space in economic geography be altered. A spatial perspective acknowledges that economic action and interac- tion are always grounded in particular places and the relations between them. Consequently, there are fundamental interdependencies between economic, social, and cultural processes within and between different places, regions, or national states. Processes are necessarily interdependent, either because they take place within the same localities, between the same regions or, exactly, because they do not (Bathelt and Glückler 2003*b*). In this understanding, proximity is important because it provides opportunities for face-to-face contact (Storper and Venables 2004; Bathelt and Schuldt 2008*b*), which can be used to develop 'relational capital' and stimulate collective learning (e.g. Amin and Cohendet 2004; Gertler 2004; Capello and Faggian 2005). By no means, however, are learning processes restricted to particular spatial configurations.

This spatial perspective is particularly relevant when analysing the knowl- edge economy. Knowledge flows are uneven in space. Knowledge exchange and transfers take place under different conditions, within and between existing networks of firms (Glückler 2008, 2011), and, at a personal level, within communities of practice (Brown and Duguid 1991; Wenger 1998) and epistemic communities (Knorr Cetina 1999). Within a particular regional context, agents do not even have to be in close contact with one another or engage in direct transactions to learn from each other or make decisions that are related to one another (Ettlinger 2001, 2003). There are two types of relationship patterns, in particular, which help us to understand these processes (see also Bouba-Olga and Grossetti 2008):

1. *Spatial proximity.* When firms operate in close proximity to one another, overlapping personal knowledge networks may develop as they share some of the same partners or contacts. In such cases, little interaction is necessary, especially since firms can also learn from observation (DeFillippi and Arthur 1998).
2. *'Relational proximity'.* Strong relational ties with friends and close colleagues in other corporate divisions or other firms in different locations can have similar consequences as spatial proximity. Ongoing communication via telephone or computer-mediated communication enables knowledge transfers over distance and knowledge spillovers between places without permanent face-to-face contact (e.g. Bathelt and Turi 2011).

2.5 Storper's Conceptualization of the Holy Trinity

One of the most sophisticated attempts to reformulate the foundations and goals of economic geography during the 1990s is that developed by Storper (1997*b*, 1997*c*). His conceptualization of the so-called 'holy trinity' has had a profound impact on our view of economic geography and serves as our main point of departure. This conception is particularly well designed to deal with the challenges and dynamics of the globalizing knowledge economy. We integrate his ideas into a general model of relational action and interaction as a basis for a re-conceptualized economic geography (Bathelt and Glückler 2003*a*).

Storper (1993, 1997*a*) argues that, despite revolutionary improvements in information, communication, and transportation technologies, localized production systems continue to play a decisive role in the global economy. He suggests that the continued importance of proximity is largely due to the advantages associated with reduced transaction costs and enhanced capabilities for organizational and technological learning in specialized agglomerations of interrelated economic activities. Apart from traded interdependencies, which are key variables in the regional science and neoclassical economics literature, untraded interdependencies play a critical role in enabling communication, adjustment, and learning processes, and accommodating knowledge flows between economic agents (Storper 1997c). They are embodied in the relations between people and the existence of conventions, as expressed in the form of accepted norms, rules, and practices. Relations and conventions are also localized because they are bound to those people, firms, and places involved and cannot easily be transferred to other places. They become region-specific and/or value-chain-specific assets and form the basis for further concentration and specialization of economic activities (Maskell and Malmberg 1999a, 1999b).

To understand the complex nature of economic production and its geography, Storper (1997b, 1997c) identifies technology, organization, and territory as overlapping constituent pillars of economic geography. They form a holy trinity through which economic and social processes and their interactions and power relations can be analysed (see Crevoisier 2001). The holy trinity is a conceptualization of economic geography that is dramatically different from regional science. It consists of the following three pillars: (a) *Technology.* Technological change lies at the heart of the dynamics of the economy. It results in the rise of new and the decline of old products and processes. (b) *Organization.* This pillar emphasizes the importance of the ways in which firms and networks of firms are organized and how these organizational structures are influenced by institutions. As such, this conceptualization can also be described as an institutional approach. (c) *Territory.* At the territorial level, it is possible to analyse the co-evolution of organizations and technologies. Through regional input–output linkages, knowledge transfers and adjustments between firms, spillover effects, and learning processes enhance the collective competitiveness of regional agents that are interrelated in the same value chain. In this way, untraded interdependencies play a decisive role in transforming technological and organizational worlds into regional worlds (Storper 1993, 1997c).

An important aspect of Storper's approach (1995, 1997c) is that he emphasizes the role of context-specific institutions. He also views social interactions, as expressed in processes of organizing, learning, and knowledge creation, as being central to analyses in social science contexts. Storper (1997b, 1997c) identifies mechanisms through which socio-institutional contexts stimulate processes of geographical clustering of industrial production, and provides an explanatory framework that concentrates on economic agents as opposed to their spatial settings. Although our view builds upon the notion of the holy trinity, it proposes a different conceptualization of the role of space and territory:

1. *From a territorial dimension to a spatial perspective.* In order to avoid deterministic interpretations of the role of space, we dissolve the territorial dimension and, instead, conceptualize space as a *perspective* (Glückler 1999). We deduct our conceptualization from a micro-perspective of economic

action and interaction, and use a geographical perspective to guide our analyses of economic processes.

2. *Integration of economic and social processes from a spatial perspective.* To reduce the temptation of analysing economic dynamics in isolation from 'spatial' relations and specificities, we use the geographical lens to contextualize all economic and social processes from the very beginning of our analysis. We do not view the economic and the social as two separate entities; nor do we treat them as abstract dimensions that are not localized. The next section develops concepts that aim to systematically integrate economic and social processes, while viewing both from an explicitly spatial perspective.

2.6 **Four Dimensions of Analysis**

In this section, we further develop the ideas and approaches discussed above into a relational framework for the analysis of economic action in spatial perspective. This framework revolves around the four basic dimensions of organization, evolution, innovation, and interaction. These four dimensions serve as the key analytical categories of a relational approach. In our conceptualization, social institutions are of critical importance in explaining context-specific behaviour and action. We refer to numerous institutional concepts, such as those discussed by Storper (1997c), Schamp (2000a, 2002), and others. They help us to understand the processes through which all four dimensions are constructed and reconstructed, and serve as the basic mechanisms underlying our relational framework.

Our conceptualization relies on a distinct geographical perspective to analyse the economic and social processes that correspond to each of the four dimensions mentioned above. This allows us to develop an interdisciplinary approach that integrates both economic and social theories. Below, we draw attention to some of the main research agendas associated with each of the four dimensions. In applying a geographical perspective, we also draw attention to the interconnections between these dimensions. The structure of the four dimensions, employed in Figure 2.1, serves as a heuristic framework to systematically apply the consequences of a relational perspective to the theoretical debates in much of the work of economic geographers and other social scientists today.[7]

2.6.1 ORGANIZATION

A basic problem of organizing industrial labour and production processes is to establish an efficient division and integration of labour (Sayer and Walker 1992). This involves the coordination of the labour force, raw materials,

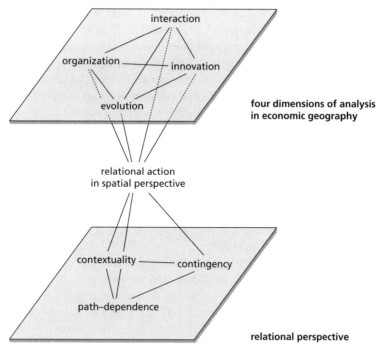

Figure 2.1. Relational conceptualization of economic action in spatial perspective

intermediates, machinery, and equipment applied within and between work-places and firms. In essence, it includes the establishment of a particular social and spatial division and integration of labour. This must be done in a way that allows for sufficient control to be exercised over the production process in order to continuously produce the same goods at high quality standards according to customer needs (Bathelt 2000). To solve the problem of indus-trial organization, decisions must be made with respect to the process tech-nologies that will be used, and the way in which the labour and production stages will be bundled together. Decisions must also be made regarding the types of intermediate products that will be produced in-house versus those that will be acquired from subcontractors and suppliers. To the extent that some vertical disintegration is intended, decisions must also be made with regards to contacting suppliers. This includes deciding the geographical location to focus on, the competencies that suppliers will be given, and the places, regions, and nations where different parts of the production chain will be located. These and other aspects of industrial organization can be analysed through the application of institutional theories, such as the transaction-cost approach in economics (Coase 1937; Williamson 1975, 1985) and the em-beddedness approach in sociology (Granovetter 1985, 1992a, 1992b).

A firm's particular solution to the organizational problem has a direct impact on the locational structure of that firm and the spatial organization of its production. In turn, the spatial distribution of potential suppliers and customers, as well as the strategies and decisions of major competitors, also has an impact on the resulting social and spatial divisions of labour. Overall, the organizational problem of industrial production is so complex that it is not possible to explain its outcome simply through the use of location factors and regional attributes. Spatial proximity and institutional affinity (or proximity) can in some technological and political contexts help to stabilize network relations between specialized firms because they reduce costs for knowledge acquisition, generate knowledge spillovers, and enable more efficient communication (Scott 1988, 1998). Depending on the institutions that shape industrial relations and organization, the existing training and education system, and other aspects of the capital–labour nexus, regional or national agglomerations can result.

These organizational structures are, however, not static. An evolutionary perspective is required to understand the dynamic nature of the organization of firms and value chains as a result of socio-institutional relations (Nelson and Winter 1982; Swedberg and Granovetter 1992). Whether a firm develops a vertically integrated or a largely disintegrated production structure and the specific regions in which subcontracting relationships are established also depend on the firm's experience and particular sequence of organizational decisions made in the past. Learning from experience enhances organizational reflexivity.

At the same time, organizational structures are embedded in social, cultural, institutional, and political structures and relations that cannot be separated from the economic sphere. The existence of accepted rules, habits, norms, and other institutional arrangements creates a reliable environment for interactive learning (Hodgson 1988; North 1991), and has a direct impact on the organization of innovation and production processes. The organizational structure of a firm and its development are also related to the formal institutions and authorities that create societal standards and laws (e.g. Baum and Oliver 1992). Therefore, the spatial organization of production is a result of complex negotiations and temporary compromises between firms and formal institutions. In other words, it takes place within the context of particular power relations (e.g. Taylor 1995; Allen 1997; Berndt 1999).

2.6.2 EVOLUTION

There are at least two forms of change that are not evolutionary (Nelson 1995*b*; Glückler 2007*a*): First, when change is random, future events are independent from previous events such that there are no inferences from a given course of development on the future. Second, when change is determined, the outcome of a certain development is also independent from the sequence of events. More radically, even, equilibrium theory determines a stable equilibrium which, as a final outcome, is both, independent from the start conditions as well as from the sequence of events (Martin and Sunley 2006). Change is evolutionary, however, when future events are not independent from past events and when the sequence of events makes a difference in the outcome.

The evolutionary dimension[8] is of great importance because it allows for an analysis of the impact of historical structures and processes on current decisions. Evolutionary change is a function of both path-dependence and contingency. Path-dependence refers to a pattern of cumulative causation whereby a certain sequence of events creates unequal propensities for future events. Though path-dependent change allows us to draw inferences from the present to future states of development, change is always subject to contingency. Economic processes are contingent in that the agents' strategies and actions may deviate from existing development paths. Economic action in open systems is not *ex ante* determined and, thus, cannot be predicted through universal spatial laws (Sayer 2000). Evolutionary concepts of change assume that economic and social processes are experience-based, cumulative, and reflexive in nature. They are path-dependent in that they follow particular histories of decisions, actions, and their consequences. In this respect, there is a remarkable convergence of evolutionary perspectives in economics, sociology, and economic geography (Bathelt and Glückler 2000).

Evolutionary economics supposes that techno-economic change defines a development path that follows particular routines and heuristics (Dosi 1982, 1988; Nelson and Winter 1982; Nelson 1995*b*). As part of this, the direction of technological change is pre-structured by existing technologies, albeit not in a deterministic way. Existing technologies are products of past decisions about innovation and previous technologies. Through this, processes of selection, mutation, variation, and chance are initiated in order to create knowledge and new technologies that might increase efficiency. Past choices generate opportunities for present actions and, at the same time, limit the set of feasible solutions because former decisions cannot easily be reversed.

Approaches in economic sociology have extended this techno-economic view by applying aspects of socio-institutional embeddedness (Zukin and DiMaggio 1990). Granovetter (1985) has pointed out that economic activities are deeply embedded in structures of social relations. This means that firms cannot be analysed as independent entities but must be viewed within their respective socio-economic contexts; that is, they are closely interconnected in communication and adjustment processes with their suppliers, customers, service providers, and state authorities (Grabher 1993*a*).

This is closely related to the role of institutions. Institutions do not only restrict the possibilities of economic action (North 1991). More importantly, they also create a basis for mutual communication, collective learning, and joint problem-solving, without which a technical and social division of labour and economic interaction would not be possible (Giddens 1984; Hodgson 1988). Formal and particularly informal institutions, such as stabilizations of interaction based on conventions, accepted rules, and habits, are of great significance because they invigorate and further stimulate localized production systems at different spatial levels. Embeddedness is not spontaneous but is experience-based and develops over time from a historical process. Contextual economic relations are the result of previous and ongoing experience in durable economic transactions. Through the same process, they also form the basis for future path-dependent and context-specific developments. From an evolutionary perspective, informal institutions can be transformed into formal institutions, such as stabilized social relations based on laws. They are then typically integrated into an organizational context, such as a government agency, from which they are inseparable (e.g. Amin and Thrift 1995).

In the field of economic geography, recent work on the rise of new industrial spaces and the process of geographical industrialization also tends to adopt an evolutionary perspective (Storper and Walker 1989; Scott 1998). These studies integrate findings from evolutionary economics and the embeddedness approach into a specific spatial development perspective, albeit sometimes only implicitly. In their model of geographical industrialization, Storper and Walker (1989) argue that novel industries have few specific locational requirements in their early growth stages. New firms are thus relatively free in terms of deciding where to locate. This occurs because the particular inputs required do not exist anywhere and, instead, must be acquired from whatever capital is at hand. There are numerous regions that could house the new industry. Over time, a handful of regions may come to specialize in the new industry and, thereby, stimulate processes of selective clustering. Due to their superior growth performance, such clusters can actively shape their locational environment according to the firms' specific needs. They may, for instance, encourage the development of a specialized supplier sector and create a labour market that meets the particular skill requirements. The firms in these clusters thus develop a competitive advantage over firms in other regions. This supports further agglomeration and specialization in existing clusters. A more complex understanding of industrial and regional development paths and their socio-institutional contexts can be achieved if the effects of localized capabilities (Storper 1995; Maskell and Malmberg 1999*a*, 1999*b*) and untraded interdependencies (Storper 1995, 1997*c*) are included in the analysis (Bathelt 2002).

2.6.3 INNOVATION

This dimension is closely associated with processes of knowledge creation, the development of new technologies, and the effects of technological change, especially in a spatial perspective. Innovation refers to the market launch of inventions and new products or services and may be described as 'the first positive sanction of the user' (Akrich et al. 2002: 188). Many traditional concepts in economics and geography fail to adequately understand the mechanisms by which new products and processes are created, innovations are introduced into established markets, and generate new markets. This is largely because technological change is viewed either as a given, being external to the models used, or as a predictable outcome of a linear research process.

Evolutionary interpretations, such as those of Dosi (1988) and Storper (1997c), recognize that the process of generating new technologies requires a more multifaceted conceptualization. From this perspective, the creation of new technologies is an interactive social process, characterized by a particular social division of labour within a firm and between different firms of the value chain, as well as between firms, universities, and governmental research facilities. This process is characterized by continuous feedback from various stages in research, testing, and production; reflexive patterns of economic behaviour; and interactive learning between the agents involved. Innovative activities are risky in that researchers do not know if they will succeed. Thus, uncertainty plagues the innovation process. Successful innovations are often associated with the creation of new or modified knowledge. The process of generating new technologies and knowledge is path-dependent in that it depends on the actors' experiences. Further, search activities are often limited to a particular class of techno-economic problem-solving mechanisms. Innovation processes of firms, therefore, follow particular technological trajectories in which search processes are stimulated and directed by existing routines, heuristics, and cognitive scripts (DiMaggio 1997).

The particular spatial organization of innovation depends on a number of influences. These include the degree to which production processes are vertically disintegrated, the existence of nearby firms that could become partners in innovation, the type of knowledge needed in the innovation process, and the degree to which knowledge is localized, or sticky. The spatial organization of innovation is also deeply influenced by experience with previous innovation processes. Many new technologies are incremental in character and have not been developed in integrated research processes in large globally organized firms. In addition, specialized industrial agglomerations support the types of innovation processes that rely on an extensive social division of labour. In this case, spatial proximity enables regular personal communication, joint problem-solving, and adjustments between the people and firms involved. These interactions stimulate information spillovers and processes of knowledge creation (Storper and Walker 1989; Maskell and Malmberg 1999a, 1999b; Storper 1997c; Bathelt and Glückler 2000). This is particularly well developed if a large number of firms of the same value chain are involved in this social division of labour and if they share the same local socio-institutional context (Crevoisier and Maillat 1991).

National states have a particularly large impact on the structure of technology and knowledge creation because they define the primary institutional settings for the development of national innovation systems (Lundvall 1992; Nelson 1993; Edquist 1997). These national innovation systems are characterized by different cultures, organizational structures, degrees of vertical integration and centralization, routines and habits in technological trajectories, and capabilities in terms of enabling regional adjustments to localized capabilities. At the regional level, national innovation systems are being modified and adjusted to local cultures (e.g. Saxenian 1994; Schoenberger 1997), institutions, and production specificities, and thus result in region-specific innovation and development paths.

2.6.4 INTERACTION

Interactions between individual and collective actors in economic contexts are another crucial element of the relational framework. One important conclusion from the preceding discussion is that the particular organization of production and the processes of generating innovation are a result of ongoing interaction. This also operates as an enabling force for further interaction between people in various workplaces, firms, and formal institutions. An evolutionary approach helps us to understand how the nature and extent of interaction changes over time according to ongoing experiences between the organizations involved in innovation. The processes of interactive learning, creative variation, and collective knowledge production can thus be viewed as conceptual tools that link organization and innovation, thereby generating an evolutionary dynamic (Figure 2.1). Interactions of various kinds between economic agents at different spatial and organizational levels enable firms to modify and refine heuristics and routines along existing trajectories, or develop new technologies that lead towards new development paths.

Interaction and learning are at the core of the reflexive economy (Lundvall and Johnson 1994). This means that the outcomes of previous actions are recorded, checked, and evaluated in a systematic way in order to draw conclusions for further improvements regarding future actions. Indeed, empirical studies have shown that production and innovation are social processes, characterized by a particular social division of labour. This social character increases in importance as technologies become more complex and sophisticated, and as specialization and segmentation increase. As such, the process of learning by interacting has become a central analytical focus in economics, sociology, and economic geography (Lundvall 1988; Gertler 2004). Learning by interacting refers to the processes by which systematic communication and adjustment between producers and users particularly results in incremental improvements in product and process technologies, as well as in organizational routines.

The existence and acceptance of both formal and informal institutions are necessary prerequisites for stimulating interactive learning between economic agents. Routines, conventions, and habits with respect to technologies and resources allow producers to communicate with their suppliers and customers, and to collectively decide upon product and process adjustments in particular projects (Storper 1997c). Interactive learning also has distinct consequences for the spatial organization of production and innovation because conventions and social relations are continuously being restructured through feedback between agents. These adjustments require the co-presence of agents, which can be efficiently achieved through co-location. Some conventions may not be easily transferable over large distances to other social contexts (Maskell and Malmberg 1999a, 1999b). As a consequence, we see the development of clusters, which are characterized by close inter-firm interaction, proximity, and learning. These clusters facilitate the efficient transfer of information and knowledge (Storper 1995; Asheim 1999; Bathelt 2005a, 2005b). This encourages the development of shared technological attitudes and expectations between local actors and, over time, stimulates trust-based linkages (Crevoisier and Maillat 1991). Thus, despite the development of new forms of global organization of production, substantial interaction still takes place within national and regional socio-economic contexts (e.g. Dicken 1994; Zeller 2001).

2.7 **Conclusion**

Since the late 1980s, the development of new ideas, conceptions, and models has stimulated a reorientation of research practices in economic geography. In this context, a relational view has emerged that is particularly well suited to analysing processes of knowledge creation and exchange. These processes are central to understanding the dynamics of the globalizing knowledge economy. As will be discussed in Chapter 4, the use and application of knowledge can be conceptualized by applying a relational framework: It is contextual and path-dependent in that interpretations of knowledge depend on the context in which knowledge is being used, and on how it has been used in the past; decisions about the future use of knowledge are, nevertheless, open-ended as agents can make choices that deviate from former developments.

Drawing on Storper's holy trinity (1997*b*, 1997*c*), we have developed four dimensions from the basic propositions of economic action to be applied in our analysis, that is, organization, evolution, innovation, and interaction. These interrelated dimensions serve as a heuristic framework to systematically apply the consequences of a relational perspective to the theoretical debates in the work of economic geographers, economists, and sociologists throughout the 1990s. The point of departure in our conceptualization is that those economic and social processes that fall into our four dimensions are analysed using a distinctive geographical lens. This allows us to develop an approach to economic geography that integrates both economic and social theories. Our conceptualization does not treat space and territory as entities that are research objects in themselves, or separate from economic and social influences. Similarly, we do not intend to theorize space or identify spatial laws but, rather, look for explanations of human action in localized economic processes. Alternatively, we apply an understanding of space as a perspective. This geographical lens draws our attention towards particular localized representations of economic processes and their outcomes.

The relational conceptualization does not attempt to establish a comprehensive general theory that is capable of explaining and predicting all possible outcomes of social and economic processes in space. Rather, this framework presents an interdisciplinary and multidimensional relational view that can be applied to a large number of research problems, related to questions of localization and specialization of industries in specific regional or national settings; how these settings are connected with developments in other places at a global scale; how firms interact to overcome localized problems or communicate with distant agents operating under different institutional conditions; or how interaction patterns lead to different innovation paths in different places. One central issue on the agenda of relational economic geography is to provide a better understanding of how institutions shape contextual action in the knowledge economy, as well as the ways in which contingent action helps to transform existing and new institutional forms. This is quite important because dynamic institutions continuously enable and constrain human action. Since they are sometimes territorial in character and vary between places, regions, or nations, they are of great significance in understanding different processes and structures in spatial perspective.

3 Structure, Agency, and Institutions

3.1 **Introduction**

The relational perspective developed in Chapter 2 focuses on the analysis of economic practices at the micro level – be it related to specific actors or the social relations between them. Such an analysis necessarily leads to a number of important questions regarding the relationship between structure and agency, and the role of macroeconomic and societal conditions. It also raises questions about the types of methods that may be most usefully employed in a relational approach to the study of economic development. In this respect, we deviate from previous work that relies on actor–network theory (Latour 1986) or the theory of social systems (Luhmann 1984), which focuses largely on the flows of action and communication, while neglecting the agents themselves and the institutions guiding them.[1] The relational approach, in contrast, includes individual and collective economic agents, the economic practices and relationships in which they engage, and the role of social institutions at different scales.

This chapter discusses the role of economic agents, their rationalities and strategies, and how these lead to specific practices of economic interaction. Our purpose is not only to link agents with economic practices but also to conceptualize institutions as important mediators between the micro and macro levels, and the local and global scales, of analysis. This is important because it allows us to develop an integrated view of the dynamics of micro- and macroeconomic processes and their interrelations. It also engages with ongoing debates in the social sciences regarding the utility of quantitative versus qualitative methods. While it seems that many of these discussions remain fixed upon the dualism between qualitative and quantitative research, we encourage a combination of both approaches and suggest ways that this can be achieved. While we are sceptical that exclusive macro-statistical studies, which operate at a high level of sectoral and spatial aggregation, are sufficient in understanding the full complexity of economic and societal developments, we present examples of how qualitative and quantitative analyses can be usefully combined (see, further, Chapters 6 and 8). Based on this conceptualization, Part II of this book will discuss qualitative and quantitative studies that analyse local, trans-local, and global knowledge-flow dynamics in different spatial and sectoral contexts.

Following this rationale, this chapter is organized as follows: We begin by discussing the role of economic agency, the type of agents included, and their rationalities. This leads to a discussion of the role of agency versus structure, and of the relationship between micro and macro levels of analysis. We attempt to resolve these dualisms by introducing institutions as a concept that mediates between different levels and scales of analysis. This is followed by a discussion of how institutions allow for and guide economic and societal change, and under which conditions they support hysteresis. Finally, we develop a conception of markets as expressions of social institutions, in a context that is not dominated by optimal decision-makers and fully rational individuals. We discuss how markets are made in a relational perspective and, based on this, engage in the debate about the role of quantitative versus qualitative methods in empirically studying these phenomena.

3.2 **Agency and Rationalities**

An important question when analysing economic action is, of course, which actors should be included in our research and how. At the core of our relational perspective are individuals who make economic decisions and interact with others in research, production, and transaction processes, that is, workers, managers, consumers, and politicians. Their activities are assumed to be generally purposeful, although they may have unintended consequences (e.g. Hudson 2004). It is questionable, however, whether it is possible to limit the analysis to these individual actors. In an economic context, there are important collective actors, such as firms, governmental bodies, and other organizations, which also require consideration. These types of collective actors differ from individuals and cannot be reduced to them (also Maskell 2001a; Oinas 2005). Firms, for instance, operate differently from individuals because managers and workers may perform particular roles in their business life, and engage in complex processes of negotiation and decision-making. Firms are also organized around structures and routines that are independent from the individual agents who operate inside these organizations (Nelson 1995a; Lawson and Lorenz 1999).

The conceptual foundations of relational action are based on an institutional perspective (Amin 1999), in which the goals and preferences of economic action are not predetermined by the assumption that actors are rational, utility-maximizing individuals (Hodgson 2003). In reality, individual and collective agents are embedded in structures of socio-institutional relations and actor–networks that influence their decisions and actions (Granovetter 1985). They are, for instance, involved in specialized producer–user networks and cannot easily change their transaction partners and production programmes from one day to the next (Grabher 1993*a*).

Furthermore, there are various rationalities at work, which yield differences in economic performance (Amin 1999). Agents may choose between an instrumentalist rationality (which focuses on reactive problem-solving in a stable environment), a procedural rationality (which breaks problems down and solves them in a stepwise manner), or a recursive rationality (which tries to anticipate changes and actively shape the environment). The predominance of a particular rationality depends on the agents' contexts and experiences.[2] At the same time, '... individuals engage in multiple networks associated with different rationalities, and these different networks... [can be] overlapping networks' (Ettlinger 2003: 161). Therefore, economic relations also include social, cultural, and political rationalities that affect economic strategies and decision-making. As opposed to traditional approaches, the relational conception is capable of integrating multiple rationalities and complex contexts of economic action. Multiplex relations link people in many different ways as neighbours, friends, and business partners (Uzzi 1997). They provide a means of engaging resources from one type of relationship to another, and transferring institution-based trust into interpersonal trust and vice versa. Based on such dynamics, economic, social, and cultural relations define a creative 'field' that stimulates entrepreneurship, learning, and innovation within regional agglomerations and between them (Scott 2004).

In some of the literature on regional networks and the 'cultural turn', there is a tendency to overstate the social dimension while neglecting economic considerations in explanations of economic action. At least implicitly, networks are sometimes portrayed as if they were ultimately democratic, consisting of altruistic agents engaging in 'friendly' exchange relationships (for a critique, see Sayer 2001; Clark et al. 2004). Without denying the importance of the socio-institutional context, a relational conceptualization does not ignore the fact that economic agents are generally interested in enhancing their personal wealth (Taylor 2004*a*). Indeed, this is the main driver of economic action and interaction. Competition, rivalry, market interaction, and 'market-making' are, thus, important aspects that shape economic action in a relational perspective.

In short, the relational approach suggests that economic agents act according to economic *and* non-economic goals and strategies, as well as feelings and emotions (Ettlinger 2004; Massey 2004). The results of this deliberate action include intended and unplanned spatial outcomes which, in turn, impact the next round of decisions (Werlen 1995; Bathelt and Glückler 2003*c*). To understand the underlying processes and rationalities of economic action, it is important to adopt a micro perspective that emphasizes the contextual, path-dependent, and contingent nature of economic action and interaction.

3.3 **Duality of Structure and Agency**

A relational perspective puts an emphasis on economic action and the contextuality of that interaction within structures of socio-institutional relations. This, however, does not make it a reductionist micro-perspective that is blind to wider societal structures and dynamics. In a way that closely corresponds to structuration theory, a relational perspective aims to theorize social and economic practices beyond the micro–macro-divide. Giddens (1984) conceptualizes action as a continuous flow of purposeful conduct in the *durée* of everyday life. In this context, agents are able to monitor and reflect upon their action. The rationality of social action refers to the ability of actors to provide a rationale for their actions. Here, Giddens (1984) distinguishes a discursive and a practical consciousness from which actors draw their ability to find reasons for their actions. But action also has a recursive quality. Through the course of action, agents continuously reproduce the conditions that enable their actions in the first place. This leads to a reflexive dynamic, which Giddens (1984) refers to as the stratification model of action. Thus, much like a relational approach, Giddens' model (1984) points to the limitations of adopting either a pure micro perspective or a pure macro perspective in mutual exclusion (Glückler 1999).

- *Limitations of a Micro Perspective*

A central limitation is that social interaction cannot be fully grasped through an analysis of the acting individuals alone. Unacknowledged conditions and unintended consequences of action, which are unavoidable given the lack of complete information in interaction contexts, constrain any explanations of macro-social phenomena from the perspective of the consciously acting individual (Thompson 1989).

- *Limitations of a Macro Perspective*

At the other extreme of the micro–macro-dualism, approaches such as structuralism or functionalism are also incomplete in their explanations. The employment of a priori assumptions about the existence of functional mechanisms in macro-social systems leads to an implicit determinism in that social action is explained as simply a product of specific functional constraints or a priori principles. This perspective tends to reify concepts of social structure as real entities and dismisses the realm of contextuality and purposive social action. In addressing the conceptual duality of structure and agency, Giddens (1984: 2) suggests a potential solution to the macro–micro-dualism: 'If interpretative sociologies are founded, as it were, upon an imperialism of the subject, functionalism and structuralism propose an imperialism of the social object. One of my principal ambitions in the formulation of structuration theory is to put an end to each of these empire-building endeavours. The basic domain of study of the social sciences, according to the theory of structuration, is neither the experience of the individual actor, nor the existence of any form of societal totality, but social practices ordered across space and time' (see also Thompson 1989). The theorem of the duality of structure and agency resembles the relation between language and speech (Werlen 1995). While speech is situated in space and time, language is virtual, timeless, and without subject. Language is neither directed towards a specific actor nor can it be ascribed to a specific actor. The same applies to social structure. Though individual agency constitutes social interaction, social structure has only a virtual existence. Structure is comprised of rules and resources, around which individual agency takes place in a recurrent fashion. In this way, interaction is structured and structure is continuously reproduced. Structure, however, only exists in social interaction (Thompson 1989). Social structure is a virtual order of transformational relations that continuously reproduce social practice (Giddens 1984).

In line with structuration theory, the relational perspective focuses on institutions in order to include macro-social structures in the analysis of economic relations. We understand institutions as forms of ongoing and relatively stable patterns of social practice that owe their existence to either purposeful constitution or unintentional emergence (Hartfiel and Hillmann 1982). Institutions are based on habits, rules, conventions, norms, and laws that increase an actor's expectation about the likely response of another actor and thus create certainty in social interaction (Bathelt and Depner 2003; Glückler 2004b). They also enable patterns of reproduction through the institutionalization of economic action across space–time. Institutions represent a common social arena for processes of communication, collective learning, and innovation. On the one hand, institutions constrain the space for alternative actions (North 1990); on the other hand, they provide the necessary conditions under which continuous interaction is made possible (Hodgson 1988). A relational approach to economic geography acknowledges that institutions can only become real through the course of social practices and that such practices are the unit of analysis best suited to understanding the foundations of institutions. Economic action is, in other words, highly contextual in nature; it is situated within material and social relations as well as institutional contexts. Institutional contexts provide routine social orientations that motivate economic relations. They are recursively reproduced through these relations and transactions.

3.4 **Institutions as Mediators**

As argued in the context of structuration theory, institutions are critical in resolving the structure–agency dualism and in understanding the linkages between micro- and macro-levels of economic development. From a relational perspective, institutions do not primarily serve to constrain or limit economic action (e.g. North 1991). They possess important opportunity-generating capabilities regarding the interaction within and between firms, as well as across communities of economic agents (Hodgson 1998). In this perspective, institutions are defined not so much as rules but, following Setterfield (1993: 756), as the 'correlated behaviour of agents . . . that reoccurs under the same or similar conditions' (Dopfer 1991: 536). Institutions are collective in the sense that they include patterns of behaviour that cannot be traced back to individual agents.

The relational perspective is particularly well suited to analysing economic institutions in thematic, methodological, and ontological terms (Jessop 2001). Economic institutions can be understood as stabilized forms of social relations that are recursively produced through relational action (Bathelt and Glückler 2003c). Efficient communication between transaction partners in a particular environment requires the development of a shared context of formal and informal institutions. This encourages specialized users and producers to discuss and solve problems (Hodgson 1998; North 1991).[3] Such a framework does not, however, exist spontaneously. It develops over time and requires the joint experiences and interaction of agents in relation to one another. Institutions might involve a set of shared understandings of best-practice technologies, key concepts, signs, and expectations, or include tacit agreements of the solutions and practices that are suboptimal or do not work. In an economic context, the development of institutions can be strongly guided along the lines of so-called knowing communities (Amin and Cohendet 2004; Cohendet et al. 2011), such as epistemic communities (Knorr Cetina 1999) and communities of practice (Brown and Duguid 1991; Wenger 1998).

The various rules, norms, conventions, habits, and technology attitudes that affect economic action are often shaped to a significant degree by the settings negotiated at the level of the national state (Lundvall and Maskell 2000; Bathelt 2003). Even in the context of increasing economic globalization, the national state still has an important impact on the conditions under which firms operate. At the same time, globalization increasingly shapes processes of institutionalization and challenges the boundaries of the national state. This creates another dualism that institutions help mediate. Beyond this, institutions are significant in the context of regional production (Amin 1999; Asheim and Isaksen 2002) in that they enable inter-firm collaboration by translating and adjusting national conditions into regional specificities.

This suggests that different layers of institutions can support or may work against one another. The relations between 'community' and 'society', for instance, are decisive in understanding why some places grow faster than others (Storper 2004; Rodríguez-Pose and Storper 2006; Farole et al. 2010). In addition to these institutional levels, Clark et al. (2001) emphasize the context of 'family' inheritance for regional development. These endowments and inheritances include institutions and routines at different scales that support interactive learning. Family inheritance refers to the regional firms' accumulated capabilities and describes the overall ability of all firms in a region to learn individually. In contrast, community inheritance encompasses the overall capacity for interaction and learning between firms in a specific region, while society endowments relate to the overall societal opportunities and restrictions for interaction. In the short run, these inheritances are more-or-less fixed and cannot be changed by individual actors. In the longer run, however, territorial policies can influence processes of economic development by (re)defining institutional conditions at different levels. They create a set of nested scales that are neither hierarchical nor deterministic (Swyngedouw 1997). Economic action and interaction are mediated through and between these scales because activities take place simultaneously at various levels, and thus have multi-scalar influences (Bunnell and Coe 2001).

The above arguments suggest that a relational perspective does not rule out macro-theoretical considerations because economic agency is, of course, not independent from the conditions of the capitalist system. Institutions serve to mediate between both the micro and macro levels (Jessop 2001). They create a connection between the wider societal structures and economic agency. This also helps elucidate the relationship between local and global forces (e.g. Clark 2005). On the one hand, institutions shape economic practices and should, thus, be studied at the level of the economic actor (Hodgson 1998). On the other hand, the institutional context motivates ongoing relations between agents and encourages patterns of reproduction. This, in turn, influences the institutional conditions under which economic action takes place. Overall, a reflexive process of economic action and institution-building can be conceptualized (see Hudson 2004). This process involves influences from macro structures, such as the capitalist system, that are transferred to the individual level through institutions in a process of downward causation. At the same time, there is also a process of upward causation (Hodgson 2003). This process describes how micro practices are translated into broader institutional arrangements that affect the macro level.

The processes of upward and downward causation lead us to employ a dynamic perspective of institutions in order to understand how institutions change over time. While institutional change has often been viewed as a top-down process through, for instance, the introduction of new rules or government policies as in the state-centred approach of Skocpol (1979; see Hooghe and

Marks 2003), others suggest that institutions are also shaped through bottom-up processes. According to Hall and Thelen (2009: 17): '[c]hanges in rules often follow the accumulation of "deviant" behaviour'. Thelen's work (2003) on institutional conversion, for example, demonstrates how institutions come to be used in ways that differ from what they were originally built for (Streeck and Thelen 2005). Hall and Thelen (2009) provide several illustrative examples of such 'shifts from below' where incremental changes in patterns of economic interaction generate new demands regarding the general institutional framework. In a similar vein, Tsai (2010) shows how adaptive informal institutions can trigger changes in formal institutions. Using the case of reforms in contemporary China, Tsai (2007) demonstrates that such bottom-up processes of institutional change can occur even in non-democratic authoritarian states.

Giddens (1984) has described these processes of upward and downward causation as reflexive relationships between structure and agency. This does not mean that structure determines agency and vice versa, creating a vicious circle without any explanatory significance. Rather, interdependence between institutions and agency results in progressive development, where institutions mediate between individuals and wider societal structures.[4] Yet, as Murdoch (1995) suggests, there is a danger of constructing macro explanations to interpret micro-scale processes without sufficient empirical evidence. It is generally problematic to simply transfer findings from one level of aggregation to another. Therefore, interpretations of macro-scale trends in economic and societal development should be based on, at least, some micro-scale evidence related to practices of economic action and the social relations through which these practices are channelled.

Although we have just argued that institutions connect different scales and accommodate dynamic changes by mediating between structure and agency, shifts in institutions are by no means automatic or frictionless processes.

3.5 Institutional Hysteresis

Institutions play a critical role in economic interaction because they establish the basic conditions for information and knowledge exchange. Institutions can become a burden, however, if they are associated with rigid conditions that limit the perceptions and choice opportunities of economic actors. This is particularly problematic when institutions support inefficient economic or technological developments, and lead economic networks to rely on internal problem-solving and existing power hierarchies, instead of searching for best-practice solutions at a wider national and international level. Although lock-in situations can be a source of high economic returns over extended time periods, they can lead to a negative 'catch-22' situation, or one in which better technological choices are ruled out (Martin and Sunley 2006).

Although institutions are subject to ongoing incremental adjustments, negative lock-in can trigger constellations that are hostile to institutional change (Hassink and Shin 2005), which can lead to a situation that has been referred to as institutional hysteresis (Hassink and Shin 2005; Setterfield 1993). This raises a number of important issues regarding the potential problems that institutions create in terms of (*a*) processes of innovation and knowledge generation, (*b*) the persistence of inefficient institutions in supporting *practices* that are suboptimal, disruptive, or unsustainable, and (*c*) the creation of such institutions in the first place.

1. *Institutions versus innovations.* One important question that arises from the above discussion involves the way in which institutions may inhibit innovation processes. In the context of strong institutions and power relationships associated with existing economic structures, it might be difficult to introduce new technologies to the market and become a successful innovator in the face of opposing or contrary social forces. Whereas institutions, on the one hand, are strongly associated with stability and pre-existing structures, innovations, on the other hand, propose and often require changes. This problem is well illustrated in the historical context of the introduction of the electrical light by Thomas Alva Edison (Hargadon and Douglas 2001). In the case of the electrical light, the oligopoly of the then dominating gas industry had created rigid institutions that blocked off a shift towards the electrical light technology. This exemplifies that innovative success is not necessarily a direct consequence of technological superiority (David 1985). Hargadon and Douglas (2001) argue that associative points have to be found in innovation to present the design of a new product in established interpretative contexts in order to increase an innovation's initial acceptance. To accommodate this, the design of innovations should relate to existing routines, while, at the same time, offering enough flexibility to be adapted to new and changing market environments. As the case of the electrical light illustrates, innovations are more likely to succeed if they are introduced in the context of existing institutions. This provides legitimacy and incentives to change these institutions.

2. *Persistence of inefficient institutions.* Another question that arises involves the persistence of conventions that are clearly suboptimal. Setterfield (1993) identifies a number of possible explanations for this. Following a similar logic as in the classical prisoners' dilemma in economics, institutional inefficiencies might persist if they help to avoid conflicts regarding, for instance, the redistribution of resources or outcomes. Another reason for maintaining inefficient institutions involves the avoidance of economic sanctions. An industrial supplier, for instance, might choose to rely on outdated delivery systems in order to maintain relations with major customers (see also Uzzi

1996). The high cost of changing institutions is another factor that may help explain why institutional inefficiencies persist. Indeed, given that institutions are often systematically interrelated, changes in one institutional domain might require extensive investments in other domains. The interrelatedness of institutions can, thus, inhibit changes in one institutional dimension, irrespective of others (Frankel 1955).

Finally, the continued acceptance of an institution that has potentially negative economic or social consequences may, in fact, be a rational choice. This is a problem that has been discussed in the context of the socialization of negative external effects in the economy. Marquis (2003) provides an illustrative example of the persistence of such institutions from a geographical perspective. He compares the development of networks of inter-locking directorships in the largest US cities, and demonstrates that the business networks of cities that were established prior to the advent of air travel technology were significantly more locally bound than the networks of younger cities. Despite the availability of modern travel technologies in the entire urban system, new corporate board positions in older cities are filled predominantly with local directors. The persistence of this routine in older communities illustrates the basic argument of imprinting theory (Stinchcombe 1965). According to this perspective, organizations adopt characteristics in response to the environmental conditions that exist during their period of foundation. These imprinted patterns are sustained over time, and persist even through periods of significant environmental change. Since the social technology of long-distance travel was not available before the introduction of air transport, business communities had to assign local directors to their corporate boards. These imprinted practices constitute a 'locally legitimate template of action' (Marquis 2003: 656).

3. *Establishment of inefficient institutions.* While it is possible to explain how an institution that was once efficient becomes less efficient or even inefficient over time, it appears more difficult to understand why inefficient institutions are created to begin with. Setterfield (1993) offers three possible explanations to this problem: First, institutions that are substandard or disruptive might result from a hostile selection environment. This could be associated with random processes as suggested in Arthur's model (1988) of path dependence where increasing returns, at some point, lead all agents to choose the same solution over another, even if their original preference was in opposition to this. Second, inefficient institutions might be generated because their creation is easy, following a Pareto process which avoids conflict-laden choices that could involve redistribution. Third, the distinction between efficient and inefficient institutions might not be clear at the outset. Therefore, original choices might turn out to be suboptimal at a later point.

3.6 **Geography of Market-Making**

In situations of institutional hysteresis, such as those discussed above, it is a challenging task to overcome ossification and negative lock-in, and develop new institutional arrangements, best practices, and/or standards. Addressing these non-routine processes requires collective action – a process that is, itself, grounded in and shaped by institutional settings. We discuss this issue further in the context of markets and market institutions. In neoclassical economics, markets are traditionally viewed as idealized settings in which atomistic agents, possessing perfect knowledge, buy and sell products in order to maximize their individual benefits. These markets are governed by price mechanisms and exchange processes that do not require social interactions. However, as Hodgson (1988) correctly points out, markets are not free of institutions. Institutions shape the perceptions and preferences of economic agents and, thus, have an important impact on interaction patterns.

If we allow that economic agents are inherently social beings, rather than individual profit maximizers, a set of questions arise regarding our under-standing of market processes: How, for instance, can we conceptualize mar-kets as social institutions? Furthermore, how can we explain the existence of markets and how they are constructed? Transaction-cost analysis shows that not all transactions are best organized in the form of market transactions (Coase 1937). It is also difficult to understand market transactions at an auction without emphasizing the role of the auctioneer. As opposed to neoclassical conceptions, markets are characterized by structures and conven-tions, such as price norms, which support certain types of behaviour and not others (Hodgson 1988). How this operates can be understood by analysing how markets are constructed in relational ways, as has been studied in actor–network theory (i.e. Callon 1998*b*).

The rules and regularities of a market are constrained by both time and space. Since each transaction is accompanied by different degrees of risk, uncertainty, and valuation problems, on both the supply and demand side of the exchange, markets emerge as contextual social constructions. They are specific in time and space for each product or service (Callon 1998*a*). The question, however, remains as to how particular market regularities emerge? From an evolutionary and institutional perspective, a market can be defined as an institutional arrangement, based on a set of rules and conventions, that facilitates a large number of economic transactions between anonymous agents, at a cost that is lower than it would be without such an arrangement (Ménard 1995). Real markets are a composite of the price mechanism and a set of specific rules and conventions that coordinate expectations and com-pliances between supply and demand (Granovetter 1993; Hodgson 1999). These rules are made, first, by vendors and suppliers seeking to obtain new clients for their products (Loasby 2000), and, second, by regulating authorities and similar organizations that enforce compliance to prevent opportunistic behaviour and market failure (Boyer 1997). The advantage of such a market is that instead of having to renegotiate the terms of trade for each transaction, trade can proceed continuously under a set of established rules of exchange. This leads to substantial cost savings.

Once an institutional arrangement made by a vendor is acceptable for customers, the level of mutual uncertainty decreases such that scale economies become effective. As a particular set of rules and conventions becomes increasingly accepted and used by customers, the unit cost of 'making' the market lowers. Although businesses that fail to create appropriate market arrangements often disappear, those that are successful in this respect benefit from large demand and are thus imitated by other businesses (Loasby 2000). Transactions in – spatially and temporally constrained – organized markets are more efficient than ad hoc transactions, which require full negotiation on all terms of the exchange (Hodgson 1988; Sayer 1995).

Thus, the challenges facing suppliers and supporting actors, such as regulating authorities, business associations, and consultants, are to observe, explore, and develop appropriate rules and conventions of exchange that customers accept. Customers benefit from market-making because explicit rules of exchange reduce uncertainty regarding their suppliers. There are numerous institutional arrangements that suppliers employ to reduce customer uncertainty. Warranties (e.g. money-back guarantees), sample products (e.g. trial trip), subsequent improvement (cure), and performance-based fees are some of the incentives that suppliers and legislators may offer to make a market attractive to customers (Glückler 2004b). Many of these mechanisms have proven to be useful and have thus been copied and transferred to many other service and product markets. Additionally, real markets are embedded in a broader set of institutional arrangements that also draw on authoritative resources (i.e. sanctions) to enforce compliance. The most important of these arrangements are the monetary system, the rule of law, and the ordinary jurisdiction (Boyer 1997).

The abstract model of the neoclassical market would more accurately be described as a theory of exchange, rather than one of the market (Beckert 2009). It neither has a spatial nor a temporal dimension – in the sense of history and evolution. However, a geography of the economy would not be possible without costs of transportation and transaction, or without situated, contextual institutional arrangements about the terms of trade. It is exactly this temporal and spatial contextuality that transforms the (single abstract) market into (many real) markets. It also enables relational action in spatial perspective. A subfield in economic geography that pays particular attention to its cultural foundations follows the work of Callon (1998b) and others in examining how the relevant parties develop, negotiate, and impose rules and conventions in markets (e.g. Swain 2006; Berndt and Boeckler 2007;

Hall 2008; Lindner 2008). Markets are geographically and historically specific institutional arrangements constructed in a relational manner. They emerge from a complex interplay of macro-institutional legislation and politics, societal institutions such as norms of legitimacy, and the everyday negotiations and experimentations between suppliers, customers, and other parties at the micro level. Markets are, therefore, not only specific and contextual in the present but they are under permanent strain and continuous reproduction over time.

3.7 **Method Follows Motivation**

The discourse about the conceptualization of economic interaction in spatial perspective has been closely associated with debates about the choice of appropriate methods in empirical research. Proponents of cultural and relational approaches have emphasized the need for qualitative, interpretative work (e.g. Schoenberger 1997), while advocates of geographical economics clearly prioritize quantitative, statistical data analysis (e.g. Overman 2004). Our relational conceptualization does not *ex ante* prioritize one method of empirical research over another. Rather, it promotes an open, reflective, and problem-oriented approach to the use of methods. According to this view, methods should follow the motivations and goals of the research agenda, rather than vice versa. Similar to Bryman (1984), we detach our discussion of empirical methods from the debate about epistemology to overcome the dogmatic divide between quantitative and qualitative methods, which is so often contrasted in the dualism of positivist versus interpretative paradigms (Sayer 1992). Instead, we encourage a reflective application of both qualitative and quantitative methods as long as they are well suited to the particular research questions, objects of knowledge, and empirical units of analysis under investigation.

This approach is in line with the strategy of triangulation. The basic idea of triangulation is to challenge an empirical reality with different alternative ways of analysis. Triangulation involves a combination of different methodologies in studying the same empirical phenomena (Denzin 1978). Depending on the criteria set, different techniques of triangulation can be distinguished, such as the triangulation of data, researchers, theories, or methods of data collection, analysis, and interpretation (Webb et al. 1965; Jick 1979; Harrigan 1983; Denzin 1989; Miles and Huberman 1994; Yeung 1997; Wengraf 2001). Overlaps and comparisons of alternative theories, data, and methods allow the researcher to control for the limitations associated with different individual techniques. This helps reduce potential biases in empirical observations that are due to the specific method applied. Over the last decade, triangulation has gained increasing importance in economic geography (Cochrane 1998; Hughes 1999; Winchester 1999; Crang 2002, 2003; Glückler 2004*b*; Bathelt and Kappes 2009). The combined use of distinct methodologies increases the validity of empirical findings since the same or similar findings result from the use of different methods. When findings are contradictory, triangulation also offers the opportunity to strive for more context-specific explanations of a phenomenon (Jick 1979). The use of mixed methods does not a priori lead to more reliable and valid findings. It will still be necessary to define the grounds for appropriate research designs in each context of analysis and to reflect and adjust each method to the theoretical or empirical problem at hand (Baxter and Eyles 1997). In the remainder of this chapter, we revisit some important streams of methodologies and illustrate how they can be applied within a relational framework to analyse economic interaction.

3.7.1 QUALITATIVE RESEARCH

Qualitative, intensive methodologies (Sayer 1992) or process-based approaches (Yeung 2003) have found much support in recent years and have increasingly been used to study economic interaction in spatial perspective (Crang 2002, 2003). They are very well suited to capturing the contextuality and meaning of human action, social relations, and institutional conditions in economic processes (Mullings 1999; Oinas 1999) and to elaborate causal explanations in the sense of critical realism (Sayer 1992, 2000; Winchester 1999; Downward et al. 2002). For many research questions, interview-based qualitative methods are indispensable.

   This can be illustrated in the analysis of trust (Glückler 2005). While trust lacks universal meaning, it is constituted in subjective cognition and contextual interaction. It thus emerges as an informal institution in situated contexts of economic relations. As a consequence, trust has different meanings for different agents and varies substantially across cultures. Since trust cannot be measured directly, empirical research needs to find adequate indicators and ways of observation. In the context of business research, trust has been studied through quantitative indicators related to reciprocity, that is, the number of repeated transactions within the same relationship (Gulati 1995), and commitment, that is, the concentration of resources on one relationship (Kollock 1994). The causal ambiguity here is that while these indicators may be important effects of trust, they may also be the result of different or even opposite phenomena. Firms may repeatedly interact with other firms not only because they trust each other but also because they may bear high exit barriers, that is, high switching costs when changing partners. Alternatively, firms may commit their resources to one partner not only because of trust but also because they are dependent on that partner and lack sufficient opportunities to trade with alternative partners. Trust and dependency certainly do not represent the same qualities of a relationship. Survey-based methods are often unable to control for the contextual qualities of trust. In order to develop a deeper and more contextual understanding of the qualities of trust, it is necessary to seek conversation, create imagination, and empathize with the agents under investigation. Understanding the motivations, rationalities, and strategies behind economic action and interaction thus requires a similar methodological approach. In summary, qualitative research complements a relational perspective of the economy because it is sensitive to the contextuality of economic interaction, and to the perceptions and interpretations of the agents involved.

3.7.2 QUANTITATIVE RESEARCH

Quantitative methods are typically used for extensive research (Sayer 2000). Instead of developing (grounded), theory from the empirical field (Eisenhardt 1989; Glaser and Strauss 1967), extensive research seeks to test (universal) theories by means of finding regularities in large numbers of repeated and standardized observations (Sayer 1992).[5] Quantifying methods and statistical testing have been harshly criticized in some research. This is often grounded in fundamental dualisms rejecting aspects such as positivism, objective knowledge, the quantifiability of social phenomena, the belief in cause as regularity, universality, or the neglect of contextuality (Clark 1998; Downward et al. 2002; Yeung 2003). Despite our epistemological scepticism (see Chapter 2), we do not reject quantitative methods per se. Instead, we suggest selecting and adjusting quantitative methods in such a way that an adequate fit to a particular research problem is achieved.

Some critics have correctly pointed out the problem of theorizing micro phenomena while measuring the same phenomena at higher levels of aggregation across spatial, organizational, or sectoral units (e.g. Bahrenberg et al. 1985). It has been shown that this approach leads to ecological fallacies (Robinson 1950). Nonetheless, efforts to make controlled observations of an empirical field can be very helpful and, in fact, complement qualitative findings: In a study of the New York apparel industry, for instance, Uzzi (1997) developed a contextual understanding of the meaning and benefits attributed by entrepreneurs to trustful and long-term business relations with their suppliers. In a consecutive quantitative analysis, Uzzi (1997) analysed the impact of the specific composition of the network of business relations for each firm and found evidence of a phenomenon referred to as the paradox of embeddedness. This paradox suggests that, although individual relations based on trust and reciprocity are beneficial for firms, a dense portfolio of cooperative relations beyond a certain threshold can turn these benefits into increased mortality risks, as networks become excessively rigid and exclusive. From similar work, we can conclude that quantitative methods offer at least two opportunities for empirical research: First, they enable us to examine the sometimes paradoxical macro effects of aggregated micro events (Giddens 1984), as exemplified in Uzzi's study (1997). Second, they help us to empirically assess the contingency of causal explanations that emerge from qualitative fieldwork. By observing the empirical co-occurrence of phenomena, which have been identified in empirical fieldwork as meaningful, it is possible to develop an understanding of the non-contextuality of a contingent relation between these phenomena. In this respect, and if appropriately employed, quantitative research can add to the understanding of critical realist research in important ways – especially if causality is a matter of both contingency and the extent of non-contextuality of necessary relations. Chapter 8 will make use of this research strategy in the context of corporate internationalization.

3.7.3 SOCIAL NETWORK ANALYSIS

From a relational perspective, social network analysis represents a particularly interesting and appropriate technique within the realm of quantitative methodology to study patterns of social and economic relationships. It assumes that the structure of social relations between actors conveys systematic conclusions and expectations about individual and collective action (Mizruchi 1994). This method builds on the identification and analysis of a social network in economic context, understood as 'a specific set of linkages among a defined set of [agents], with the additional property that the characteristics of these linkages as a whole may be used to interpret the social behaviour of the [agents] involved' (Mitchell 1969: 2). This definition situates relations at the centre of analysis and suggests that a specific structure of relations may be used to make inferences about individual and collective action (Knoke and Kuklinski 1991). From this perspective, structure is not something that exists in the virtual realm; it is a tangible context of social interaction (Granovetter 1985). This view helps to bridge the dualism between structure and agency, as previously discussed, because it treats structure in such a way that allows it to be studied empirically and in direct association with human interaction (Mizruchi 1994; Glückler 2001a). This is particularly interesting in the context of the knowledge economy, as much empirical work has demonstrated the impact of network structure on the action of individuals.[6] Network analysis differs from traditional structural analyses in that it explicitly takes actors and their intentions into consideration. Hence, the contingency of structural effects on economic action is fully acknowledged when studying concepts such as social capital, where the impact of network structure is dependent upon the actors' objectives (Burt 1997; Portes 1998; Sandefur and Laumann 1998) and their specific institutional and market contexts (e.g. Rowley et al. 2000). While quantitative methods of social network analysis have been used extensively in the social sciences (e.g. organization studies, sociology, psychology, or ethnology), they have long been neglected in economic geography and economics (Grabher 2006). Such techniques have only recently been used in the analysis of intra- and inter-firm dynamics in a spatial perspective (e.g. Glückler 2007a, 2008, 2010a; Ter Wal and Boschma 2009).[7]

Over the past decade, our own research has covered many different sectors of economic interaction, including manufacturing industries – such as automobile suppliers, chemical producers, high-technology ventures, and metal fabricators – as well as service branches – such as advertising, consulting, IT services, photography, and TV/film production. We have conducted hundreds of interviews with representatives of firms, business associations, public administrations, planning departments, chambers of commerce, regulating authorities, and experts in many different countries, including Argentina, Canada, China, France, Germany, Spain, the United Kingdom, and the United States. Without 'close dialogue' (Clark 1998), conversation, and personal involvement, it would have been impossible to develop a contextual understanding of these industries and places, let alone an understanding of what drives people to pursue their economic goals and relate to one another in networks of relationships. In fact, none of the empirical findings reported in this book could have been produced without in-depth qualitative fieldwork. While the empirical examples provided in Chapters 5, 7, and 9 are strongly based on interview methods, Chapters 6, 8, and 10 explicitly draw on mixed-method approaches, where quantitative methodologies based on network surveys are combined with interview techniques. Through this, we aim to demonstrate an open, reflective, and inclusive understanding of methodologies in order to realize the full potential of relational analyses, rather than supporting epistemological exclusion. This work benefits from *in situ* qualitative research as well as from triangulation with other methods such as quantitative analyses.

3.8 **Conclusion**

This chapter aims to broaden our perspective of relational action beyond individual or collective agents and their direct transaction partners to include wider societal and economic structures and developments. It begins by discussing the role of economic agents in relational analyses and the rationalities that guide them. It then develops a conceptualization of relational action that acknowledges the various ways in which economic practices are shaped by socio-institutional settings and how these structures are, in turn, continuously reproduced through economic interaction. In this respect, it also suggests the need to develop closer linkages between the level of the individual agent and the wider social and economic structures. Otherwise, past decisions and economic conditions of a specific capitalist era would be treated as exogenous events, similar to how conventional studies in regional economics and economic geography have excluded social and technological progress from their analyses of economic processes. In this context, we define institutions as patterns of social interaction that mediate between the micro and macro levels of analysis. Drawing on Giddens' structuration theory (1984), we elaborate a conception of institutions that acknowledges both upward and downward causation processes. This allows us to analyse how institutions simultaneously shape and are shaped by processes of economic interaction. The framework opens up new possibilities to integrate micro and macro phenomena in academic work, while, at the same time, highlighting the importance of micro-level research in the study of economic processes. On a related issue, we call for a mixed-method approach in conducting relational analyses. In the empirical examples provided in Part II of this book, we promote a heterodox approach that integrates qualitative *and* quantitative methods supporting discussions across these approaches, rather than their encapsulation.

4   Knowledge as a Relational Resource

4.1 **Introduction**

In the previous chapters, we have developed a relational conception of economic action based on a critique of neoclassical economic and regional science approaches, which often assume that decision-making processes are fully rational and led by price signals. Instead of assuming homo-economicus behaviour, the relational approach conceptualizes economic action and inter-action as processes that are influenced by both existing social and institutional relations and the consequences of prior relations (Chapter 2). Simply put, we suggest that institutional contexts and networks of individual and collective agents should be central to the analysis of economic structures and processes. As demonstrated in the previous chapters, this perspective is not restricted to microeconomic studies. In emphasizing the role of institutions, we also link processes of economic action to wider territorial and social structures. At the same time, our approach does not conceptualize an economy governed by trust-based linkages and altruistic agents. As argued in Chapter 3, an analysis of the transactions of goods, services, and knowledge in markets is critical to understanding economic action in spatial perspective. A relational framework is particularly useful in understanding how markets are created and how the institutional frameworks that develop govern these markets.

Further clarification is, however, needed on the role of resources in a relational conception of the economy. As indicated in Chapter 1, critiques of constructivist theories could easily be transferred to the relational framework, and questions could also be raised regarding the degree to which resources and the material reality still matter in this approach. The role of resources in the economy is central to our understanding of economic development, and we conceptualize this role in a number of consecutive stages:

- First, we investigate the ways in which knowledge can be conceptualized in a relational framework, and respond to questions concerning the creation and diffusion of knowledge in a spatial perspective. This is important because knowledge has become a core driver of the economy, and processes of acquiring, generating, and transferring knowledge are critical to the competitiveness of firms.

- Second, we undertake a broader exploration of the role of resources in relational economies, and suggest that the relationship between natural resources – namely, the localized materials in Weber's classical analysis (1909) – and the material infrastructure cannot be ignored in our investigation of economic action. Extending this conceptualization, we provide a relational understanding of how these resources are valued, and how they impact economic decision-making.
- Third, we provide a conceptualization of resources such as power and social capital, which are produced through practices of social relations and, thus, cannot be controlled or appropriated by individual agents.
- Finally, we look at how different types of resources affect one another in economic practice and how shifts in the settings and structures of one resource type may affect other resources.

4.2 **Substantive versus Relational Thinking of Resources**

This chapter ultimately argues that a relational conception is more useful than a substantive conception in understanding the generation and application of different resources. A relational approach also leads to a more accurate representation of the variety of different uses and values assigned to resources in the reflexive economy (Storper 1997c). Firms produce outputs by procuring and transforming inputs, yielding value added. In conventional economic analysis, three types of inputs or production factors are distinguished – land, labour, and capital. Yet, in the context of the reflexive economy, the existing heterogeneity of strategies and technological developments, associated with firms in different spatial contexts, cannot be explained by variations in the composition and use of production factors alone. Strategic differentiation, innovation, organization, and the economic success of firms are strongly influenced by other factors that can be conceptualized as resources to be used in the production process. Aside from machinery, equipment, and financial capital, there are other forms of capital – such as experience, knowledge, social capital, and power – that enter production. These resources create additional challenges in the production process as they are not purely technical in nature and, thus, require more than just technological expertise. They are socially constructed entities that rely on collective processes of resource generation and application. This shift in perspective has fundamental consequences for the exploitation and use of resources, as well as for our understanding of how they operate.

Table 4.1. Substantive versus relational understandings of resources

Resource types	Substantive understanding	Relational understanding
Knowledge	Knowledge as a precondition for economic success characterized by inherent, predetermined consequences	Knowledge as a (frequently unanticipated) result of collective interpretations and recombinations
Material resources	Resources as production factors characterized by predefined input–output relationships	Resources as bundles of possible services characterized by contingent returns
Power	Power as the inscribed capacity of an actor to dominate by means of resource control	Power as the social practice of building networks and enrolling other actors in joint projects
Social capital	Social capital as the universal capability of an actor to exploit networks according to her/his own goals	Social capital as the set of opportunities which results from the existence of social relations with other actors

Source: Adapted from Bathelt and Glückler (2005: 1547).

This chapter applies this view to the analysis of resources, encouraging a shift from a substantive towards a relational understanding of resources. This is accomplished by identifying the limitations of the conventional substantive view, again using a somewhat stylized approach. We find that resources are used and/or produced in a relational manner, that is, in context-specific social processes. This leads to further resource heterogeneity, which then becomes the basis of competitiveness and economic success. We illustrate this by elaborating three key propositions: First, the generation and use of resources rely upon interactive learning and decision-making. Second, these processes are shaped by shared interpretative schemes. Third, the generation and use can (and do) change over time, depending on the context. Through this, the ultimate use and value of resources is contingent. Moreover, we demonstrate that relational resources cannot always be appropriated by individual actors. In what follows, we explore four types of resources that have become increasingly important in the contemporary knowledge economy: knowledge, material resources, power, and social capital. The central goal of our discussion is to elucidate the relational character of each resource type (Table 4.1) and demonstrate how this plays out in a spatial perspective.

4.3 **Relational Knowledge Creation**

The distinction between resources and their possible services suggests that the value and use of material resources are not predetermined but, rather, depend upon their particular social context. Substantive concepts of resources thus have difficulty explaining the processes by which firms gain competitiveness and become innovative. This is particularly relevant in processes of knowledge generation that are internal and external to the firm (Maskell 2001*a*). Interdependencies between the knowledge basis and the structure and strategy of a firm generate a reflexive process of specialization through which particular capabilities are continuously reproduced and extended. At the same time, knowledge is not just the result of the former productive use of resources; it can be viewed as a relational resource in and of itself.

A distinction is often made between explicit, codified knowledge and implicit, tacit knowledge, which is not codified or not codifiable (Nonaka 1994; Gertler 2001). Codified knowledge is knowledge that is, for instance, written down in the form of rules or formulas. Although it can be transferred relatively easily, the comprehension of such knowledge often requires additional scientific knowledge and experience, which are not necessarily available in codified form. These might be practices that involve tacit knowing as conceptualized by Polanyi (1967: 4) who famously stated 'that we know more than we can tell'. According to Polanyi (1967), tacit knowing results when agents focus their complete attention on an event or signal and, in the anticipation of the event, do not consciously notice the trigger that caused it. In an economic context, this view helps us understand routines of problem-solving, as well as the management and control of complex production processes.[1]

In the knowledge-creation view of the firm (Nonaka et al. 2000), which can be viewed as a generalization of the resource-based view (Wernerfelt 1984), knowledge is the decisive asset of a firm, and knowledge creation is the key mechanism through which firms produce and sustain competitiveness. From this perspective, knowledge is viewed as the key resource of the developing reflexive or learning economy (Lundvall and Johnson 1994; Boekema et al. 2000; Strambach 2004). Recent work has also demonstrated the importance of adopting a knowledge-based view of localized industry networks or clusters (Maskell 2001*b*; Bathelt 2002; Malmberg and Maskell 2002); adequate explanations cannot be based solely on analyses of the material linkages between firms and resource locations. Knowledge is not a resource that guarantees economic success, nor does it have inherent, predetermined consequences as a production input. We often can identify situations that are characterized by a surplus, rather than a shortage, of knowledge. The solution to a particular problem has to do with the way in which different sorts of knowledge are combined (Lundvall and Johnson 1994). To accomplish this, it is necessary to identify the relevant body of knowledge (know-what), find capable partners (know-who) that are well suited to the particular problem context (know-why), and recognize how to effectively combine and use this knowledge (know-how).[2] This description clearly reveals the relational character of knowledge. Knowledge is socially constructed; it might even become irrelevant outside of a particular context of interaction if external actors are unable to comprehend this knowledge.

As opposed to material resources, the stock of knowledge can be extended through intensive usage (Maskell 2001*a*). The notion of knowledge as 'stock' is, however, problematic in the context of a relational conceptualization. A relational approach implies that the use and value of knowledge – or that of other resources – are fundamentally open and constantly changing. Thus, as Ibert (2007) suggests, it might be more appropriate to give up the notion of stocks altogether. Our approach supports this position and, thus, uses the term 'stock' only as a temporary reference point to describe the amount and value of accumulated resources at a specific time and place. Knowledge differs from material resources and products particularly in two aspects:

1. *Price determination.* Knowledge cannot be treated as though it were an ordinary commodity that can be exchanged through market transactions. The trade of knowledge is difficult because of the challenges associated with specifying its exact supply and demand. Even in the case of explicit, codified knowledge, it is an arduous task to establish a market price. For a potential buyer to determine the value of a particular set of codified knowledge, s/he must be familiar with its contents. One could argue that once the potential buyer knows the contents, s/he has already acquired the commodity and, thus, no longer needs to purchase it.[3] The evaluation of new explicit knowledge is associated with two further difficulties. On the one hand, sufficient tacit knowledge is necessary to interpret and integrate new knowledge in a useful way (Maskell and Malmberg 1999*b*). On the other hand, an actor needs to possess enough experience-based, non-codified knowledge in order to recognize the potential of new knowledge. This makes it difficult to clearly differentiate between explicit and implicit forms of knowledge, as the two are usually combined (Johnson et al. 2002).
2. *Transfer of knowledge.* Another way in which knowledge differs from material resources and products relates to the particular spatial dynamics of knowledge exchange. Tacit knowledge is embodied in people, machines, and other technical systems, which makes it difficult to transfer (Polanyi 1967). Experienced workers, for instance, know exactly how to adjust the production process in their firm to produce maximum quality. It is not easy to transfer this type of knowledge to third parties. Tacit knowledge is also localized in that it is restricted to the actors, firms, and places where it exists and is used (Maskell and Malmberg 1999*b*; Bathelt and Glückler 2003*a*). Amin and Cohendet (2004: 102) emphasize, however, that '[t]he "stickiness" of knowledge in these sites . . . stems from the unique interactions and combinations of bodies, minds, speech, technologies, and objects that can be found there. . . . It has little to do with "native" practices or locally confined assets.' In addition, explicit knowledge that is codified can also be quite 'sticky'. This is especially the case when codified knowledge is adjusted to the conditions of a specific context. Contextualized or embedded knowledge, which is enriched by

localized knowledge, is, in turn, less prone to ubiquitification (Maskell and Malmberg 1999*b*). Therefore, tacit and even contextualized codified knowledge generate a competitive advantage to the regional actors who share it (Asheim 1999; Belussi and Pilotti 2001; Gertler 2003).

The recent 'practice turn' in economic geography convincingly demonstrates the need to shift our perspective of knowledge towards a practice view of knowledge circulation (Faulconbridge 2006; Ibert 2007). This is very much in line with a relational approach, which views knowledge not as a clearly specified object with predefined applications and uses but as fluid and in a constant state of flux. Knowledge is regularly communicated and discussed with other agents, which can lead to new and different interpretations regarding its applicability, or reinforce its application to existing purposes. It is, therefore, impossible to store or sell knowledge like other products in discrete transactions; knowledge is situated within specific contexts, and generates opportunities for economic action within these contexts. This requires meaningful interpretations and translations (e.g. Latour 1986) across cultural, political, or institutional boundaries. In this sense, the increasing importance of consulting and other knowledge-intensive businesses is a reflection of the need to acquire new knowledge practices and processes, as opposed to knowledge products.

The above discussion demonstrates that while the use of knowledge is contextual and path-dependent, it is also contingent. During the process of transforming data and information into knowledge, such information is continuously being interpreted and evaluated with respect to a specific context. The degree to which such knowledge is important to a firm depends upon a host of factors: the firm's particular technology and market context; its strategies and capacity to absorb new knowledge; its previous experience with integrating new knowledge; and the extent to which the actors inside the firm are able to recognize the potential of this knowledge in extending their overall competencies (Cohen and Levinthal 1990; Malecki 2000; Bathelt et al. 2004). There is no agreed best way to apply new knowledge originating from different industries or technology fields; it can be used and evaluated in different ways. With respect to existing practices, it can cause incremental, discontinuous, or even no changes at all, although incremental changes might be the typical consequence of relational action and interaction.

4.4 Spatiality of Knowledge Creation

The creation of knowledge is a spatially sensitive process that requires a spatial perspective of analysis. Equally, knowledge practices are not abstract processes (Ibert 2007). They are bound to particular people and occur in and between specific places (Meusburger 1998, 2008; Faulconbridge 2006). Given the spatial overlap of different flows of economic and social interaction, and the inclusion or exclusion of different people in various functions and locations, knowledge creation logically varies from place to place (Bathelt and Glückler 2003b). Taking this one step further, a relational reading of place (Amin 2004) implies that local knowledge is not just locally produced or solely based on close-by resources; it depends on and is shaped by systematic linkages with other parts of the world through media reports, international business travel, transnational communities, and so on. In light of this, Amin (2004) and Massey (2004) argue for a new relational, non-territorial politics of place that extends beyond a limited number of seemingly local issues to include external actors that are connected to a specific place as a result of shared stakes and responsibilities (see Chapter 11).

New knowledge does not simply appear out of nowhere. It has a history in the sense that it is based on existing knowledge, and created through a process whereby different kinds of knowledge are integrated, transformed, and re-interpreted in meaningful ways (Nonaka et al. 2000). The process of knowl-edge creation can also be understood as one of knowledge transformation, as Nonaka and Takeuchi (1995) have convincingly demonstrated in the case of large firms. This so-called SECI process involves different sources of tacit knowledge that are explicated, recombined, internalized into the technical systems and employees' routines, and further transformed through processes of learning and socializing. Although it has been recognized that the articula-tion of tacit knowledge is important in enabling learning (Tracey and Clark 2002), the transformation of implicit into explicit knowledge does not follow a linear or sequential trajectory. Through this transformation, production can be organized at a lower cost over time (Lawson and Lorenz 1999). With respect to the role of resources, the processes of knowledge creation and transfer are associated with specific spatialities:

1. *Spatiality of knowledge transfer.* This process clearly shows why knowledge has become important as a resource in economic life. Organizational deficits and miscommunication at some stage can interrupt the transformation and recombination of existing knowledge pools resulting in a lack of innovation and loss of competitiveness. Given the potential problems that can occur at a single firm site, it is easy to imagine how much greater the barriers and risks for miscommunication might be in an inter-firm innovation context involv-ing actors from different countries and regions (Gertler 1997, 2001). Such innovation processes are important, however, in order to prevent firms from missing out on technological and strategic developments in other market regions and national states (see Chapter 10). If firms focus too exclusively on regional networks and neglect market and technology trends elsewhere, a lock-in situation could result (Grabher 1993b; Hellmer et al. 1999; Clark

and Tracey 2004). This could undermine the reproduction of a firm's knowledge basis (Bathelt 2002). In an international innovation context, however, the agents involved speak different languages and act according to different norms, rules, and other institutional practices. They are not able to automatically exchange the details of new knowledge between one another and they cannot participate in each other's local buzz or information flows (Fujita et al. 1999; Storper and Venables 2002; Bathelt et al. 2004). In order to benefit from long-term learning and knowledge transfers, it is, therefore, necessary to develop a common institutional basis that enables processes of interactive knowledge generation in trans-local, interregional, and supranational contexts (Storper 1997c; Depner and Bathelt 2003a). This can be accomplished through the development of a multinational or transnational firm structure (Dicken et al. 1994; Dicken 2003; Grabher and Powell 2004; Glückler 2008, 2011), which helps firms integrate different socio-institutional and cultural frameworks into their competence profile, and offer products in one market region that are based on experience gathered in other regions.

2. *Spatiality of knowledge creation.* The process of knowledge generation further demonstrates that new knowledge is socially constructed in a timely manner (Amin and Cohendet 2004). This process involves various stages that require different organizational structures to be efficiently executed (Nonaka et al. 2000). The process of articulating various types of tacit knowledge and recombining this knowledge into a new product conception might, for instance, be best organized in a project team of experts who get together for a limited time period to achieve a clearly defined goal (Grabher 2002a). In contrast, the process of learning and perfecting production routines might be better performed in the context of a more permanent organizational form such as a workplace within a firm. Such an environment also enables the formation of small, flexible teams that are able to conduct short-term problem-solving. Routine problem-solving that extends individual experiences and competencies might even be organized in the context of virtual user communities (von Hippel 2001; Jeppesen and Frederiksen 2006; Grabher et al. 2008), which share general goals, experiences, or visions, along with a particular technological expertise. Such interaction can take place without direct face-to-face contact.

Nonaka et al. (2000) use the Japanese concept of 'ba' to refer to the organizational contexts in which individuals interact at a specific time and place (Lee 2001; Kostiainen 2002; Amin and Cohendet 2004). These contexts are fluid and, due to reflexive social practices, constantly changing. The existence of 'ba' allows information to be interpreted in a meaningful way and eventually results in new knowledge. Although 'ba' is a social concept, its empirical manifestations are associated with distinct spatialities. It can be a physical place, where the technicians in a firm get together to discuss a machinery failure, or an Internet platform, through which engineers regularly exchange ideas about new product designs. In this sense, firms can be understood as dynamic configurations of 'ba', although these principles are not restricted to intra-firm organizational contexts. A practice interpretation leads to a relational dynamic in the sense that places of learning affect the learning patterns of agents, whose actions and interactions, in turn, structure the places of learning (Ibert 2007).

4.5 **The Social Construction of Material Resources**

When we talk about material resources, we usually think of raw materials, intermediate products, machinery and equipment, as well as the different kinds of infrastructure used by firms. These resources are limited in terms of their availability, and are used up through consumption. In this respect, there is a remarkable difference between material resources and the other types of resources discussed. Knowledge, power, and social capital do not diminish when used. In fact, the application of these resources can further strengthen and extend them, as new knowledge, power, or social capital is generated. According to neoclassical economics, the material resources that drive economic action face a shortage problem (Peteraf 1993). From a substantive view, these resources are production factors that can be acquired by firms, and are subsequently exploited according to their needs. In a relational understanding, material resources cannot automatically be viewed as factors with an inherent use value and predetermined application. Accordingly, resources can be used in many different ways and for many different purposes. The use value of a resource depends upon the social context within which goals and capabilities are shaped. Resources can be defined as bundles of possible services, as expressed by Penrose (1959). It is important to differentiate between resources and their respective services because it is possible to acquire and characterize resources independent from the purpose they serve. It is the particular use that determines the way in which they enter the production process as inputs, how valuable they are, and how they strengthen a firm's competitiveness. Penrose (1997: 31) prefers the term resource over production factor, as the latter does not allow for a distinction between the factor itself and its possible services: 'Strictly speaking it is never resources themselves that are "inputs" in the production process, but only the services that the resources can render.' Examples of this can be found when products are used in different, sometimes unrelated contexts. A specific paint, for instance, that is used to mark highway surfaces costs several times as much as it normally would when it is applied as a resistant coating in the context of the aerospace industry.

A relational concept of resources has important consequences for our conceptualization of firms. In conventional economic analysis, firms are defined in terms of the outputs they produce. A resource-based view, in contrast, defines a firm according to its inputs. In this view, firms are defined as bundles of resources, and can be characterized by their specific resource profile (Mahoney and Pandian 1992). From this understanding, we can analyse how different combinations of resources shape a firm's economic success (Wernerfelt 1984). Only by distinguishing between material resources and their potential applications, it is possible to understand the heterogeneity of firms, output specificity, and deviating strategies.

Resources are not only bundles of potential services but also assets for future returns. Firms do not necessarily gain higher returns because they have better resources than others. Their improved performance is also a consequence of using their resources in a different or superior manner (Maskell 2001a). This again directs our attention to the specific practices at hand. In sum, the distinction between a substantive and relational understanding of resources becomes quite clear. Whereas the former concept defines resources as objective production factors characterized by predefined input–output relationships, the latter emphasizes the multiplicity of potential services associated with these resources. The particular use of resources does not only depend on their physical characteristics; it is also influenced by a number of contextual conditions, some of which are described below:

1. *Firm-specific competencies.* Each firm has an accumulated set of knowledge, capabilities, and experience, which have developed over time and shape the identification of particular uses for the resources at hand. It is through these specific competencies that firms are able to integrate resources into the production process in a certain way.

2. *Mental model.* The competencies of a firm are part of its overall mental model or dominant logic (Prahalad and Bettis 1986). This interpretative framework impacts the way in which existing competencies are used, and enables a joint understanding of knowledge pools. The interpretations that are associated with a firm's internal and external information flows indicate its organizational capabilities. The routines that have become established over time strongly influence these interpretations, and the way in which new information is processed and transformed into action. According to Nelson and Winter (1982), organizational routines are the skills of a firm. Through the development and diffusion of new interpretative schemes, it is possible to reinterpret existing knowledge and attach it to new uses, or find new innovative services for existing resources.

3. *Market conditions.* The potential returns of an innovative use of resources also depend on the productive opportunities and constraints in the market (Penrose 1959). These productive opportunities determine

which competencies can be combined or synchronized. This depends on the overall competition, demand, and value-chain-related environment, associated with supplying innovative resource applications and processing the resources further. External market conditions may also constrain the development and use of resources. This depends, for instance, on the market power of key players, or institutional constraints such as dominant technological standards.

The above considerations clearly demonstrate that a firm's products, strategies, interactive capabilities, and technological trajectories can neither be explained by nor reduced to the mix of material resources used. On the contrary, the productive and innovative use of resources depends upon the combination of adequate resources, the competencies of a firm, the mental models that are applied, existing market conditions, and the respective socio-institutional context.

This relational conceptualization of resources shares some important similarities with the concept of non-human actants in actor–network theory (Latour 2005; Jöns 2006). These include technologies, infrastructures, and other non-human artefacts. Actor–network theory describes how these entities affect and stimulate human action, and thus become a subject that can trigger certain reactions. Our relational perspective does not, however, view material resources as being on the same level as agents and their social relations. In this perspective, economic action and interaction are, in essence, intentional and led by institutional conditions (Chapter 3). Accordingly, the effects of material resources are not predetermined or engrained but depend upon the context in which agents are confronted with these resources, the intentions and strategies of the agents, and how they apply them.

4.6 **Power Structures versus Power Relations**

Substantive concepts view power as the characteristic of an economic actor or organization based on the ownership and control of material resources. According to this perspective, agents either have power or they do not. By controlling access to these resources, some actors in economic processes dominate others. As a consequence of this understanding, critical analysts have described multinational firms as being extremely powerful, due to their size and ability to regulate access to resources and labour in international markets. This line of argument can be found, for instance, in discussions about the power of firms versus national states (e.g. Dicken 2003). Without denying the importance of this work, such arguments are based on a limited notion of power. Power cannot be viewed as an 'inscribed capacity' that an actor possesses based on ownership of resources (Allen 1997, 2004). Using a geographical lens, we find numerous examples of asymmetrical distributions of material resources that do not necessarily determine the outcome of economic action. It can, for instance, be quite difficult for a firm to coordinate its production activities in remote branch plants located in different countries even if resource access is under the full control of the headquarter. There are also many reports of international mergers and acquisitions that fail because it is not possible to synchronize the activities of the different workplaces, despite centralized resource control. This is not to say that there is a simple binary geography of power, either as being centred in a localized industry context, such as a cluster from where it radiates, or as being placeless and omnipresent in the global circuits of everyday practices (Allen 2004). In a relational view, power works through different layers of social relations, leading to multiple spatialities.

Drawing on actor–network theory (Latour 1986, 2005; Thrift 1996; Jöns 2003), a relational conception of power is based on a reflexive understanding that views power as both the cause and consequence of human action (Scott 2001; Allen 2004). The consequences of power are not determined by ownership. Rather, its impact on economic structures and processes cannot be forecasted. Taking inter-firm relations in networks or clusters as an example, we find that such relations are shaped by existing power asymmetries that cause patterns of dominance and dependence and affect actors' abilities to react to changing markets and institutional structures (Grabher 1993*a*; Taylor 2000*a*; Bathelt and Taylor 2002). It is, however, problematic to view power asymmetries in only negative terms. Under real world conditions, it is hard to identify a network of firms characterized by symmetrical power relations. Such a distribution of power could, in fact, hinder problem-solving and lead to a situation where debates are prolonged and decisions are postponed. In contrast, the existence of power asymmetries creates opportunities for efficient problem-solving and flexible adjustments in production (Taylor 1995; Lowey 1999; Bathelt 2002). Power asymmetries create a sort of hierarchy and dominance within a network, which helps to settle conflicts between actors and accelerate decision-making processes. This can lead to problems, however, if the agents have too much trust in a given hierarchy, and develop blind confidence in the decisions of dominant firms (Granovetter 1985; Kern 1996). In such cases, agents run the risk of being locked into an inefficient technological trajectory.

This leads to the question what – if not resource control – the mechanisms are that support consistent behaviour within an economic context and allow participating firms to act and grow collectively (see also Chapter 5). In the case of a cluster, we argue that the internal actors, as well as those outside the cluster, must recognize the cluster as an entity that is sufficiently different from its environment and act accordingly. In this view, clusters have causal power because network relations have an 'emergent effect' (Yeung 1994; Dicken et al. 2001; Yeung and Lin 2003); that is, they make the cluster visible to others. This implies that the combined effects of network relations within the cluster are greater than those of the individual powers of its actors. This type of power is referred to by Latour (1986) as the 'powers of association', or 'power as relationships' (Allen 1997; Taylor 2000a). In actor–network theory, actors that are viewed as having power can build networks and develop them further by enrolling other actors (e.g. Murdoch 1995; Smith 2003). Therefore, power is – similar to social capital – embedded in all network relations and, at the same time, created through them.[4]

In a regional industry context, such as a well-developed cluster, social relations are constantly being produced and reproduced through ongoing communication between the actors, similar ways of solving problems, joint decisions about which technologies to use, and the like. This is not a simple diffusion of information from one end to the other. Rather, it should be viewed as a translation process where messages are being transferred through social relations to other actors, who then evaluate the information according to their own goals. During this transfer, the messages are constantly being reinterpreted, giving each actor the opportunity to change its contents (Latour 1986). Within such a structure of social relations, the role of building networks can change over time and is not necessarily limited to a specific number of actors. This becomes even more complicated if we consider the role of structure and spatiality in power relations:

1. *Bringing structure back in.* It is, of course, difficult to establish coherence within a cluster through social relations alone. Material and non-material resources, such as non-human artefacts (e.g. particular technologies or symbols), tools (e.g. manuals or reports), and accepted rules, enable human actors to engage in and maintain social relations (Murdoch 1995; Dicken et al. 2001). The importance of these resources in stabilizing social relations reflects the power of technologies in the sense of Foucault (Allen 1997), or the facilitative power circuit (Clegg 1989; Taylor 2000a). Material and non-material resources are the glue of social relations (Latour 2005).[5]
In a cluster context, particular process and communication technologies serve to stabilize interactions between the actors and firms, as they share the same problems, have similar day-to-day experiences, and develop a mutual understanding. In an intercultural context, non-human artefacts – such as technologies – and existing norms and rules are particularly critical in supporting the interaction between people and the achievement of common goals. Material and non-material resources also shape the course of action. Otherwise, messages could easily be misinterpreted by other actors and technologies used in a different fashion. According to this perspective, a regional industry cluster can be viewed as a temporarily

stabilized set of social relations and accepted material and non-material resources (Chapter 5).

2. *Spatiality of power relations.* Since the coherence of a regional industry configuration and its ability to work are dependent upon the day-to-day interactions of its actors, distance and visibility are of great importance (e.g. Crang 1994; Depner and Bathelt 2003*a*). Geographical proximity enables the installation of control regimes, which support interaction between firms through a multitude of micro-practices and technologies. Ongoing interaction also provides important feedback about the actions of a firm in relation to that of others. This can, of course, be accomplished relatively easily within a small territory or cluster context. It is, however, less clear how social relations can be maintained if the actors lack regular contact with one another due to the geographical distance between them. As demonstrated above, it is not an easy task to exercise power over distance (Murdoch 1995; Allen 1997).[6] The exercise of power across space requires the introduction of effective technologies and routines that do not rely on proximity to encourage, for instance, continuous checks on the outcomes of a firm's orders in its different branches and locations. New forms of temporary or virtual proximity, such as regular business travel and Internet platforms, can support communication and interaction processes across large distances (Chapters 9 and 10). As emphasized by Dicken et al. (2001: 104), '[t]he ability of actors to reach across space and act at a distance ultimately depends upon entraining other actors and the necessary material objects, codes, procedural frameworks and so on that are required to effect the activation of power'.

This is, of course, an important issue in the relationships between headquarter locations and their foreign branches. A motivation behind the establishment of international production networks is their capacity to integrate foreign actors and exercise power over distance. Due to problems that are related to cultural differences, however, interpretations could be quite heterogeneous and knowledge transfers between actors may be slowed down. In an intercultural context, network-builders and boundary spanners are thus quite decisive because they are able to enrol others in networks and have the potential to communicate between the people involved. They can provide an understanding of heterogeneous habits and attitudes (Clark and Thrift 2003; Coe and Bunnell 2003; Smith 2003). These are people who have experienced different cultural contexts and, from this, are able to understand the different expectations and patterns of behaviour, and to negotiate them between the actors. Overall, global executive travelling, Internet 'thinking studios', and mobile, transnational 'epistemic communities' of business people have given rise to new geographies of circulation, which are characterized by coherent, stable interactions and power relations (Thrift 2000*b*; Amin and Cohendet 2004). There is no reason to assume that the rising knowledge economy will only be a regional phenomenon (Tracey and Clark 2002).

4.7 **The 'In-Betweens' of Social Capital**

A substantive understanding of resources presupposes that resources have objective, inherent values, and that they can be assigned to specify actors based on property rights. In the previous discussion of material resources, knowledge, and power, we have already demonstrated that a substantive conceptualization can be quite problematic. In the case of social capital, it is virtually impossible to develop a useful substantive perspective. In contrast to physical capital, social capital cannot be attributed to individual actors or firms. Generally speaking, it refers to the opportunities that allow actors to draw from the quality and structure of their relations with other actors in order to pursue individual objectives (Glückler 2001*b*; Bathelt and Glückler 2003*a*). Social capital – and, in a similar way, power – is thus constituted through the very relations between the actors involved, and is a result of ongoing social practices. Actors do not have the universal capability to exploit networks according to their own goals. They cannot possess or build social capital without the active involvement of others. This concept introduces a perspective that acknowledges non-pecuniary resources as a fundamental source of power and influence, and integrates these resources into a framework of multiple forms of capital (Portes 1998).

Social capital can be conceptualized at the micro and macro levels. At the *macro level*, formal institutions, such as behavioural patterns based on the state constitution or legal norms, make up the social capital of a society (Putnam 1993, 1995). This social capital indicates the level of impersonal trust, that is, the trust of individuals in the solidarity and cooperation of other – unknown – individuals in that society. Since this concept is based on institutions that define an overall level of reliability and certainty within a society, social capital reduces transaction costs and raises social welfare. The Word Bank's 'Social Capital Initiative' and other comparative studies suggest that a positive correlation exists between the level of social capital in a society and its economic welfare (Knack and Keefer 1997; La Porta et al. 1997; Grootaert and Bastelaer 2001). There are, however, numerous problems associated with these approaches. First, the cause-and-effect relationships are ambiguous (Knack 1999), as it is unclear whether economic welfare stimulates trust, or whether trust generates welfare. Second, the methodology is based on aggregates of individual self-evaluations about their perceived trust in the overall level of cooperation in a society. Since social capital has been defined here as a resource that develops from relations between actors, it is questionable whether samples of unconnected individuals can yield any significant insight into the quality of social capital. Third, by focusing on mean levels of trust in a society, this methodology makes it difficult to draw meaningful conclusions about the unequal distribution of social capital. A macro-level conception does not enable context-specific, spatially sensitive analyses, and is therefore not suitable when treating social capital as a resource of firms at the regional scale.

At the *micro level*, social capital can be conceptualized as personal trust that exists in a particular community or social network. Coleman (1988) – one of the founders of the concept (see also Bourdieu 1986) – defines social capital as an accumulated history in the form of social structure, which can be employed by individuals to achieve their own goals. In this perspective, resources are always built collectively, while returns can be attributed to specific individuals. Attempts to conceptualize social capital as a private good are, therefore, unlikely to succeed because the concept addresses social interaction rather than individual resource endowments (Putnam 1995). If we view firms from this perspective, they can no longer be viewed as isolated actors. Instead, they are integral elements of a wider structure of social relations with customers, suppliers, state agencies, and lobby groups (Grabher 1993a; Podolny and Page 1998). Social capital provides a number of advantages – or externalities – to the members of a network. First, it enables the formation of mutual expectations and responsibilities, which can be viewed as some form of credit to be claimed in the future. Second, firms have access to additional information flows within their respective networks. Third, social capital supports the formation of joint values and norms based on identity and repeated interaction. These institutions are important because they allow interaction to take place in a coherent fashion and encourage the formation of reasonable expectations within the network (Hodgson 2003). As a consequence, opportunistic behaviour becomes less likely and transactions become more efficient (Coleman 1988; Collier 1998).

The formation and impact of social capital varies according to the structure of social relations. In Coleman's view (1988), it results from the relatively closed nature of social systems. Only if the set of relations between agents is sufficiently closed – or redundant (Grabher 1994) – can shared institutions be built, monitored, and sanctioned. Since actors in a closed network are linked to many of the other actors, information, opinions, and knowledge circulate widely within that network and contribute to the development of mutual trust. At the same time, however, such networks can also be problematic. First, internal cohesion has negative consequences for non-members since they remain excluded from information flows. Second, closed networks generate opportunities for freeriding in the sense that individuals may enjoy the benefits of group resources simply because they belong to the network, but do not share their own resources with the group (Portes 1998; Portes and Sensenbrenner 1993). Third, closed networks can cause technological lock-in and, as a result, stagnate if important external information is missed (Kern 1996; Clark and Tracey 2004).

The theory of structural holes defines social capital in a different way, that is, as a set of opportunities that are derived from bridging relations (Burt 1992, 1997). It suggests that advantages in terms of information and control will be enjoyed by agents, able to bridge otherwise unconnected networks. In other words, agents are expected to take control of the exchange relations between the networks. In this conceptualization, social capital is not attributed to the overall network of social relations but to individual brokers who are capable of establishing bridging relations. Since brokerage fosters strategies of exploitation and opportunism, open networks face further challenges regarding the formation and reproduction of joint values and norms. In sum, it is important to distinguish internal bonding relations from external bridging relations, and integrate them into a balanced network of internal and external ties. Networks can only maintain openness for external markets and innovations – a prerequisite for longer term competitiveness – if they are systematically linked to other networks (Chapter 9).

In a spatial perspective, it is necessary to exercise caution when attributing social capital a priori to local or regional scales. Institutional structures and economic practices define the spatiality of social capital and embedded relations (e.g. Glückler 2001*b*), and not space per se. There are, of course, institutions and organizations that support the formation of social capital at a national level (Putnam 1995; Grootaert and Bastelaer 2001). Furthermore, studies have shown that social capital can also develop at the regional level (Putnam 1993). Whether social capital is constituted locally, regionally, nationally, or whether it cuts across geographical scales depends, however, on the actual patterns of interaction, as well as the institutions that enable and constrain economic action (Giaccaria 2009). A micro-level conception supports a more detailed analysis of social capital and is helpful in explaining spatial variations in localized production configurations. Regional industry clusters can, for instance, create high levels of social capital between firms based on shared institutional frameworks and repeated face-to-face interaction (Amin 1999). If, however, social networks become too close and exclusive, the risk of neglecting external relations may rise. This could have a negative impact on resource availability and innovation capacity in the long run (Bathelt et al. 2004; Florida et al. 2002). Hence, social capital can also have negative effects (Carroll and Stanfield 2003).

The overall impact of social capital consequently depends on the combination and integration of bonding and bridging relations within and across localized networks. In the context of global production and trade networks, executives are increasingly confronted with the uncertainty of establishing access to and finding appropriate partners and clients in new market regions. In knowledge-intensive business services, social capital plays a decisive role when firms enter international markets (Chapter 8). This is due to the fact that foreign competitors face considerable problems in overcoming the local clients' uncertainties (Glückler 2005, 2006; Armbrüster and Glückler 2007). Networks between individuals in corporate networks, or between firms, are, nonetheless, often international in character (Chapter 10). The type of social capital used and maintained by these business services can by no means be reduced to the regional level. Otherwise, these firms could not be successful in international markets.

A relational perspective that extends beyond the individual actor and considers the context of economic interaction is necessary in understanding the formation of social capital. Individual agents can only use social capital if mutual interdependence and interactions with others exist. This corresponds with the concept of power discussed before. All actors involved create these resources, and mutually influence both the extent and distribution of the resulting returns.

4.8 **Conclusion**

The arguments discussed in this chapter emphasize the relational quality of resources, particularly those which have become increasingly important in the knowledge economy. We have systematically explored the shortcomings of conventional substantive understandings of resources and shown how these can be overcome by employing a relational perspective (Table 4.1). In addition, the arguments presented provide evidence that there is a qualitative difference between the resource types investigated, that is, between material resources and knowledge on the one hand, and power and social capital on the other. This can be shown by distinguishing two levels of relationality:

- *Level 1 relationality*: This type of relationality refers to the fact that the generation and use of resources systematically depends on the structure of social relations and the institutional conditions that affect the course of economic transactions, the framework for interpretations, and the choice of strategies. Level 1 relationality establishes a particular context for economic action and interaction that can be applied to all types of resources. This helps to determine the types of resources that are interpreted, as well as the purpose of their usage.
- *Level 2 relationality*: This level of relationality refers to the collective character of resources and becomes apparent when distinguishing between ownership of resources and ownership of returns. As opposed to material

resources and knowledge, which can be classified as private goods (Antonelli 2003), power and social capital are collective resources that cannot be possessed and controlled by individuals. The resources themselves cannot be attributed to the general capabilities of single agents, even though they might earn a private return from them. Instead, power and social capital are collective capacities that make the individual dependent on the overall set of related actors.

If we allow that resources are socially constructed, relational entities, the question then becomes what the key advantages of this view over a conventional understanding of resources are. One important advantage of the relational conceptualization is that it helps avoid treating power and social capital as if they were private resources that can be attributed to individuals. Although the geography of the firm is mainly focused on measuring and explaining individual returns from resource use, these resources are constructed in a relational manner and thus should be understood within their overall context of economic interaction. We identify four primary advantages of applying a relational view to empirically analyse the generation and use of resources and their outcomes.

1. *Contingency of resources.* A relational view of resources acknowledges that economic interaction takes place within a particular social context. Depending on this context, there will be observable differences in the creation and exploitation of resources. As a result, there are no universal best practices regarding the use of a specific resource. In contrast, the social and institutional conditions of economic life generate differences in how agents evaluate, interpret, and incorporate resources. This leads to heterogeneity and contingency in innovation and growth paths, as well as in firm strategies.

2. *Collective use of resources.* A relational perspective also corresponds with the view that the economy is increasingly structured by processes of learning, imitation, creation, organization, and bargaining – all of which are collective in character. Advanced economies are characterized by a deepening of the social division of labour in production and research. This is a result of the growing complexity of economic structures and processes, and their systematic reflexivity. In applying a relational view, we are able to understand the processes through which resources are shaped collectively, and how this affects their value.

3. *Spatial perspective of relational resources.* A relational view has further consequences for our understanding of economic structures in a spatial perspective. Since informal institutions and structures of social relations can vary between places, a perspective that emphasizes the social construction of resources sheds light on differences in the generation and use of

them, even on a small scale. Such differences can occur despite the existence of similar factor conditions and prices. This does not mean, however, that our understanding of resources is restricted to the local level. Collective learning processes and knowledge generation are increasingly embedded in wider international networks of social relations. Processes, such as the exchange of implicit knowledge and the control of complex configurations of production, can be organized quite efficiently within a local or regional context – due to the advantages of sharing the same interpretative schemes and engaging in face-to-face communication – but they are not limited to that context. It is necessary for economic actors to acquire resources over large distances from different regional and national environments in order to gain access to new markets and exchange information about technological innovation. In our view, the ownership and control of resources do not provide a sufficient basis upon which to organize the efficient use and exploitation of resources at an interregional and international level. To understand the mechanisms that enable international production configurations, we need to view power as a social practice, and analyse the role of technologies in establishing stable social relations.

4. *Mutual interdependencies between resources.* Finally, the relational view of resources presented in this chapter helps us to understand how resources affect one another in such a way that positive returns from one resource type can be transferred to generate further positive returns from another. New combinations of material resources, for instance, also increase knowledge about particular technologies and markets. Through this process, further innovations are likely generated, existing power networks shaped, and new ones created. This parallels conceptions put forward by Coleman (1988) and Bourdieu (1986), which suggest that certain forms of capital may be used to compensate for or develop other forms of capital. The development and use of existing resources may contribute to the improvement and re-contextualization of other resources.

In sum, resources do not serve a predetermined purpose; they are socially constructed and can be employed in different ways. The contextual nature of resources, along with the mutual interdependencies between them, indicates the profound contingency and relationality of resources and technological trajectories. As a consequence, it is important to exercise care in portraying resources in a mechanistic way, as though their final application and use value were predetermined.

Part II
Relational Clusters of Knowledge

5 Know-How and Industrial Clusters

5.1 Introduction

Part I of this book has focused on developing a relational conceptualization of economic action and interaction in spatial perspective. This chapter will begin to apply this perspective to the analysis of industrial agglomerations or clusters. This research focus follows a long tradition in economic geography and other social sciences regarding the question of why industries often co-locate in particular regions, cities, or places, and subsequently form specialized industrial regions. Porter's introduction (1990b) and discussion of the cluster concept has, in many ways, pushed the debate surrounding agglomeration processes, and revived older debates on industrial location. This work has also been decisive in strengthening the policy relevance of clusters and related concepts, which are now widely used to support regional and national economic development policies (Chapter 11).

One particular problem in the literature on regional competitiveness and networking is that many of its propositions are based on the assumption that networked clusters within a region per se have a positive effect on regional economic performance and well-being. Another problem in traditional conceptions is that explanations of clustering processes focus on regional transaction linkages and associated cost advantages. A substantial critique has developed in recent years regarding the explanatory limitations of Porter's work (1990b), as well as that of others who have applied his diamond conception in a more or less rigid way (Martin and Sunley 2003; Asheim et al. 2006; Simmie 2006). Much of this critique focuses on inconsistencies in the model, its failure to adequately address social processes and institutional relations, and the weakness of its spatial perspective.

Malmberg and Maskell (2002) develop a set of questions that need to be dealt with before one can begin to address the question of how networks between local actors can be created. These include the following: (*a*) Why do industrial clusters exist and how do they evolve? (*b*) How do the firms belonging to a particular cluster become competitive and what are the key factors supporting their growth? (*c*) What are the core processes that ensure the reproduction of agglomerations and enable specialization processes? The answers to these questions lead to a discussion of the various dimensions of industrial clusters. Here, we define clusters as regional concentrations of complementary firms and competitors, linked within a value chain through traded and untraded interdependencies. In short, we could say they are built around the technological know-how of a localized value chain or parts thereof. The respective firms establish the vertical and horizontal dimensions of the cluster. The dynamic relations between regional firms along those dimensions strongly depend on the role of institutions and power relations, which form two other analytic dimensions. In addition, external relations in the form of vertical and horizontal linkages with agents in other regions and countries are key to understanding the growth dynamics of clusters (this aspect will be developed in more detail in Chapter 7).

In this chapter, we employ a relational perspective to discuss the various cluster dimensions and how they support one another, drawing particular attention to the individual and collective agents that operate within clusters. We also highlight the trade-offs associated with these relations. We then use the case of the chemical industry in different cities in China's Yangtze Delta region to illustrate the effects of these cluster dimensions, and how they are influenced by institutional conditions. Although the chemical industry does not have producer–user relations that are as strong as those in other sectors, and thus forms a specific type of cluster, we argue that this multidimensional relational framework is useful in comparing different clusters and identifying the impact of institutional variation on regional growth trajectories. This is done by analysing the recently established Shanghai Chemical Industry Park (SCIP), Nanjing Chemical Industry Park (NCIP), and Ningbo Chemical Industry Zone (NCIZ). Our analytical focus is to investigate the different institutional settings and traditions in these locations.

5.2 **The Horizontal Cluster Dimension**

Whereas many studies of clusters focus on vertical input–output relations along the value chain, Malmberg and Maskell (2002) have stressed the importance of the horizontal dimension, which consists of regional firms that produce similar goods and compete with one another. This dimension can play a decisive role in the early stages of cluster formation and specialization, as historical developments in Italy and Germany have shown. Porter (1990*b*, 2000) has demonstrated that strong competition is an important incentive for innovation and product differentiation. While the firms in a cluster do not necessarily have close contact with one another or intensive input–output relations, co-location is still beneficial because they are able to stay informed about their competitors' products and the production factors they use (Malmberg and Maskell 2002). Due to their

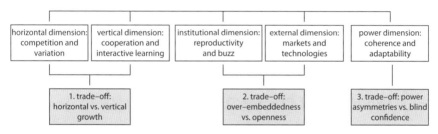

Figure 5.1. The ecology of cluster dimensions and trade-offs

co-presence, production conditions are basically the same. This provides firms with an opportunity to effectively compare their performance with that of their competitors (Figure 5.1).

Overall, this creates rivalry between the respective firms and, according to Grabher (2001: 354), 'preserves the richness of the organizational ecology and, hence, provides a more diverse "genetic pool" for the evolution of new organizational mutations'. Heterarchies provide a particular organizational structure that draws from a combination of redundancy, complementarity, reflexivity, and innovation, yet also benefit from rivalry. Functional heterarchies are groups of businesses characterized by a high degree of diversity and rivalry between the different divisions and business segments (Grabher 2001). In order to avoid separation and ensure sufficient consistency and coherence between the separate units of the group, common tags are created and project cooperation is emphasized. This serves to establish a relatively homogeneous set of norms, rules, and practices, which are accepted by the different units of the heterarchy. When similar organizational principles apply between separate firms in a cluster context, this can be viewed as a locational heterarchy characterized by a similar dynamic.

In a cluster, comparisons are based on systematic observation and information flows between competing firms (Maskell and Lorenzen 2004). This creates incentives for product differentiation and variation, and becomes a basis for technological learning. A prerequisite for such innovative activities is that the firms in a cluster have a certain degree of overlap in their activities and that they are aware of each other's conditions of production; that is, they share a similar knowledge base (Nooteboom 2000). This strongly supports Marshall's celebrated notion (1927) of 'industrial atmosphere' as 'something that is in the air' and limited to the people within a particular region. These knowledge flows will be explored more systematically in Chapter 7 when we discuss local knowledge flows, or 'buzz', versus trans-local or global 'pipelines' (Bathelt et al. 2004; Owen-Smith and Powell 2004; Storper and Venables 2004). The main point, however, is that horizontal relations within a cluster greatly benefit from spatial proximity as well as cultural (institutional) affinity (Lundvall 1988; Gertler 1993). Even in the absence of direct contact, firms are aware of their competitors and understand their actions because they operate under the same rules and conditions.

5.3 **The Vertical Cluster Dimension**

The vertical cluster dimension consists of firms that are complementary to one another and interlinked through a network of supplier, service, and customer relations. Marshall (1920: 225) provides one of the earliest descriptions of how variety at the horizontal level stimulates growth in the vertical dimension: 'if one man starts a new idea, it is taken up by others and combined with suggestions of their own; and thus becomes the source of further new ideas. And presently subsidiary trades grow up in the neighbourhood, supplying it with implements and materials, organizing its traffic, and in many ways conducing to the economy of its material.' Once a specialized industry cluster has been established, the participating firms develop a demand for specialized services and supplies. As Krugman (2000) points out, this demand creates a strong incentive for suppliers to be near these firms because they represent important markets. In locating close to these markets, suppliers can gain economies of scale and distribute substantial parts of their production at a low cost (i.e. low transportation costs). According to Krugman (1991), the existence of a large pool of specialized labour in a region, along with a high demand for such labour, increases its attractiveness for other workers and firms in that particular area of specialization. The vertical dimension is thus very important in understanding the continued growth of an established cluster (Malmberg and Maskell 1997, 2002). Both dimensions are important for the formation of a specialized labour market, which may be at the core of a cluster's success and internal knowledge spillovers (Malmberg and Power 2003; Scott 2006).

In contrast to Krugman's model (1991, 2000), industrial clustering is, however, not merely based on cost considerations, economies of scale, or other kinds of traded interdependencies. As the work of Storper (1995, 1997c), Lawson (1999), Maskell and Malmberg (1999a), and others demonstrates, we need to go beyond traded interdependencies in order to understand the processes underlying regional specialization and concentration. In emphasizing 'localized capabilities' and Dosi's concept (1988) of 'untraded interdependencies', this research tells us that socio-institutional settings, inter-firm knowledge flows, and interactive learning play a decisive role in regional innovation and growth processes (Gordon and McCann 2000; Bathelt and Glückler 2003a; McCann 2008).

A large body of literature suggests that complex innovation processes rely heavily on supplier–producer–user interaction and corresponding learning processes (Lundvall 1988; Gertler 1993, 1997). As such, innovations must be viewed as a result of social relations and knowledge circulation between firms, rather than simply a product of individual endeavours. Along with Granovetter (1985), the relational conceptualization suggests that economic activities are embedded in structures of social relations. This means that firms are closely interconnected in communication and adjustment processes with suppliers, customers, and formal institutional settings (Grabher 1993a). As such, they must be viewed not as independent entities but as part of their respective socio-economic contexts. Many firms establish close, long-term relations with important suppliers and core customers based on reciprocity and trust. This does not, however, imply that embeddedness is a purely spatial phenomenon that automatically develops as a result of co-location or proximity (Oinas 1997; Glückler 2001b).

Malmberg and Maskell (1997) argue that a firm's competitiveness is based on a set of product- and process-related competencies. Such competencies can be partially based on what Maskell and Malmberg (1999a) call localized capabilities, which include specialized local resources, skills, as well as shared trust, norms, routines, and other local institutional structures. Some firms use these local resources and competencies to specialize production. This, in turn, has an impact on existing local supplier relations since it requires adjustments in the products and processes of these firms. Over time, their combined effects shape the labour market, organizational routines, and best practices within a region. They also serve to further develop localized capabilities. This can lead to a specific regional competence (Lawson 1999), or regional competitive advantage (Porter 1998, 2000). It also serves as an incentive for specialized suppliers, producers, and customers to relocate facilities to these regions, which then stimulates cumulative regional growth (Bathelt 2005c).

There is a trade-off, however, between the horizontal and vertical dimensions of a cluster that can reduce a region's growth rate or weaken its competitive base in the long term (Figure 5.1). Incentives for suppliers to locate within an industrial cluster are high if the social division of labour in the local production system is well developed and sophisticated (Malmberg and Maskell 2002). At the same time, the deeper the social division of labour, the fewer the opportunities to compare and observe competitors, which is a necessary feature of a strong horizontal cluster dimension. Only through continued agglomeration processes can the vertical division of labour and horizontal opportunities for variation and differentiation be extended simultaneously.

5.4 **The Institutional Cluster Dimension**

The institutional dimension is related to the production and reproduction of social relations within an industrial cluster, and to the cluster's long-term existence (Figure 5.1). Institutions have a profound impact on regional growth opportunities and the direction of a region's growth trajectory. This will be a central focus in our empirical study of the chemical industry in the Yangtze Delta region (Zeng and Bathelt 2010). As discussed in Chapter 3, we view institutions as correlated behaviour of economic agents, or established patterns of social relations (Setterfield 1993). Within this framework, two types of institutions jointly shape economic patterns and decision-making: formal and informal institutions. Whereas informal institutions are related to stabilizations of economic interactions based on conventions, norms, traditions, experience, trust, or reciprocity – which are often tacit in nature – formal institutions demonstrate behaviour based on codified laws, rules, or regulations (see also Chapter 3). The creation of institutions within a cluster helps to stabilize producer–user relations, shape the nature of economic decisions, and influence the overall growth trajectory of a cluster (Bathelt and Zeng 2005).

As a result of regional specialization and agglomeration, particular localized sets of rules and regulations might be established to shape the direction of economic action. The establishment of rules, norms, laws, and other institutional arrangements generally reduces uncertainty in economic transactions, and allows the actions of others to become more predictable. On the one hand, informal and formal institutions restrict the possibilities of economic action (North 1990). On the other hand, and more importantly, they create a basis for mutual communication, collective learning, and joint problem-solving, without which a social division of labour and economic interaction would not be possible (Hodgson 1988). In the context of an industrial cluster, the creation of institutions stimulates the development of shared technological attitudes and expectations, increases stability in producer–user linkages, and stimulates trust-based linkages (Granovetter 1985; Crevoisier and Maillat 1991; Bramanti and Ratti 1997). Amin and Thrift (1995) conclude that localized production systems are particularly successful and stable if a large variety and high density of specialized institutions, referred to as 'institutional thickness', develop.

According to Storper (1997c), regional technology districts provide a particularly strong basis for cumulative technological learning, collective action, and problem-solving due to the role of untraded interdependencies, which are established through conventions, existing economic relations, and social practices. Untraded interdependencies serve as a prerequisite for complex, technologically sophisticated innovation processes that involve a distinct social division of labour. The goals of such interactive innovation processes are not predetermined; they are continuously shaped and redefined by the firms involved, and influenced by the outcomes of their prior actions. Conventions and relations are, therefore, only preliminary in character, as they are restructured on an ongoing basis in close communication with all of the actors involved. Adjustments of conventions and relations require the co-presence of the respective actors and firms, which can be efficiently conducted in a localized context (Storper 1997c). They cannot be easily transferred over larger distances to other social contexts (Maskell and Malmberg 1999a). As a consequence, clusters can develop and become stronger over time, characterized by close inter-firm interaction, proximity, and systematic interactive learning (e.g. Morgan 1997).

5.5 **The External Cluster Dimension**

Industrial clusters do not, however, exist in isolation. They often depend on external markets and apply technologies developed in other contexts. A number of studies have identified the disadvantages associated with intensive, long-term network relations between firms (Grabher 1993b; Bathelt 2002; Bathelt and Taylor 2002). Uzzi (1997), for instance, finds that close social relations between suppliers and their customers are positive only to a certain extent. More specifically, if too many suppliers are embedded in close customer relations with the same customers, market failure may ensue. This problem, which Uzzi (1997) refers to as 'over-embeddedness', implies a second trade-off between socio-institutional embeddedness and openness; that is, between the internal and external dimensions of a cluster. Whether and how such a trade-off operates depends upon institutional conditions and power relations, and is, thus, related to the other cluster dimensions.

It is, of course, important for economic actors to be embedded – to some degree – in internal structures of social relations. If these linkages are too close, too exclusive, and too rigid, such social relations can, however, pose a threat to the competitiveness of a firm or an entire group of firms. Granovetter (1973) tells us that strong ties between firms might cause a cluster to become isolated. Strong ties typically do not bridge the gap between different networks, and are unlikely to ensure openness in an existing system of social relations. A reliance on strong internal ties can, therefore, block off the diffusion of important breakthrough innovations that have been developed outside of the regional industrial cluster (e.g. Bathelt 2001a). In light of the above discussion, the success of an industrial cluster clearly hinges upon a mixture of internal and external knowledge flows (see, specifically, Chapter 7).

The degree of openness has to be large enough to allow for a maximum amount of external innovation and growth impulses. Yet, at the same time, the cluster has to be sufficiently closed in order to benefit from a maximum amount of regional interrelatedness.

In response to a similar problem, the milieu school suggests combining the positive effects of internal communication with those derived from external information flows (Crevoisier and Maillat 1991; Bramanti and Ratti 1997). According to Maillat (1998), the actors need to establish systematic linkages with external information sources in order to maintain the flow of important information about market trends and new technologies within the milieu. Otherwise, a milieu could become stagnant (Schamp 2000b). Scott (1998) argues that growth processes in a cluster heavily depend upon the extent and mix of spatial transaction costs. In his analysis, large superclusters are especially likely to develop if transactions are characterized by a hybrid cost structure; that is, a structure wherein some transactions involve low spatial transaction costs, while others entail high costs. In such a situation, low spatial transaction costs would lead to trade relations with other world regions, and firms would receive growth triggers from outside the cluster. High spatial transaction costs in other business segments would encourage cluster-based transactions. Only through the combined effects of both, routine transaction processes could transfer external growth impulses to the localized production system, which would then be disseminated through internal transaction networks. This implies that the performance of localized production systems depends on the right mix of local and non-local transactions and that strong growth can only result if external markets are linked to the production cluster (Bathelt et al. 2004).

Despite the significant role of this dimension, external relations are not a primary focus of our empirical case study of Chinese chemical industry clusters below. This is due to two processes: First, the chemical industry in China primarily concentrates on the fast growing domestic market. Second, through foreign direct investment (FDI) and global corporate networks, which play an important role in this industry, external linkages to new technologies and knowledge are not a major problem for these firms.

5.6 **Power Relations**

The existing power relations between economic actors and the circuits of power involving the various cluster components – and their regulatory environment – represent another important cluster dimension (Clegg 1989; Taylor 1995). Studies on regional production networks often suggest that firms have harmonious relations with one another based on an equal distribution of power (see also Chapter 4). It would, however, be difficult to identify a regional ensemble characterized by symmetrical power relations. In fact, such a distribution of power can provide a barrier for problem-solving and lead to a situation where conflicting views of individual actors are excluded from collective action in the network. This could delay technological learning and innovation processes. In contrast, the existence of power asymmetries generates opportunities for efficient problem-solving and flexible adjustments in production towards external market changes (Grabher 1993*a*; Taylor 2000*b*). In other words, power asymmetries are not necessarily negative as they create a kind of hierarchy within the cluster network, which can help to settle conflicts between actors and speed up decision-making processes.

There is, however, a danger that firms might develop too much trust in a given hierarchy and rely on dominant actors in strategic decisions. The trade-off, in this case, is between power asymmetries and blind confidence. Granovetter (1985) suggests that too much trust gives rise to opportunist behaviour and malfeasance. If networks are overly hierarchical and dominated by a few actors, technological lock-in can result (Grabher 1993*b*). Over the long term, the development of too much trust can cause structures of blind confidence and gullibility to spread within a network (Kern 1996). Such a situation can lock actors into an inefficient technological trajectory. A certain amount of distrust with respect to traditional technologies and prominent decision-making structures might thus be beneficial in reducing the risk of collective failures and regional decline (Bathelt and Taylor 2002).

With respect to power relations, there is no simple binary logic of good versus bad, strong versus weak, or hierarchical versus non-hierarchical. Economic agents do not have a predetermined power capacity; their power depends on the reaction of others regarding, for example, their suggestions, commands, or future visions (Latour 1986, 2005). Power relations are fluid, affected by constant struggles and negotiations between agents with a different resource base and different perceptions of what strategic decisions to make (Chapter 4).

An individual can be said to have power if the person is capable of motivating others to engage in joint action. So-called boundary spanners and gatekeepers may, for instance, be powerful in successfully transferring knowledge between agents that operate in different contexts, and do not realize the importance of differences in knowledge or institutional settings (Coe and Bunnell 2003; Depner and Bathelt 2003*b*). In the context of an entire cluster, power refers to the ability to mobilize agents to act coherently, possibly with shifting internal responsibilities and shifting leads between cluster firms in setting product or technology trends within the cluster or value chain.

Clegg's work (1989) clearly shows that the capacity to make joint decisions and solve problems interactively depends on the dynamics of the daily practices of domination and subordination (Allen 1997). This form of power asymmetry can be viewed in terms of power circuits, through which disharmony and conflicts arise, and new rules are negotiated that lead to temporary stabilizations in causal, dispositional, and facilitative power circuits (Taylor 1995, 2000*b*).

1. *Causal circuit.* In a cluster context, this circuit describes how day-to-day interactions affect asymmetrical control over resources and establish a certain structure of social relations, including hierarchies of power relations. This structure defines so-called 'standing conditions', which could be defined as the maximum degree of heterogeneity or inequality in resource access that is accepted by the agents. In a cluster, these standing conditions create a more or less stable situation and suggest that power relations must be continuously negotiated.

2. *Dispositional circuit.* In the dispositional circuit, Clegg (1989) describes how social relations are negotiated and sustained. At the core of this power circuit are the rules of interaction, which define membership and legitimacy, and pre-structure social relations leading to territoriality. In the context of a cluster, this can be supported through industry associations, private clubs – within which managers and entrepreneurs socialize with one another – or formal networks that develop based on a regional or national policy initiative, involving, for instance, a local university. Ongoing interaction leads to the development of routines, accepted norms, and commitments in this circuit. They act as 'compulsory passage points' in the sense of Clegg (1989), which enable coordinated, consistent action. Due to the constantly changing conditions in the causal power circuit, these rules are under pressure for ongoing incremental adjustments.

3. *Facilitative circuit.* The conditions for a more durable stabilization of social relations between the firms and agents in a cluster are implemented and negotiated through the working of the facilitative power circuit. Through this circuit, particular labour regimes and technological paradigms are defined and detailed in a way that cannot be changed by the individual firms in the cluster. These decisions are largely made outside of the cluster and can only be partially influenced or controlled by its actors (Taylor 1995). They are particularly associated with the dominance of the national state, or the conditions associated with being integrated into global production networks (Chapters 8 and 10; Miao et al. 2007; Sun and Wen 2007; Wang and Lee 2007).

These power circuits are subject to ongoing changes in their conditions and structures. They are able to temporarily reproduce a particular cluster context and its associated power relations, as long as the agents tolerate existing asymmetries of resources and outcomes. If this is not the case, the emergence of power struggles could threaten the coherence of a cluster (Bathelt and Taylor 2002). This conceptualization will be applied in the following section to analyse the development of the chemical industry in China's Yangtze Delta region.

5.7 **Yangtze Delta Chemical Industry**

Due to the financial crisis in Asia and its consequences following 1997 (Zeng 2000, 2001), policymakers felt that it was premature to concentrate primarily on the industries of the 'new economy' and, instead, placed greater emphasis on 'old economy' industries, such as machinery and automobile production (e.g. Depner and Bathelt 2005), as well as the chemical industry, including pharmaceuticals. Taking this policy shift as the starting point of our enquiry, the remainder of this chapter investigates its effects on the chemical industry in the Yangtze Delta region. Through an examination of three newly developed chemical industry parks in Shanghai, Nanjing, and Ningbo, our central goal is to determine whether increased support and investment have led to the development of new industry clusters, and how this policy shift has shaped the regional divisions of labour in the Yangtze Delta region (Figure 5.2).

With industrialization and liberalization, China has become a vibrant destination in the globalization process of the chemical industry (Dong 2007). On the one hand, FDI continues to grow, particularly focused on the coastal areas (e.g. Sun and Wen 2007). On the other hand, the Chinese government has invested a great deal of money in the extension of the chemical industry. This has become even more pronounced since the 1997 financial crisis in Asia, which dealt the Chinese economy a devastating blow. General economic growth has had a strong impact on the development of the chemical industry in the Yangtze Delta region, where large shares of industrial users are concentrated (Mu 2006). The chemical industries in Nanjing, Shanghai, and Ningbo have substantially increased in national importance, and the Jiangsu, Shanghai, and Zhejiang provinces have developed into major locations of this industry. Between 1997 and 2006, the gross production value in these provinces grew from 302.5 billion Yuan (37.8 billion US$) to 1,603.1 billion Yuan (213.7 billion US$). Its national share in employment and gross production value increased from 15.5 to 17.6 per cent and from 25.9 to 30.3 per cent, respectively (Table 5.1).

Although cluster dimensions do exist in agglomerations of the chemical industry, the structure of supplier relations is somewhat different from that found in other industries. Regional producer–user networks tend to be narrower in character, and do not involve intensive horizontal and vertical interaction. Suppliers establish close transactional relations with their main customers, but often do not engage in intensive interaction or joint product development. These relationships often appear to be relatively standardized, but are stable since the firms specialize in the complex production of chemicals, which are sometimes dangerous to handle and expensive to transport (Bathelt 1997). The establishment of chemical industry parks in the Yangtze Delta region serves as a good example of this. Here, new industrial parks have

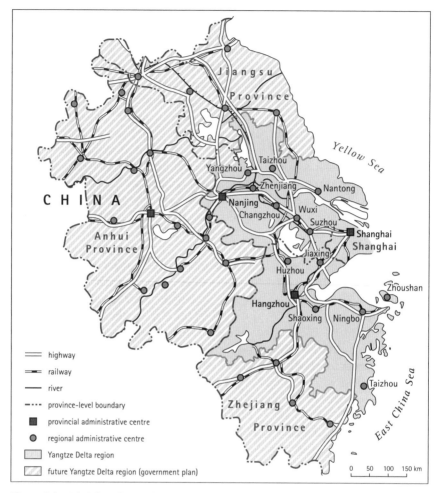

Figure 5.2. Administrative setting and city–regions in the Yangtze Delta region

been built that focus on the production of petrochemicals and organic chemicals. The strategy of these parks is to select and attract firms from a certain value chain to develop close transactional networks and spur broader economic growth.

From this discussion, it is unlikely that fully fledged clusters already exist in the Yangtze Delta chemical industry. Rather, we can identify initial clustering tendencies as a result of the enormous investments undertaken in the industry. These include investments by the central and provincial governments, by large state-owned chemical firms, as well as substantial FDIs. Although knowledge regarding the origins and initial stages of cluster development is still limited (e.g. Feldman and Francis 2004; Henn 2006; Atherton and

Table 5.1. Gross production values of the Yangtze Delta chemical industry, 1983–2006

Year	Gross production value by province (billion Yuan)[1]				
	Shanghai	Jiangsu	Zhejiang	Yangtze Delta region	China
1983	8.90	7.63	3.41	19.94	74.11
1985	14.82	10.43	5.21	30.46	109.40
1990	26.88	40.58	16.54	84.00	325.76
1995	70.11	128.53	58.77	257.41	955.67
2000	120.50	210.65	129.84	460.99	1623.31
2005	264.00	593.35	447.55	1304.90	4248.36
2006	309.10	740.03	553.93	1603.06	5293.51

Note: [1] 1 US$ = 8 Yuan (2005 and before) /7.5 Yuan (2006).

Source: Adapted from Zeng and Bathelt (2010).

Johnston 2008), it is important to point out that such development is fundamentally shaped and directed by the specific institutional conditions that exist within the regions. These conditions vary substantially within the Yangtze Delta region, as expressed in different local traditions and business cultures. The province of Zhejiang with Ningbo, for instance, developed networks of entrepreneurs that started up many successful ventures involving substantial risks, especially since the Chinese economy opened up (Wei et al. 2007). These businessmen formed close guanxi networks through which they were able to split risks, and also mobilize large amounts of private capital for economic projects. Due to these private initiatives, the provincial and central governments played a limited role in economic development. In contrast, Nanjing, which is located in the province of Jiangsu, was dominated by large state-owned firms with strong linkages to the central and provincial governments (Ong 2007). In the chemical industry, these dominant firms tried to protect their leadership within China through close business–state relations, while private risk-taking was less common than in Zhejiang. Shanghai also had a strong tradition of large state-owned firms that developed close government linkages, especially with the provincial government. In the late 1990s, however, the focus radically shifted towards an opening policy based on the integration of FDI, technology transfer, and the embedding of western business cultures (Wang 1996).

Due to these specific institutional settings, we expect clustering tendencies to lead to different growth trajectories. Because of the impact of varying formal and informal institutions, different types of decisions and interaction patterns are favoured in the regions. The analysis shows that the formal institutional conditions – related to the nature of investments, basic infrastructure provided, and governmental policies – are quite different between

Table 5.2. Cluster structure and the institutional set-up of the chemical industry parks in Shanghai, Nanjing, and Ningbo, 2009

Characteristics of the industrial structure	Shanghai Chemical Industry Park (SCIP)	Nanjing Chemical Industry Park (NCIP)	Ningbo Chemical Industry Zone (NCIZ)
Business model	Pudong model (late 1990s): orientation towards foreign investments/technologies; local implementation of foreign business culture	Sunan model (1980s): development primarily led by collective/state-owned enterprises; effective use/allocation of national resources	Wenzhou model (early 1990s): development led by local private enterprises; market-oriented cost-efficient investments based on local guanxi networks
Dominant ownership structure	Joint-venture firms/wholly foreign-owned enterprises	Mixture of collective/state-owned firms and foreign enterprises	Local private enterprises/few large state-owned firms/joint ventures
Product focus	Petrochemicals/organic chemicals and downstream processing (value-chain focus)	Petrochemicals/organic chemicals with downstream linkages (no planned value-chain development)	Mixture of specialty chemicals/organic chemicals
Goal of establishment	Greenfield development of integrated chemical park according to western ideals/prototypes, built around a value-chain concept	On-site modernization of state-owned enterprises	Relocation of existing inner-city chemical firms
State of development	Early state of development; initial sophisticated investments completed; fast growth	Dual structure: established firms and initial park development; medium growth with potential	Early state of development; less sophisticated but profitable firms; medium growth
Origins of bulk resources	Imports from the Near East, Africa, Indonesia	Pipeline flows from Shandong; imports from the Near East	Imports from the Near East, Africa, Indonesia (smaller quantities)
Regional linkages	Adjustments of foreign operations to Chinese settings; few local material linkages	State-driven networks; few local material linkages	Guanxi networks/financial linkages; few local material linkages
International linkages	High degree of internationalization; access to foreign corporate networks	Medium degree of internationalization; access to foreign and national corporate/state networks	Limited degree of internationalization; primarily local enterprises
Research/advanced services	Research activities envisioned, including on-site university/college branches	Research not as important, but off-site linkages to universities/colleges	No detailed plans to create research linkages envisioned

Source: Adapted from Zeng and Bathelt (2010).

the three cases. It also suggests that the dominance of certain informal institutional arrangements has had a substantial impact on the actions and decisions of firms. Key factors in the following analysis include the type of industrial park and infrastructure set up, goal of development and cluster policy, horizontal and vertical firm structure and investments, producer–user linkages, and power relations (Table 5.2).

The research presented draws on a variety of sources, including statistical data, academic literature, business/news reports, and government publications. More importantly, it is based on a qualitative research design[1] that seeks to uncover the processes and motivations behind the establishment and development of chemical industry parks in the Yangtze Delta region, as well as their structure of internal and external social relations. Between 2003 and 2007, over fifty interviews were conducted with representatives of firms and local experts in the larger Shanghai region, as well as in Wuxi, Nanjing, and Ningbo. These included park developers, Chinese firms, and the most significant foreign investors in each industrial park (Zeng and Bathelt 2010).

5.8 The Shanghai Chemical Industry Park

The institutional conditions for the growth of the chemical industry in the Shanghai Chemical Industry Park (SCIP) are unique, as the scale of this Greenfield development would be difficult for other countries to emulate, especially in Europe and North America.

5.8.1 INFRASTRUCTURE

Since 2004, the SCIP has developed into a modern world-scale industrial site for chemical production with a size of 29.4 km^2. The industrial park is located in Caojing about 50–60 km south of Shanghai's city centre, at the north side to Hangzhou Bay (Festel and Geng 2005; Krumberger 2005; Shanghai Economic Commission 2004, 2007). Shipments of crude oil or basic chemicals can be received via integrated jetties and harbour facilities. The park is a fully developed industrial area equipped with infrastructure, such as streets, internal pipelines, public utilities, and environmental protection facilities, all of which are provided by the Shanghai Chemical Industry Park Development Corporation, which operates and manages the park. Once completed, the SCIP will be connected with an older petrochemical park in Caohejing in the west.

5.8.2 STRATEGY/GOAL OF DEVELOPMENT

The goal of the development corporation is to develop the SCIP into an integrated site of petrochemical/organic chemical production and to provide a basis for the continued growth of the manufacturing sector in China. Further, the aim is to turn the park into a central hub of the chemical industry in South East Asia. The design and strategic planning of the SCIP were based on a broad analysis of chemical industry parks in Europe and North America. First, an ethylene cracker forms the heart of the SCIP producing basic organic chemicals. In selecting new investment projects, the development corporation prioritizes operations that establish long-term material linkages with other facilities in the park in order to further process basic chemicals. Through this, the SCIP has a potential to establish strong local producer–user networks as a basis of future cluster development. Second, the institutional set-up has been designed to offer a large variety of services to the tenants in the park. The logistical infrastructure for the supply and delivery of chemical goods has also had a high priority. Third, the park aims to pursue an integrated environmental protection strategy. Fourth, the park management aims to develop into an integrated agency that deals with all problems and requests from local firms through a one-stop service philosophy (Shanghai Chemical Industry Park Development Corp. 2005). Representatives of the development corporation insist that the growth of the park is not supposed to be based on low-cost production but on its integrated long-term goals and settings. One of the means through which to establish initial trust with new tenants has been to engage some of the long-term service providers and suppliers of the new firms in ongoing infrastructure projects. The provincial government is also directly involved in and supportive of the development of the park and has a permanent on-site office. In sum, the SCIP is designed to develop into a cluster-type structure based on vertical linkages, external corporate ties, and a sound institutional set-up. As will be argued below, however, it remains unclear whether a fully developed cluster would be a realistic expectation for further growth.

5.8.3 POPULATION OF FIRMS/INVESTMENTS

In 2004, there was only one older Chinese chemical firm in full operation in the SCIP. Many new facilities were, however, under construction, including foreign investments by Air Liquide, BASF, Bayer, BP, Degussa, and Huntsman, as well as investments of Chinese groups such as Sinopec, SPC (Shanghai Petrochemical Corporation), and GPCC (Gaoqiao Petro-Chemical Corporation). Many projects were joint ventures of foreign–Chinese co-leadership. In 2004, the German Bayer group officially opened its first operations in the

SCIP (Shanghai Chemical Industry Park Development Corp. 2005). The firm's overall investment into six new plants was viewed as a major trigger for development. The structure of the SCIP will drastically change in the future as more chemical production facilities will be under operation. In 2006, the park already hosted fourteen chemical firms with a labour force of 3,250 employees. By 2007, contracts for investment projects of more than 8.8 billion US$ had been signed, more than half of which (4.5 billion US$) related to investment projects of the German BASF and Bayer groups (Kreimeyer 2005; Stachels 2005; Shanghai Chemical Industry Park Development Corp. 2007).

5.8.4 PRODUCER–USER NETWORKS

During the time of this research, most industrial operations in the SCIP were not closely interlinked with each other or with other regional firms. Most bulk resources, especially crude oil, were imported from the Near East, Africa, or Indonesia, and were shipped through the park's jetties. The interviews indicated that the firms were still heavily dependent upon corporate networks for the supply of specialty chemicals, know-how, and high-end services. In addition, direct linkages to foreign-owned chemical firms with customers in China were generally weak or non-existent. In particular, firms that were established as WFOEs (wholly foreign-owned enterprises) tended to ship their products to specialized traders that would, in turn, distribute these products to user industries. These were typically located in Hong Kong or in the centre of Shanghai. They operated as knowledge brokers by connecting otherwise unconnected firms, or as structural holes in the sense described by Burt (1992). This strong reliance on knowledge brokers could slow down learning processes based on producer–user interaction. According to one manager, decisions to invest in a WFOE project were generally based on former experience in China as well as the desire to avoid knowledge spillovers to Chinese competitors. Chinese firms also seemed to have customer relations that were relatively loose and rarely focused on aspects of learning and innovation. This appears to be an additional burden for the future development of dynamic clusters. In sum, local transaction networks were often underdeveloped or non-existent.

The empirical research generally indicated that firms were only partially informed about other investment projects in the SCIP, or possibilities for future interaction. Local information flows also appeared to be weak. One might expect, however, that information flows through informal networks and producer–user relations will become stronger over time as more tenants settle in the SCIP. Since the new projects involve different combinations of Chinese and foreign chemical groups, intended and unintended knowledge flows between these projects will likely develop, especially since some Chinese and foreign firms are simultaneously involved in projects with different partners. Many of the interviewees shared this view. Although local buzz was still low and did not travel easily between the different locations in the region, other information flows through private friendship networks of foreign expatriates, who live in the same urban quarters in Shanghai, already existed to some extent.

5.8.5 POWER RELATIONS

The structure of power relations in the SCIP is still quite fluid and in the process of formation. At the individual-firm level, foreign chemical firms have increasingly decided to establish WFOEs in the SCIP to avoid conflict with and dependence on large Chinese groups and different levels of government. Instead, these operations depend more on corporate relations and external control functions, as well as the specialized traders that provide market access for these firms. To some extent, the new tenants follow the structure of Chinese–foreign joint ventures or joint ventures between different foreign corporations. Although it is too early to draw conclusions regarding the power relations of these firms, they are likely influenced by tensions between their member firms, which relate to different interests and a limited experience of cooperating with one another. At the cluster level, the structure of social relations translates into segmentation tendencies and a lack of joint goals, which could provide a basis for collective action.

5.8.6 FUTURE INSTITUTIONAL SUPPORT

To support the training and qualification of employees, a plan was developed to establish branches of the East China University of Science and Technology and the Shanghai Research Institute of Petrochemical Technology in the SCIP. German firms had begun to sponsor the introduction of new programmes in vocational training schools that adopted the German dual training system, combining practical and conceptual knowledge. These and other projects were aimed at securing a constant inflow of skilled labour. In the future, these developments promise to support increases in production capacities and employment. One of the goals of including these training and research facilities in the park has been to stimulate on-site research linkages. Altogether, the institutional conditions in the SCIP support the development of a new major centre of chemical production, albeit not in the form of a fully fledged industry cluster.

5.9 **The Nanjing Chemical Industry Park**

The institutional setting for the development of the Nanjing Chemical Industry Park (NCIP) was quite different from that in Shanghai, despite its similar focus on large-scale development goals.

5.9.1 INFRASTRUCTURE

The NCIP represents the core of chemical production in the Nanjing region (Zhong 2007). It is located on the northern banks of the Yangtze River, about 30 km north of the city centre. Large parts of the total area of 45 km^2 are reserved but not yet developed. Firms benefit from direct access to the Yangtze River, through which large shipments of crude oil and other resources are received. In addition, harbour facilities allow large ocean tankers to make their way through the Yangtze River (Krumberger 2005). The region's labour market benefits from access to several universities and research institutes located in the city of Nanjing, which offer specific programmes in chemistry and chemical engineering. Aside from the SCIP, the NCIP is the only *strategic* chemical industry park in China that has received the approval of the central government.

5.9.2 STRATEGY/GOAL OF DEVELOPMENT

Prior to the economic opening policy, Nanjing was already an important centre of chemical/petrochemical production in China, due to the activities of the formerly state-owned Sinopec group and its subsidiaries. The NCIP was established to complement and strengthen Sinopec's production competencies, and support the development into a key petrochemical production base in China. As opposed to the SCIP, the NCIP aims to maintain or strengthen the region's role within China, and does not include a vision beyond the national market. The NCIP is designed to focus on petrochemical and gas-based production, basic organic chemicals, polymer products, and new materials (Nanjing Chemical Industry Park Corp. 2005). As such, the park overlaps with some of the core areas of production in the SCIP. Our research suggests that this is seemingly not a major problem, as demand is growing at a faster pace than production (Perlitz 2005). In the future, however, increased competition between both chemical industry parks could potentially develop.

5.9.3 POPULATION OF FIRMS/INVESTMENTS

The industrial park hosts older plants of Chinese chemical and petrochemical firms, as well as more recent foreign investments by firms such as BOC (now

Linde), BP, Celanese, DSM, Dystar, and Sasol Chemicals (Festel and Geng 2005). The NCIP is also surrounded by older Chinese firms such as the Nanjing Chemical Company, Yizheng Chemical Fibre Company, and Jinling Petrochemical Corporation, the latter of which is located directly across the Yangtze River. The largest and most prospective investment project in the NCIP is the 50/50 joint venture between BASF and the Sinopec subsidiary Yangtze Petrochemical Co. (YPC) – named BASF-YPC Company (BYC) – which opened in 2005 (Kreimeyer 2005; Kurz and Schmidkonz 2005). Building upon some earlier smaller joint investments in the region, the decision was made to invest in a large integrated production facility with related downstream productions in Nanjing. The original investment allowed the firm to observe and further investigate the joint venture partner and, thereby, overcome potential barriers for future cooperation. The project occupies a territory of 2.2 km^2 and produces exclusively for the Chinese market (Tichauer 2005). The total number of new jobs created through the Nanjing project is, however, moderate with about 1,400 positions (Perlitz 2005). Interestingly, the site of BASF's new facilities is located outside of the originally designated territory of the NCIP. Although BASF-YPC cooperates closely with the park authorities and emphasizes its commitment to the overall development, the location of the new facilities suggests that the firm intends to remain independent from the park.

Similar to the SCIP, the growth of the chemical industry in Nanjing is driven by investments from German and other European multinationals, accompanied by formerly state-owned Chinese firms in large vertically integrated joint ventures. In industry branches such as petrochemicals, which are viewed as being strategically important, market entry in the chemical industry is highly regulated by the central government (Perlitz 2005; Cheng and Bennett 2007). Having a Chinese joint venture partner in such industry branches is advantageous because firms benefit from established distribution channels. Some older Chinese firms in the region, which ran into financial problems in the 1990s, have been acquired by foreign producers providing them with new technologies and finance. Although the institutional conditions in the NCIP seem supportive for further growth, they do not provide as strong a basis for consistent development as the SCIP, due to the heterogeneous nature of its structures and related frictions.

5.9.4 PRODUCER–USER NETWORKS

Consistent with this evaluation, our research shows that the new chemical operations in the Nanjing region are not strongly linked with other regional firms through transactional networks. Both input and output linkages are largely national in character with little regional interaction. The structure of the industrial park resembles that of a sheer agglomeration of firms, rather than an industry cluster with horizontal and vertical linkages between the firms. Despite this, the growing number of chemical firms, including the operations of established Chinese firms in the surrounding region, may provide new opportunities for the development of regional supplier networks in the future. Presently, most firms still have strong input linkages with their foreign home base. One of the disadvantages of Nanjing relates to its limited local market potential, compared to southern China's Guangdong province and the Shanghai region. Nanjing operations concentrate a substantial part of their sales and marketing workforce on these market regions.

5.9.5 POWER RELATIONS

Similar to the SCIP, the structure of operations in the NCIP remains quite fragmented, despite its long history. Most chemical firms operate according to their own plans leaving little room for collective endeavours. This makes it difficult to generate a strong sense of a cluster. In terms of the individual-firm level, power relations differ from the SCIP in two interesting ways: First, existing joint ventures seem to function well, since the foreign and Chinese managers have learned to overcome, or work around, initial frictions. These firms are better equipped to exploit existing networks and market connections in China. Second, large established Chinese groups operate in traditional ways with government bodies and are still quite reliant on their inputs and direction. Unlike the first group, the second is associated with clear hierarchies and stronger power asymmetries.

5.9.6 FUTURE INSTITUTIONAL SUPPORT

Despite some overlap in the production chain between the chemical parks in Nanjing and Shanghai, and the massive investments in Shanghai to become the Chinese and South East Asian leader in the chemical industry, one should not overstate the competition between the industrial parks, as demand in the regional and national manufacturing sector is rapidly growing. In recent years, the SCIP has been more successful in attracting large investments than the NCIP. This seems related to the fact that the chemical industry park in Nanjing has grown organically, having produced some infrastructural shortages over time. In contrast, the institutional set-up of the SCIP is more coherent and offers advantages to a larger number of potential investors than the NCIP. In terms of the future infrastructure, on-site research activities will likely be weaker in the NCIP than in the SCIP. These conditions suggest that future growth in the NCIP may be somewhat slower than in the SCIP. A well-developed cluster structure will not necessarily evolve under these conditions.

5.10 **The Ningbo Chemical Industry Zone**

The Ningbo Chemical Industry Zone (NCIZ) is again characterized by a rather different institutional configuration, opening different opportunities for regional growth compared to those analysed in Shanghai and Nanjing.

5.10.1 INFRASTRUCTURE

The NCIZ was established in 2003, on the south side of the Hangzhou Bay, to support the establishment of a new chemical industry cluster (China Petroleum and Chemical Industry Associatiion 2007). The NCIZ is located 24 km west of the deep sea harbour and tank facilities in Beilun and 14 km northeast of the city of Ningbo. It has a scheduled size of 56.2 km^2, of which 60 per cent is still undeveloped. About half of the remaining area is occupied by a large older Sinopec petrochemical plant. The services available in the NCIZ include logistics, utilities, environmental protection, and other support services (Ningbo Chemical Industry Zone Corp. 2007*a*, 2007*b*).

5.10.2 STRATEGY/GOAL OF DEVELOPMENT

The NCIZ's original goal was to support the development of a value chain focused on the production of petrochemicals and downstream organic chemical production, similar to that of the SCIP and NCIP. To achieve this goal and generate cost advantages, a specific support policy for foreign investors was introduced. The idea behind the development of the industrial zone was to link new production capabilities with the existing Sinopec operations. In reality, however, the new tenants are neither linked with each other through input–output flows nor attracted to the zone based on cost advantages. Instead, they are located there because the city of Ningbo decided, in the late 1990s, that chemical production should be relocated from the urban core to the new chemical industry zone. As a result, twenty to twenty-five firms moved to the NCIZ.

Unlike the chemical industry parks in Shanghai and Nanjing, the central government has not declared the NCIZ a designated industrial park of strategic national importance. The chemical industry zone nonetheless receives political support from different government levels, and, in particular, the local government.

5.10.3 POPULATION OF FIRMS/INVESTMENTS

The NCIZ hosts about thirty mostly small- and medium-sized firms with a total labour force of 9,400 people, two-thirds of which are employed in the

Sinopec petrochemical plant, which was established in 1975. Overall, the NCIZ has not yet been successful in attracting major foreign investments. In the area of petrochemical production, the joint venture LG Yongxin was established between the South Korean LG group and the Chinese firm Yongxin. Aside from this joint venture and a relatively small branch of the Dutch Akzo Nobel, the industry zone developed into a location of Chinese chemical firms. Although the development of the NCIZ has been partly influenced by the presence of large state-owned firms or joint ventures, the majority of firms were independent start-ups, based on substantial amounts of capital available in the region related to the success of earlier local entrepreneurial ventures. Access to these funds requires that close linkages are developed with existing guanxi networks in the region. The impressions from the interviews and background knowledge about local business practices comparable to the Wenzhou model (Wei et al. 2007) suggest that such privately financed investment projects by regional business people will continue to play an important role in the future.

5.10.4 PRODUCER–USER NETWORKS

Most firms in the NCIZ are relatively small, and do not form a value chain or parts thereof. They have no local customers and only limited market relations in the province. In addition, most firms do not have close supplier linkages with other firms in the industry zone and the region. As such, the industrial zone shares few similarities with a cluster that is well developed along multiple dimensions. In most firms, production is largely standardized and technologies are relatively old. The firms operate in specific niche markets, which they can serve well. They have established social relations with major customers or traders; yet these relations are not located nearby. The limited regional customer base and relatively large distance to other economic centres in the Yangtze Delta region are clearly some of the main disadvantages of Ningbo.

5.10.5 POWER RELATIONS

The structure of power relations in Ningbo is complex. In terms of the individual-firm level, small single-plant operations dominate. They are characterized by clear hierarchies and are headed by individual entrepreneurs and owners. These operations are central to the competitiveness of the firms because they provide access to critical market knowledge and are embedded in guanxi networks that have strong linkages with finance and distribution networks. Since part of the guanxi networks, which provide finance, are located in the Ningbo region, the firms that are locally embedded are indirectly linked with each other. This does not, however, translate into collective production capabilities because the firms are not part of the same value chain. The large Chinese–South Korean joint venture LG Yongxin is characterized by similar networks and tensions between corporate cultures and firm–state relations, as is also the case in Nanjing.

5.10.6 FUTURE INSTITUTIONAL SUPPORT

In terms of future development prospects, the NCIZ has a number of advantages compared to the industrial parks in Shanghai and Nanjing: First, it is open to small investments. Second, compared to the situation in Nanjing, local government support is strong and environmental protection is a high priority. Finally, the new Hangzhou Bay bridge, which cuts down driving time between Shanghai and Ningbo from 4 to 2 hours, may become an important catalyst for further economic development and the strengthening of traditional business ties between both regions (Chiang 2007). Ningbo might become part of the new periphery of Shanghai. Although the NCIZ is not as modern and well developed as the SCIP, it has considerable growth potential because of its new link with Shanghai and the entrepreneurial local business culture.

To increase the potential for further growth, local authorities are trying to develop a plan to establish a new pipeline to Nanjing for the purpose of transporting petrochemical products. It is still unclear, however, whether this investment project will be realized under the new priorities of the central government. The development of the NCIZ has also been criticized by the provincial government because local firms have only created a limited number of new jobs. In terms of research linkages, plans to support or create such linkages at the regional level are not well developed. Any trend towards the establishment of such linkages would, thus, likely depend on the decentralized initiatives of individual firms. In 2007, investment activities came to a standstill related to the lack of consistent government support, especially from the provincial and central levels. The development of a future cluster structure appears unrealistic under these conditions.

5.11 Conclusion

This chapter elaborates a multidimensional cluster conception in order to understand why clusters exist, grow, and how they reproduce themselves. It has been argued that industrial clusters are built in a relational way around the technological know-how of localized value chains or parts thereof.

Chapter 6 shows that this conception cannot easily be transferred to the context of service industries. As illustrated in the case of the Yangtze Delta chemical industry, however, this conception can be used as a heuristic tool to investigate local/regional concentrations of industries, identify their strengths and weaknesses, and draw conclusions regarding their future growth potential. The empirical analysis offers compelling evidence of the growth of the 'old economy' in the Yangtze Delta region in recent years, especially as it relates to the chemical industry and its new industrial parks. The three chemical industry parks in Shanghai, Nanjing, and Ningbo were designed to become world-scale facilities, each having a projected size of 30–55 km^2. As summarized in Table 5.2, these parks are characterized by different institutional set-ups and structures, which lead to different growth trajectories. These paths have been particularly shaped by the institutional arrangements of specific local business models: (*a*) Since the 1980s, the Sunan model, led by collective or state-owned enterprises, supported the development in Nanjing; (*b*) since the early 1990s, the Wenzhou model in Ningbo spurred diversified start-ups and subsequent growth processes, without strong influence from the state; and (*c*) since the late 1990s, the Pudong model has shaped Shanghai's successful integration of foreign investments in the local economy and associated technology transfers.

Although the development is still at an early stage, we anticipate that most industrial park developers will not stick closely to the goal of developing an extended chemical value chain. Whether the chemical industry parks have the potential to grow into networked industry clusters is, therefore, questionable. To avoid further stress on natural resources and the overall environmental quality in the region, the central government has, since the late 2000s, reduced its financial support for further investments in the chemical industry. Given that land in the Yangtze Delta region has become increasingly scarce and too valuable for large-scale resource-intensive industries, a new goal has been launched to foster the growth of the chemical industry in western and central China. As the details of this policy have not yet crystallized, and since its feasibility is still a topic for debate, the growth prospects of the chemical industry parks remain unclear. Due to their different institutional set-up, the development prospects are likely different, and contingent upon the government's future decisions regarding this industry:

1. If the government decides to continue and extend its economic opening policy and free-market focus, Shanghai would likely have the strongest growth potential of the three parks. The SCIP is closely linked with international markets through corporate ties of foreign investors and their producer–user networks. It is also designed to become an international hub for the chemical industry in South East Asia.

2. If the government establishes a different policy aimed at strengthening Chinese raw material producers through interventionist policies and trade barriers, Nanjing might have the largest growth potential. Policymakers and developers of the NCIP are already concerned with extending and protecting Nanjing's tradition as the primary centre of petrochemical production in China, building upon domestic resource access and linkage networks.

3. The outcome will again differ if the government cuts its financial subsidies for investments in the chemical industry altogether. In this case, Ningbo could have the highest growth potential, as its development is less dependent upon this type of financial support. In Ningbo, firms have been able to mobilize capital through private networks within the region.

4. Finally, if government support in the Yangtze Delta region is reduced to a minimum and shifts towards inland locations, cities in western provinces – as opposed to the three chemical industry parks discussed here – might have the largest growth potential in the future.

6 Know-Who and Urban Service Clusters

6.1 Introduction: Knowledge as Social Relationship

In Chapter 5, we employed a relational perspective to revise existing cluster conceptions leading towards a knowledge-based understanding of the competitive advantage of co-located firms in Chapter 7. In essence, this perspective suggests that industrial clusters offer locational advantages in the creation and circulation of technological know-how. In Chapter 4, we discussed the significance of knowledge as a relational resource – an insight that will now be applied to explore the differences between industrial and service clusters. While Chapter 5 has argued that industry clusters may strongly benefit from technological spillovers (know-how), this chapter extends the relational perspective to service clusters by investigating social networks of opportunity (know-who). The approach is linked to discussions in Part III of the book, which further expand our understanding of geographical knowledge circulation from permanent locations, such as city–regions, to temporary clusters (Chapter 9) and configurations of geographically distributed operations (Chapter 10).

This chapter argues that urban agglomerations of specialized knowledge services require a different explanatory approach than industrial clusters because several of the arguments developed in cluster theories do not apply to these services. First of all, knowledge services are not produced in extended value chains. Hence, the notion of local externalities to co-location in backward and forward linkages is empirically less relevant. Moreover, knowledge services do not produce the same kind of innovation as discussed in conventional cluster theory. Innovation is neither technological in nature nor is it organized in internal laboratories or separate business processes. Instead, new knowledge is systematically acquired through client relationships, and is thus inseparable from daily service work. Simply put, local transactional linkages are overemphasized in the context of knowledge service firms. This raises the question of why knowledge service firms cluster in cities. To answer this question, we shift our analytical focus from backward production linkages to forward market relationships, from technological know-how to relational know-who, and from cost to opportunity.

The chapter explores the idea that firms enjoy network externalities through co-location at different spatial scales. Urban agglomerations create size and diversity and, thus, convey the advantage of reputational spillovers. This line of argument highlights the importance of know-who and the economic significance of reputation in such contexts. Moreover, it suggests that the better connected a city is to other cities in an urban network, the higher the likelihood of local firms of being referred to business opportunities in other places. After developing the conceptual argument from a relational perspective, the chapter uses a quantitative empirical approach to demonstrate how economies of overview operate in the management consultancy market in the metropolitan region of Frankfurt/Main. A quantitative network approach is particularly useful in capturing the contingency of the relational mechanisms at work across a large number of individual business relationships (Chapter 3).

6.2 From Value Chains to Value Shops

Over the past several decades, knowledge-based business services have grown substantially. Their growth has not, however, been evenly distributed across space, as such services continue to concentrate in major metropolitan regions (Bennett et al. 1999; Bryson 1997; Keeble and Nachum 2002; Wood 2002*b*; Haas and Lindemann 2003; Glückler and Hammer 2010). Although part of the variation in the spatial distribution of industries can be explained by natural cost advantages (Ellison and Glaeser 1999; Roos 2005), the major differences in spatial clustering can only be understood as a consequence of external economies. External economies are 'services (and disservices) rendered free (without compensation) by one producer to another' (Scitovsky 1954: 143). They are outside the reach of the firm and depend on the size of the industry, the region, or the economy (Stigler 1951). Local externalities are usually associated with market size or scale economies (Krugman 1991), transactional cost advantages (Scott 1988), or technological spillovers (Jaffe et al. 1993; Audretsch and Feldman 2004). The following sections criticize the industrial bias in existing arguments about agglomeration advantages and develop six hypotheses for a novel relational account of urbanization advantages for professional knowledge-based services in cities. These hypotheses are then empirically investigated.

Alfred Marshall's trilogy (1956 [1890]) of agglomeration advantages has fundamentally influenced cluster theory and has been applied in many contemporary research contexts, including Krugman's work (1991) on geographical economics. Marshall (1956 [1890]) identifies three advantages of geographic agglomeration: specialized suppliers, labour market pooling, and knowledge spillovers. The California school of economic geography later revisited the original work of Coase (1937) and Williamson (1979), and applied transaction cost considerations to the geographic organization of value chains. This application is most notably expressed in Scott's conception (1988) of new industrial spaces, which suggests that, under the conditions of a post-Fordist production regime characterized by the increasing disintegration and social division of labour, the transaction costs between organizations are best minimized through geographical co-location.

This argument has mainly been applied to the context of manufacturing, although Scott (1988) also acknowledges the role of professional business services. In the case of knowledge services, however, the concept does not translate very well because the organizational logic of value creation fundamentally differs from the production of tangible commodities. Stabell and Fjeldstad (1998) view professional services in the context of so-called value shops, as opposed to value chains. In contrast to the linear assembly of a fixed set of activities, the notion of the 'value shop' describes the problem-specific alignment of resources, and the scheduling of activities in response to client problems. The shop metaphor implies that the specific and often unique alignment of problem-solving resources is essential for the management of the value-creation process. In the context of professional services, the value-creation process cannot be organized in a sequential chain of activities because it is often bound to a specific location (Sampson and Snape 1985; Boddewyn et al. 1986), that is, problem-solving activities cannot be produced in locations other than where they are actually delivered. This largely impedes a spatial division of labour in order to exploit scale economies in upstream activities. A brief review of the empirical findings illustrates the inadequacy of value chain configurations in the context of knowledge services:

- *Backward linkages*: Compared to firms in manufacturing sectors, knowledge-intensive business service firms maintain only limited vertical relations along the value chain. In the context of the London consulting sector, for instance, Nachum and Keeble (2001) found little evidence of vertical supplier relations since service production for the majority of consulting firms was organized within the company, and often by just one individual. Intermediary services and goods purchased from suppliers are often unrelated to the strategic value-adding competence of consulting services and, therefore, do not offer competitive advantages based on co-location.
- *Horizontal linkages*: Unlike backward linkages, horizontal linkages have been recognized as important competitive factors in the consulting market (Strambach 1994; Lilja and Poulfelt 2001). Networks of cooperative partner firms extend market opportunities, sustain revenue growth, enhance service range and quality, and broaden the knowledge base. Empirically,

however, patterns of cooperation seem only weakly related to spatial proximity (Coe and Townsend 1998). It is, therefore, the functional synergies, rather than geographic co-location, that drive cooperation.

- *Forward linkages*: Intuitively, geographical co-presence appears to be an indispensable condition for a firm's choice of location. Indeed, there is some empirical work that indicates that knowledge-intensive business services are located in close proximity to their customers (Bryson and Daniels 1998; Hermelin 1998; Bennett et al. 2000). The bulk of the literature suggests, however, that locational proximity is far less important than one would assume (Schamp 1986; Tordoir 1994; Wood 1996). Illeris (1994) suggests that highly specialized services are independent from a client's location because a high degree of specialization and sophistication yields premium fees, thus making transportation costs a marginal consideration. Spatial proximity, which is necessary in the course of cooperation in the consulting process, is established through temporary travel and residential stays at client premises, rather than through permanent co-location (Rallet and Torre 1999). In the context of business consulting, empirical work shows that the majority of clients are often located outside the service provider's region (Schamp 1986; Daniels 1991; Daniels et al. 1992; Keeble et al. 1992; Bryson et al. 1993, 1997; Strambach 1995; Wood 1996). In other words, it is not only the suppliers but also the clients that neglect spatial proximity to their providers (Schickhoff 1985). De Lange's research (1993) demonstrates that although business services and client firms locate in the same type of location – that is, the large urban centres – they do not co-locate in the same places. Business service firms thus do not follow their clients. And in the work of Strambach (1994) and Wood (1996), business development is clearly more constrained by access to social networks than by geography. These findings lead to the following hypothesis: the quality of a client relationship is independent from geographical proximity (H1).

6.3 **From Local to Network Externalities**

If direct face-to-face relationships or transactions are not important at the local level, the question becomes: why do so many knowledge-intensive business service firms cluster in metropolitan cities and regions? The world city hypothesis offers an explanation of the urban agglomeration of knowledge services based on the nodal function of a city in the global network economy (Friedmann 1986; Sassen 1994; Felsenstein et al. 2002). World cities are not simply big urban centres with large endowments of infrastructure and population; they are important nodes of governance, control, and innovation.

One important indicator of their centrality is the concentration of specialized management functions, knowledge-intensive services, financial organizations, and advertising agencies (Taylor 2004*b*). Analyses by the research group on 'Globalisation and World Cities' (GaWC), as well as studies conducted on the world system of cities (Smith and White 1992), suggest that urban centres are strongly interconnected through overlapping location patterns of multinational business service firms (Taylor and Hoyler 2000; Taylor et al. 2002; Taylor 2004*b*) and international passenger air traffic (Smith and Timberlake 1995). Although knowledge service agglomerations often extend beyond the boundaries of global cities to cover larger metropolitan regions, the effects of centrality and connectivity may not be equally distributed. The global city is the original place for urbanization advantages and connectivity within the urban network, whereas the geographical extension of a surrounding metropolitan region often complements the functions of the central city, albeit not in the sense of Christaller's hinterland (1933) of central places. It is, therefore, hypothesized that the advantages of international connectivity are limited to the central city and do not fully apply to the surrounding metropolitan region. In other words, firms located in the city are hypothesized to be more international than firms located in the rest of the metropolitan region (H2).

This relational perspective extends current agglomeration theory by moving beyond the issue of local externalities to examine the positive network externalities for a city as a result of its connectivity with the international city system. A network externality refers to the fact that the value of a unit of a good increases with the number of units sold: 'the utility that a given user derives from the good depends upon the number of other users who are in the same "network"' (Katz and Shapiro 1985: 424). The utility of an urban business location may thus be viewed as a firm's accessibility to other firms (strategic partners and clients) in other locations. A city that is highly connected within the city system thus provides accessibility advantages to its firms beyond the local reach. In the context of urban network externalities, large cities form the nodes of a global network economy; the more interconnected a city is within the city network, the greater the benefits for the firms located in that city. In contrast to agglomeration theory, this view also suggests that cities establish urbanization advantages because they realize trans-local network externalities in the global network economy. Indeed, empirical work demonstrates that cities with a higher level of connectivity in the world city network enjoy advantages regarding policy programmes (Capello 2000). If we allow that network connectivity yields external effects to the city as a whole, the question then becomes: to what extent do cities yield returns to individual firms seeking trans-local interconnections? If metropolitan or world cities represent key nodes or spatial gateways to the global network economy, firms located in these cities should, on average, benefit from international business access and perform better than firms located elsewhere. Drawing on the world city thesis, the argument can be extended to claim that world cities yield a location premium to business service firms. This leads to the hypothesis that firms located in the city enjoy higher rates of employment growth than firms located in the rest of the metropolitan region (H3).

Finally, if the network connectivity of a city is the cause of enhanced firm performance, Hypotheses 2 and 3 should exhibit a significant degree of association. In order to test the relationship between firm internationality and firm performance, a fourth hypothesis can be developed: the more international a firm, the higher will be the average rate of firm growth (H4).

6.4 **Economies of Overview**

Contemporary agglomeration theory is characterized by an additional conceptual basis – namely, a particular emphasis on know-how. Knowledge spillovers yield technological externalities, whereby knowledge gains occurring in one firm increase the productivity of the other firms, without full compensation. The literature is replete with theories about the conditions for increasing local knowledge externalities along a range of different dimensions, including, for instance, competition (Jacobs 1969; Porter 1990a; Glaeser et al. 1992; Malmberg and Maskell 2002) versus monopoly (Marshall–Arrow–Romer externality, Glaeser et al. 1992), localization (Marshall 1956 [1890]; Porter 1990a) versus urbanization (Jacobs 1969), and traded (Scott 1988; Williamson 1981) versus untraded interdependencies (Storper 1997c).

We find that all of these theories prioritize technological know-how and production efficiency over business opportunity. As previously suggested, the absence of localized vertical and horizontal production linkages in management consulting reduces opportunities for technological knowledge spillovers. More generally, the innovation process in knowledge services differs from technology production, as knowledge firms do not generate innovation in internal laboratories but are always in close interaction with their clients. Clients are not only the source of knowledge; they are also the vehicle through which expertise, innovation, and revenue are generated. Management consulting, in particular, has established a largely unspecified and non-transparent marketplace in which highly specific services are offered (Glückler and Armbrüster 2003; Armbrüster 2006). In order to reduce uncertainty between consultants and clients and avoid market failure, personal trust and reputation are extremely important, as they initiate and sustain business relationships (Keeble et al. 1992; Clark

1993; Glückler 2005). In this context, know-how is not the only source of economically relevant knowledge; know-who (Lundvall and Johnson 1994) is also a vital form of knowledge that relates to the interconnection of people and the quality of their relationships. The essential entrepreneurial value of know-who is that it yields business opportunities and provides advantages of overview. Johannisson (1990) emphasizes an entrepreneur's interest in maximizing business opportunities, as opposed to simply minimizing costs. Economies of overview relate to 'the demarcation of an action frame where overview facilitates the identification and subsequent exploitation of opportunities' (Johannisson 1990: 35). In contrast to the management of costs where scale economies are the guiding principle, economies of overview refer to business opportunities. Economies of overview increase with geographic proximity and agglomeration since a greater number of actors and potential multipliers are in direct reach. Local buzz, that is, the spillovers of information and gossip in a localized community, has the potential to open up new opportunities for firms, and thus is a potential catalyst for firm growth (Marshall and Wood 1992; Gertler 2003; Storper and Venables 2004).

Economies of overview are even more important when services are highly specialized. One lesson that can be derived from conventional economic geography is that the more specific a service is, the wider its minimum catchment area will be in order to meet sufficient demand and cover production costs (Christaller 1933). Whereas Johannisson (1990) conceptualizes economies of overview as a purely local externality, such economies may also be viewed as a trans-local network externality. Extending this notion accordingly, Martinelli and Moulaert (1993) developed a multilevel conception, which suggests that 'economies of overview can only be realized if synergies between elements stemming from different spatial levels and forms are achieved' (Moulaert and Djellal 1995: 109). In the context of knowledge services, being located in metropolitan agglomerations can generate returns due to access to trans-local resources, such as global networks of clients and knowledge flows. In this context, empirical work has found that consulting firms in London are more globally oriented than their decentralized counterparts, in terms of international revenues, overseas offices, and staff recruitment (Keeble and Nachum 2002). Metropolitan locations might be advantageous for knowledge-intensive business services not only because of their proximity to clients but also because of their access to extra-regional business opportunities. With increasing specialization, management consulting services will face decreasing local demand, which makes it more difficult to grow exclusively on the basis of clients that are located in the hinterland. Consultants thus need to find new business on a wider national or international scale. A well-connected urban centre might offer better economies of overview that lead to better access to trans-local social networks. Thus, one would expect firms in urban centres to have more clients outside of the region than firms in the rest of the hinterland (H5).

6.5 **Reputation as Geographical Shortcut**

Beyond the mere existence of overview economies, this section investigates the mechanisms of their operation. A number of questions emerge from the above discussion: First, how do consultants in an urban centre manage to gain clients in other regions? Second, to what extent does geographic remoteness influence business development? And, third, what are the core mechanisms driving client acquisition? Geographical co-location clearly facilitates face-to-face contact, and thus reduces the costs of canvassing clients locally. In such contexts, a consultant can contact, meet, and present proposals to a greater number of potential clients than would be possible across a larger distance at the same cost. One would, therefore, expect direct client acquisition to take place more frequently at the local level. With increasing distance, the opportunity costs of relationships rise, since the number of equally preferred but more proximate contacts grows (Sorenson 2005). Beyond opportunity costs, meetings with potential clients at a greater distance also incur travel expenses, and thus render direct client acquisition more risky and costly. In this context, the problem of market failure will be discussed to identify reputation as a critical social mechanism for market growth and geographical expansion.

6.5.1 THE LIMITS OF PRICE

According to Akerlof's so-called 'lemons principle' (1970), markets can collapse under conditions of uncertainty if price is the only transaction mechanism. Such findings correspond with the consulting market. In this context, clients are well aware that consulting firms differ from each other in terms of their levels of competence, quality, and commitment. Since consultants cannot signal the quality of their service prior to its provision, prices do not regulate and clear the market (see also Chapter 4). A large number of empirical studies support this argument. They show both that consulting firms do not compete on prices (Dawes et al. 1992; Clark 1993, 1995; Lindahl and Beyers 1999), and that clients do not choose providers on the basis of prices (Kaas and Schade 1995; Glückler and Armbrüster 2003). In the United Kingdom, for example, Bryson (1997) found that only 1 per cent of the surveyed client corporations chose their consultants primarily on the basis of prices. The major problem for clients relates to the uncertainty of investing money, time, and effort in a consultant that might lack competence or behave opportunistically in a given project. Since price is not a sufficient condition for the consulting market to work, complementary mechanisms are required to reduce uncertainty and enable sustained transactions between consultants and clients.

Institutions describe stabilized patterns of interaction based on rules, conventions, habits, or norms of social interaction (Chapter 3). They entail behavioural patterns that constrain certain alternatives and enforce others so that mutual expectations about the behaviour of others are increased (Beckert 1996; Dosi et al. 1999). As a result, institutions contribute to the patterning and stabilization of social interaction at two different levels: the societal and the personal level. First, at the societal level, rules and norms help build a general level of trust. Through this, formal and informal institutions facilitate interaction among anonymous actors and allow for social and economic exchange at the level of a national state or beyond. Second, certain habits and conventions contribute to the formation of personal trust. Although limited to specific relations, these habits and conventions serve to stabilize patterns of interaction among actors who continuously reproduce these patterns. Given the clients' uncertainty in management consulting, there is, however, a deficit of legally enforceable rules, professional standards, and so on. In this market context, economic exchange will mainly be constrained to structures of social relations that are constituted and reproduced in ongoing day-to-day interaction. Joint cognitive and cultural schemes (DiMaggio 1997), habits and routines (Nelson and Winter 1982), conventions (Storper 1997c; Lindkvist and Sánchez Hernández 2008; Sánchez Hernández et al. 2010), trust (Lorenz 1999; Nooteboom 2002), and reputation (Uzzi 1997; Murphy 2003) are all mechanisms that improve mutual expectations in economic exchange.

6.5.2 EMBEDDING MARKET RELATIONS

Social practice institutions have been addressed from various perspectives and have received a range of different labels. Most prominently, the concepts of embeddedness (Granovetter 1985), untraded interdependencies (Storper 1997c), and social capital (Coleman 1988) have nourished our understanding of how the patterns and rules of social relations matter for economic exchange. These approaches all criticize conventional economics for neglecting the role of informal institutions in theory building and treating them as non-economic factors, market imperfections, or humane 'fetters on the rapacious tendencies of the market' (Storper 1997c: 29). In contrast, this perspective argues that economic action is embedded in ongoing systems of social relations, which simultaneously enable and constrain economic transactions. Unlike goods and production factors, however, these patterns of social interaction cannot be traded (Arrow 1974). In response to this, Storper (1997c) has usefully conceptualized such processes as untraded interdependencies between economic actors. In a similar vein, trust and cooperation are viewed as sources of social capital that reduce transaction costs and can be used as resources in economic processes, including, for instance, innovation and learning (Chapter 4). We address these approaches jointly because they are dedicated to the same essential phenomenon: the relevance of social practice institutions for economic exchange (Glückler 2004, 2005). Given the increasing complexity of the contemporary economy, these socio-institutional cues are not fossils of a traditional society, as some modernists might argue. On the contrary, 'in many ways, capitalist markets are more intertwined with "nonmarket" forces than ever before' (Storper 1997c: 30).

The embeddedness concept critically reflects the atomistic treatment of individual action in the social sciences and examines the essential relationality of all social and economic action, that is, its contextuality, contingency, and path-dependence (Bathelt and Glückler 2003b; Glückler and Bathelt 2003a; see Chapter 2). However, the embeddedness concept has been repeatedly criticized for its theoretical infiniteness (Staber 1996; Oinas 1997; Uzzi 1997; Luhmann 2000; Glückler 2001b). While economic action is regarded as fundamentally embedded in social relations, it remains unclear how embeddedness evolves, whether economic relations vary by degree of embeddedness, and what implications this might have for actors and firms. In analysing the market mechanisms of professional service firms, it is thus necessary to develop a detailed understanding of how embeddedness is empirically constituted and how it evolves over time.

According to Granovetter (1985), embeddedness describes the extent to which exchanges between actors are expressions of social relations (relational embeddedness), and the ways in which these relations are part of a wider structure of social relations (structural embeddedness). This, of course, leads to the question of how embeddedness evolves in specific exchange relations between individuals and firms. We suggest two institutions of social practices that potentially operate as market mechanisms in the consulting market: First, personal trust, as a source of relational embeddedness, and, second, reputation, as a source of structural embeddedness. Trust has been discussed widely over the past few decades (Barber 1983; Zucker 1986; Shapiro 1987; Nooteboom 1996; Lorenz 1999; Das and Teng 2001; Glückler and Armbrüster 2003; Glückler 2005). It is most commonly understood as the expectation that another person will cooperate despite the fact that they have an opportunity and an incentive to act opportunistically (Nooteboom 2000: 107). Personal trust is in principle dyadic. It is limited to direct experience with other transaction partners and evolves slowly over time (Lorenz 1999). Although trust institutionalizes existing relations, it is not sufficient to explain how new relations are formed. More specifically, if consulting firms operate on the basis of trust, how can they find new clients?

6.5.3 PUBLIC VERSUS NETWORKED REPUTATION

Reputation becomes a particularly important factor when we look at how new clients are acquired. In this chapter, reputation is viewed as an essential mechanism to expand business, bridge social and geographical distance, and participate in global markets. Briefly defined, reputation is the expectation of future performance based on the perception of past behaviour. For reputation to be established, three conditions must be fulfilled (Glückler 2005): First, reputation only makes sense in situations characterized by incomplete information. Indeed, if the quality of a product was fully known before the product's purchase, it would not be necessary to evaluate earlier products (Shapiro 1983; Weigelt and Camerer 1988). Second, reputation is only helpful in situations where the same kinds of transactions are repeated (Kreps and Wilson 1982). Third, reputation for a specific behaviour can only develop if that same type of behaviour is consistently displayed in all transactions (von Weizsäcker 1984). Under such conditions, positive reputation can be a very valuable way to access information, financial or other resources, as well as referrals for new business. In fact, the resource-based view of the firm goes so far as to treat reputation as a resource itself (Mahoney and Pandian 1992). In empirical research, however, reputation has received limited and sometimes only superficial attention (Kollock 1994: 320). Consequently, its precise role remains somewhat elusive in the context of economic exchange (von Weizsäcker 1984: 1104):

> This social mechanism is quite fundamental for economic cooperation and productivity in a world of incomplete information. It is partly a substitute for the price mechanism but it also appears to be a complement of it. It is not yet well understood by economists. When and where does it arise? Where does it fail?

The conventional conception of reputation has proven to be insufficient for empirical analysis. Although reputation has received increased attention in game theory and the management literature, three implicit assumptions are problematic (Kreps and Wilson 1982; Shapiro 1982; Weigelt and Camerer 1988; Roberts and Dowling 2002): First, reputation models usually presuppose that the past behaviour of an actor is observable and assessable with respect to its quality. Second, it is typically assumed that the reputation of an actor is public, that is, equally well known to everybody (Table 6.1). Third, the behaviour of an actor is thought to produce only one overall reputation, as opposed to multiple and perhaps contradictory partial reputations. Such assumptions lead to empirical problems because the quality of a firm's performance may not always be measurable and, moreover, not necessarily

Table 6.1. Public versus networked reputation

Indicators	Public reputation	Networked reputation
Diffusion	*Public*, that is, broadcasting over media/business press	*Network*, that is, communication within trust relations (word of mouth)
Scope	*Unlimited*, that is, public	*Limited*, by membership in a personal network
Reliability	*Thin information*, that is, low reliability due to unknown origin of judgement	*Thick information*, that is, high reliability due to trusted contact towards the origin of judgement

Source: Adapted from Glückler (2005: 1744).

be known by all potential clients. Beyond this, a firm may have competing reputations. Since reputation is uncertain in character, reliability and credibility largely depend upon the communication channel through which they circulate.

Two significant types of reputation must be distinguished (Glückler and Armbrüster 2003; Glückler 2004*b*, 2005): First, reputation is public when it circulates freely. Clients can learn about the reputation of firms through so-called reputation industries (Fombrun 1996), that is, newspapers, industry journals, contests, or opinion polls. Public reputation is easily available but may not be very reliable, as indicated in Uzzi's study (1996: 680) on the New York apparel industry: 'manufacturers can play hit-and-run for years before their reputation catches up with them'. In short, public reputation is information that is in the public domain; it is either published by or communicated freely in the media and the press. Second, reputation is networked when new clients learn about a firm's performance through trusted contacts within their social network (Table 6.1). Unlike public reputation, networked reputation does not circulate freely; rather, it works as an informational spillover restricted to mutually entrusted members of a specific network, where one member transfers his or her direct experience with a particular business partner. The concept links with ongoing research on social network mechanisms and conveys one potential resource that contributes to what Uzzi and Gillespie (2002) call network transitivity. Their concept describes a mechanism through which actors obtain competencies or resources from one actor, which then increase the returns from a relationship with another actor. Networked reputation is one of the ways through which a consultant may take advantage of network transitivity. It offers more reliable and credible information on potential transaction partners: '[b]etter than the statement that someone is known to be reliable is information from a trusted informant that he has dealt with that individual and found him so' (Granovetter 1985: 490). The difference between these two kinds of reputation is clearly reflected in practice, as indicated in the following interview with the partner of a Frankfurt-based management consultant:

One has to distinguish qualitative and quantitative aspects here. Public reputation brings more contacts, however, the recommendation is, of course, far more sustainable. There is nothing better. If somebody recommends us, you can be almost sure that it works. In contrast, a contact over public reputation is only attention and you still have to really win the client. If you don't know, that certainty is a decisive criterion in consulting, and if there is nobody around to give you this certainty – except from what you read in the newspaper, where you can read a lot – then you miss an important aspect. I have to gain this certainty either by personal presentation or by referral.

In management consulting, networked reputation essentially takes the form of personal recommendations and client referrals. Since referrals reduce uncertainty between mutually unacquainted business partners, consultants save time and money on repeated meetings and travel. Reputation may therefore ease business development over long distances, and increase the spatial reach of a firm. Combining the advantage of reputation networks with the network externality of overview economies, it may be argued that the more internationally linked a city, the more likely it will be that referrals transcend local networks and offer business opportunities in other places. This is exactly the kind of effect that is most desired by consultants. It is thus hypothesized that remote clients are acquired more frequently through personal reputation networks than geographically proximate clients (H6).

6.6 **The Frankfurt Location Premium**

The conception and the corresponding hypotheses developed above have been applied to the empirical context of management consulting in Frankfurt/Main (or Frankfurt, for short). The Rhine-Main region forms the second largest consulting agglomeration in Germany, with over 4,500 consulting firms operating in the mid-2000s. While the region accounted for 8.8 per cent of the national GDP, during the same period, the consulting sector had a share of 11 per cent in national consulting sales. At the same time, and throughout the 1990s, the region experienced substantial annual growth of 10 per cent of new consulting firms through firm formation – a rate that is far beyond the national average. The city of Frankfurt is characterized by very high connectivity scores within the European network of urban centres, and thus belongs to the 'major spines' of highest city network centrality (Taylor and Hoyler 2000). The case study region complies with the precondition of high connectivity necessary to test the previously formulated hypotheses. It differs from other metropolitan regions in Europe in that it is a polycentric region with various city centres (Figure 6.1). The empirical analysis is based

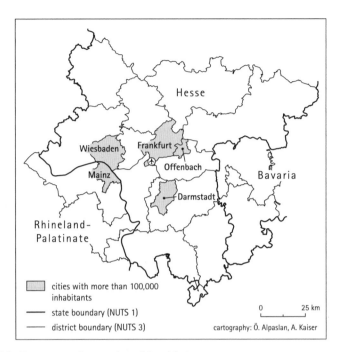

Figure 6.1. The metropolitan region of Frankfurt

on a standardized network survey that was carried out in 2003. The survey collected data from 213 consulting firms at two different levels: the level of the firm and the level of nearly 1,000 individual business relationships. For a detailed discussion of the methodology, see Glückler (2007*b*).

Following Hypothesis 2, we test the relationship between the connectedness of world cities and the inclination of firms towards international business. Table 6.2 displays the results of Student *t*-tests for differences of mean values between Frankfurt (city) and its surrounding region. The table shows that Frankfurt firms are significantly more international than firms in the rest of the region. While 57.3 per cent of the firms in the surrounding region have international projects or operations, more than three-quarters of all firms in Frankfurt operate internationally. Furthermore, less than half of the clients in the region are international, whereas firms located in Frankfurt have nearly 60 per cent of their clients abroad. This finding clearly supports Hypothesis 2, as well as the world city argument that urban interconnection yields location advantages to knowledge services. Table 6.2 also supports Hypothesis 3, which suggests that firms will perform better if they are located within the urban centre. Firm performance was measured as the rate of employment growth over the time period between 1997 and 2002.[1] Conceptually, employment growth is an adequate measure of performance since the scope for improved capital/labour ratios in consulting is limited. If firms acquire more business

Table 6.2. Student *t*-tests for differences of means between the core city and surrounding metropolitan region

Variables	Group variable	N	Mean	S.E.	T	d.f.	Mean difference
International operations (percentage of firms)	Region	89	0.573	0.053			
	City	98	0.765	0.043	-2.825^a	174.165	-0.192
International clients (percentage of firms)	Region	87	43.667	3.900			
	City	98	59.520	3.478	-3.044^a	183.000	-15.854
Employment growth (CAGR)	Region	45	0.033	0.029			
	City	62	0.089	0.013	-1.754^b	60.583	-0.056
Firm age (year of establishment)	Region	89	1993.865	1.049			
	City	98	1992.633	0.871	0.040	185.000	2.960

Notes: [a] $p < 0.01$;
[b] $p < 0.10$; CAGR, compound annual growth rate of employment.
Source: Adapted from Glückler (2007b: 956).

and work on more projects, they necessarily need to extend their headcount. Consulting companies located in Frankfurt grew by 8.9 per cent per year, compared to a growth of 3.3 per cent in the surrounding region. Though only weakly significant, the metropolitan centre seems to enjoy a location premium. This premium is, of course, only a black box and leaves open the real nature of the comparative advantage of an urban location. The question thus becomes: what is the cause of this growth differential? Following Hypothesis 4, we would expect internationality to enhance firm performance. If world cities are more interconnected than other cities in the overall network, then international orientation in these world cities should provide a comparative advantage to firms located in these centres.

In order to assess this relationship, a multiple linear regression analysis is used to test the effects of firm location, international business, client orientation, and repeat business on employment growth (Table 6.3). Indeed, model 1 finds that firm location significantly affects annual employment growth. Despite a low level of significance, the locational growth differential cannot be rejected. Model 2 clearly refutes a positive association between firm internationality and employment growth. Neither the proportion of international clients nor the number of international offices/branches increases the likelihood for enhanced firm growth. Therefore, the link between the world city network hypothesis and positive returns for individual firms cannot be supported. Instead, model 3 shows a positive effect of repeat business growth on employment growth. This effect is also maintained in the final model 4, where firm location and the growth of repeat business are significant. In sum, consultants enjoy at least two pecuniary advantages from ongoing client relations (Glückler 2005): First, long-lasting accounts secure a continuous

Table 6.3. OLS regression coefficients for the estimation of employment growth

Variables	Model 1	Model 2	Model 3	Model 4
Intercept	−.8.812[a] (3.155)	−.9.641[c] (2.727)	−.8.536[a] (2.629)	−.9.569[a] (3.093)
Firm location	0.052[c] (0.028)			0.047[c] (0.028)
International operations (number)		0.045 (0.028)		
International clients (number)		0.000 (0.000)		
Repeat business (share, %)			0.073[a] (0.024)	0.072[b] (0.028)
Firm age	0.004[a] (0.002)	0.005[a] (0.001)	0.004[a] (0.001)	0.004[a] (0.002)
Statistics				
R^2 (adjusted)	0.085	0.076	0.126	0.131
F	5.909	4.485	9.797	6.155
P	0.004	0.005	0.000	0.001
S.E.	0.144	0.136	0.134	0.142
d.f.	106	126	122	103
N	107	127	123	104

Notes: [a] $p < 0.01$;
[b] $p < 0.05$;
[c] $p < 0.10$ (standard errors in parentheses). Dependent variable: CAGR, compound annual growth rate of employment. Size has no significant effect on average employment growth.
Source: Adapted from Glückler (2007b: 956).

stream of income through repeat business at reduced marketing costs. Second, established relations are fundamental sources of new business referrals. Strong ties and enduring relations with key clients therefore seem to offer significant growth opportunities for consulting firms.

The metropolitan region of Frankfurt is a very heterogeneous, polycentric region with four other major cities. It was therefore important to employ additional alternative models to test whether the location premium was actually a function of the central city of Frankfurt or of a combined urban region consisting of the major five cities. The results, however, were insignificant and thus re-enforced the models presented in Table 6.3. More specifically, firms that were located in Frankfurt grew at a higher rate, during the boom of the late 1990s, than did firms located in the rest of the region. In conclusion, employment growth is higher in the urban centre than in the surrounding region, and contingent on the ability to increase repeat business with existing clients. At the same time, however, it is important to note the variation in the strength and significance of these results, and the fact that model 4 only explains about 13 per cent of the overall variance in the data. Nonetheless, one cannot expect to fully account for a performance indicator such as firm growth with a set of only three specific variables.

6.7 **Geography of Reputation**

The empirical survey also asked each consultant to specify, for each individual client relation, whether their clients had been acquired through a personal recommendation, and whether those clients had already referred the consultant to another client afterwards.[2] In terms of the empirical weight of personal recommendations and so-called reputation networks (Glückler and Armbrüster 2003; Glückler 2004b), the results were surprising: 45 per cent of all clients were gained through some form of networked reputation, that is, through the referral of another client or other third party. More than 40 per cent of the clients had themselves spread successful referrals, and thus contributed to the business development of a focal consulting company. Comparing clients that referred new contacts with those that did not, it turns out that the likelihood for a referral increases with the duration of a client relationship, and its relative contribution to the consultancy's revenues. Those that had referred new business by recommendation had already bought services from their consultancy for over 5.5 years, as compared to only 3.5 years for those that had not. Moreover, those that had referred new business contributed 19 per cent to a consulting firm's revenues compared to an average of 14 per cent of the non-recommenders. The analysis for individual clients across all client networks demonstrates that these important relationships are not only intensive and beneficial for their own operations but that they are also sources of reputational spillovers. In other words, close and enduring relations, as well as big client accounts, clearly improve new business development.

Following earlier empirical findings, Hypothesis 1 expects that there will be no significant difference between local clients and remote clients in terms of the quality of the relationship and tie strength. Table 6.4 reports the results from logistic regression analysis. To predict the likelihood for client location within the metropolitan region, tie strength (i.e. the duration of a relationship, the frequency of contact, and the share of revenues that a client contributes) and referrals were defined as independent variables (Glückler 2007b).[3] Model 1 displays the effects of tie strength on the likelihood that a client will be located in the same region. It shows that both the frequency of contact and the duration of a relationship only slightly improve the odds, and at a low level of significance. In fact, if we test the corresponding bivariate models, none of the three variables of tie strength is significantly associated with client location. We can, therefore, conclude that business relationships do not depend strongly on geographical constraints. This finding is particularly interesting given that many of the arguments in cluster theories are based on the assumption that proximity makes a difference for the intensity and quality of personal contacts. Hence, the results support Hypothesis 1.

Table 6.4. Logistic regression models for the estimation of client location

Variables	Model 1	Model 2	Model 3
Intercept	0.163 (0.241)	0.237[b] (0.119)	−.107 (0.221)
Duration of relation	0.032[c] (0.017)		0.017 (0.016)
Frequency of contact	−.176[c] (0.103)		−.188[c] (0.097)
Share of revenues	−0.002 (0.005)		
Firm location		−0.320[b] (0.137)	−0.378[a] (0.140)
Referral		−0.290[b] (0.137)	−0.270[c] (0.142)
Statistics			
−2 log-likelihood	1078.415	1197.483	1155.059
X	6.378[c]	9.261[a]	15.734[a]
R^2 (Nagelkerke)	0.011	0.014	0.025
Hit ratio (%)	51.9	55.2	56.2
N	783	871	845

Notes: [a] $p < 0.01$;
[b] $p < 0.05$;
[c] $p < 0.10$ (standard errors in parentheses). Dependent variable: client location (1 = metropolitan region; 0 = elsewhere).
Source: Adapted from Glückler (2007b: 957).

Instead of focusing on the geography of direct relationships, the argument about metropolitan locational advantage concentrates on the geography of indirect relationships and economies of overview: finding clients and raising business opportunities through referrals. Following Hypotheses 5 and 6, we explore the relationship between firm location and the geography of reputation. Hypothesis 5 suggests that firms in the urban centre have relatively more clients outside the region than firms in the surrounding metropolitan region. In fact, a *t*-test for differences of means supports this expectation. While consulting firms in the metropolitan fringe had 47.8 per cent of clients outside the region, consultants in Frankfurt had 55.4 per cent of their clients, and thus significantly more, outside the region.[4] If the argument about the importance of reputation networks and their concentration in the urban centre is correct, we would also expect the data to support Hypothesis 6. The key comparative advantage of the urban centre rests on a high density of trans-local social networks. These networks provide economies of overview with necessary referrals to trans-local clients. Again, the sample data support this hypothesis. Clients outside the region were more often acquired through referrals than were clients within the region. While nearly half of the external clients (49 per cent) were gained through reputation networks, only 42 per cent of the local clients were gained through referrals.[5]

Given that these comparisons measure the individual effects separately, the data set was further investigated through multivariate logistic regression models in order to determine the combined effects of the independent variables. In Table 6.4, models 2 and 3 display the multivariate logit coefficients for the aggregate regression models. Model 2 confirms the direction and strength of association between firm location, referrals, and client location. This indicates a joint effect in the sense that (*a*) when a consulting firm is located in Frankfurt, its clients are more likely to be located outside the region, and (*b*) when a client has been referred to the consulting firm, that client is also more likely to be located outside the region. When tie strength is added, the suggested interpretation is further strengthened. Whereas the variables of tie strength in model 3 are either less or no longer significant, the effect of firm location becomes even more pronounced and highly significant. It is important to note that the models are not intended to optimize the overall explanatory power of the models, but, rather, to demonstrate the combined effects of firm location and referrals, in order to support the argument that trans-local reputational spillovers are concentrated in urban centres.

6.8 **Conclusion**

This chapter has reviewed the shortcomings of current agglomeration theory in the context of knowledge services. It has argued that cities do not only offer local externalities based on traded interdependencies but also trans-local economies of overview based on reputation networks. In general, local advantages have been widely studied and well understood in the literature. In this context, we should keep in mind that often at least 40 per cent of the client base is located within the same region; there is also evidence that knowledge service firms grow within their regional customer base in less connected, secondary cities and regions (Daniels and Bryson 2005). Despite the intuitive appeal of the geographical proximity argument, this chapter demonstrates that the quality of client relations is not strongly dependent on physical co-location. Given that specialized knowledge services follow a value creation logic, in which resources are uniquely aligned to solve specific problems and produce tailored solutions (Stabell and Fjeldstad 1998), face-to-face collaboration with clients does not necessarily depend on permanent co-location; it may also be facilitated through temporal travel across distance (see Chapter 9).

In essence, this chapter has argued that, apart from being a source of local linkages, urban centres are important localities for trans-local business opportunities. The survey revealed that Frankfurt firms acquired more clients outside the region than firms located outside the metropolitan centre, and that these clients were gained through reputational spillovers or interpersonal referrals. Local reputation networks of this kind generate trans-local network externalities in that they circulate referrals to clients in other places. At the same time, however, our regression models explain only a limited portion of the overall variance of the dependent variables. These results indicate a contingent, rather than a deterministic, relation (Sayer 2000) between consultancy location in the urban centre and the propensity to find business opportunities outside the region. This does not deny the fact that firms located within the surrounding region may also find access to external business opportunities. The literature on knowledge intensive business services has identified various mechanisms regarding the extension of business to other regions, such as referrals from ongoing repeat business or piggybacking strategies through non-equity partnerships with other consultancies (O'Farrell and Wood 1999). According to these results, trans-local reputational spillovers in the urban centre represent an important mechanism driving trans-local business development.

The empirical findings suggest a geography of reputation, where the dense, diverse, and trans-locally connected urban communication networks spread reputation farthest, thus yielding trans-local business opportunities to local firms. At the same time, this geography of reputation connects the concept of local economies of overview (Johannisson 1990) with the implicit notion of positive network externalities in the world city network approach. One of the reasons why knowledge services tend to cluster in urban centres is because these centres generate business opportunities across space. This analysis contributes to broader debates about agglomeration economies and to our understanding of the dynamic interplay between local externalities and global linkages (Bathelt et al. 2004; cf. Chapter 7). The recursive interdependence of local and global relations constitutes an understanding of the city as a Neo-Marshallian node (Amin and Thrift 1992; Nachum and Keeble 2003).

The analysis has also shown that the city offers a location premium. On average, Frankfurt firms enjoyed stronger employment growth than firms located in the surrounding metropolitan region. The exact causal direction of this location premium remains unclear though. Since overview and reputation advantages are measured at the level of individual relationships, it is difficult to test the effects of these economies of overview on performance at the firm level. Future research is, therefore, necessary to test the effects of overview economies and reputation networks on firm performance. The findings suggest that the metropolitan region does not produce homogenous advantages as a whole. Instead, the urban centre clearly dominates as the primary locus of opportunities and trans-local reputational spillovers. The Frankfurt/Rhine-Main region is an especially interesting case because it is one of the few metropolitan regions in Europe that has a polycentric structure. An even more pronounced decay between the urban centre and its hinterland might be found in mono-centric metropolitan regions such as London, Paris, or Madrid.

7 Local Buzz and Global Pipelines

7.1 Introduction: The Paradox of Globalization

This chapter further contributes to the discussion of industry and service clusters in Chapters 5 and 6. As previously mentioned, one of the major problems in the literature on economic agglomeration and clustering processes is that it focuses almost exclusively on local relations and networks, to the relative neglect of interregional and international linkages to important markets and knowledge pools. The goal of this chapter is to develop a more comprehensive conception of clusters, which suggests that the growth of a cluster depends on systematic linkages between its internal networks, conceptualized as 'local buzz', and its external knowledge and market connections, referred to as 'global pipelines'.[1] We develop this conception by applying a relational approach that emphasizes the dynamic relationship between local and non-local processes of knowledge circulation. This knowledge-based conceptualization suggests a shift from a substantive to a relational conception of clusters. It calls for a deeper investigation into the internal and external contexts of economic interaction, and finds that regional growth processes in clusters largely depend on systematic reflexive relationships between local and trans-local knowledge flows and transaction relationships.

Interestingly, a similar line of thought can be developed if we use the dynamic linkages in economic globalization processes as the starting point of our analysis. Although the exchange of goods and knowledge across regional, national, and cultural boundaries is becoming noticeably easier thanks to modern technologies, we are faced with the paradox that global economic success still depends on the utilization of local and/or regional resources. Research demonstrates that closely interconnected regional concentrations of firms from a particular sector, along with supporting suppliers and service providers, continue to attract new firms to that sector. A considerable part of global economic production is located in such clusters. This apparent contradiction can be explained when one takes a closer look at the opposing processes of the dissemination (ubiquitification) and localization of knowledge (contextualization), which form the backdrop to economic globalization. During the process of globalization, new knowledge about product technologies and organizational forms is disseminated as firms set up production facilities in foreign countries similar to those in their home countries. Firms are able to export knowledge because they are in a position to standardize the knowledge developed in the original locations and to commit this in writing in a way that can readily be transferred to other locations and countries. But the corollary of this is that the regions in which this knowledge has been created may lose their competitive edge and first-mover advantages.

This is, however, accompanied by a process of knowledge localization, through which the competitive capability of regions is strengthened. It entails the adaptation of new technologies. As a consequence, old is combined with new, and is coupled with the specific knowledge of experienced employees. This combination of knowledge produces small, incremental changes in the technologies used, which, in turn, contribute to further changes over time. The results are interdependent innovation processes that lead to the perfection of production processes. This line of argument suggests that the positive effects of localizing new knowledge can be enhanced if firms do not act in isolation, but, instead, are located close to other firms of the same value chain (suppliers, service providers, and customers), and are intertwined with them through producer–user linkages. The concepts of local buzz and global pipelines suggest that while economic success often has local roots, it also crucially depends on combining local and trans-local, or global, linkages. This is exemplified through the case of the Munich film and TV industry cluster in Germany, which, despite experiencing steady growth during the 1980s and 1990s, has suffered from a serious crisis since 2001. This chapter argues that the crisis relates to the cluster's structural weaknesses, which are largely due to insufficient local networks and information flows, as well as limited access to large international markets in Europe and North America.

7.2 Local Buzz: Creating Meaning and Membership

Locating within an industrial cluster has advantages that are not readily available to firms situated elsewhere. Co-location and face-to-face contact within a cluster give rise to a particular information and communication ecology, which has been variously referred to as its 'industrial atmosphere' (Marshall 1927), 'noise' (Grabher 2002a), or 'buzz' (Bathelt et al. 2004; Storper and Venables 2004). This buzz consists of specific and continuously updated information, intended and unintended learning processes in both organized and accidental meetings, the application of shared interpretative schemes, common understandings of new knowledge and technologies, as well as shared cultural traditions within a particular technology field (Figure 7.1). These

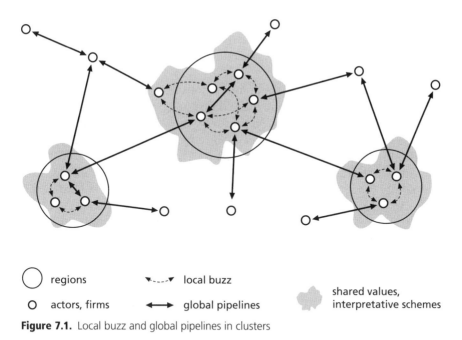

Figure 7.1. Local buzz and global pipelines in clusters

Legend:

- regions
- actors, firms
- local buzz
- global pipelines
- shared values, interpretative schemes

features stimulate the establishment of conventions and other institutional arrangements. Actors contribute to and benefit from this buzz by just 'being there' (Gertler 1995, 2004).

Participating in a cluster's buzz does not require particular investments. Information and communication is received by actors that are located within the cluster region and participate in its various social and economic spheres (Grabher 2002a). Receiving information, news, rumours, gossip, and trade folklore about other firms located in the cluster is virtually automatic. Codified and tacit knowledge flows circulate at a high pace, density, and intensity. Such flows may take place in the context of negotiations with local suppliers, in phone calls during office hours, while talking to neighbours in the garden, over lunch with colleagues, and so on. The nature of this buzz is spontaneous and fluid. Co-presence within the same economic and social context creates many opportunities for personal meetings and communication between local agents, and links actors in a variety of ways – as, for instance, friends and business partners (Uzzi 1997). As Ettlinger (2003: 161) observes, 'at any point in time individuals engage in multiple networks associated with different rationalities, and these different networks . . . [can be] overlapping networks', thus stimulating one another. This observation draws attention to an important prerequisite for the growth of an information and communication ecology: namely, the existence of overlapping networks. This buzz is, however, not just related to unintended encounters between local agents; it also includes a universe of planned and scheduled meetings, sometimes with rigidly planned agendas. The decisive point is that institutional cohesion and spatial proximity generate numerous possibilities for frequent meetings and communication.[2]

Firms systematically learn about innovations and strategic changes that are being developed or executed by their competitors, suppliers, and customers. Intensive monitoring and observation serve to create rivalry and stimulate activities, such as imitation, reverse engineering, and product differentiation (Maskell 2001*b*; Malmberg and Maskell 2002). As Powell et al. (2002: 294) conclude in their empirical study of venture capital (VC)–biotechnology firm clustering, 'there are real advantages that accrue to firms and venture capitalists to being "on the scene" – unplanned encounters at restaurants or coffee shops ... or news about a seminar or presentation all happen routinely in such settings. The combined impact of access to "news" and more effective monitoring help explain the pattern of VC clustering.'

Co-location within a cluster helps firms to understand local buzz in a meaningful way because it stimulates the development of a particular institutional structure that is shared by participants. This can result in the development of 'communities of practice' in the cluster (Wenger 1998; Brown and Duguid 1991; Gertler 2001). Firms develop similarities regarding language, technology attitudes, and interpretative schemes, which encompass a combination of tacit and explicit knowledge elements (Lawson and Lorenz 1999; Grabher 2002*b*; Lundvall et al. 2002). This serves as an important sorting mechanism, helps actors recognize relevant signs and information, and assists them in making use of this information in ways that are similar to other cluster actors. Over time, experience in cooperations with regional actors can stimulate the development of (professional) trust (Harrison 1992; Lorenz 1999). In some clusters, this trust might become the default value in inter-firm communication and transactions (Maskell and Malmberg 1999*a*). This can develop into a valuable localized capability stimulating further growth. Start-up and spin-off firms, as well as other firms that locate close to these clusters, might inherit this trust as an advance payment (Lawson and Lorenz 1999; Malmberg and Maskell 2002).

This is not to suggest that each agglomeration of firms creates automatic, useful information about technologies, their development, applicability, and markets. Of course, agents can only know *ex post* how valuable the information is that they received through local buzz. Furthermore, the above argument does not imply that agglomerations always create the same sort of buzz. Intensive local buzz is neither a direct consequence of co-location nor is all buzz equally relevant to the firms of a cluster. Local buzz most likely serves as a particularly meaningful source of information if a cluster is characterized by a mixture of well-developed horizontal, vertical, institutional, power, and external dimensions along a value-chain focus (Chapter 5). The particular mix of local buzz and trans-local pipelines also varies across value chains, technologies, and market segments. Whereas some industries (e.g. fashion products) might require more buzz than others (e.g. steel production), some industries (e.g. biotechnology) may depend more heavily on pipelines (see Tracey and Clark 2003).[3] The model of buzz and pipelines presented in this chapter is especially relevant for knowledge-intensive or knowledge-driven industries.

7.3 Global Pipelines and Trans-local Connectivities

Amin and Cohendet (1999, 2004) persuasively demonstrate that a cluster cannot realize its growth potential in the long run if firms rely exclusively on internal markets and knowledge circulation through local buzz. This work builds on a much older literature which analyses the relationship of intra- versus interregional production linkages. In regional economics and regional science, this work is based on regional input–output and export-base models (e.g. Isard 1956; see Lloyd and Dicken 1972; Richardson 1978). Accordingly, exclusive local relations can pose a threat to the competitiveness of a firm or a group of firms. Uzzi's empirical work (1996, 1997) on the organization of production in New York's textile industry reveals that close social relations of suppliers and customers are positive only to a certain extent (see also Sofer and Schnell 2002). Following Granovetter's work (1985), close, long-term customer relations are generally advantageous because they enable both customers and suppliers to benefit from learning processes and to react quickly to market shifts. But this scenario can quickly change if the majority of firms are closely linked with the same few customers. According to Uzzi (1996), firms are more likely to fail the more a group of suppliers is strongly embedded in relations with the same set of customers. This phenomenon of over-embeddedness corresponds to lock-in effects, blind confidence, and gullibility, all of which threaten the collective success of cluster firms.

In the literature, there is now a growing acknowledgement of the importance of tapping into external markets and engaging in trans-local interaction (e.g. Bramanti and Ratti 1997; Maillat 1998; Scott 1998; Bresnahan et al. 2001) in order to avoid 'entropic death' (Camagni 1991*a*). Despite this growing awareness, the structure of interaction and the ways in which such linkages are established and maintained remain poorly conceptualized in the cluster literature (Humphrey and Schmitz 2002). Tracey and Clark (2003: 11) correctly suggest that 'geographical clusters can no longer be (if, indeed, they ever could be) thought of simply as closed local systems'. The rising knowledge economy clearly is not a regional or regionalized phenomenon (Tracey and Clark 2002). Indeed, it is often the trans-local, and sometimes even global, interactions that are central to the individual and collective competitiveness of cluster firms.

Owen-Smith and Powell (2002, 2004) use the term 'pipeline' to refer to such linkages. In contrast to the type of communication and interaction that occurs within a cluster, the knowledge flows and interaction in trans-local pipelines differ from local buzz. They are targeted towards certain, often predefined, goals and are planned in advance. Unlike local buzz, trans-local pipelines do not occur automatically and do not result from the spontaneous meetings of actors, which have a mutual understanding and share the same interpretative schemes. They are, in fact, quite risky and require particular investments into new linkages with other firms (Bathelt et al. 2004).

Once a potential partner from outside the cluster has been found, it is necessary to determine how much information to give to that partner, and the degree to which the activities of that firm should be monitored or controlled. Podolny (2001) suggests that networks can also be viewed as prisms of the market, and not just as pipes. This is because the quality of the existing network partners of a firm allows third parties to make judgements about the status of that firm. This helps these parties to decide whether or not to develop a link with that firm. The resulting interaction is greatly influenced by the level of existing trust between the firms. Unlike local relations between cluster firms, there is no pre-existing shared trust from which the new partners can benefit (Maskell and Malmberg 1999a). Instead, the establishment of trans-local pipelines requires that new trust be created – a lengthy process that involves substantial costs and investments (Harrison 1992; Lorenz 1999). In order to facilitate cooperation in particular projects, partners at both ends of a pipeline must develop joint interpretative schemes and common institutions. This is, of course, no simple task, as the cultural contexts in which firms operate may have different roots (e.g. Schoenberger 1997).[4]

Determining the precise value and location of external knowledge, and building pipelines to access that knowledge, is only part of the challenges of attempting to stimulate a firm's innovative capability.[5] An important prerequisite for the successful establishment of pipelines is a firm's ability to assimilate incoming information and effectively apply it within its internal divisions of labour. Cohen and Levinthal (1990) have labelled this firm-specific ability as 'absorptive capacity' (Malecki 2000). In the case of a large multi-locational firm, this capacity largely depends on the way in which information is transferred across and within the departments and subunits of a firm. This information may be removed from the point at which the pipelines enter the organization. The role of internal gatekeepers and boundary spanners becomes crucial for translating externally produced knowledge into a form that can be internally understood by the relevant departments or individuals (van den Bosch et al. 1999; Giuliani 2005). Such individuals are similarly important in global corporate networks (Chapter 10).

7.4 **The Dynamics of Local Buzz and Global Pipelines**

Overall, the particular combination of local buzz and trans-local pipelines generates a dynamic of knowledge creation within a cluster that provides the potential for enhanced learning capabilities and future economic growth (Bathelt 2007).[6] The argument here is that both local buzz and trans-local pipelines have only limited effects if they remain separated spheres (Figure 7.1). Although the particular character of buzz and pipelines – or closure and range – may differ between industries and shift over time (He 2006), the combination of both concepts provides new grounds for explaining the high degree of dynamism in processes of knowledge creation and innovation in different clusters (Bathelt et al. 2004; Bathelt 2005b). As argued above, local buzz in clusters has only a limited or even marginal impact in the absence of trans-local pipelines. The more strongly the actors in a cluster are involved in establishing and maintaining trans-local partnerships, the more information about new markets and technologies is pumped into the respective local networks. Of course, formal contractual alliances between firms from different regions and national states can differ in terms of how they enable and channel information flows and transactions. Without this influx of external knowledge, there is a danger that firms could pin their hopes on the wrong technologies and lose their competitive edge. Pipelines, which are open or 'leaky', function as sprinklers supporting the diffusion of information within the cluster (Owen-Smith and Powell 2004). This stimulates additional buzz and serves as a basis for further product innovation and differentiation initiatives.[7]

In the absence of local buzz, in turn, pipelines are of limited use because they predefine and, in part, restrict the way in which new knowledge is applied. Local buzz in a cluster assists firms in sifting through the mass of available information in order to isolate elements that are particularly important for the development of technologies, while discarding elements that have little prospect for success. This saves both time and money, and speeds up innovation processes. The current role of Stanford University in Silicon Valley usefully illustrates this point, as it is an important place where engineers originating from the United States, India, Taiwan, and other countries meet. As such, Stanford University plays a key role in the development of a common knowledge base and industry background, which can become the basis for the establishment of networks and global pipelines between Silicon Valley and other parts of the world in the future – empirically observable elements of which are already crystallizing (Hsu and Saxenian 2000).

Zademach and Haas (2008) use the term 'echoing' to describe how multinational or transnational firms extend their global networks to take advantage of buzz-and-pipeline dynamics. These firms set up branches in different world regions and develop pipelines with distant markets. By establishing these branches, they tap into various regional and national knowledge pools, and take part in the local buzz in different places (Faulconbridge 2007).[8] Internationalization can, thus, be viewed as a strategy that allows firms to benefit from multiple local information and communication ecologies.[9] In transferring knowledge back to the original cluster locations (and other regions), these firms benefit enormously from knowledge inputs, and also transfer some of this knowledge via linkages and sprinkler effects to other cluster agents (Figure 7.1).

Intensive local buzz encourages firms to recognize the significance of trans-local pipelines and acquire knowledge about the establishment of new pipelines. In other words, this cluster approach can be viewed as an extension and reinterpretation of export-base models in regional science and traditional economic geography (Isard 1956; Lloyd and Dicken 1972; Richardson 1978; Schätzl 1978). At a micro-scale, external knowledge resources may enter a cluster and stimulate rounds of internal recombination, through which innovation and growth impulses result. Access to external resources thus strengthens internal capabilities in a cluster.[10]

7.5 Genesis of the Munich Film and TV Cluster

Empirical work has shown that media industries and, in particular, film and TV production are often important drivers of urban economic growth (Scott 2000a; Krätke 2002). Indeed, most industrialized countries feature well-developed media industry centres that generate high incomes as well as skilled jobs for agents embedded in the project ecologies of these industries. Drawing on the case of Munich, Germany – a well-established centre of the film and TV industry in Germany – this chapter presents what, at first glance, seems to be an industry success story. Upon closer investigation, however, the case of Munich reveals deep-rooted problems (Bathelt and Gräf 2008). Although Munich is the most important centre of the film and TV industry in Germany, our investigation illustrates that its structure of social relations is relatively weak. This is apparent in terms of both the cluster's internal networks, which could drive creative recombination and innovation, and its linkages with external markets, which could provide important growth impulses to the region.

This vulnerability is by no means obvious, however, as the Munich film and TV industry has a long tradition. While Berlin was the undisputed centre of film-making until the end of World War II, Munich established itself as an important production site for high-quality feature films (Horak 1996). After World War II, Munich developed into the dominant location of the newly established German

Table 7.1. Establishments and sales in the Munich film, TV, and advertising industry, 2001–4

Media industry branches	Establishments		Sales (1,000 Euros)	
	2001	2004	2001	2004
Broadcasting[1]	48	51	3,475,000	3,457,924
Film/TV/post-production	987	1,043	2,213,868	2,105,908
Film distribution and other services	105	104	2,626,075	776,819
News agencies/journalists	1,409	1,647	134,775	130,995
Subtotal	2,549	2,845	8,449,718	6,471,646
Advertising	1,979	2,084	1,710,000	1,404,026
Total	4,528	4,929	10,159,71	7,875,672

Note: [1] Public broadcasters are not included.
Source: Adapted from Bathelt and Gräf (2008: 1945).

film and TV industry, challenged only by Cologne, Berlin, and Hamburg (Ernst & Young 2006). According to the sales tax statistics, the film and TV industry in the city and county of Munich consisted of a total of 2,845 establishments and had sales of 6.47 billion Euros in 2004 (Table 7.1). As shown by Gräf (2005), Munich's film and TV industry developed into a fully fledged industry cluster, characterized by well-developed vertical, horizontal, and institutional cluster dimensions (Industrie- und Handelskammer für München und Oberbayern and Landeshauptstadt München 2003; Mossig 2006).

The main factors underlying the growth of the Munich film and TV industry closely relate to a set of favourable conditions that developed in the post-World War II period. First, the reconstruction of the German film and TV industry shifted away from its former core Berlin due to the geographical isolation and unclear future of the city at that time. Although Munich was already an important media location in the early 1900s, with activities in fine mechanical, optical products, and motion picture production (Biehler et al. 2003), it further benefited from Berlin's uncertain future. Second, the growth of the Munich cluster profited from the relative 'closedness' of the German TV market, which can also be observed in other national TV markets (e.g. De Laurentis et al. 2003). Third, the growth of Munich's film and TV industry cluster was also based on traded interdependencies, related to low transaction costs and economies of scale. Film and TV producers, for instance, were able to exploit existing infrastructure and build upon large pre-existing project networks of media specialists. Fourth, a unique institutional structure developed parallel to this growth consisting of funding and training organizations, such as the FilmFernsehFonds Bayern (FFF), Bayerische Akademie für Fernsehen (BAF), and Hochschule für Fernsehen und Film München (HFF). This institutional structure supported the growth of the cluster relative to other German media locations. Finally, Munich received important growth impulses due to the introduction of the so-called dual broadcasting system in 1984, through which private/commercial TV was established (van den Berg et al. 2001; Mossig 2006).

These factors help explain why Munich developed into a leading national centre of film and TV production. They do not, however, explain why the cluster remains only marginally important in international terms. With the economic recession in 2001, the negative effects of poorly developed linkages with media markets and locations outside of Germany became increasingly obvious. In addition, the effects of shrinking advertising expenditures in the manufacturing sector extended beyond the advertising industry (Jentsch 2004) to include private broadcasters. Furthermore, the bankruptcy of the Kirch Group – a fully integrated media group headquartered in Munich – caused disarray in the film and TV industry. Overall, these problems are clearly reflected in the available sales figures. From 2001 to 2004, sales in the Munich's film and TV industry decreased by 23.5 per cent, from 8.45 billion Euros to 6.47 billion Euros (Table 7.1).

Using this as our point of departure, the following analysis examines local and non-local communication patterns and market linkages in the Munich film and TV industry cluster. The analysis is based on extensive fieldwork, including explorative interviews, discussions with experts, field observations, and semi-structured interviews, which were conducted between 2002 and 2004 during three research trips to Munich. Overall, sixty-five semi-structured interviews were conducted with actors from different value chains in the film and TV industry and other media institutions, including specialized industry associations and academies. The majority of the interviews were conducted with key actors in different film and TV production chains, such as producers and post-production executives. In order to measure the effects of local influences and compare them with non-local influences from other German and international media locations, respondents were asked to describe the nature, frequency, and importance of these linkages and evaluate their significance (Gräf 2005; Bathelt and Gräf 2008).

7.6 **From Growth to Crisis**

This section demonstrates that the genesis of the Munich film and TV industry cluster in the post-World War II period was neither unproblematic nor free of conflict. The growth of the cluster since the 1980s, which was primarily driven by the introduction of commercial/private TV and the respective growth of the Kirch Group, gave rise to initial dilemmas. These were reinforced by the advertising crisis and the dissolution of the Kirch Group at the turn of the Millennium.

The Kirch Group was originally established and led by one person: Leo Kirch. He launched a successful media operation in the late 1950s by buying and trading film rights. After the introduction of the dual broadcasting system in 1984, Kirch started up, acquired, or integrated several broadcasters, such as Sat.1, ProSieben, the pay TV channel Premiere, Kabel1, the sport channel DSF, and the news channel N24, as well as production firms (e.g. ndF – neues deutsches Fernsehen) and other related activities (Frankfurter Rundschau 2002*a*, 2002*b*). The vertically and horizontally integrated Kirch Group developed into one of the dominant actors of the German film and TV industry. A central part of the Kirch Group and an important basis of the Munich TV industry was the ProSiebenSat.1 Media AG, a conglomerate of several TV stations with total sales of 2.16 billion Euros, in 2000, and about 3,200 employees (Kurp 2005).

As a result of this growth, many production and post-production firms (e.g. MET and TV Werk) located their facilities in Munich to be close to these broadcasters, which were their main customers. Consequently, they developed close local contacts. Since the late 1990s, however, the development has exhibited signs of stagnation. The cases of film studios, such as Plazamedia and the Bavaria Filmstudios, which increasingly rent out studio space to low-budget TV shows and series, indicate that the TV production networks have begun to face a 'creativity dilemma'. On the one hand, they need to be more creative and innovative to tap into new markets and gain new customers. On the other hand, they have introduced cost-cutting measures leaving few resources for innovative thinking.

The post-World War II growth in the film sector was less spectacular than that of the TV sector even though movie production also benefited from the growing cluster dimensions. Despite some notable exceptions, such as 'Das Boot' and 'The Lives of Others', the poorer performance of this sector is largely due to the limited international recognition of Munich's motion picture industry. Indeed, most motion pictures produced in recent years have been primarily directed towards the German market and have not received international attention. An 'identity dilemma' has thus developed while the pre-World War II tradition of film production is fading away. This tradition is still being used to promote the city as an international media location; however, TV production has become the core business in Munich, and resources and infrastructure have become increasingly specialized to serve private/commercial broadcasters.

At the turn of the Millennium, crisis tendencies in Munich became particularly obvious. The Kirch Group ran into severe financial difficulties due to a number of structural problems and failures. These included false growth predictions in pay TV, financial losses of private broadcasting channels, the acquisition of overpriced film rights for sports events, overly hierarchical decision-making centred on Leo Kirch, and a tendency towards closed, over-integrated group networks. As a consequence, many people lost their jobs and numerous bankruptcies, restructuring activities, and management buyouts had occurred by the time the Kirch Group declared bankruptcy and was eventually dissolved in 2002 (Frankfurter Allgemeine Zeitung 2002, 2003a).

The decline and eventual dissolution of the Kirch Group coincided with a dramatic drop in industrial advertising expenditures. This advertising crisis severely impacted the activities of the private broadcasters in Munich (Frankfurter Allgemeine Zeitung 2003b). It caused many employees to be laid off and restructuring activities to be undertaken within the broadcasters. Production firms that were closely tied to the private broadcasters suffered most from the crises. Such firms fell under heavy cost pressures, as the number of film and TV productions decreased, and the broadcasters reduced prices for external production contracts. This led to a situation in which many producers were caught in a vicious circle. In response to the crisis, they focussed on cost efficiency and high productivity measures, instead of trying to come up with new, creative ideas that could have supported them in getting access to new markets outside the Munich film and TV industry. The dissolution of the Kirch Group also caused production companies to be spun out into the market of independent film production, thus creating more competition in this segment. As a result, markets became tighter and production firms began giving up their specialization in particular segments. Movie producers also started to subcontract work to Eastern Europe to take advantage of low-cost production in these countries (i.e. the Czech Republic and Baltic States).

In contrast, the negative effects of these crises were less visible in the public broadcasting sector, which is not connected to the Kirch Group and does not depend as much on private advertising expenditures.

7.7 Local Communication and Information Flows in Munich

This section argues that the effects of the recent crisis are not temporary in character; rather, they are indicative of deeper structural problems in the film and TV sector, which serve to block off regional knowledge flows and opportunities for recombination in the development of new film and TV formats. The structural problems relate to weak local networks and knowledge flows, as well as insufficient extra-local connections with other media centres, especially in foreign growth markets. In order to adequately explore this problem, this section provides an analysis of internal communication patterns and information flows, focussing, in particular, on segmented value chains and fragmented communication patterns.

1. *Segmented value chains.* The relatively low density of local communication and information flows is related to the fact that the existing value chains in Munich are highly segmented (Gräf 2005). This segmentation occurs along three dividing lines: by media branch, TV format, and broadcasting group. First, despite the use of similar technologies and tasks, there are different contexts of motion picture production between different media branches (i.e. advertising, movie, and TV production), which are associated with different problem-solving activities and routines. Interaction between these branches is limited. Second, different TV formats (i.e. film, documentary, series, and show) require specific technical skills and vary in terms of creativity, organization, and sequence. This also results in divided value chains. Third, segmentation is particularly strong between private and public broadcasting groups. There are two broadcasting groups in the Munich film and TV industry that have developed their own producer and supplier networks, that is, the Kirch Group (including ProSieben, Sat.1, Kabel1, and Premiere) and the public broadcasting services (Bayerischer Rundfunk and a regional ZDF branch), including the Bavaria Film network. These networks were established in mutually exclusive ways and could be classified as quasi-integrated in character, similar to the network configuration described by Leborgne and Lipietz (1991). Although the firms in these broadcasting networks were often independent in terms of ownership, their decision-making processes were not. Our research empirically demonstrates that these firms made collective decisions and conducted business with each other, locking out firms from other broadcasting group networks (Bathelt and Gräf 2008).

   The result of such segmentation tendencies was the development of parallel project networks, which were relatively closed and had little overlap. Each broadcasting group relied on an almost proprietary set of scriptwriters, production firms, actors, cameramen, and the like. Due to segmentation and specialization tendencies, individual agents had few opportunities to shift between different branches of the industry throughout their career. There are, however, some tendencies that seem to indicate that this could partially change in the future. First, we encountered some firms and freelancers that did not clearly belong to any particular broadcasting group (e.g. MET and TV60). Instead, they formed their own kind of network, which was characterized by more open information exchange and the development of new ideas. Second, the exclusive character of the broadcasting group networks has begun to dissolve, since production companies, such as ndF, try to conduct business with all types of broadcasters and cover the whole market. Core actors, such as the Bavaria Filmstudios, could play an important role in the process of creating more diversified project networks because they already have contracts with each of the groups. Thus far, however, they do not mediate between them.

2. *Fragmented communication patterns.* Overall, firms in the Munich film and TV industry seemingly benefit less from local buzz than expected. Many interviewees mentioned that they have relatively little contact with other specialists in their industry, and rarely go to trendy bars and cafes, which are well-known meeting places for the media business. They rely, instead, on personal networks, which either they or their close colleagues had established, to get new information about the industry and its market. Information exchange with these colleagues takes place on a daily basis in the office. Although transaction and project networks are influenced by such communication, general information exchange is neither fully systematic nor ubiquitous. Although it seems exceptionally strong within particular 'communication islands' and is usually found in the respective office spaces, it does not easily spread to other localities and circles. According to our interviews, this is because unintended, less organized meetings and interactions, where diverse information flows between different organizations can occur, are less important. Overall, this creates fragmented communication patterns. As indicated below, even within the various cores and localities of the Munich film and TV industry (Figure 7.2), there are social practices that limit information exchange and knowledge flows:

- *Media Park Unterföhring.* Along a stretch of several hundred meters close to the S-Bahn station Unterföhring, there is a large concentration of media firms, including ProSiebenSat.1 Media AG, Bayerischer Rundfunk, and the Bavaria Filmstudios. Despite their close physical proximity, there is hardly any interaction between the employees of these organizations. The firms' policy is to fully concentrate on themselves and ignore their neighbours. Employees from other firms are not allowed access to each other's dining halls and cafes. In-depth information exchange in the Media Park Unterföhring is thus non-existent. The only strong local linkages that exist are those between the broadcasters and some of the production firms, which produce for them on a virtually exclusive basis. The Media Park Unterföhring is characterized by a high degree of anonymity and lacks public meeting places, such as street cafes or restaurants, where individuals can interact.
- *Geiselgasteig.* The Bavaria Filmstadt in Geiselgasteig is also characterized by a large concentration of TV and film-related firms, including smaller broadcasters (i.e. RTL II and Tele 5), numerous studios for film and TV production and shows (i.e. Bavaria Filmstudios), as well as Bavaria

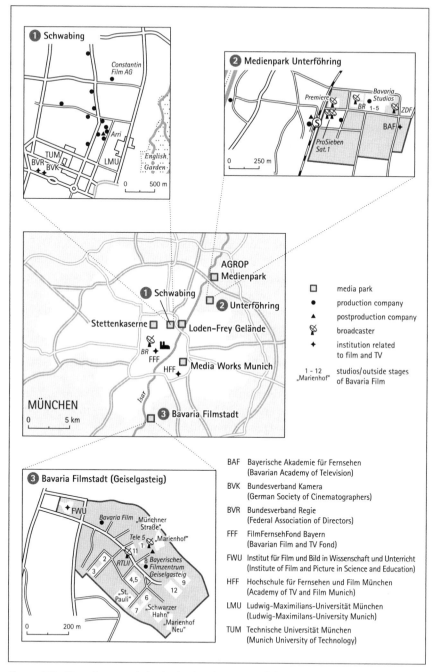

Figure 7.2. Sites, firms, and the institutional context of the Munich film and TV industry clusters

Filmproduktion and independent film producers. At first glance, Geiselgasteig appears to be more open than Unterföhring. There are meetings places, such as cafes and places, where people from different firms can sit together and have lunch. As noted by our interviewees, people also meet on the streets and chat. The film and TV specialists interviewed in Geiselgasteig also confirmed that this location was more conducive to communication and interaction between individuals than Unterföhring. However, they also pointed out the limitations of such communication, which were similar to those in the Media Park Unterföhring. Firms, such as RTL II and Tele 5, appeared insular in their activities and generally ignored the existence of others.

- *Communication islands.* There are, however, small communication islands in different parts of Munich, such as TV Werk, parts of Schwabing, and – at an earlier stage – the former Stetten barracks and the Lodenfrey area, where intensive, open communication patterns have developed (Gräf 2005). Such areas appear trendy and 'hip' to media people. They were described as places where established ideas are constantly combined with new ones, existing routines challenged by new combinations, and creative ventures tested. These communication islands seem to be more like homes than workplaces to the employees. At the same time, however, our interviewees commented on the closed nature of these locations, and suggested that they do not interact intensively with other areas in their respective industries in Munich.

- *Differentiation between media centres in Germany.* Segmentation tendencies can also be identified in relations with other German media centres. This is especially obvious in the area of TV production. Although most TV films, series, or shows involve agents from other German media centres – and even though joint funding of films through the Länder (states or provinces) requires that substantial inputs are acquired from within the respective regions – such linkages did not form across the different media groups. This is due to the rivalry that exists between these groups and their tendency to isolate themselves from the others. As a result of the distribution of the group networks, Munich TV producers have closer contact with Berlin or Leipzig, as opposed to Cologne, which is home to the competing media group RTL-Bertelsmann. Seemingly different local cultures have developed around the two private media groups in Cologne and Munich, partially grounded in rivalry, that have given rise to scepticism about each other's activities. One producer in Munich, for instance, described his counterparts in Cologne as being somewhat arrogant despite the fact that they were involved in low-budget, less creative project work.

Overall, this shows that while there are processes in the Munich film and TV industry cluster that can be described as local buzz, information flows and knowledge transfers appear limited to particular circles of people or segments of the industry. The research suggests that these linkages are highly fragmented according to media sector, TV/film genre, media group, and location. The result of these communication and interaction patterns is that information flows are selective and opportunities for creative recombination and innovative ideas limited.

7.8 **International and Inter-sectoral Linkages**

Although local networks of communication and interaction are important, the economic success of clusters often depends on the development and maintenance of trans-local pipelines, such as access to international markets and finance (Bathelt et al. 2004; Bathelt 2005*b*). International market access is especially important in the film or TV industry as it generates potentially large growth opportunities. Depending on the particular type of film or TV project, and the financial support required, projects initiated in Munich may involve firms from other German or international media centres. Similar to the observations of Grabher (2002*b*), personal address lists and private cellular phone numbers have become decisive anchor points in the know-how-driven processes of exchanging, distributing, and acquiring information. Of course, these networks are not purely local. They have developed over time and are based on the actors' personal experiences and backgrounds. Nonetheless, these networks often have a particular face-to-face history, which has helped to establish joint interpretative schemes over time. As will be demonstrated below, such international linkages and market access are surprisingly weak in Munich, which consequently limits the inflow of ideas and new contracts.

In the area of *TV production*, there are relatively few linkages with foreign markets, such as those of the public broadcasters with their Austrian, Swiss, and French counterparts. The joint French – German TV channel ARTE, located in Strasbourg and Baden-Baden, is an exception. Most linkages are related to joint shows or the exchange of TV formats, such as crime series. The successful licensing of TV programmes, such as 'Derrick' – a crime series that has been dubbed and sold to many countries worldwide – is rare, and the establishment of licensing agreements with foreign broadcasters is often not systematically planned in advance. Exceptions have occurred seemingly arbitrarily. If such agreements were to be expanded in the future, more TV productions would have to be done in English because there is not much demand for German or dubbed TV formats in other countries. The interviewees viewed the TV market as mainly a national market with many 'cultural particularities'. One TV producer explained that it is very difficult to sell German formats to other countries. It seems that the public broadcasters stopped their efforts to establish international linkages. According to a leading representative of one broadcaster, such attempts were made in the past, but '[t]he Brits are too egoistic, the Eastern block has no money, [and] Italy is too chaotic . . .' There were only a few co-productions, and these mainly focussed on the joint financing of TV formats. The Munich media sector is rarely involved in the actual production of joint documentaries and TV films, an activity which is typically carried out elsewhere. One interviewee described such co-productions as being difficult because they often involve conflicts associated with divergent interests.

Surprisingly, initiatives to provide better access to the Eastern European markets through the organization of co-productions or licensing were not very strong. Such access could become important in the future as the Eastern European media markets have only recently opened up and are likely to grow. Interaction is strongest in the area of studio production and decoration, due to the low labour costs in Eastern Europe. In contrast, attempts to attract US and other foreign movie productions to Munich have been less successful.

There are joint international activities in the area of *movie production*, but these activities are primarily focussed on co-financing. German distributors, for instance, carry a substantial portion of the costs of the Hollywood Majors, which produce 'blockbusters' for global markets (Scott 2002). This tradition of co-financing dates back to the pre-World War II period. As opposed to co-financing, international co-productions are rare. They sometimes occur when international involvement makes it possible for German producers to access additional funds or tax pre-emption, as in the case of Canada. Since the 1980s, German movies have occasionally been successful in international markets (e.g. 'Die Blechtrommel', 'Das Boot', 'Lola rennt', or 'Das Leben der Anderen'). Low-budget, high-profile German movies (so-called Autorenfilm) associated with independent directors, such as Rainer Werner Fassbinder, have also received much attention by international critics, but did not sell to a large audience. Despite these successes, there has not been a concerted effort to engage in co-productions with Hollywood producers. According to our interviews, the Hollywood Majors are not very interested in such cooperation as they do not require external support. Contacts with German producers are typically accomplished through subsidiaries and not the Majors themselves. Such contacts develop, for instance, when US producers want to produce at European sites.

Producers also have difficulty launching German movies in the US market. Aside from aspects of consumer taste and other cultural factors, the US market seems relatively closed and difficult to access. As one interviewee pointed out, it is difficult for foreign films to receive favourable time slots in the movie theatres without the cooperation of the Hollywood Majors. German productions would, therefore, likely be more successful in entering the North American market if they could actively involve US partners in co-financing and/or co-production. Under the lead of German producers, such arrangements are, however, virtually non-existent. Contacts with the Hollywood Majors are usually initiated through them, and take place under the lead of one of their subsidiaries.

There are, however, some producers in the Munich media industry cluster that have a very strong focus on international co-productions and try to implement international co-financing arrangements. As one film producer mentioned, networks are primarily established during international festivals and fairs. Co-financing networks include partners from the United States, Canada, England, and Australia, while co-productions primarily take place in Eastern Europe and Canada, due to cost advantages and tax incentives. Due to the difficulties of accessing financial resources in Germany, international productions rarely take place in Munich, despite the long history of such endeavours (e.g. productions of Alfred Hitchcock and Luchino Visconti in Munich).

This leads to a 'global–local dilemma'. Although there are some independent producers that establish creative, technical, and financial pipelines with markets in other countries, the Munich cluster barely profits from these linkages because it cannot establish a strong local platform for production activities.

Similar to the trend in studio production and decoration, *post-production* is increasingly subcontracted to Eastern European low-cost locations (Cole 2008). There is often no direct connection between the Munich producers and foreign post-production firms. One major German producer, for instance, typically hires Munich firms for post-production activities. At the same time, this producer creates strong cost-cutting pressure which, in turn, encourages post-production firms to seek out partners in Eastern Europe. Such practices strengthen the networks of potential future competitors in Eastern Europe. The former Werk Group, which had established a large international production network with subsidiaries in many cities and countries (e.g. Frankfurt/Main, London, New York, and Los Angeles), is an interesting exception (e.g. Krätke 2002). Overall, most post-production firms interviewed were surprisingly passive regarding the acquisition of new contracts, and had few external contacts with customers in other regions or countries.

In general, the results of this research indicate that there are only a few international linkages or pipelines that would be able to direct additional contracts, substantial growth, leading international artists, and creative ideas to Munich. Such access would be particularly important as Munich's project networks already tap into a substantial part of the national resources of the film and TV industry. This structure could result in further stagnation and structural dilemmas, which have emerged and become clearer with the end of the expansion period of private/commercial broadcasters.

International sources of finance are also not well developed in the Munich TV and film industry. Although film funds and co-financing arrangements with foreign partners are more important in the segment of *movie production* – compared to TV production – budgets are limited. Our interviewees were particularly concerned about private film funds in Germany, international market access, and funding for their films, particularly with respect to the US market. Although there are numerous private film funds located in Munich, it is difficult for local independent filmmakers to access these resources. As illustrated in the complaints of one producer, these funds are mostly invested in big Hollywood productions because the rate of return is higher and more secure than that expected from German films. In Hollywood, this source of financing is sometimes also referred to as 'stupid German money' (Kurp 2004). Overall, the success of some German movies in foreign markets has had a limited effect on the budgetary situation of the production firms. It has neither become easier to acquire financial funds nor has the amount of available funds grown.

7.9 **Conclusion**

This chapter has used the case of the Munich film and TV industry cluster to empirically demonstrate that regional growth patterns cannot easily be understood if the underlying structures of social relations are not adequately examined. This draws attention to the benefits of a relational approach to economic action and interaction in spatial perspective. The initial growth of the Munich film and TV industry cluster was a result of the introduction of private/commercial TV in the mid-1980s and a sound institutional infrastructure, which developed from the city's tradition in film production. The cluster also benefited from national specificities related to language, consumer taste, and other cultural factors that created national entry barriers, similar to those in other national TV markets. Although these conditions could have led to optimistic growth projections, this research argues that the favourable conditions for growth in the Munich film and TV industry cluster in the post-World War II period have been overshadowed by its existing structural weaknesses. The advertising crisis and the dissolution of the Kirch Group after the turn of the Millennium served to enhance these weaknesses.

Building upon a relational buzz-and-pipeline conception of clusters, we argue that a cluster's economic success is not only based on internal networks of communication and producer–user interaction, it also depends on a strong external dimension, involving market and technology linkages with actors in other regions and countries. The particular combination of local buzz and trans-local pipelines generates a reflexive process of knowledge creation within a cluster, generating enhanced learning capabilities and dynamic growth.

Cluster firms obviously benefit less from local buzz than expected, due to the existence of highly segmented value chains. Although communication islands exist in different parts of the city, they do not interact intensively with one another and are unable to function as hubs for widespread information transfers. Furthermore, linkages with external markets and access to international finance are surprisingly weak, thus limiting the prospects for future economic growth. At all stages of film and TV production, attempts to acquire new partners abroad are underdeveloped. The existing lack of financial resources seemingly serves to aggravate this situation. Although some producers have established trans-local pipelines in creative, technical, and financial fields, the Munich film and TV industry cluster does not benefit much from these linkages. Additional sources of finance – apart from broadcasting services and public film funds – are not well developed.

Given these structural weaknesses, the future prospects for creative recombination, new ideas, and additional growth impulses in the Munich film and TV industry seem limited. There are, however, opportunities for institutional renewal related to the dissolution of the rigid networks of the former Kirch Group after its acquisition by the US billionaire Haim Saban. Such a development could lead to more intensive information and communications flows in the future. It could also become a focus of additional policy initiatives. The strengthening of internal networks may also require that agents extend external business relations both with other media locations in Germany and international media centres. These are just some of the ways how cluster policies could support further regional development in the media sector – an issue that will be discussed in greater detail in Chapter 11.

Part III
Knowledge Circulation across Territories

8 A Relational Conception of Firm Internationalization

8.1 Introduction: Bridging Distance

Part III of this book analyses the problems of establishing and maintaining economic relations, especially in the context of knowledge circulation across space. Chapters 6 and 7 moved us beyond simple local–global dualisms to develop a more accurate understanding of how firms in local clusters benefit from trans-local interconnections to access diverse resources such as knowledge or technology. Building on these discussions, this chapter extends the relational perspective to the issue of bridging distance in order to interact with remote places and markets. In many cases, firms are not single-plant operations but have multiple international locations to ensure continuous access to markets and critical resources. The questions that follow from this are: How do firms establish a presence in new markets, and what are the organizational challenges associated with market entry? This chapter challenges the atomistic view of most conventional theories of firm internationalization and develops a relational conception of firm internationalization and foreign market-entry. While the chapter critically engages with internationalization theory to address the emergence of permanent foreign locations, Chapter 9 examines more temporary forms of coping with geographical distance in economic interaction.

In an increasingly global economy, many firms must expand their business relations to international markets in order to increase their market share, gain access to critical resources, achieve cost efficiency, and secure strategic assets. Since the 1960s, economics and management theories have developed a wide range of conceptual approaches to explain the internationalization of multinational firms. At present, firm internationalization has become a more complex phenomenon than initially theorized in these early approaches. To begin with, the international expansion of firms has proceeded not only in traditional manufacturing-based businesses but also in services, especially in knowledge-intensive services such as investment banking, legal services, advertising, accounting, and management consulting. Second, firm internationalization is no longer solely restricted to large firms; it increasingly involves medium, small, and even micro businesses. The example of the born-global companies, which are launched as transnational corporations from the very beginning, usefully illustrates one aspect of the various forms and processes of internationalization (Chetty and Campbell-Hunt 2004). The contemporary notion of the 'transnational firm' is, thus, more complex than the traditional model of the post-World War II multinational corporation (Jones 2003).

This chapter addresses the shortcomings of conventional approaches to the study of firm internationalization by developing a relational conceptualization of the internationalization process. It also conducts an empirical test of this alternative conception of market entry. A mixed-method approach to fieldwork is used to examine the impact of the specific context – namely, the social network of a firm – on the choice of the organizational form of market entry. Our argument begins by criticizing foreign direct investment (FDI) theories and stage theories of internationalization for their atomistic perspective of firm decision-making and international expansion. It then proposes a relational approach to firm internationalization and introduces a network conception of internationalization that takes inter-firm relations as the starting point for the analysis of firm expansion. The argument leads to a relational conception of international market entry based on ethnographic fieldwork in three major European cities: London, Frankfurt, and Madrid. This is followed by the presentation of a statistical model, which lends further support to our conceptualization.

8.2 **Atomism in Theories of Internationalization**

Since the late 1970s, two theories of internationalization have come to dominate academic debates: (*a*) the theory of multinational enterprises (or FDI theory) and (*b*) the Uppsala stage theory of internationalization. Our critique of these approaches is derived from a relational perspective that brings together many contemporary arguments that are based on conceptions such as embeddedness, social capital, and untraded interdependencies. Following Granovetter (1985), the major pitfall in theorizing economic action relates to its explicit or implicit atomism. According to this view, theories are atomistic if the analysis of individual action is exclusively based on internalized norms (i.e. over-socialized form) or the application of external assumptions such as formal rationality or profit maximization (i.e. under-socialized form). Whereas atomistic conceptions of human action ignore the complex interplay between economic action and the particular socio-institutional context in which agents are embedded, a relational perspective acknowledges that individual action is fundamentally shaped by such contexts (Storper 1997*c*; Bathelt and Glückler 2003*b*).

Among the many concepts of firm internationalization, the eclectic paradigm is most prominently associated with the work of Dunning (1977, 1988, 2000). His so-called O-L-I model is eclectic because it integrates distinct explanatory approaches from different theories into one single framework. According to this perspective, the selection of a specific form of international operation, in a particular target market, is the result of a combination of three advantages: First, a firm must have specific ownership (O) advantages that compensate for the general liabilities associated with being foreign, as well as the competitive position of rival domestic firms in the target market. Second, the location (L) advantages of the target market must be identified and evaluated with respect to the firm's strategy (Dunning 1977). Third, it is necessary to determine whether the O-advantages can best be realized through internalization (I) – which involves I-advantages – or through external cooperative or market transactions. Given the imperfections of good and factor markets, positive transportation costs, heterogeneity of demand, and increasing returns to scale, internalization is an alternative organizational strategy to reduce transaction costs (Coase 1937). The internalization of O-advantages becomes more efficient than trade when the transaction costs of market relationships are higher than the costs of hierarchical inter-firm linkages (Rugman 1980; Bradach and Eccles 1989).

In the so-called Uppsala School (Johanson and Vahlne 1977, 1990, 1992; Johanson and Wiedersheim-Paul 1975), firm internationalization is viewed as the process by which firms' gradually increase their commitment to a foreign market. Previous empirical work suggests that local experience-based knowledge leads to incremental advances in market knowledge and, thus, to a stepwise establishment of an international organization (Johanson and Vahlne 1977). The process of internationalization unfolds in a series of stages, where firms gain experience, build management competence, and reduce uncertainty in order to incrementally increase investments in a target market (Johanson and Vahlne 1977; Erramilli 1991). Although the individual stages and their sequence are conceptualized differently in various approaches, most approaches identify a gradual intensification of operations from indirect to direct export, and from licensing arrangements to own international production.

The theory of the multinational enterprise addresses the firm-specific advantages that can be used to improve a firm's competitiveness in a foreign market. At the same time, it discusses the location-specific advantages of a target market based on a country's immobile resources. Rather than focussing on the normative aspects of efficient resource allocation, stage theory concentrates on the very process of an international engagement. In emphasizing processes of learning and past experience, stage theory predicts an incremental increase in the activities of firms as a result of accumulated market-specific knowledge. Despite adopting an explicitly process-based approach, stage theory shares some common ground with the more normative theories of resource allocation in that it also demonstrates a bias towards internal resources, strategies, and competences (Johanson and Wiedersheim-Paul 1975; Johanson and Vahlne 1977). In other words, it does not analyse the internationalization process of a firm in light of the specific context in which a firm chooses to internationalize. Without denying the utility of these theories in explaining both the selection of a target market and the choice of an organizational form of market entry, the following section suggests that such approaches miss important aspects of firm internationalization because they treat firms as analytically independent from their respective socio-institutional contexts. This argument will be developed in the context of management consulting.

8.2.1 UNDER-SOCIALIZED CONCEPTS OF MARKET SELECTION

In conventional theories, the selection of an international target market is an under-socialized form because it is viewed as a process of rational decision-making by atomistic firms. Stage theory, moreover, suggests a gradient of psychic distance that influences the pattern of international expansion.

Market selection as rational decision-making

FDI theory conceptualizes international market selection as a normative, efficiency-led rational decision. Firms identify their specific competitive edge and look for those location-specific advantages of a market that provide the best production or sales conditions. Markets are, thus, systematically screened, compared, and assessed with respect to efficiency gains. According to this perspective, a firm always chooses the market that best facilitates the realization of its goals (e.g. the highest sales potential, lowest labour costs, or highest concentration of specific technological knowledge). In stage theory, market selection is also the result of independent rational decision-making processes. In order to minimize uncertainty, firms often choose to extend their operations to culturally proximate – often neighbouring – markets. This is because it is easier to compensate for a lack of specific market knowledge in such contexts than in more remote markets. Market risk is, thus, viewed as the key parameter of market selection. Increasing experience conveys specific knowledge which, in turn, allows for a gradual intensification of market commitment. Both FDI and stage theory are expressions of optimal or rational market selection models. Firms compare potential target markets, assess locational advantages, and choose the best match. Both approaches are atomistic because market selection is explained, first, through conditions that are internal to the firm and, second, by general market characteristics. In other words, external firm-specific conditions and networks are ignored.

Past empirical research does not provide substantial support for these approaches (Coviello and Martin 1999). According to O'Farrell and Wood's study (1998) of British consulting firms, for example, service firms rarely engage in any form of systematic market assessment or formal processes of decision-making. In this context, market selection and the form of market entry are largely constrained by inter-firm relations with clients or strategic partners. Only 6 per cent of the firms surveyed in the study employed active strategies of comparative market selection (O'Farrell et al. 1996: 114). The work of Westhead et al. (2001), moreover, reveals that international exports are mainly a reaction to either demand from abroad or existing domestic clients. Such reactive internationalization suggests that market selection is not the result of rational decision-making processes but related to contextual business relations. A recent empirical study of medium-sized manufacturing firms in Germany illustrates the importance of social networks and personal relationships, rather than rational market-screening procedures, in the actual choice of a target market (Scharrer 2000). These findings suggest that conventional theories underestimate the relevance of specific social networks.

Market selection and psychic distance

Stage theory argues that psychic distance influences the geographical patterns of international expansion. Psychic distance is defined as 'the sum of factors preventing the flow of information from and to the market' (Johanson and Vahlne 1977: 24), including, for example, differences in language, education, business practice, culture, or industrial development (Gertler 1997). Given the uncertainty of an operation in a market with cultural, legal, and business institutions that are very different from the firm's home base, early international activities are likely to target similar and often neighbouring markets. Stage theory, thus, predicts the extension of international activities from countries with a high level of psychic proximity to those with more psychic distance (Bell 1995; Buckley and Casson 1998). Empirical work on different business service sectors challenges this argument (Sharma and Johanson 1987; Bell 1995; Coviello and Martin 1999). It shows that actual geographical patterns of expansion do not necessarily follow a gradient of psychic distance. Instead, markets that promise the highest growth or sales potential are often targeted first.

In the case of management consulting, the psychic distance argument is questionable on both empirical and theoretical grounds. On the one hand, Sharma and Johanson (1987) argue that the market selection of business service firms is independent from the problem of psychic distance because associated investments tend to be lower and less market-specific than in manufacturing firms. Whereas manufacturing firms have pronounced sunk costs through the installation of machinery and production facilities (Clark and Wrigley 1995), a consulting firm may start operation with rented office space. The limited specific investments lower the risk of a local market operation and thus permit international operation trials in more remote markets with a higher degree of psychic distance. On the other hand, the marketing and provision of management services requires fundamental knowledge of local business culture, regional/national and sectoral market conditions, and management methods (Wood 2002*a*). Market-specific adaptation is, therefore, far more decisive for consulting firms than for standardized manufacturing operations: 'Selling milk or cars in a foreign country requires, for example, specific labelling or a special advertising campaign. Offering an advanced management service in another country requires perfect knowledge of the client and environment, in order for this service to be unique and its success or failure will be influenced considerably by the success or failure of the process of cultural adaptation carried out' (Rubalcaba 1999: 290).

In light of recent empirical observations, we expect psychic distance to play an important role in the internationalization of consulting firms. British and French consulting firms, for example, demonstrate a pronounced international market presence in countries of their former colonies, whereas German firms are particularly active in Austria and Switzerland (Hofmann and Vogler-Ludwig 1991: 24). Spanish consultants, moreover, engage quite intensively in South American markets (Alpha Publications 1996). While these general references do not provide sufficient evidence of the psychic-distance hypothesis, it seems more compelling to analyse the logic of market selection as a reaction to opportunities from external relations with clients and other stakeholders than as a function of internal evaluations of uncertainty. Bell's work (1995) suggests that business service firms choose their markets 'on the back of their clients'. In the process of following their clients, many business service firms react to the internationalization path of their existing clients or new offers of foreign clients in their respective markets. In other words, Bell's study offers little support for the argument that the gradient of psychic distance explains market selection (Bell 1995: 67).

8.2.2 UNDER-SOCIALIZED CONCEPTS OF MARKET ENTRY

After the decision to internationalize and the choice of a specific destination, the major part of internationalization theory is dedicated to the form of market entry. In this stage, the approaches implicitly assume atomistic decision-making procedures. FDI theory, for instance, interprets the choice of the organizational form as a make-or-buy problem following transaction-cost economics. According to this perspective, firms tend to internalize operations when the internal hierarchical organization incurs lower transaction costs than the market. Decisions about the appropriate form of market entry are, consequently, atomistic. Empirically observable processes of market entry do not, however, always follow this logic. According to a study by O'Farrell et al. (1996), only 20 per cent of the firms assess alternative entry forms before the final establishment. Despite ongoing efforts to isolate the determinants of organizational choice (Brouthers and Brouthers 2000; Hennart and Park 1993), the actual choice of the organizational form remains contingent upon conditions that exist in the business and market environment. Market entry is, thus, a highly context-specific procedure (Erramilli 1991).

Stage theory suggests that market entry is initiated through exports, and that organizational commitment gradually increases with market experience over time. The precise nature of the relationship between market experience and the form of market entry has not, however, been determined in the literature on service firms. Firms neither choose similar organizational forms nor does the development of an operation follow a single pattern of organizational stages (Buckley et al. 1992). Instead of viewing exports as the first stage of international activities, Young (1987) documents the increasing importance of alternative organizational designs, such as licensing agreements and joint ventures. Moreover, the internationalization process does not always unfold in a direction that increases commitment. Firms may skip certain hypothesized stages or revert to less committed forms of engagement during times of economic downturn (Cannon and Willis 1981; Turnbull 1993; McDougall et al. 1994). Given the heterogeneity of organizational designs and the flexibility of organizational development, stage theory has been criticized for being overly deterministic, as it postulates a fixed sequence of stages regardless of the context in which a firm operates (Reid 1983).

Aside from the fact that organizational forms are not always chosen on the basis of rational decision-making processes, management consulting does not produce the full range of options regarding organizational designs. Although unbounded service production can be distinguished from processes of service provision, which may be stored in certain media (e.g. plans, software, and reports), in the case of consulting, the places of production and service provision cannot be separated. Consulting is clearly a locationally bounded service (Sampson and Snape 1985; Boddewyn et al. 1986) that requires the physical co-presence of consultants and clients. As a consequence, management consulting services are hard to trade internationally and exports do not represent a sustainable form of international operation (Vandermerwe and Chadwick 1989; Buckley et al. 1992; Erramilli and D'Souza 1995). Only the travel of consulting professionals permits a temporary provision of services across borders.

8.2.3 FOCUS ON LARGE MANUFACTURING FIRMS

Apart from their implicit atomism, both conventional approaches largely focus on the internationalization process of large manufacturing firms (Coviello and Munro 1997; Grönroos 1999). Since the internationalization process discussed here refers to service firms that involve mostly small- and medium-sized operations, these approaches offer limited analytical leverage. The international expansion of small- and medium-sized enterprises (SMEs) often follows a pattern that differs from and cannot be easily represented by these approaches. For SMEs, the decision to launch operations abroad is riskier than in the case of large firms. Given that the required investments are higher relative to the available firm resources, a potential failure in a new market would be more expensive (Buckley 1993). Erramilli and D'Souza (1995) demonstrate that the likelihood of a service firm investing abroad increases when the firm size increases and the capital intensity of the planned operation is in decline. And, since SMEs often lack financial and management resources, a shortage of financial resources may lead to the choice of less appropriate organizational entry forms. Decision processes based on a lack of managerial resources tend to be short term and spontaneous (Buckley 1993). These structural conditions make it more difficult to launch an international operation, especially in the case of an initial international establishment. According to one British study, many SMEs fail in their first attempt to expand internationally and only manage to establish foreign operations after repeated trials (Buckley et al. 1988). Overall, FDI theory is not particularly helpful in explaining the internationalization processes of small- and medium-sized business service firms (O'Farrell and Wood 1998). Other research also notes the limitations of stage theory and shows that a general pattern of successive stages is not suitable in understanding the internationalization of service firms, especially knowledge-intensive business services (Sharma and Johanson 1987; Erramilli 1990; Westhead et al. 2001).[1]

8.3 A Network Approach to Internationalization

The critique of atomistic conceptions of firm internationalization directs attention towards contextual factors, including the relationship between firms and other economic actors, such as suppliers, clients, and strategic partners. This relational perspective parallels recent developments in the study of global production networks (Henderson et al. 2002), as well as in the Uppsala School. Johanson and Vahlne (1992), for instance, describe the process of foreign market entry as a problem of access to networks of new business relations. The network approach to internationalization has been primarily developed in the industrial marketing and international business literature (Johanson and Mattsson 1987, 1993; Sharma and Johanson 1987).

This perspective views the market as a network of exchange relations between producers, suppliers, customers, and competitors. These relations serve very different purposes (Johanson and Mattsson 1987): They may, for example, reduce the cost of production or transactions; contribute to the development of new knowledge and competencies; lead to, at least partial, control over other actors; serve as bridges to unrelated third actors; or help to mobilize partners against a third parties. In a dynamic perspective, networks undergo constant changes by breaking up established contacts and forming new ones. In contrast to internationalization theory, the network approach prioritizes external relations over internal conditions and assets. In line with the concept of resource dependence (Pfeffer and Salancik 1978), access to other firms' resources is critically important in turning market opportunities into internal competencies and competitive advantages. A firm's position in a network is, thus, of significant strategic value; it becomes an intangible resource. In sum, the network approach argues that international market entry depends more on a firm's network position than on the institutional, economic, or cultural conditions of the host market. A business network serves to form 'bridges to foreign markets' (Sharma and Johanson 1987: 22).

From the perspective of inter-firm relations, Johanson and Mattsson (1987) articulate an alternative approach to the study of international expansion. This approach complements the network perspective by performing a contextual analysis of specific internationalization paths. Johanson and Mattsson (1987) emphasize the role of external resources in gaining opportunities to internationalize. Network relations are not, however, always an enabling force; they can also block internationalization (Coviello and Munro 1997). Altogether, the processes of network formation and a firm's position in a network have an important impact on the form and direction of international expansion. The form of market entry is thus viewed as a consequence of business relationships that have evolved over time, rather than the result of rationally selected optimal solutions (Blankenburg Holm et al. 1996). Similar to FDI and stage theory, the network model was developed in the context of manufacturing firms. Although it has only been applied in few case studies, the empirical findings demonstrate the qualitative influence of existing firm relations on the strategic and organizational decisions of firms in international expansion (Coviello and Munro 1997; Coviello and Martin 1999; Chetty and Blankenburg Holm 2000). As such, the model increases the explanatory power of other models.

The processes of internationalization are complex and unfold in contingent ways (Strandskov 1993). Analyses of the interrelationships between consulting firms and their client and partner organizations, as well as their contingent internationalization processes, call for an alternative approach (O'Farrell et al. 1995; O'Farrell and Wood 1998). A relational perspective that acknowledges existing sets of inter-firm relations promises to be particularly instructive in analyses of market entry. If we allow that networks shape internationalization processes, the question becomes: How, and in what ways, do different kinds of networks affect forms of internationalization and market entry? In contrast to conventional theories, we suggest that social networks, which are external to the firm, are central to processes of internationalization in knowledge-intensive project-based businesses. In supporting this claim, we also aim to identify the causal mechanisms linking the social context of firms with their choices of market entry.

8.4 A Relational Conception Explaining International Market Entry

The empirical foundations of our research are derived from a combination of diverse sources of observation and multiple methods. The analysis is based on a study of consulting firms in the metropolitan regions of London, Frankfurt, and Madrid between 1999 and 2003 (for detailed discussion of the methodology, see Glückler 2005, 2006). All three metropolitan areas are major agglomerations of consulting services in their respective countries (Table 8.1). Given our interest in the actual context and process of international market entry, local affiliates and subsidiaries of foreign international firms were used to represent the main unit of analysis. The study is based on two different data sets that allow us to pursue a mixed-method approach: seventy-three semi-structured interviews with managers of consulting firms and a set of 111 consulting firms for which interview data was coded into numerical categories and combined with additional survey data.[2] The quantitative and qualitative analyses are designed to deliver complementary evidence. Based on ethnographic fieldwork, the next section develops an argument about differential entry risks and the role of network contexts in reducing the risks of market entry. The findings are then tested in a statistical model to assess the contingent relation between the contextuality of social networks and the organizational form of market entry.

8.4.1 MARKET-ENTRY CHALLENGE: HIDDEN EXPERIENCES

International market entry is not an easy venture. It becomes even more challenging when firms do not pursue expansion as a proactive strategy, but are pressured to internationalize to maintain their business with an existing

Table 8.1. Key economic indicators of the case study regions

Indicators	Frankfurt	London	Madrid
Inhabitants (*millions*)	5.2	7.3	5.0
% of national population	7	12	13
% of GDP (*estimates*)	9	20	16
% of national consulting firms	11	22	45
% of national turnover in consulting industry	11	n.a.	n.a.
% of employees in consulting industry	n.a.	36	56

Note: n.a. = not available.
Source: Adapted from Glückler (2005: 1734).

client. The repeated enforcement of international market expansion by existing clients is nicely illustrated in the following statement made by a managing director of a German consultancy firm in Frankfurt: 'We do not globalise because we think we get more through that. Instead, our clients say "we are global, so you have got to be global, too, otherwise we do not work with you."' Given the uncertainties facing consultants in international markets, the step to launch foreign operations is subject to major barriers. Existing research on internationalization often fails to develop a comprehensive understanding of unsuccessful international ventures. In this respect, the Frankfurt study reveals two interesting cases, both of which provide clear examples of the challenges of successful internationalization. In the first case, a top German management consulting firm tried to enter Spain in a market-seeking mode.[3] The company, founded in 1992, grew rapidly and was able to acquire international client corporations. After three years, the firm expected to sustain its growth through international expansion. The CEO reported the experience as follows:

We had started to go to Spain. We sent a consultant and pursued client acquisition for about two years. We invested a whole lot of money but it is not easy to get a foot in the market. It turned out that one [should] better know the local context. We had to learn the lesson that the Spanish market is less open to consulting than the German one. Only the real global players could succeed... except that one follows a client just as a competitor of ours has done. Their client went to Spain... so that the consultancy simply followed in the market. Today, this client remains the focus apart from the additional local business... Ok; the background was that we had a colleague whose wife was Spanish. Since personal relations play an important role in Spain and since that lady belonged to the inner circle in Madrid, we thought to send them to Spain... Yet, we never won a project and after a while we decided not to continue these efforts. Our colleague, by the way, stayed in Spain.

In the second case, a multinational logistics consulting firm in Frankfurt was forced to open an office in the US market in order to be assigned by a major car manufacturer. After two years of business, however, the company exited the market because of a lack of new business development. The company's managing director described the situation as follows:

> The management suddenly changed with somebody who was evidently consulting averse. Our...business was 95% with that client. We had always tried intensively to diversify and win new clients in the US but the rules of the game seemed different from the European logistics market. Size matters, niches are not sustainable. And we certainly were a niche player.

Whereas the first case demonstrates the difficulties of developing new local client relations without current business in the market, the second case suggests that a client-following mode of entry may only provide a short-term basis and may lead to full dependence on a single client. Acquiring new clients in a foreign market is one of the most critical challenges in internationalization processes. According to our interviewees, prior attempts to launch foreign operations also failed in a number of instances. These incidents support the argument that processes of internationalization do not unravel in a linear way but follow sequences of trial, error, and success.

8.4.2 MARKET-ENTRY FORM: TWO KINDS OF ORGANIZATIONAL RISKS

The organization of a new international operation may take different forms. It can include the establishment of subsidiaries and affiliates, the acquisition of wholly-, majority-, or minority-owned local companies, and the formation of joint ventures, strategic alliances, or loose non-contractual forms of inter-firm cooperation (Daniels 1995; O'Farrell and Wood 1999; Samie 1999). From an empirical standpoint, the proportion of loose cooperation networks in the overall volume of international revenues is limited. For the analysis of market-entry forms, only foreign direct investments were considered and two organizational modes of entry distinguished: An investment is classified as a Greenfield investment when an international consultancy sets up *de novo* subsidiaries or affiliates; it is classified as a Brownfield investment when the firm enters the market through an acquisition, joint venture, or majority-participation in local firms. Each of these modes of market entry is characterized by inherent benefits and risks. The following section stresses the importance of considering organization-specific risks in understanding the impact of social relationships on organizational design. The analysis of opportunities and threats associated with Greenfield and Brownfield investments is drawn from the managers' rationales and experiences, as reported in the interviews (Table 8.2).

Table 8.2. Greenfield versus Brownfield market-entry: opportunities and threats

Opportunities/threats	Type of market-entry	
	Greenfield	Brownfield
Opportunities	Internal transfer of professional standards and knowledge	Purchase of existing business relationships and personnel
	Full control over organization development and international intra-firm coordination	Profits from day 1
		Speedy entry and fast growth
		High potential market share
Threats	Slow growth	Post M&A integration failure
	Lack of local contacts	Threat to firm reputation
	Time lag until break-even	Overpriced target company

Source: Adapted from Glückler (2006: 384).

A Greenfield market-entry enables the internal transfer and control of professional standards, work routines, and organizational cultures. According to many consultants, this represents a strong argument in favour of growing organically into a new market. The core competencies of a consulting company are the knowledge of its professionals, the reputation of the firm, and the quality of the client network. When firms grow through Greenfield investments, they are able to maintain the quality of their recruitment standards and can consistently integrate local professionals into the existing organizational and knowledge architecture. An important upshot of organic growth is that firms can ensure internal cohesion and continuity with their clients at an international level, and thereby sustain their consulting reputation. An additional benefit of Greenfield entry relates to its involvement with smaller investments, as opposed to mergers and acquisitions (M&As). Investments in renting office space and expatriating professionals can be done in a stepwise manner so that the risk of financial losses can be controlled. The downside of Greenfield investments is that internal firm organization and recruitment, as well as external market relationships, must be fully developed from scratch without local knowledge. This involves several challenges: First, a Greenfield venture has no local business contacts. Given that the reputation effects associated with existing business contacts are crucial in acquiring new clients, a firm may face severe barriers to business development that could threaten the venture in the medium term. Second, in developed markets, where competition is high and size becomes a factor of competitiveness, incremental organic growth may be too slow to establish a competitive position.

The advantages of a Brownfield market entry can compensate for the drawbacks of Greenfield entry. M&As are attractive ways to acquire a range of client and industry relationships with just one financial transaction. By purchasing a local consulting firm, an entrant may 'get a foot into the door', integrate established professionals, and achieve a considerable market share. One managing director of an American human resources consulting firm in Madrid justified his decision for an acquisitive market entry by arguing that, in his business, human resources (the number of capable and well-connected people) were quite limited in any country. One would have to buy these specialists out, pay superior salaries, hope that these people assemble a coherent and competitive staff, and wait many years for the new firm to grow and generate profits. New contacts, thus, need time to evolve before the company sees any return on its investment. Another respondent suggested that Brownfield investments are beneficial because they provide opportunities for quick growth and immediate profit gains, whereas *de novo* establishments take a long time to break even. In turn, a Brownfield entry bears the risk of purchasing 'hot air', as the managing director of a Swedish human resources consultancy in Madrid graphically phrased it. The hot-air argument comprises two components: First, since client relationships are central to the competitiveness and market success of a consulting business, these external relationships influence the value and purchase price of a target firm. The CEO of a technology consultancy in Frankfurt explained this as follows:

What is a consulting company worth? The computers or the office equipment? No, the value of a consulting firm is determined, first, by its employees. They are highly mobile, however, and fly away if the integration fails after a merger. The second determinant is the client network. So you can avoid making cold calls and saying 'Hello, you do not know us, but could we come for a presentation?'

Second, competitive resources are fundamentally reflected in the human capital of the acquired firm and the relational capital associated with its client portfolio. Although human capital is highly mobile and sensitive to changes in a firm's governance and organizational structure, relational capital is often strongly bound to the respective specialists that create the relationship. Consequently, problems in post-acquisition integration can quickly lead to a situation where professionals, their knowledge, and their relational capital leave the new organization. Our empirical work shows that not all market entries were successful on their first attempt. Various firms tried to establish operations beforehand, but failed. Respondents referred to numerous examples where takeovers of local firms resulted in 'disastrous' experiences. Some technology- and IT-related consulting services had to internationalize through M&As because of the speed of market growth during the 1990s. Geographical expansion and local acquisitions were the only way to keep up with this speed. The economic downturn since late 2000 has again stimulated change, and growth must now be managed more carefully. One managing director of an American technology consultancy in London regretted the decision to conduct an M&A. In the due diligence procedure, speed had been given more weight than accuracy, which led to unforeseen problems of post-merger integration. The firm later shifted its expansion strategy towards organic growth by acquiring enough business in a market from the outside before entering it.

These divergent lines of argument go some way in illustrating the contingencies of entry mode choice. However, the analysis of entry-form-specific opportunities and challenges points towards a strategic decision-making problem that relates to a trade-off between two kinds of risks: A Greenfield investment, which runs the risk of new business development failure, and a Brownfield investment, which avoids this risk by purchasing these relationships but then faces the problem of acquiring overpriced target firms and post-merger integration failures. Integration problems can be very harmful and threaten the entire venture if local professionals decide to leave the new operations and take their knowledge and client base with them. The question then becomes: How do firms choose between these risks, and how does the market-entry context influence such risks?

8.4.3 MARKET-ENTRY CONTEXT: SAFEGUARD AGAINST THE RISK OF BUSINESS DEVELOPMENT FAILURE

What general lessons can we draw from the above-described trade-off problem, and how might a relational perspective inform our analysis of this situation? Aside from the two cases mentioned above, access to social network contacts and business relationships seem to be a crucial factor in other sample cases. To further explore this, we have defined two distinct types of market-entry contexts based on the interviews conducted. When an entry process drew on business relations from client or other business partner networks, this context was labelled relational entry. Alternatively, when firms invested in a region without drawing on prior contacts or existing network relations, this context was labelled atomistic entry.

In an atomistic entry context, firms organize their market entry on their own, rather than through the support of existing business networks. Although market-seeking emerged as the dominant motive in our interviews, some firms pursued a resource-seeking strategy for international expansion in order to improve their level of competence and innovativeness. Atomistic entries support the arguments of conventional internationalization theory, which suggest that firms develop corporate strategies, make optimal decisions, and venture into the most profitable markets. Since no external relationship constraints or opportunities seem to exist, explanations of internationalization processes are exclusively based on the firm and its resources. However, as discussed in further detail below, cases of atomistic entry were not very prominent in the sample. Conventional theory tends to prioritize firm-specific competitive advantages over the ability to acquire new clients in a market. As previously demonstrated, however, one of the most important barriers to internationalization is new business development. Given that sustainable local business contacts can only be acquired through local presence, consulting firms take substantial risks in opening offices in a target market. And, since the development of a new client in the consulting business can take several months to a year or longer, considerable financial commitments must be made in advance. Yet, given the project-based nature of the consulting business, consultancies are rarely able to establish a financial buffer for their future business. The risk of venturing into a new market under atomistic conditions is, therefore, extremely high. Indeed, as the CEO of a German technology consultancy in Frankfurt explained: 'You must have very large savings in order to finance a market entry over one year in advance. I do not think that many firms can afford this. In fact, we could not.' Since creating a new client base is a lengthy process, atomistic entry contexts revealed a tendency to foster Brownfield entry. Through the acquisition of local firms, the buying firm was able to take over local client networks and avoided the risk of business development failure; it did this, however, at the cost of potential post-merger integration failure.

A relational entry context is characterized by existing client relationships. The study showed that the more a consultancy serves internationally operating client firms, the more likely it is to benefit from an opportunity to be pulled abroad. It is important to note, however, that the client-following mode does not, in itself, say whether a firm deliberately followed or whether this occurred in response to an existing client demanding international service provision. As soon as the business volume in a host market exceeded a certain threshold, a local presence was ventured. As indicated by the marketing director of a Swedish technology consultancy in London, market selection and time of entry depend on the client organizations' internationalization path: 'Where our clients want us, that is where we will go.' Relational entry is not, however, synonymous with the client-following mode (Samie 1999); it also includes other types of business networks.

Our study identified a second entry path, whereby current or former employees (alumni) who had worked abroad for other firms referred business contacts from earlier employers to their latest employer. One German-based technology consulting firm was, for instance, referred by a former employee to jobs in Indonesia, Egypt, and Brazil. Dense network contacts also helped facilitate market entry into markets with pronounced cultural dissimilarities and over a large geographical distance. This finding poses an empirical challenge to atomistic arguments about psychic distance and cultural proximity.

The third type of business network identified in the study involves so-called piggybacking (Terpstra and Yu 1990; O'Farrell et al. 1996). In this case, consulting firms enter a market 'on the back' of strategic partners or collaborators. When a service firm enters a foreign market and requires additional capacity to service their new clients, they refer partner firms from their home base to these projects. They, therefore, serve as bridges for consulting firms to new markets. The attraction of a piggyback strategy is twofold: First, it provides access to a remote network of clients and business opportunities through one partner firm, and, second, it helps to avoid an early entry risk. The downside, however, is that client access tends to be mediated through the incumbent firm and, therefore, remains indirect. Overall, diverse sources of referrals within an existing business network are an alternative way to reduce the risk of business development failure. Unlike atomistic entry, a firm does not need to take a new risk by acquiring an existing local company, that is, the risk of post-merger integration failure. Instead, the firm enjoys the advantages of a Greenfield investment and maintains full control over internal organizational and professional standards. At the same time, it benefits from its existing linkages in the market and the potential reputation effects within social networks that create multiplier effects and generate new business (Glückler and Armbrüster 2003; Glückler 2005; cf. chapter 6).

8.4.4 INTERNATIONAL EXPERIENCE: SAFEGUARD AGAINST THE RISK OF POST-MERGER INTEGRATION FAILURE

The argument that relational entry contexts protect against the risk of business development failure and foster Greenfield entry is an important but still static explanation. From a dynamic perspective, one might expect multinational corporations to be less constrained by local business networks when entering a new market. The more international entries experienced by a corporation, the higher its expertise in managing and organizing a new entry process. A firm's historical experience in entering new markets can, therefore, be expected to reduce its dependence on a relational entry context. Over time, internationalizing firms should therefore be exposed to lower risks of failure, even if the entry context is atomistic. Internationalization theory typically draws on internal, firm-specific advantages in order to explain different modes of entry. The empirical findings discussed here suggest, however, that external inter-firm relationships and a firm's prior internationalization experience have an important impact on the choice of the market-entry mode. Drawing on individual firm experiences, we test this relational account in a statistical model representing the whole sample of foreign consulting affiliates in London, Frankfurt, and Madrid. The model estimates the effects of market-entry context (atomistic or relational) and of international experience (number of countries with an own subsidiary) on the probability for a firm to choose the organizational mode of Greenfield entry.

With respect to market-entry context, our statistical analysis suggests that the majority of firms were pulled into new international markets through their clients. Fully two-thirds of firms used existing business relations in order to gain access to new local markets. The decision to internationalize was mostly a reaction to an opportunity that resulted from within the existing networks of clients, employees, or strategic partners. Only one-third of the firms had no contacts to draw on and entered under atomistic conditions in one of the three city regions investigated. In terms of international experience, the number of countries with prior entries ranged from 1 to 130 countries, with a median of 8 countries. Figure 8.1 displays the estimated probabilities for a firm to enter a foreign market via Greenfield investment. These probabilities were estimated through a logistic regression model (for more detail, see Glückler 2006).[4] The graph illustrates that Greenfield entry becomes less likely, first, if a firm enters a new foreign market under the conditions of an atomistic entry, and, second, with the increasing multinational presence of a firm. Firms that entered a new market through a Brownfield investment had, on average, operations in twice as many countries as Greenfield entrants. Moreover, firms entering under atomistic conditions had twice as many foreign operations as firms entering under relational conditions. In sum, it appears that a relational entry context and Greenfield entry are important drivers in the early phases of internationalization, but less decisive in later phases. International experience increases the knowledge and competence of how to conduct due diligence processes and how to manage post-merger integration process without risking the exit of local personnel and their client contacts. The more international a consulting firm grows, the better its management competence in M&A integration and the smaller the relative risk of a market entry.

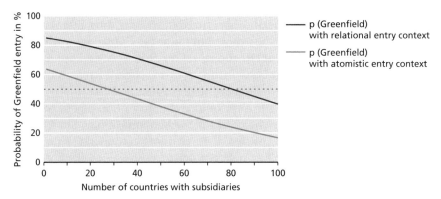

Figure 8.1. Estimated effects of a relational model on the probability of Greenfield investment

This reasoning suggests that increasing international experience reduces the risk of post-merger integration failure and makes Brownfield entry more likely over time. At the same time, international experience reduces the dependence of firms on relational links with their respective business environments based on the creation of internal competences. Taken to its logical extension, young firms with little international experience and relational market-entry context will likely internationalize through Greenfield investment, whereas large, multinational firms under atomistic entry conditions will likely enter via Brownfield investments through M&As. These findings support the central argument developed from the qualitative interview material – namely, that social networks minimize the risk of business development failure and allow for controlled investments in setting up foreign operations. Moreover, increasing international experience compensates for the lack of relational access to a host market. Multinational firms generally have the experience and competencies needed for successful atomistic market entries by acquiring and integrating local companies.

8.5 **Conclusion**

Existing empirical research on the international expansion of business service firms has demonstrated that international market selection and foreign market entry are strongly influenced by existing client relations and business contacts (O'Farrell et al. 1996; O'Farrell and Wood 1998; Coviello and Martin 1999; Westhead et al. 2001). This chapter builds on this work by formulating an argument about the impact of the social context on the choice of market-entry form. In so doing, it challenges conventional internationalization theories.

Instead of explaining market-entry modes by firm attributes or firm-specific assets, our approach directs attention to the relational environment of firms. The empirical analysis reveals two significant findings: First, it provides evidence of the systematic influence of social networks on the choice of an organizational mode of market entry, thereby supporting the arguments of a network approach to internationalization. Given the challenges associated with choosing between the risk of a business development failure through Greenfield market-entry and the risk of a post-merger integration failure through Brownfield market-entry, the analysis confirmed that a relational entry context reduces the risk of business development failure by providing direct market contacts. In the relational entry context, firms thus tend to choose Greenfield investments to avoid the risk of M&A integration failures. Second, the regression model confirms that the impact of a relational entry context is strongest for young and less experienced firms in the course of international expansion. In other words, internationalization experience reduces the risk of M&A integration failures because firms develop competences to manage due diligence procedures and post-merger integration. Consequently, when multinational firms know how to integrate a foreign firm in a controlled way, they take advantage of the local knowledge and client base through Brownfield investments.

A relational approach to firm internationalization stresses the importance of the particular socio-institutional context in which firms make decisions to enter into a new market. This perspective challenges the distinction between three separate decisions usually discussed in the O-L-I internationalization theory. In fact, the existing network of relationships influences, first, the decision to internationalize, second, the selection of a target market, and third, the choice of the market-entry form. If internationalization is a result of the external business relationships of a firm, these three aspects merge into one single decision complex. Finally, and in a wider context, this research links to other studies that focus on the impact of a relational context on economic decisions and processes. Baker and Faulkner (2004), for instance, find that relational contexts are important to reduce the probability of capital losses in the course of investments. If investors draw on pre-existing social ties, the probability of losing capital in an investment drops significantly.

While the context of social relations has been shown to systematically affect the action framework and organizational decision-making, it would be incorrect to conclude that social networks determine strategic action. Provided with the same set and quality of external relations, economic actors will still differ in their ability and style of using these relations. Therefore, internal organizational conditions as well as the strategic context of an organization are important in understanding how social relations are built and used.[5] Future research should thus aim to simultaneously assess the impact of both relational and firm-specific variables in order to integrate both streams of theories. Nevertheless, the coherence of qualitative and quantitative findings presented in this study points towards potentially fruitful methodological avenues to study firm internationalization in business services.

Whereas this chapter focuses on service firm internationalization processes and decisions, Chapter 9 raises the question of how firms in existing international networks, or with linkages to international markets, can establish or maintain regular knowledge flows about market and technology developments in, as well as beyond, networks. At the centre of our examination is the role of leading international trade fairs, which are conceptualized as temporary clusters that facilitate knowledge circulation, support existing production networks, and assist firms in finding partners for new networks.

9 From Permanent to Temporary Clusters

9.1 **Introduction**

The cluster conception developed in Chapter 7 suggests that a cluster's growth potential depends on a combination of both internal knowledge flows and transactions, or local buzz, and access to extra-regional national and international networks, or trans-local pipelines. The question that remains is: how do firms establish trans-local linkages with partners and markets on a global scale? Chapters 8 and 10 identify two potential avenues by which firms may gain access to international markets and technologies: First, firms may find new customers through existing networks, based on reputation effects, or through their contact networks in global value chains. Second, they might establish a global corporate network of branch operations and rely on intra-firm knowledge flows. Such opportunities may not, however, be sufficient. This is particularly true for young firms that operate under relatively isolated conditions, such as in stand-alone facilities located in peripheral regions.

This chapter suggests that leading international trade fairs are critical events that bring together agents of a particular industry, technology field, or value chain from virtually all parts of the world. In addition to supporting knowledge flows about markets and innovations, these events create opportunities for agents to find new transaction partners and establish networks on a global scale. Participants at international trade fairs discuss and present new developments and exchange information and knowledge about products, markets, firms, and leading individuals in given areas of expertise. The temporary co-presence of many agents at such events does not only open a vast range of possibilities for face-to-face interaction; it also gives participants an opportunity to directly observe and experience new products, technologies, and designs. We refer to the professional information and communication ecology at these events as global buzz (Maskell et al. 2006; Bathelt and Schuldt 2008*b*), which consists of a variety of interrelated components that facilitate learning and knowledge exchange. Global buzz includes a wide range of information and knowledge sources, such as news, strategic information, experience, rumours, recommendations, and speculations about an industry or technology branch. It is exchanged in an extremely intensive form over a limited time period, and results from both intended and unintended meetings between producers, users, suppliers, and other industry experts. Global buzz depends upon reciprocal communication patterns and the direct – albeit temporary – co-presence of economic agents (Bathelt and Schuldt 2005; Borghini et al. 2006).

Employing a relational perspective, this chapter views international trade fairs as expressions of the new geographies of circulation that enable knowledge creation and dissemination over distance (Thrift 2000*b*; Amin and Cohendet 2004). We begin by exploring the specific ecology of information and communication processes at these events, focussing particular attention on the action and interaction of exhibitors and visitors. In conceptualizing international trade fairs as temporary clusters, we then offer an illustration of such clusters through an empirical analysis of two major flagship fairs in Germany. At the end, we conclude and provide an outlook how global information and knowledge flows can also be accommodated through computer-mediated communication, and how virtual and temporary global buzz may reinforce one another providing the basis for new forms of global research, production, or marketing networks in the future.

9.2 **The Phenomenon of Global Buzz**

Global buzz is an extremely complex and somewhat ambiguous concept. As such, it is difficult to measure empirically, and cannot be easily condensed into a single variable. Global buzz does not refer to just one communication style, such as an informal, group-based conversation (e.g. Asheim et al. 2007); it is an all-embracing, yet specific constellation of components that, together, generate a professional information and communication ecology. Encompassing multiple aspects of the information and communication processes that occur during international trade fairs, the concept of global buzz stresses the mutual reinforcement of the various components through five core mechanisms: (*a*) the co-presence of global supply and demand, (*b*) intensive face-to-face communication, (*c*) possibilities for dense observation, (*d*) intersecting communities and visions, and (*e*) multiplex meetings and relationships (Bathelt and Schuldt 2008*a*). Whereas the components of global buzz are inextricably linked, for the purpose of clarity, we describe each of the elements separately.

9.2.1 DEDICATED CO-PRESENCE OF GLOBAL SUPPLY AND DEMAND

The trade fair grounds establish a spatial constellation through which a specific ensemble of agents meet and interact, both in sequence and simultaneously. International flagship fairs are events that bring together leading as well as less well-known agents from an industry branch, technology field, or value chain. Centred on the displays of existing products, prototypes, and innovations, trade fairs are a place where suppliers, producers, users, interested experts, media representatives, and other multipliers get together to exchange news about the present and future development of their business. The physical co-presence of many specialized firms from a particular value chain, and the continuous face-to-face communication between these specialists generate a unique milieu for the exchange of experience and knowledge. In such contexts, specific information about technologies, markets, strategies, and solutions is discussed in a variety of planned and unplanned meetings (Borghini et al. 2004).

Despite considerable variation in the roles and expectations of the individuals participating at trade fairs, participants reveal a strong sense of dedication to the activities that take place on the fair grounds for several days in a row (Blythe 2002; Bathelt and Zakrzewski 2007). Removed from their normal workplace and routines, participating agents can take advantage of new time slots that are not blocked with particular tasks. They can concentrate on all aspects of the trade fair without the typical interruptions associated with day-to-day work situations. The number of appointments scheduled during such events, and the amount of time spent observing other exhibits or participating in informal meetings, depends, however, on the function and position of the firms' representatives.

Given the nature of these 'get-togethers', the focus on exploring an industry's state of the art, and the freedom from routine administrative issues, agents tend to be more relaxed than in an everyday work situation. As such, they are open to new ideas, and are willing to critically compare their own economic practices with the practices of others. This environment is, thus, highly conducive to the adaptation of different experiences, as well as processes of learning and knowledge dissemination (Bathelt and Schuldt 2005; Schuldt and Bathelt 2008). Media representatives and other multipliers, such as specialized user groups that are rarely in direct contact with producers, also play an important role during trade fairs (Entwistle and Rocamora 2006; Rinallo and Golfetto 2006). They have a substantial impact on the success of trade fairs, as well as the public image of exhibitors, because of their role in broadcasting their impressions to a larger audience after the events.

9.2.2 INTENSIVE TEMPORARY FACE-TO-FACE INTERACTION

Unlike other modes of communication, attendance at international trade fairs necessitates face-to-face contact with a multitude of participating agents, through which a diverse mix of information and knowledge can be sorted, classified, and interpreted. The work of Storper and Venables (2004) illustrates the importance of face-to-face interaction in transferring complex messages, getting immediate feedback, and responding further. As demonstrated in the field of social psychology, face-to-face communication involves important non-verbal cues that help not only in the transmission and comprehension of complex messages (informational function) but also in building confidence between speakers and listeners (integrative function) (Short et al. 1976). Face-to-face communication helps diminish information asymmetries, as there are many ways of enquiring about the reliability of new information and the trustworthiness of other agents. It also helps in evaluating potential future partners and reducing the risks of interaction. Firm representatives grasp important additional information when talking to their peers and observing their facial expressions and gestures; this is extremely useful in making judgements and sorting information (e.g. Watzlawick et al. 2000). In this context, it is thus possible to obtain an initial read on the mindsets and opinions of other agents, and make some preliminary decisions about their compatibility for future business relations.

The value of trade fair participation also relates to the fact that firms do not necessarily need to be in direct contact with a specific information source in order to have access to that information. Participants may hear from other agents about new developments and decide themselves whether or not it is useful to personally inspect these innovations. Although all firms benefit from the decentralized character of information flows and the multiplicity of information channels that exist during international trade fairs, there are notable differences between trade fairs. In design-intensive industries, for instance, the symbolic and emotional aspects of the exhibits are particularly important: In such contexts, face-to-face contact is of critical importance in acquiring knowledge, which is largely tacit and contextual in nature. Discussions with peers often provide a stimulating arena for the development of new visions, uncoupled from standard corporate routines and pressures for homogeneity. In technical trade fairs, by contrast, interest in the actual exhibits can be limited, especially if it is difficult to evaluate technical properties through visual inspection. Personal meetings are, however, still important at these types of fairs because they help to maintain positive business contacts with customers and suppliers from other parts of the world (Backhaus 1992; Sharland and Balogh 1996; Prüser 2003).

9.2.3 TEMPORARY POSSIBILITIES FOR DENSE OBSERVATION

Important insights can also be obtained from observing exhibitors and visitors at international trade fairs. Practices involving the close inspection of other exhibits, peer observation, 'being part of the crowd', and watching the reaction of other visitors give agents an opportunity to collect ideas and impressions that are used to revise or confirm existing strategies regarding the production programme. Trade fairs are events that attract leading as well as 'unusual' or 'exotic' agents, providing plenty of opportunities for learning-by-observation (Blythe 2002; Borghini et al. 2006). In the area of consumer products, it is extremely valuable to be able to directly experience, touch, or smell the products. In creative industries, particular colour and design variations stimulate associations and help observers to imagine reconfigurations involving their own products and designs. In contrast, firms in technology-oriented fairs are more interested in strategic information on system architecture that can affect medium- and long-term policies.

While looking through the exhibits of competing or complementary firms, agents are also able to evaluate the goals of other firms' trade fair participation and their corporate identity. This may be in line with a firm's pre-existing expectations of a competitor, or it may deviate from such beliefs, indicating that the firm might have begun to operate in a different market context. Similar to the role of gestures and facial expressions in face-to-face communication, a competitor's trade fair exhibit can be viewed as a visualization of that firm's broader philosophy within the industry. The unique combination of exchanging arguments about new developments and observing the effects on other agents can be applied to one's own production. This provides immediate insights that cannot be acquired through other means.

9.2.4 INTERSECTING INTERPRETATIVE COMMUNITIES, SHARED UNDERSTANDINGS, AND OVERLAPPING VISIONS

In general, international trade fairs attract different, yet closely interrelated, communities that have in-depth knowledge about many aspects of the products, technologies, and value chain portrayed (Entwistle and Rocamora 2006; Skov 2006). Both communities of practice and epistemic communities meet during these events (Wenger 1998; Knorr Cetina 1999), which leads to large conglomerates of shared understandings, repertoires, and visions about the wider business context.

These communities draw on similar specializations and work experience, and meet regularly or periodically (Power and Jansson 2008). As such, they share a similar institutional basis that allows them to efficiently exchange and interpret knowledge, generate new ideas, and further develop competencies. They may also share swift trust related to the norms and goals acquired through their training (e.g. Knorr Cetina 1999). These focused communities provide a valuable source of knowledge that cuts across the strict boundaries of corporate structures (Lawrence et al. 2006).

By no means, however, do trade fair participants share the same background. Their backgrounds are often heterogeneous, reflecting differences in technology, specialization, and business focus. Participants that are experienced in production might, for instance, be interested in discussing problems of product quality or production failure, while others, such as sales specialists, interact mostly with customers and are eager to learn more about demand changes and new trends. The point to emphasize here is that the visitors and exhibitors at international trade fairs are characterized by, at least, some degree of common knowledge or cognitive proximity (Nooteboom 2000). Thus, despite their many differences, the knowledge base of most participants is close enough to facilitate efficient transfers of information. The unique mix of similar, overlapping, and complementary knowledge at trade fairs, thus, stimulates important learning processes.

Overall, active participation and membership in focused communities makes it possible for firms to distinguish between more and less valuable knowledge, and to sort through the innovations of other firms that call for further exploration. Not only do interaction processes benefit from a shared institutional basis; ongoing meetings, discussions, explorations, and interpretations also serve to reproduce and further develop this institutional basis.

9.2.5 MULTIPLEX MEETINGS AND RELATIONSHIPS

Within these networks of contacts, agents are linked in different ways with each other as business partners, colleagues, peers, or community members. Resources can, therefore, be transferred from one type of relationship to another. Multiplex ties and diverse possibilities for meetings at international trade fairs provide firms with access to new information, speed up the transfer of knowledge, and enable connections to relevant knowledge pools (Uzzi 1997). During a trade fair, information is constantly transmitted from one agent to another. While acquiring new knowledge, participants act simultaneously as recipients and broadcasters of global buzz. Participants profit from the large variety of meetings with different groups of agents. The potential advantages of applying this knowledge become clearer as the trade fair evolves and interpretations are drawn from the various meetings.

Such meetings are particularly valuable for firms that are seeking entrance to new markets and partners to support them in this endeavour. These often spontaneous encounters are also useful in checking out the 'chemistry' between two parties and establishing some initial communication – if only to rule out the possibility of future communication.

These events involve feelings and emotions (Massey 2004), and participants generally look forward to 'having a good time'. While the development of conventional trust between business partners may take a long time, the existence of swift trust and repeated meetings during international trade fairs form a solid basis upon which to build business relations. Trade fairs constitute a setting in which participants can quickly shift from negotiations to observations, and from straight business talks to private conversations – all within a period of two or three days. In this sense, trade fairs provide unique opportunities for multiplex encounters on a global scale.

9.3 Trade Fairs as Temporary Clusters

The orthodox literature on clusters fits rather uneasily with the more recent work on market organizational forms. Whereas the former has traditionally viewed clusters as durable or permanent entities,[1] the latter strongly suggests that temporary forms of economic interaction, such as projects and similar temporary coalitions, have become increasingly important in the knowledge-based economy (Lundin 1995; Taylor 1999; Grabher 2002*a*). In the following sections, we argue that international trade fairs, conventions, and other professional gatherings have characteristics similar to those of permanent clusters, albeit in a temporary and periodic form. They can thus be conceptualized as temporary clusters and characterized along several dimensions (Maskell et al. 2004, 2006). Trade fairs help firms to systematically acquire information about competitors, suppliers, and customers. Through regular attendance at such events, firms learn about potentially suitable partners and may even initiate durable inter-firm collaboration, or new pipelines, in research, production, and/or marketing (Figure 9.1). Like permanent clusters, temporary clusters are characterized by distinct vertical and horizontal cluster dimensions, although real transactions may not take place (Malmberg and Maskell 2002).

Vertical interaction with suppliers and customers consists of information exchange about recent trends, experiences, and requirements for future products and services. Firms arrange meetings with established suppliers located in different regions and nations to discuss technological changes in product specifications, developments in markets, and future conditions. They also identify new suppliers that exhibit interesting modifications of products and indicate opportunities for new applications. This creates a rich arena for learning processes. This is particularly true when technical personnel from different firms specializing in the same areas meet regularly at such events, as a basis for interactive learning and problem solving develops. Although these types of exchanges can take place at scheduled meetings during convention hours, other meetings are more spontaneous and occur in combination with social events such as joint dinners. Members of existing communities come together at trade fairs, extended communities are formed and reproduced, and common interpretative schemes are developed as technologies shift towards new directions.

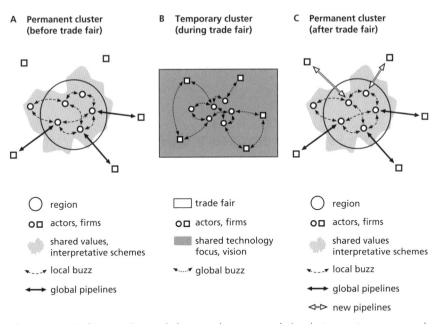

Figure 9.1. Pipeline creation and the complementary relation between temporary and permanent clusters

Systematic customer contact is a key component of the vertical interaction during trade fairs. As pointed out in the literature on trade fairs, firms intensify social relations with their customers and try to contact new customers to market their products, display new developments, and discuss potential contracts (e.g. Ziegler 1992; Meffert 1993). There is, however, another aspect of producer–user interaction that is increasingly emphasized in the literature on innovation (e.g. Lundvall 1988; Lawson and Lorenz 1999), and also applies to trade fairs and conventions (e.g. Prüser 1997). Scheduled meetings between producers and their customers taking place during a trade fair provide vital sources of information for further product improvements and new developments. Producer–customer interaction during trade fairs can, therefore, improve a firm's longer term competencies and competitiveness; it is not just a source of short-term sales.

Trade fairs also bring together competing firms, which are less likely to interact. In providing multiple opportunities for firms to observe and compare their products and strategies with those of their competitors, they have a distinct horizontal dimension. Firms systematically look at the exhibits of their competitors, make note of product designs, modifications, innovations, and new fields of application. They collect and consider available information that can reveal new products or changes in strategies that competitors may be planning. It is sometimes even possible for representatives of competing firms to discuss general technological problems or industry trends during trade fairs. Similar to permanent clusters, the corridors, cafés, bars, and similar meeting points are important places for information exchange in temporary clusters.

Parts of these screening and observation processes are less systematic, as firms try to get an overview of recent and ongoing trends or developments in their business. This information is of great importance because it allows firms to determine whether or not they are on the right track. This, in turn, helps firms make decisions about their technological focus and future investments, and serves to stimulate reflexive practices. In sum, international trade fairs and conventions bring together leading-edge firms from different parts of the world where they establish distinct, yet temporary clusters. They also create opportunities for firms to select suitable partners for innovation and knowledge creation.

This is illustrated by analysing the structure of information and interaction patterns between exhibiting firms and their suppliers, customers, competitors, and complementary firms at two leading international flagship fairs in Frankfurt/Main, Germany (Bathelt and Schuldt 2005, 2008b):

1. *Light and Building – International Trade Fair for Architecture and Technology (L+B.)*. This is a well-known trade fair for products in the areas of lighting, electrical engineering, and house and building automation. In 2004, it had a total of 1,920 exhibitors, 57 per cent of which originated from other countries. Of its 116,000 visitors, 70 per cent came from other countries.
2. *International Trade Fair for the Meat Industry (IFFA)*. IFFA is one of the world's leading trade fairs for firms in the area of meat production and processing. In 2004, 852 firms exhibited their products at this trade fair, almost half of which originated from other countries. Additionally, more than 60 per cent of the 57,000 visitors came from outside Germany.

Both events can be characterized as business-to-business fairs, where firms present their exhibits to other firms and not primarily to end customers. The empirical results presented below are based on 142 interviews with owners, leading marketing managers, product developers, and engineers at these trade fairs, the selection of which was based on a systematic random sample of exhibiting firms.

9.4 Information Flows and Communication during International Trade Fairs

In analysing the information and communication processes at L+B and IFFA, a particular hierarchy of interaction between firms becomes apparent (Table 9.1). Interaction with existing and potential customers appears to be

Table 9.1. Goals of trade fair participation at L+B and IFFA, 2004

Goals of trade fair participation	Firm responses at L+B[1]		Firm responses at IFFA[2]	
	Number (n = 51)	Share (%)	Number (n = 51)	Share (%)
Being there	33	64.7	34	66.7
Making new customer contact	31	60.8	32	62.7
Dealing with existing customers	31	60.8	25	49.0
Presentation of innovations	21	41.2	16	31.4
Sales and orders	4	7.8	1	2.0
Accessing new markets	—	—	4	7.8

Notes: [1]L+B = Light and Building – International Trade Fair for Architecture and Technology; [2]IFFA = International Trade Fair for the Meat Industry.
Source: Adapted from Bathelt and Schuldt (2008b: 859).

the most important incentive for firms to participate in trade fairs. Approximately 60 per cent of the firms interviewed mentioned that the most important goals for their participation at L+B and IFFA are: (*a*) to inform customers of their presence, (*b*) to make new customer contact, and/or (*c*) to maintain and intensify contact with existing customers. Another important reason for participating is to present innovations (Ausstellungs- und Messe-Ausschuss der Deutschen Wirtschaft 1996, 1999). In contrast, the traditional sales function has seemingly become less important at these trade fairs. Customer interaction is, however, not the only type of interaction that firms have during these trade fairs. Direct and indirect contact with competitors is also highly ranked, while contact with suppliers is ranked as being less important.

9.4.1 INTERACTION WITH CUSTOMERS

To convene and interact with customers is clearly the most important incentive behind a firm's decision to participate in L+B or IFFA. Firms systematically contact their existing and potential new customers before the trade fair to inform them about their presence and invite them to visit their exhibits. These initial contacts are usually fairly standardized and not customer-specific. In order to maintain a flexible time schedule, most firms at L+B do not make appointments a priori unless a customer specifically requests one. There is, however, a difference between the fairs in terms of how customer contact is made. Much of the customer interaction at IFFA involves technical conversations and consultations, which means that specialists must be available during the trade fair. In this case, it is often necessary to make appointments in advance.

Interaction with potential future customers

We identified two types of meetings that differ in terms of communication with potential future customers. In the first case, customers simply pass by the producers' exhibits to acquire general information about the production programme and its characteristics. The second type involves customers that enquire about solutions for particular problems that exist or are likely to occur in the foreseeable future due to changes in production. While the first type of interaction is not very specific, it is useful in identifying potentially interesting customers and their needs. This approach helps to establish databases of possible customers that may be contacted at a later date. Whereas the second type of interaction is less frequent, such contacts serve as a potential basis for intensive future interaction and transactions. This is especially important in trade fairs that focus on technical aspects, such as IFFA. Such interaction serves as a precondition for the development of trans-local pipelines with transaction partners in other parts of the world, and fosters the knowledge-creation process (Maskell et al. 2006).

Interaction with existing customers

Meetings with existing customers can also be classified into two groups. Such meetings are either meant to discuss the particular circumstances of the business relationship or to exchange general information to intensify that relationship. In the first case, communication between firms assumes the character of negotiations, and takes place in a separate facility. Although the importance of technical fairs as places where orders are made and contracts signed seems to be decreasing (Backhaus 1992; Meffert 1997), large firms and market leaders at L+B and IFFA received a substantial number of orders.

In the second case, general information about markets and technological innovations within the industry is exchanged. Although individual conversations might not release much new information, such interaction provides exhibitors with substantial knowledge about customer needs, and an opportunity to detect market and technology trends throughout the course of a trade fair. Often people have been in contact with one another for many years, and exchange private information with their partners. As a certain level of trust develops, the information flows in these interactions become quite detailed and multiplex in nature (Uzzi 1997).

In terms of product and strategy development, the acquisition of information about customer experience is of central importance. About 80 and 50 per cent of the respondents at IFFA and L+B, respectively, mentioned that the most intensive information exchanges are about a firm's experience with their products, comparisons with the products of competitors, and ideas about how to further develop products.

Circumstances of getting together

Producer–user interaction usually takes place during the official fair hours. Contact is made or meetings are scheduled at the producers' exhibits. In a case where a firm introduced complex new machines and equipment to the market, customers were invited to register for a day trip to the producer's development centre to see how the machines operate under regular working conditions. About 70 per cent of the respondents suggested that they also aim to meet customers for dinners and other informal events to discuss design variations and technological aspects in a more relaxed atmosphere. While meetings are often scheduled for the purpose of having fun and socializing with customers,[2] business-related discussions inevitably occur, as it is difficult for peers to get together without talking about their professional experience. Such meetings help key personnel get to know one another on a personal basis. The multiplex nature of these meetings leads firms to develop expectations about how their partners conduct business. This ultimately reduces the risks of future transactions. Some interviewees indicated that they test out how they fit with their business partners and with whom they share the same 'chemistry'.

There are, however, substantial differences in how informal meetings with customers are structured. On the one hand, large exhibitors at L+B and IFFA typically organize evenings with customers, sometimes including an entertainment programme. During these events, the commitment involved and type of information exchanged is not very specific. Small- and medium-sized firms (especially those at L+B) are, on the other hand, more spontaneous in meeting with their customers and more interested in getting to know them on a personal level than larger firms. Large internationally organized firms use trade fairs as a forum to bring together personnel from different regions and countries to exchange their experience in different market contexts, support the formation of stronger bonds between the subunits, and support the development of corporate solidarity (Backhaus and Zydorek 1997; Kirchgeorg 2003). Some interviewees noted that such intra-firm gatherings are useful in spreading important new information about markets and customer needs throughout the firms' worldwide operations. Employees are, thus, able to build up intra-firm networks of experts who they can contact later if particular questions or problems arise.

Approximately half of the respondents mentioned that they accidentally meet customers at important trade fairs. The opportunity for unplanned meetings largely depends on how often firms participate in important trade fairs and how well they are established. According to the firms at L+B and IFFA, between 50 and 80 per cent of all customer contacts were with existing customers. This points to the importance of trade fairs in both maintaining and intensifying existing customer networks (Prüser 1997; Zundler and Tesche 2003).

Customer information through third parties

Exhibitors also acquire information about potentially new or important customers through interaction with other customers or partners. About 90 and 50 per cent of the firms interviewed at IFFA and L+B, respectively, mentioned that information flows through third parties occur on a regular basis, although this information may be biased. As one manager pointed out, one must be experienced in evaluating this information properly, or know the people in advance to be able to interpret the content of such conversations. In addition, important information about customers is acquired through systematically scanning their respective exhibits in the event that they also present products at the fair. This gives firms an opportunity to obtain ideas about trends in designs, and the need for innovative efforts (Ausstellungs- und Messe-Ausschuss der Deutschen Wirtschaft 1999). Personal inspection of the customers' exhibits also allows firms to gather experience that could not be acquired through conversation alone (Backhaus and Zydorek 1997; Goehr- mann 2003*a*).

Almost all firms at L+B insisted that customer contact is extremely impor- tant because, as one project manager put it, 'such dense information is only available during trade fairs (*translated from German*)'. Furthermore, 'during a trade fair, you get to know whether it is worthwhile developing an idea further which you had on your mind'. According to some respondents, another advantage of trade fairs is that they meet other customer groups with whom direct contact is rare in day-to-day operations (Backhaus 1992; Prüser 2003). During L+B, for instance, producers of luminaries regularly exchange ideas with architects who are usually not the buyers of their products. Others try to get media coverage by making contact with representatives of national and international media.

Observed differences in the evaluation of trade fairs seem to be related to the character of customer communication in various industries. Whereas exhibitors at IFFA have frequent personal contact with their customers to guarantee smooth production, L+B exhibitors have fewer regular contacts and, thus, heavily rely on this forum for interaction.

9.4.2 INTERACTION WITH COMPETITORS

Most respondents also noted the importance of opportunities to exchange information with, or acquire knowledge about, competitors during a trade fair. Although participation in trade fairs is the most direct and fastest way to get an overview of the market and the competitive environment, not all firms acquire information in the same systematic way. On the one hand, small firms often do not have enough personnel at their exhibits to thoroughly scan and observe competitors' exhibits. On the other hand, some important market leaders seem overly confident and, for this reason, spend little time observing their competitors. In adopting such an attitude, firms could easily overlook less visible but significant market trends.

Direct contact

Direct contact with competitors usually occurs during official trade fair hours when representatives visit the exhibits of other firms. Such meetings typically remain at a general level, involving short conversations about current business conditions and recent developments in the industry (e.g. Dahl and Pedersen 2003; Maskell et al. 2004). During IFFA, direct meetings with competitors are rare, however, and information exchanges limited because of fierce competitive conditions. Firms often compete by publicly stating that their products are superior to those of their competitors, which creates an atmosphere of rivalry between firms. In contrast, information exchange with competitors seemed more open at L+B. People were fairly relaxed and did not hesitate to talk to some of their competitors. This openness relates to the fact that the lighting industry is highly segmented and differentiated. As such, firms usually specialize in particular market segments and have only partial market overlap. In such design-intensive industries, producer flexibility is greater than in the area of producing specialized machinery, which cannot be redesigned within short time periods.

Competitor information through third parties

More than half of the exhibitors mentioned that they receive additional information about the actions and strategies of their competitors by talking to customers and other firms (Kirchgeorg 2003). These information flows are not necessarily akin to passing secrets. They tend to be fairly general in nature, and mostly serve to complete the picture that firms already have of their competitors. Comparative comments about the products of competing firms may, nevertheless, be useful in drawing conclusions about a firm's strengths and weaknesses.

Learning through observation and comparison

The best way to obtain information about competitors is simply by observing and comparing their exhibits. This allows firms to learn about their competitors' products, modifications, input materials, and visions (Strothamm 1992; Prüser 1997; Fuchslocher and Hochheimer 2000; Meffert 2003). This information gives firms an opportunity to evaluate their own products and technological progress in relation to what is going on in other parts of the world. They get an overview of the market, about variations in products, materials, and designs, and acquire a lot of information in a concentrated form. They also get an impression about their competitors' overall production programme, appearance, and philosophy (Backhaus and Zydorek 1997; Meffert 2003).

According to one product manager, two-thirds of his personnel were at the trade fair just to watch the competition.[3] Although this is an extreme example, the systematic scanning and analysis of other exhibits is generally an important task because it encourages firms to engage in more critical product evaluations. Firms can use this information to make more informed decisions regarding future investments and product policies.

Although product and machinery changes are often introduced to customers during a major trade show,[4] other participating firms are usually aware of these developments beforehand. Our interviewees were nevertheless excited to see the details of new designs and how the customers would respond to them. The relevant literature suggests that practices to keep new information secret prior to the fair can help flagship fairs maintain their importance (Dahl and Pedersen 2003; Goehrmann 2003*b*). Although some of the details regarding innovations may not be known in advance, firms are usually quite knowledgeable about their competitors' past and present actions. New products and solutions are also a hot topic during a trade fair, which helps firms evaluate the importance of these innovations. Even if a firm does not identify any novelties during a trade fair, its presence at the fair is still useful in confirming that it has not missed important new developments.

9.4.3 INTERACTION WITH COMPLEMENTARY FIRMS

Many of the firms at L+B and IFFA explicitly mentioned that they acquire information about complementary firms that operate in different countries or sell products in related market segments. Contact with such firms can be useful when partners for joint marketing campaigns or sales are needed. This is important if firms intend to enter new markets in different countries. In this case, firms systematically scan other exhibitors to identify potential partners and begin initial discussions. Particularly when their experience in foreign markets is limited, firms use trade fairs as an opportunity to sort out or initiate potential trans-local pipelines with other firms (Bathelt et al. 2004). The firms interviewed at L+B and IFFA often develop such contacts over several consecutive trade fairs and learn about their potential partners over a longer time period before closer contact is established (Power and Jansson 2008). Regular attendance at international trade fairs promotes the development of latent networks, which can be activated and used when needed (Grabher 2002*a*; Maskell et al. 2004).

9.4.4 SUPPLIER INTERACTION

In contrast to customer and competitor interaction, contacts with suppliers are less important for the exhibitors at L+B and IFFA. Exhibitors thus spend less time and effort dealing with existing and potential suppliers, despite the fact that both fairs include firms from virtually all stages of the value chain. Although the limited significance of supplier interaction can be largely attributed to the exhibitors' customer-oriented focus, the high costs of participation also encourage firms to cut back on the number of employees working at their exhibits, which leaves little time to scan the supplier sector.

That being said, suppliers systematically visit the exhibits of existing and potential customers. This does not usually lead to in-depth discussions or problem-solving activities, as most exhibitors do not have supply-side managers at hand to engage in such conversations. Nonetheless, all of the interviewees at L+B and half of the respondents at IFFA said that it is advantageous to have personal contact with suppliers during the fair. In particular, small creative producers (especially at L+B) are interested in meeting with their suppliers. International trade fairs are often the only opportunity to make direct contact with innovative suppliers from different countries. Interviewees mentioned that the high density of suppliers during the fair generates a multitude of opportunities to make new contacts. This provides firms with an opportunity to preselect suppliers that seem compatible and leave a good impression. An additional and more thorough scan tends to occur after the trade fair.

Many interviewees indicated a preference for a separate trade fair specialized in materials and supplies over a full-coverage fair. Such a fair would give firms more time to communicate with existing and potential new suppliers. Overall, our research suggests that many firms do not fully exploit opportunities to acquire supplier information at trade fairs due to practices of selective communication.

9.5 **Conclusion**

This chapter suggests that international trade fairs play an important role in the global economy. Such events can be usefully characterized as temporary clusters that develop a unique information and communication ecology, referred to as global buzz. While trade fairs have traditionally been viewed as important events for conducting business and negotiating contracts with customers and suppliers, as a microcosm of an entire industry (Rosson and Seringhaus 1995), they also enable firms to systematically acquire information about trends in the world market and the state-of-the-art in production and innovation. Communication with specialists from the same or related technology fields helps firms develop new ideas and strategies for production and innovation. Through intensive interaction and observation, these events become catalysts for identifying and/or setting important trends. International trade fairs also provide multiple opportunities to deepen existing networks and establish global pipelines (Figure 9.1).

Why have international trade fairs become central nodes in the global political economy? One of the most important reasons relates to the fact that such events compress an industry's entire world market into a single place – albeit for a limited time period (Bathelt and Zakrzewski 2007). Agents accustomed to interacting at a distance get to know one another and become part of communities. The multitude of planned and unplanned meetings that take place between specialized agents strengthen and reproduce an industry's institutional basis. Firms use these occasions to present their latest products to customers and structure their innovation processes so that novelties are readily introduced to the market. As such, these events often serve as pre-defined deadlines for the creation of new products, machines, or designs, thereby structuring the timelines of intra-firm innovation projects.

The unique gathering of specialized agents at international trade fairs generates a dynamic information and communication ecology that is highly conducive to processes of global pipeline formation and knowledge creation. Participants at these events automatically benefit from a densely knit web of specialized information and knowledge flows. The multidimensional structure of this global buzz gives firms a general overview of the industry and an opportunity to scrutinize emerging trends, as reflected in the exhibits of competitors and complementary firms. Firms can also evaluate their own activities and achievements by comparing themselves to others. This information is useful in making decisions about future strategies and products. Global buzz creates openness and swift access to external knowledge pools, embedded in a variety of different industry settings and/or world regions. Firms simply benefit from the large variety of relevant ideas that circulate during these fairs. This includes both explicit knowledge – exchanged in the form of presentations, discussion forums, and special exhibits – as well as tacit knowledge – mediated through the design of products and exhibits. The associated knowledge flows are diffuse and goal-oriented in character.

9.6 **Outlook: Virtual Buzz through Computer-mediated Communication**

Recent research demonstrates that economic interaction and problem-solving processes occur on a daily basis, regardless of regular or even occasional face-to-face contact. To suggest, however, that virtual interaction will eventually eliminate the benefits accrued from geographic proximity, or to say that 'the world is flat' (Friedman 2005), makes little sense when evaluating complex economic realities (Leamer and Storper 2001; Stiglitz 2006). Instead, modern information and communication technologies allow distant and close collaboration to simultaneously occur. The organization of Internet-based user-communities can, for instance, play a decisive role in day-to-day problem-solving, brainstorming, and related innovation processes (von Hippel 2001; Jeppesen and Molin 2003; Grabher et al. 2008). Virtual spaces create opportunities for firms to overcome the limitations of spatial proximity in economic interaction and provide agents with important networks for information and knowledge exchange.

The comparative advantages and disadvantages of computer-mediated communication versus face-to-face interaction have been intensively studied in social psychology and form the basis of competing theories. Traditional studies on these issues point to the structural differences between computer-mediated communication and face-to-face interaction. Drawing on these insights, social presence theory suggests that the lack of non-verbal and physical cues in computer-mediated communication prevents users from gaining important information about the characteristics, emotions, and attitudes of other agents. This leads to communication that is less understandable and less effective (Walther et al. 2005). This line of argument is, however, challenged by two alternative conceptions: First, social information processing theory rejects the notion that computer-mediated communication is inherently impersonal and that relational information is inaccessible to users. Instead, it assumes that individuals deploy whatever communication cues are at their disposal when motivated to form impressions and develop relationships (Walther et al. 2005). Second, equilibrium theory similarly posits that communicators dynamically adapt levels of gaze, proximity, and other behaviours indicative of intimacy to normative levels based on culture and need for affiliation until an equilibrium level of comfort is achieved (Olson and Olson 2003). This can provide the basis for the establishment of social relations.

The systematic use of computer-mediated communication enables complex interaction that can stimulate network formation even without permanent face-to-face contact. If we include video-based computer-mediated communication formats and the combination of these virtual encounters with occasional planned face-to-face meetings, the range of possibly efficient configurations involving local and non-local face-to-face and computer-mediated exchanges drastically widens. Studies of team-based collaboration show that innovation over distance can be successful. Such collaborative endeavours can fail, however, if they are organized in an unfavourable context or with misguided expectations.

Drawing on their study of communication processes and outcomes, Wainfan and Davis (2004) suggest that the group structure in computer-mediated communication is often broader, yet more agile, than in face-to-face teams. Accordingly, there is greater breadth in collaboration themes due to a wider involvement of experts. Although it might be harder to form social networks in computer-mediated communication compared to face-to-face contexts, it is also more difficult to distract or deflect participants' attention by involving them in side conversations. In reducing non-verbal cues, other factors such as common ground, power, and status become much less important. In the localized context of a firm, contextual cues such as seating position, office location, and even clothing have been found to influence communication patterns during employee meetings (Dubrovsky et al. 1991). Individuals using computer-mediated communication feel less constrained by conventional norms, rules of behaviour, and other 'social baggage' (Sproull and Kiesler 1991).

While analyses of the nature of group processes mediated through face-to-face interaction and computer-mediated communication differ with respect to the mode of communication, task type, and individual and group characteristics, researchers have found consistent results across different experimental conditions (Wainfan and Davis 2004). It is consistently reported that synchronous, text-based conferencing groups take longer to complete assigned tasks than face-to-face groups (McGuire et al. 1987; Reid et al. 1997). Consensus frequently follows a leader's push for his or her preferred solution, while interaction patterns in computer-mediated communication settings show more evenly distributed participation. This effect also emerges during video-conference collaboration, despite its closeness to face-to-face interaction. Depending on the context, this can be an advantage at the beginning of a decision-making process, or a disadvantage in finalizing a project under time constraints.

With less overall participation and more difficulty reaching consensus, studies have shown that computer-mediated communication participants make more explicit proposals, defer less to high-status members, and are less inhibited than face-to-face collaborators (Dubrovsky et al. 1991; Hollingshead and McGrath 1995). Rice (1984) finds that, when confronted with a dilemma, face-to-face groups begin by analysing the problem, whereas computer-mediated communication collaborators start discussion by proposing a solution. In some cases, group members in computer-mediated communication suggest solutions before even listening to the thoughts of other participants. Studies also suggest that anonymity decreases the pressures to conform in computer-mediated communication settings (Baltes et al. 2002). Ideas are, thus, more likely to be evaluated in terms of their individual merit, regardless of the status of the person presenting them.

In the context of innovation projects in multinational firms, Song et al. (2007) uncover some interesting findings regarding the nature of collaboration and its outcomes. Their study finds that knowledge dissemination between agents is greatest when both settings are combined (see Chapter 10). Whereas certain parts of the innovation process seem to require face-to-face meetings to develop new ideas and concepts, other parts benefit from work at dispersed workplaces with regular computer-mediated communication adjustments. Permanent co-location may, therefore, foster knowledge dissemination within the research process, but impede knowledge dissemination between research and production. In response to inefficiencies of computer-mediated communication and the importance of geographic proximity, corporate actors increasingly explore organizational structures combining both aspects, thus enabling knowledge generation over distance. For Torre and Rallet (2005), a solution lies in the temporary mobility of individuals, rather than permanent co-location. In the case of business air travel, for example, problems can be solved through the mobility of individuals, as in the case of the Irish software cluster (e.g. Wickham and Vecchi 2008). Another example are transnational communities that organize global production and marketing networks as the case of the Indian Palanpuris family networks (Henn 2010) or South American immigrant networks (Portes et al. 2002). In other cases, individuals collaborating in projects may only need face-to-face contact during particular phases of the innovation process, such as times of high complexity and uncertainty. During these periods, temporary face-to-face interaction or 'organized proximity' is critical (Rallet and Torre 2009). At other stages of the innovation cycle, interaction via computer-mediated communication may be sufficient.

Organized proximity is a relational concept that urges greater interaction among the members of a project or value chain. It refers to the establishment of a collective culture that generates shared interpretations of new information even if the agents are located in different places. Such commonality in thinking and solving problems is critical to knowledge generation and innovation.

10 Global Knowledge Flows in Corporate Networks

10.1 **Introduction**

In Chapter 9, temporary proximity has been conceptualized as a way of facilitating knowledge exchange between actors otherwise separated by location. According to this, temporary clusters offer opportunities for observing competitors, acquiring clients, and obtaining critical know-how over distance. In contrast to this conception of temporary proximity, Chapter 8 has developed a relational conception of permanent forms of corporate expansion and international market entry. Chapter 10 builds upon this and concludes Part III of the book by engaging with the consequences of internationalization in terms of knowledge-sharing practices across the spatially dispersed units of multinational corporations. In this chapter, we develop a relational approach to knowledge-exchange practices and apply this to the empirical context of corporate knowledge transfers, using methods of social network analysis. More specifically, we explore the enabling and constraining forces underlying interpersonal and international exchanges of expertise between qualified knowledge workers. While this chapter concludes by identifying the implications of a relational approach for management practices and corporate governance, Chapter 11 extends these implications beyond corporate boundaries to address broader regional governance and relational cluster policy.

Given that knowledge is incomplete and unequally distributed throughout society, a long-standing economic problem involves 'the utilization of knowledge not given to anyone in its totality' (Hayek 1945: 520). Most modern corporations operate from various geographically distributed locations. And all multi-locational firms confront managerial challenges, which tend to be particularly pronounced in business models that are grounded in expertise services. Under conditions of geographically separated expertise, the accumulation and transfer of diverse knowledge is, thus, central to establishing a competitive advantage over nationally operating competitors. There are two potential advantages of successful knowledge transfers: First, to reuse (exploit) specific expertise in broader markets and, second, to transform this expertise into new knowledge (innovation). Professional service firms that fail to transfer decentralized inimitable knowledge via corporate networks miss out on essential opportunities for global business development. Against this backdrop, this chapter investigates the conditions under which processes of global knowledge sharing are enabled or constrained.

In the following sections, we develop a strategic framework for the analysis of such conditions. We also draw attention to a dilemma regarding the way in which non-trivial experiential knowledge is generated and shared across geographically distributed corporate units. Drawing on the concept of know-who (see also Chapter 6), we then propose an analytical approach to study knowledge transfers. This is followed by an overview of our empirical case study – a transnational technology consultancy firm. Using this case study, we conduct visual as well as quantitative analyses of an entire global corporate knowledge network. In doing so, the vulnerability of international knowledge flows is revealed and empirical evidence of the impact of geographical dispersion on the establishment of organizational knowledge islands provided. Finally, we analyse the impact of diverse management programmes on international knowledge exchange, discuss opportunities for technical and social approaches to knowledge management, and summarize the study's main findings within the context of a relational conception of economic action.

10.2 **Knowledge as a Global Competitive Advantage**

Multinational and transnational knowledge-intensive firms are increasingly faced with a particular managerial challenge: to make localized knowledge available across their different locations in order to enhance the use and reuse of best practices, update innovation processes, and prevent other units from 'reinventing the wheel'. In contrast to manufacturing firms, where global competitive advantages are primarily found in scale economies that derive from international integration (Porter 1986), expertise service firms are much more limited in their spatial division of labour due to their close interaction with clients, which are often located nearby. In general, the greater the need for individual expertise and the greater the specificity of services, the less scale economies can be gained from global integration (Aharoni 1996; Glückler 2005).

Multinational professional service firms consequently look for different global competitive advantages than manufacturing operations. In recent years, two sources of such advantages have become increasingly important (Løwendahl 2000). The first benefit that may be derived from a firm's global presence is a positive reputation and an ability to use this reputation to win new clients in new markets (Chapters 6 and 8). The second advantage is the ability to access a broader pool of knowledge and professional experience. In this context, one of the key synergies to be realized involves the accumulation of knowledge and the internal transfer of distributed knowledge bases. This is important not only in terms of reusing expertise but also in terms of transforming this expertise into new knowledge. Professional service firms, therefore, miss out on critical opportunities for global business development if they fail to transfer inimitable knowledge through their corporate networks.

This chapter combines a relational understanding of knowledge and a network perspective to study the circulation of expertise within multinational service corporations (Borgatti and Cross 2003; Bathelt and Glückler 2005). We define expertise as the cognitive combination of declarative and causal knowledge with professional experience. The creation and transfer of knowledge are often treated as two distinct processes. Whereas knowledge creation is recognized as an innovation process, knowledge transfer is frequently referred to as the diffusion of existing knowledge (e.g. Caspers and Kreis-Hoyer 2004). This distinction underestimates the innovative potential of knowledge transfer because it views such transfers in terms of knowledge replication. This chapter challenges this interpretation and suggests that the very act of transferring knowledge is, in fact, part of the innovation process because the exchange of existing expertise stimulates new ideas and solutions. Learning is a collective process in which knowledge is shared, articulated, and reinterpreted in ways that inspire new ideas (Lawson and Lorenz 1999). As such, the transfer of knowledge is an important component of the innovation process.

10.3 **The Expansion–Coherence Dilemma**

From a geographical perspective, the organizational challenge of transferring expertise between geographically distributed sites can be framed as a dilemma involving, on the one hand, the acquisition of knowledge diversity and, on the other, the loss of organizational coherence through corporate expansion (Glückler 2008, 2010b). This predicament can be conceptualized as an organizational choice between two polar extremes, where a firm either concentrates all of its resources in just one location or completely scatters its resources across space. The first extreme offers the advantage of organizational coherence. When all corporate production and uses of knowledge are co-located, communicative friction is minimized and local externalities are efficiently exploited within the firm.

The recent cluster literature focuses considerable energy on the dynamics of geographical clustering in response to collective learning and knowledge sharing between firms (Malmberg and Maskell 2002). In essence, it suggests that knowledge activities cluster in response to positive local externalities. First, geographical proximity, along with specific institutional characteristics, produces leaky information networks that yield spillover effects. According to this general line of argument, knowledge spillovers are positively associated with co-location (Jaffe et al. 1993), the size and mobility of the labour pool (Almeida and Kogut 1999), and the magnitude of strategic alliances among firms. Geographical proximity increases the visibility of each firm in a way that allows community membership to become more important than structural position. Other recent work emphasizes the sustainability of industrial agglomerations in the absence of local externalities when knowledge is complex. This is because complex forms of knowledge are more difficult to communicate across space, as the effects of distance apparently limit knowledge transfers and learning (Sorenson 2005). Although geographical proximity does not alone produce knowledge spillovers if actors belong to different epistemic communities (Lissoni 2001), organizational coherence is said to develop more easily if a firm's activities are concentrated in one location, as this encourages the reuse and transformation of expertise. The clustering of such activities also brings with it opportunity costs related to context redundancy. In other words, knowledge is based on a similar socio-economic context that tends to discourage diversity. Thus, despite the fluid circulation of knowledge, its concentration within one pool runs the risk of lock-in processes and a decline in innovation in the long term (Bathelt et al. 2004; Lazer and Friedman 2007).

The second option of complete dispersion offers advantages of knowledge diversity. It is suggested that the principle of geographical separation is a source of such diversity. When expertise is continually reused in different contexts, contextual variation can trigger new knowledge generation processes. Geographical separation may thus be conducive to innovation. More specifically, advantages of diversity through geographical knowledge distribution become more pronounced when expertise is produced and transformed in the context of client interaction, rather than during isolated laboratory research. In business services, different social, institutional, cognitive, and material contexts provide fertile ground for the emergence of distinct solutions. Given that firms work intensively at particular client sites, learning opportunities tend to spread across different places, turning every project location into a learning site for distinct expertise. Though much of this localized expertise will not be applicable in other contexts, some of it may help to improve problem-solving capabilities in other locations. And even if localized expertise does not directly solve problems in other locations, it may still be valuable through recombination with other localized expertise to produce new knowledge. Whereas research is often a planned and goal-directed process, many innovations are the result of unintended research outputs. Indeed, knowledge that is considered useless in one context may become useful in another. In the late 1980s, for instance, Pfizer conducted research to develop a new medication for the treatment of angina; the actual discovery was, however, later developed into what is now known as Viagra – a drug for the treatment of erectile dysfunction. Thus, while the discovered drug failed to cure angina, it offered side effects that were conducive to successful commercialization (Chesbrough 2003).

In reality, few organizations are prepared to devote much energy to the development of such 'false negatives'. Consequently, the unintended benefits of many research endeavours remain undetected. In contrast to technology development in closed permanent laboratory settings, which is capital-intensive and long term in character, client-driven knowledge services are characterized by considerable mobility. They change places by virtue of client location. In comparison, projects in business services tend to be more short term and geographically flexible than those in manufacturing (Ibert 2003; Glückler 2004*b*). Hence, an organization that offers specialist expertise to develop customized solutions for specific problems greatly benefits from its ability, first, to make localized knowledge available to other locations and, second, to recombine localized knowledge from different places into accumulated expertise and further innovations. According to Porter's notion (1986) of global markets, knowledge transfer represents one of the few strategic opportunities to attain global competitive advantage. The drawbacks associated with the geographical distribution of organizational units relate, however, to the costs of maintaining organization-wide comprehension and circulate knowledge (Glückler 2008). Opportunity costs can be defined as the costs of failing to mobilize localized knowledge to other contexts and losing potential benefits by not reutilizing and recombining knowledge. Whereas innovation potentials increase the more geographically diverse a knowledge base becomes, so too do the costs of circulating, reusing, and recombining this distributed knowledge. As demonstrated in previous research on global research and development (R&D) in multinational firms, unbalanced corporate strategies may threaten organizational coherence. According to Blanc and Sierra (1999: 200), 'too wide a dispersion of R&D activities may give rise to leakage of corporate coherence'. Therefore, if an organization becomes too dispersed, it may lose its capacity to effectively interpret and communicate distributed knowledge. In this context, the organization would likely break up into a set of firms that operate as separate knowledge islands. Similar to the exploitation–exploration problem theorized by March (1991), the knowledge-based firm faces a dilemma between geographical expansion and organizational cohesion of its knowledge base. At a given degree of geographical distribution and a given regime of knowledge circulation, the firm has to assess the benefits between two investment alternatives: to set up another geographical unit (*expansion*) or to enhance inter-unit communication (*cohesion*).

This expansion–cohesion dilemma is used as a conceptual framework to explore the conditions underlying international knowledge transfer empirically in the following sections.

10.4 **Relational Knowledge – Knowing Who Knows What**

Lundvall and Johnson's typology (1994) of economically relevant knowledge has often been used to discuss the differences between know-what or know-why on the one hand, and know-how or know-who on the other. While the former two are largely codifiable, know-how and know-who are difficult and sometimes even impossible to codify. Know-how refers to the often tacit knowledge of knowing how to use know-what for certain purposes. Know-how both defines and is defined by the social context (Gertler and Vinodrai 2005). Given its collective constitution and socially specific meaning, a key challenge involves the transfer of know-how within a multi-locational or multinational organization (Gertler 2003). The fourth type of knowledge, know-who, has, thus far, received limited scholarly attention. Empirically, however, organizational learning is fundamentally a function of know-who – that is, the social relationships that people draw upon to retrieve know-how and to enhance their learning process (Borgatti and Cross 2003). Similar to know-how, know-who cannot be traded. Drawing on Arrow's argument (1962), Lundvall and Johnson (1994: 29) state that 'you cannot buy trust, and if you could buy it, it would be of little value'. In analysing the transfer of unique expertise within an organization across different geographical locations, it is thus necessary to understand the underlying architecture of interpersonal relations through which such expertise is channelled. According to the interdisciplinary debate about knowledge management, there are at least three common barriers to knowledge transfer (Argote et al. 2003). These barriers relate to the type of knowledge being exchanged, the actors involved, and the relationships between the actors in a specific social context.

10.4.1 KNOWLEDGE PROPERTIES

In the relevant literature, considerable scholarly emphasis has been placed on different kinds of knowledge and their suitability for transfer and imitation. In general, tacit or sticky types of knowledge are more costly to transfer than explicit forms of knowledge (von Hippel 1994; Szulanski and Jensen 2004). Empirical research suggests that property rights are also associated with barriers to knowledge transfer. Whereas private knowledge (e.g. patents and licenses) is protected from spillovers, public agencies often actively promote the transfer of knowledge (Uzzi and Lancaster 2003; Owen-Smith and Powell 2004). Some studies also find that causal ambiguity, which is closely associated with the stickiness of knowledge, hampers knowledge transfer (Lippman and Rumelt 1982; Szulanski 1996; Argote et al. 2003). In other words, when knowledge is context-specific, collective, causally ambiguous, and experience-driven, its transmission and reutilization in different contexts becomes more costly. The case of MILECS nicely captures such complex and context-specific types of knowledge. It is therefore well suited to the analysis of interpersonal knowledge transfer.

10.4.2 PROPERTIES OF THE UNITS UNDER STUDY

Another identified barrier to the transfer of knowledge involves the characteristics of the actors under investigation. At the level of the individual agents, key sources of friction in knowledge transfer often relate to status, qualification, competencies, motivation, attitudes, and the like (see also Chapter 9). The most prominent concept in this regard is absorptive capacity, which describes the capability of an organization or its individuals to identify, incorporate, and commercialize new knowledge (Zahra and George 2002). At the level of the firm, absorptive capacity is often measured as the proportion of R&D expenditures in overall revenues (Cohen and Levinthal 1990; Tsai 2001). The same measure has, however, also been used to assess organizational innovativeness, which introduces the problem of associating absorptive capacity and innovation in a tautological manner. In response to this issue, alternative indicators have been defined, including the participation of firms in academic publications as a measure of an organizational inclination towards external knowledge pools (Cockburn and Henderson 1998). Another popular measure is the similarity of organizational designs and knowledge bases between two firms (Lane and Lubatkin 1998). As discussed below, a relational perspective of know-who within a distributed organization offers another way of defining absorptive capacity.

10.4.3 PROPERTIES OF THE RELATIONSHIPS BETWEEN UNITS

Reframing absorptive capacity in relational terms reveals an additional barrier to knowledge transfer that lies in the quality and structure of relationships. From an empirical standpoint, the structure of communication often diverts from formally designed organization charts (Krackhardt and Hanson 1993). People share different kinds of dyadic relations. Some may be 'arduous and barren', while others are 'intimate and fertile' (Szulanski 1996; Szulanski and Jensen 2004). Aside from the quality of individual relations, the structure of the overall set of relations in and between different organizational units also affects the ease and direction of knowledge transfers. In this sense, absorptive capacity is a function of the communication structure within the firm. On the one hand, closed and redundant communication structures tend to reiterate existing knowledge at the expense of absorbing external knowledge (Grabher 1993b; Bathelt et al. 2004). On the other hand, completely open and non-coherent networks are as deficient as closed ones because they cannot process and collectively transform new knowledge into innovative products. This means that every organization must find a specific mode of organizational communication that ensures the development and exchange of coherent internal knowledge development, as well as sufficient connections with the environment. This can be achieved either through intra-firm or inter-firm communication.

Given that the maintenance of network relations requires resources, inter-unit relations are costly and only beneficial if projects are to fulfil tasks that require tacit knowledge, that is, if there is a transfer problem (Hansen 1999). We investigate this problem within the context of the microcosm of personal knowledge transfers between the globally distributed workplaces of a globally operating firm. MILECS[1] – a knowledge-intensive technology consulting firm that depends on the accumulation and reutilization of tacit knowledge and individual expertise to yield competitive advantage – is an ideal case study for two reasons: First, it displays a strong pattern of geographical dispersion, as roughly 200 consultants and engineers are distributed across fifteen offices in ten countries across four continents. Second, in order to benefit from its international structure of locations, MILECS depends on its ability to mobi-lize existing localized knowledge and reuse it in other places. Following on the arguments developed in the previous sections, the empirical analysis pursues two goals: First, the aim is to visualize the knowledge 'architecture' (Amin and Cohendet 2004) of the corporation as represented by the personal exchange relations between its employees, and to find ways to assess the degree of integration and vulnerability of these exchanges. The second goal is to explore the contingent conditions that either impede or enhance inter-office and international knowledge transfers in relation to the three dimensions of knowledge transfers discussed above: the properties of knowledge, the proper-ties of the units, and the properties of the relationships between the units.

10.5 **The Evolution and Structure of MILECS**

MILECS was founded as an engineering service firm in the early 1970s and, over the first years, primarily grew 'on the back' of some international clients, which triggered initial internationalization (Chapter 8). When the firm was more established, the founder promoted the establishment of a partnership governance model and began to sell shares to his senior colleagues. After opening a few European offices during the 1980s, the internationalization process accelerated when MILECS launched operations in Latin America, India, and the United States, along with some minor representative offices. Given the limited size, yet extended geographical dispersion of the corporation, the management of knowledge transfer soon became a key issue. In 1997, MILECS founded a holding company dedicated to the collection and redistribution of the financial assets required for the development of an international organization between the local offices. Each national subsidiary was required to pay an annual contribution and report financial results to the holding firm. The holding company, in turn, set up international training programmes and other forms of corporate communication (e.g. newsletters). As one partner suggested, the training programme soon became a key element of MILECS' approach to global quality and knowledge transfer:

The backbone of our company is a global training system, which is the same for all employees world-wide. These trainings cover all areas of competence in the firm. They bring people together from all offices and help create the networks for tomorrow . . .

In 1997, the partners launched an online computer-mediated knowledge management system (KMS). Additional staff was recruited to operate and support the system, which offered a variety of information services including biographical employee data, a project directory with detailed documentation, literature, tools and software, a global newsletter, and chat and email services to facilitate knowledge exchange between employees on a global basis. By 2000, the firm had grown to thirty partners and more than 200 consultants. As decision-making among the multiple owners became more challenging, and the 'new economy' hype reached a climax, the management board decided to sell all operations to a publicly traded software firm, which had expanded massively through mergers and acquisitions with a market capitalization of over 1.5 billion Euro. Though the founders of the two firms had repeatedly worked together in projects, the decision turned out to be disastrous. Only a few months later, when the 'new economy' bubble burst, the software firm 'burnt' the entire capital reserves and went bankrupt.

In 2003, MILECS' partners managed to redeem their stakes and, thus, prevented the firm from exiting the market. In their struggle for survival, the management installed a rigid cost-control regime and cut down on all forms of international support for the organization. This intervention had far-reaching consequences. First, the firm cut half the costs, slimmed down the holding structure, and relinquished cost, profit, and investment autonomy to the international subsidiaries. Second, programmes for international knowledge transfer, including international training for novices, specialized practice group meetings of leading experts, as well as softer forms of knowledge exchange such as the global newsletter, were frozen. Any training that continued to take place was held nationally. Third, the management stopped delegating senior staff to overseas operations, thereby impeding the transfer of experience-based business and management know-how. Fourth, the computer-supported KMS was abandoned and converted into little more than a project archive. This was largely due to an external assessment of the initiative, which showed its limited value in terms of knowledge transfer. Most employees did not enjoy searching the database, nor were they professionally committed to it. The system merely served as an internal directory to retrieve information about projects and the colleagues responsible for these projects. From one day to the next, each national subsidiary was treated as an independent business. The legacy of this remains visible today, as indicated in the following statement by the CEO:

When we managed to buy the company back, we were urged to control costs and to cease the support for internal exchange across offices [...]. Today we have consolidated financially, but we do not benefit from our internationality.

At the same time, this self-inflicted crisis was aggravated by a generation shift, through which many of the most senior partners retired – and with them many of the established client accounts.

In 2005, two years after turnaround, MILECS had consolidated with around 190 employees; it was, therefore, in a position to reconsider its competitive position in the marketplace. Acknowledging its unique international presence vis-à-vis its competitors, the CEO found that MILECS did not adequately exploit its international character. The firm's partners did not circulate or reuse their distributed expertise, nor did they economize on cross-selling opportunities due to local access to global client accounts in other markets. The CEO explained that 'we never wanted to be the largest player. We have always been striving for quality and technology leadership'. In order to achieve higher value-added related to the high degree of internationality, the holding management and the global advisory board decided to relaunch the promotion of international knowledge transfer, an idea long desired by many of the partners.

The research conducted began at this particular juncture. Having overcome a major financial crisis and consolidated its operations, the firm began to assess its current state of internationality in order to commit resources to the global integration of knowledge and expertise.

10.6 **Knowledge Islands**

The above-mentioned scenario offered a unique opportunity to undertake an organization-wide analysis of corporate knowledge transfers. Having previously established an agreement with MILECS to participate in the study, a network survey was carried out in 2005 focusing on the exchange of knowledge in interpersonal relations, especially across the international offices of the firm. Essentially, the network survey invited employees to indicate all those colleagues that provided them with important information and who had been effective sources of help to solve work-related problems in the recent past. One hundred twenty-nine employees responded to the survey, that is, 69 per cent of the respective total. Most of the missing fifty-eight individuals were support staff or novices in their first year with the firm. By agreement with the management, they were not invited to complete the questionnaire (for a more detailed discussion of the methodology, see Glückler 2008, 2010b).[2]

Social network analysis offers a number of tools to describe and analyse the structure of such a network. The visual representation of the knowledge network reveals several characteristics of connectivity. The vast majority of 123 employees are mutually reachable, that is, there is always a path of linkages through which any of these individuals can contact any other within this group. The biggest mutually reachable subset of a network is called the main component (Table 10.1). Only six employees are isolated from this main component and therefore disconnected from the corporate knowledge flow. The 123 colleagues in the main component reported a total of 956 knowledge exchange relations, which corresponds to a network density of 5.8 per cent (Table 10.1). On average, every employee indicated approximately seven contacts with some exceptional individuals who are connected with up to thirty-nine colleagues in the firm. Those people that are not directly linked to each other, have an average path length to their peers of 3.1 steps, meaning that there are, on average, three linkages or, respectively, two intermediary individuals between any two people of this network.

Table 10.1. Structural characteristics of the MILECS knowledge network

Network measures	Mean	Standard deviation	Max.	Sum
Components (size)	—	—	123	7
Degree	7.411	6.203	39	956
Density	0.0579	0.2335	—	956

Source: Adapted from Glückler (2008: 133).

Beyond the importance and density of interpersonal exchanges between employees in the same local offices, there are numerous linkages between the different locations that serve as important sources of advice and expertise. Overall, every office is linked through direct contacts to at least two other offices in the corporate network. The most intensively developed linkages are between the two German offices, where intra-office and inter-office linkages are equally well developed (Figure 10.1). If one were to only look at these two offices, an almost perfect picture of a network would arise that is suited to customized responses (Cross et al. 2005). Compared to Frankfurt and Berlin, all other offices clearly fall behind in terms of the level of inter-office exchange and are much more focused on local knowledge circulation.

In light of the above discussion, it is important to explore the underlying vulnerability of the MILECS knowledge network. We approach this issue through a graphical assessment. Krackhardt and Hanson (1993) identify a number of structural problems in specific networks, three of which are particularly interesting in this context: First, the strength of networks can be undermined by imploded relationships due to patterns of communication that focus almost exclusively on intra-departmental or intra-office flows. Second, networks may be plagued by a fragile structure where a coherent

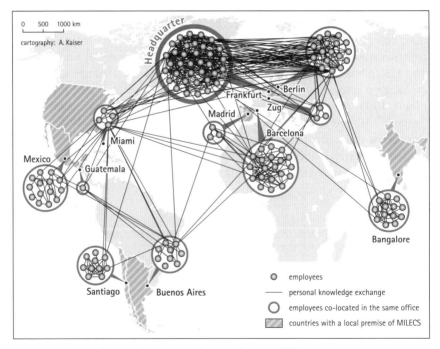

Figure 10.1. Overall network of knowledge transfers at MILECS

group maintains only one strong external communication link with another group, rather than linking up with many other groups. Third, networks may suffer from bow ties, where many employees depend on a single person but do not directly communicate with each other, and where that one person controls communication flows. Using these concepts for a first graphical assessment, some of the problems of MILECS become visible. Offices in Mexico, Argentina, Chile, and India are rich in local interconnections but weak in international knowledge transfer. Their international linkages mostly concentrate on one or a few bow ties in the sense of Krackhardt and Hanson (1993).

If the most important boundary spanners are removed one after another, the international knowledge architecture of MILECS eventually breaks down into eight separate knowledge islands (Figure 10.2). How, then, does this firm differ from a set of independent nationally operating firms? The difference lies in the roles of fifteen highly interconnected individuals. A knowledge perspective of the firm, thus, highlights the vulnerability and lack of cohesion regarding the reutilization of the core assets of the firm. The global organization of this expertise-based service firm fundamentally depends on the few individuals that bridge the distinct islands of expertise. These islands are internally connected networks of colleagues that share local knowledge in multiple ways. They rely, however, on only one or a very small number of

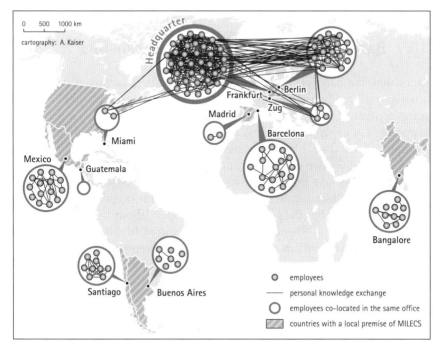

Figure 10.2. Network of knowledge transfers at MILECS without fifteen key individuals

individuals to manage the circulation of expertise and the provision of knowledge from other parts of the organization. As long as these so-called boundary spanners achieve their task of mobilizing expertise between the geographical units of the organization, the knowledge base becomes, at least partly, accessible and globally reusable (for a qualitative account on the role of boundary spanners, see Depner and Bathelt 2005; Depner 2006). The highly fragile structure of knowledge flows nevertheless puts the organization at risk of missing profit opportunities due to the disconnected nature of expertise between the units. This empirical example highlights the managerial dilemma between expansion and cohesion (Glückler 2010b). MILECS seems to have developed too much geographical diversity at the cost of organizational cohesion between the various units of the organization. This picture of MILECS is, however, not identical for all units. Indeed, it is interesting to note that the knowledge transfer between the four German-speaking offices in Germany, Switzerland, and the United States cannot be separated by omitting even the most influential employees. In this context, inter-office transfer seems to have developed in a far more robust way than in the predominantly Spanish-speaking offices. Describing and looking at the visual representation of a network, thus, allows us to draw some conclusions about the vulnerability and overall design of international knowledge transfers.

10.7 **Barriers to Global Knowledge Transfers**

To analyse the barriers to global knowledge transfers further, a first set of analyses was conducted that uses the multiple regression quadratic assignment procedure (MRQAP)[3] to test the effects of co-location, hierarchical status, area of expertise, seniority, and language on interpersonal knowledge transfers (Table 10.2). While regression models 1–4 display the bivariate statistics between the dependent and one independent variable, model 5 shows the results of a multivariate regression. The regression models suggest the following regularities: The single most important variable for knowledge transfer is, predictably, the geographical division of labour within the organization (co-location). Whenever two employees work in the same office, they are more likely to establish and maintain personal knowledge exchanges. On the one hand, this is a strategically planned result since people are co-located in organizational units exactly because they are supposed to work together. On the other hand, this finding further supports the idea that sharing geographically distributed expertise is a difficult managerial task. Co-location accounts for about 17 per cent of the variation in the distribution of knowledge transfer relations.

Table 10.2. MRQAP regression models, dependent variable: information

Variables	Model 1	Model 2	Model 3	Model 4	Model 5
Intercept	0.018**	0.004**	0.013**	−0.045	−0.063
Co-location	0.277**			0.260**	0.261**
Status level		0.007**		0.007**	0.007**
Status equality					.027**
Native language equality			0.119**	0.027**	0.026**
Language overlap					0.004
Tenure difference					−0.002
Age difference					0.003
Competence overlap					0.006
Qualification equality					−0.004
Statistics R^2 (adjusted)	0.172	0.027	0.061	0.204	0.215
P	0.0001	0.0001	0.0001	0.0001	0.0001

Note: $*p < 0.01$, $**p < 0.001$; 16,512 observations; 2,000 permutations.
Source: Adapted from Glückler (2010a).

The second important influence is status similarity between employees. There are several effects with respect to status. Generally speaking, if two employees have the same position, they are more likely to exchange knowledge. Although people with the same ranking often do not work on the same projects, they significantly engage in knowledge transfer (status equality). In contrast, the greater the difference in position between two employees, the less likely they to engage in knowledge transfers. Another effect is related to hierarchy. The higher a pair of employees is ranked, the more it engages in knowledge transfer. This means that directors, for instance, tend to engage more in knowledge exchange than consultants or other employees in lower positions. The measure used was the product of rank values for each pair of actors in the corporation (status level).

A third expectation about knowledge transfer in an organization relates to seniority. In general, one might expect an expert's age and seniority to influence their involvement in knowledge transfer. The community of practice literature suggests, for example, that new members are less knowledgeable and, thus, more likely to seek information than others (Borgatti and Cross 2003: 438). In the MILECS' case, however, neither employee age (age difference) nor seniority (tenure difference), that is, the number of years of employment with MILECS, has a significant effect on the structure of knowledge transfer.

Language is a fourth, and particularly interesting, factor affecting international knowledge transfer. While the constraint of native language on communication is intuitively appealing, the general language overlap between individuals draws a different picture (Table 10.2). If two individuals speak the same native tongue, they are more likely to exchange expertise (native language equality). If, however, two people have fluent command of at least one joint language, there is no measurable effect on their propensity to exchange knowledge (language overlap). In other words, the fact that employees are able to communicate in a language of mutually fluent command does not improve the overall knowledge exchange. In this respect, it is hard to compensate for native language differences in interpersonal knowledge transfer.

A fifth set of conditions relates to the area of expertise. One would normally assume that individuals working in the same areas of expertise maintain a more pronounced exchange of knowledge. In the case of MILECS, there is, however, only weak support for this expectation (Table 10.2). It is interesting to see that neither the same qualification nor the 'sameness' in firm-specific competences do positively affect the communication network. The notion of competence overlap refers to the degree of overlap between different actors according to their joint competences (Hansen 2002). In the case of MILECS, there is a clearly defined matrix of eight areas of expertise in which every professional locates his or her expertise. In many cases, individual employees overlap in a number of different competence fields such that the measure counts the number of joint areas of expertise for each pair of co-workers. Albeit weakly positive in bivariate regression, the effect of competence overlap on knowledge transfer is negligible and statistically insignificant in multivariate analysis.

In summary, a combined model 5 of the impact of influences produces a highly significant, though moderate, explanation of the variation in the distribution of knowledge transfers relations (Table 10.2). It suggests that interpersonal knowledge transfers within the corporate organization are constrained by co-location, and increase with status level and the equality of a pair of employees. While these effects may not be surprising, it is less intuitive to observe that seniority, age, qualification, educational background, and language skills are not related to personal knowledge transfer relations.

10.8 **Boundary Spanners – Bridging Knowledge Islands**

Having discussed some of the major constraints on knowledge transfer relations, the next step in the analysis was to address the role of management intervention. The central question, here, is: What kinds of management incentives enhance inter-office knowledge transfers? The extent to which an employee is involved in inter-office knowledge exchanges is expressed in that individual's so-called E-I value. This is measured as the relative commitment of that individual's set of relations to people outside the home office. The E-I Index can thus be calculated as the proportion of an individual's relationships with members of other groups (offices) by subtracting the number of internal ties (within the same office) from the number of external ties (with other offices) and dividing this difference by the sum of all ties.[4]

MILECS supports several programmes dedicated to enforcing international knowledge transfer, three of which are included as independent variables in a multivariate regression model: First, 'trainings' measures the number of global training sessions an employee has participated in. In the case of MILECS, sixty-eight employees (55 per cent) participated in at least one and up to thirty international training(s) (mean = 4.64). Second, 'projects' is a dummy variable that captures the assignment to international projects involving the collaboration with colleagues from offices in other countries. In sum, forty-nine individuals (38 per cent) reported to have collaborated internationally. Third, 'expatriation' is another dummy variable that measures the assignment of an employee to another office for a minimum of two months. Thirty-one employees (24 per cent) said that they had been assigned abroad for extended time periods. Beyond these individual management programmes, a combined measure is defined to reflect an employee's inclination towards international corporate contacts: 'Programme diversity' counts the number of different training, project, and expatriation programmes an employee participated in. In addition, people's attitudes towards other locations are measured in terms of the variable 'local focus' – that is, the degree to which employees reported full satisfaction about the availability and quality of knowledge in their home office. This measure is calculated as the average score of confirmation with the following four statements, each measured on a six-point scale:

(a) The information I can get from colleagues within my office as compared with other offices is first-best and fully sufficient; (b) the expertise I can consult from colleagues at my office as compared with other offices is first-best and fully sufficient; (c) I can find all contacts and information necessary to win a new client account within my office; (d) the intranet central project documentation (CPD) service is very effective for my work.

The effectiveness of the programmes on inter-office knowledge transfer is tested by means of OLS regression models (Table 10.3). In the bivariate regression models 1–3, the three forms of international encounters are conducive to an individual's future inclination to maintain inter-office knowledge transfers when measured individually. By far, the most effective tool in enforcing long-term knowledge transfers between geographically separated experts is to assign employees to foreign offices for an extended period of time (expatriation). International office deployment explains 10 per cent of the variation in an individual's E-I value in the knowledge transfer structure. Furthermore, as shown in the bivariate models 4 and 5, the combined measures (especially programme diversity) are quite conducive to inter-office knowledge relations. The individuals that experienced office deployment, international project work, and global trainings were generally more likely to have international involvement in knowledge transfers than other employees. On the one hand, the diversity of international experiences accounts for 12.5 per cent of the overall variance in knowledge transfers in the bivariate model 4. On the other hand, local focus seems to hamper internationally oriented knowledge transfers. Model 5 demonstrates that the more satisfied employees are with local resources, the less inclined they are towards knowledge exchanges with employees in other offices. This isolated effect becomes insignificant, however, in the multivariate model (Table 10.3).

Table 10.3. OLS unstandardized regression coefficients for the prediction of inter-office knowledge transfer

Variables	Model 1	Model 2	Model 3	Model 4	Model 5	Model 6
Intercept	−0.665***	−0.633***	−0.657***	−0.833***	−0.191***	−0.552***
Expatriation[1]	0.387***					0.218*
Projects[2]		0.002***				0.000
Trainings[3]			0.019***			−0.000
Programme diversity[4]				0.157***		0.085*
Local focus[5]					−0.099**	−00.061
Statistics						
R^2	0.118	0.068	0.063	0.137	0.041	0.189
R^2 (adjusted)	0.104	0.053	0.049	0.124	0.026	0.150
P	0.000	0.002	0.007	0.000	0.024	0.029

Note: *$p < 0.1$,
**$p < 0.05$,
***$p < 0.01$; 129 observations.
Independent variables: [1]assignment to another office for a minimum of two months (dummy);
[2] assignment to international projects involving the collaboration with staff from other offices (dummy);
[3] number of global trainings an employee has taken part in;
[4] sum of the binary variables training (as a dummy), expatriation, and projects (range 0–3);
[5] average score on a set of confirmations about the degree of satisfaction with the quality of knowledge available in the own office (range 0–6).
Source: Adapted from Glückler (2008: 136).

10.9 **Knowledge Management: Technical or Social?**

There are two basic strategies to support or manage knowledge transfers within and between corporations: codification and personalization (Hansen et al. 1999). The personalization strategy takes a people-to-people approach and supports the creation of networks of interpersonal relationships to circulate knowledge. The primary objective, here, is to facilitate conversation between people, for example, by offering specific spaces for meetings to exchange ideas and experiences. This strategy may support the emergence of communities of practice (Lave and Wenger 1991; Wenger 1998), or 'groups of people informally bound together by shared expertise and passion for a joint enterprise' (Wenger and Snyder 2000: 139). Members select themselves on the basis of passion and commitment for a certain topic with a strong interest in sharing and creating knowledge. With respect to this strategy, community access and composition does not depend on organizational hierarchy or divisional, functional, and regional divides within or between the corporate units. In contrast, the strategy of codification takes a people-to-documents approach and aims to maximize the reuse of existing knowledge at minimal cost. This is accomplished by archiving knowledge artefacts in information systems that can be accessed through computer networks. While codification stresses the efficient retrieval and reuse of knowledge in routine processes, personalization responds to the need for exchanging specific expertise to recombine new ideas (Hansen et al. 1999).

Information and communication technologies are often discussed as an alternative way of supporting corporate knowledge management. Although corporations invest millions of dollars in setting up knowledge management systems (Ofek and Sarvary 2001), empirical analyses point to the limitations of these systems (McDermott 1999; Roberts 2000; Hislop 2002). This work suggests that the transfer of tacit knowledge, such as personal expertise, advise, and problem-solving based on professional experience, cannot be substituted by technology (Borgatti and Foster 2003; Cross et al. 2005; Reihlen and Ringberg 2006). Indeed, it has been found that people turn to friends and colleagues five times more often than to the screen of an electronic information system (Cross and Baird 2000). Though electronic information systems leverage access to large amounts of information, extracting value from this information by means of interpretation remains fundamentally contextualized in organizational and social relationships (Weick 1985). Some radical critics neglect the very notion of managing knowledge because of its social, semantic, and cognitive contextuality (Alvesson and Kärreman 2001). It thus appears that personal communication is still central to complex transfers of knowledge, even if this communication takes place in computer-mediated form. Rather than constructing an either-or-dualism, we suggest, however, that both virtual document-to-people *and* people-to-people communication can, in combined form, be an alternative to pure face-to-face knowledge transfers (Rice 1984; Hollingshead and McGrath 1995; Baltes et al. 2002).

The quality of knowledge creation and exchange through computer-mediated communication has recently been demonstrated for user–communities in the Internet (von Hippel 2001; Grabher et al. 2008). In the context of professional services, however, empirical evidence of the use of document-based forms of communication is less convincing. According to one team of researchers, 'all strategy consultants that we studied came to grief with document-driven systems' (Hansen et al. 1999: 112). Reihlen and Ringberg (2006) find that codification and personalization work together in a complementary way. As indicated in their study of a global consulting firm, consultants use an electronic knowledge management system for three purposes: to access the contact information of other colleagues, to access project documents, and to access tools and methods. Reihlen and Ringberg (2006) also identify a fundamental problem in the system. Often, the materials retrieved from the electronic archives could not be properly interpreted or used because its contents were idiosyncratic in nature, lacking contextual information. In other cases, project documentation was simply incomplete. This often resulted in interpretative ambiguity (Amin and Cohendet 2004), which prevented the reuse of the materials and information. Overall, the technical knowledge management system studied was of limited use, even after years of operation. As Reihlen and Ringberg (2006: 338) conclude, 'even with a high degree of sharedness (practice, background, training), the consultants we interviewed had persistent difficulties in making sense of one another's computer-mediated artefacts, leading to either miscommunication or a creative but unrelated use of the information'.

At MILECS, the consultants reported remarkable support for the appropriateness of the personalization strategy. When asked about the most important sources of information to solve work-related problems (Table 10.4), they clearly prioritized interpersonal relations with colleagues and clients over document-driven information sources. Though MILECS develops specific and high-profile expertise in a particular technological domain of logistics, the consultants rated the Internet even higher than the firm-specific electronic knowledge management system. In addition, when invited for suggestions on how to improve global knowledge transfer, the majority of people reported that they would like to participate more intensively in trainings, meetings, and workshops with colleagues from other offices and countries, as opposed to simply feeding and searching virtual databases.[5]

Table 10.4. Importance of sources of information in solving work-related problems

| Source of information | Number of ratings | | | | | |
| | Not important | | | Important | | |
	1	2	3	4	5	6
Colleagues within the firm	2	5	5	10	30	76
Clients	7	7	12	16	29	57
Internet	4	14	23	48	13	26
Professional colleagues in other firms	10	32	20	32	14	20
Literature (books/business press/magazines/etc.)	8	22	32	39	17	10
MILECS Knowledge Management System	12	26	38	23	18	11

Source: Own research.

10.10 **Conclusion**

This chapter relies on a single case study to explore the structural foundations of international intra-firm knowledge transfers in an industry of expert technology services. The case of MILECS is particularly interesting because it is characterized by a pronounced geographical dispersion across four continents. The firm also faced a severe corporate crisis in its recent history, which forced the management to withdraw support for international knowledge management. In a situation where MILECS was recovering and thinking about measures to realize stronger advantages from its global presence, this research has enabled a diagnosis of its current knowledge architecture. By surveying the entire organization and using methods of social network analysis, the case study provides insights into the structural aspects of a corporate knowledge transfer network.

Relying on visual analysis, we first demonstrated the vulnerability of the knowledge network as a result of many bow ties between offices. Inter-office communication was channelled and mediated by only a limited number of boundary spanners. And, in this case, the difference between a global corporation and a set of nationally separated knowledge islands consisted of only fifteen key individuals. Second, personal knowledge transfers between every pair of employees were mainly constrained by geographical co-location, native language, and the similarity and level of hierarchical status. Knowledge transfers were, thus, independent of age, corporate tenure, qualification, and the overlap of language skills. Third, the case study suggests that international knowledge transfers can be enforced and intensified by expatriation programmes. The employees that were deployed to other offices for long periods of time (usually between several months and two years), or that participated in diverse programmes with international contacts, clearly contributed to international knowledge transfers and also displayed a stronger international orientation in their communication. In addition to their immediate effects, these management policies promise positive long-term effects for sustained international knowledge transfers.

To sum up, the expansion–coherence dilemma is a useful framework for assessing a firm's commitment to corporate knowledge management. In weighing the value of knowledge circulation against that of continuous global expansion, the framework emphasizes effective internal knowledge architectures in transnational firms. A knowledge architecture based on bottleneck effects between unconnected knowledge pools is more likely to convey private returns to the boundary spanners, along with substantial losses through unrealized knowledge reuse, than collective returns to the organization as a whole. Organizations that depend on client interaction to generate new knowledge are bound to geographically dispersed learning and should, therefore, commit substantial intelligence and resources to the effective circulation of expertise within their particular organizational geographies. While these policy implications are primarily corporate in nature, Chapter 11 addresses the wider regional policy consequences of a relational approach to the study of economic action and interaction.

Part IV

Towards a Relational Economic Policy?

11 Consequences for Relational Policies

11.1 Introduction

Having developed a relational framework for the study of economic action and interaction in a variety of spatial contexts and organizational forms,[1] this chapter highlights the key findings of this approach and draws attention to some potential policy implications. Our main objective is to provide a preliminary outline of what a relational cluster policy framework might look like, and to further illustrate the utility of this approach in investigating economic interaction from a *spatial perspective*. The defining characteristics and key advantages of the approach may be summarized as follows:

- First, the relational approach goes beyond conventional theories of economic action, which tend to view economic structures as the product of abstract optimization processes, while the spatial dynamics of economic activity are explained through discrete cost and revenue factors. In contrast, the relational approach recognizes that economic action and interaction are critically shaped by social and institutional relations, as well as the legacies of past economic decisions and established structures (Chapter 2). From this perspective, markets are social constructions that influence the spatial dynamics of knowledge flows and industry networks (Chapter 3).
- Second, a relational approach is particularly well suited to understanding the knowledge economy that is increasingly defined by intangible assets and is, thus, less easily explainable by conventional demand – supply accounts (Chapter 4). A relational perspective is useful in understanding why knowledge is shared in some contexts and not others, as well as how knowledge flows shape and are shaped by existing economic structures.
- Third, as an institutional approach that recognizes the importance of past economic action and interaction on present structures and decision-making, the relational conceptualization sheds a much needed light on the reflexive relationship between physical infrastructure and economic relations in knowledge networks (Chapter 4). While institutions play a key role in directing economic action, they are simultaneously reproduced and even modified by the intended and unintended consequences of economic action (Chapter 3).

- Fourth, in addressing spatial asymmetries in economic development, uneven flows of goods, people, and knowledge, and the spatial disparities that result from specific regional policies (see also Stiglitz 2006), a relational perspective directs attention to the roles of power and contingency in patterns of economic action and interaction. In so doing, it helps to explain why the same structural conditions in two regions can foster different strategies and forms of economic interaction, which, in turn, lead to different regional dynamics and disparities over time (Chapters 5–7).
- Fifth, the relational approach contributes to our understanding of the local–global connection in the context of the knowledge economy. While emphasizing the interconnectedness of local and trans-local knowledge flows (Amin and Thrift 1992), such processes do not produce identical structures, and not every region benefits from access to global production chains in other parts of the world (Chapters 6–10). A relational conceptualization is, thus, particularly useful in explaining regional variations in the mobilization of external agents and resources.

The above-mentioned attributes of the relational perspective have important implications for economic policy because such policy initiatives are increasingly focussed on the promotion of interactive learning and knowledge creation at different spatial scales (Bathelt and Dewald 2008). Although local networking is, of course, an important aspect of regional economic development, establishing global networks requires the attention of policymakers, as well as institutional support. The challenge for local and regional policy initiatives is, therefore, to encourage the development of global linkages, while, at the same time, reinforcing local cohesion and networking so that external triggers are provided with local support.

11.2 **Foundations of Relational Regional Policies**

To avoid the problem of spatial determinism associated with territorial policy initiatives, we extend our approach to a relational policy agenda that considers the development towards a global knowledge economy. Here, the focus of policymaking is on the economic agents in a region, as well as the context in which they operate. This includes local and non-local relationships. First, this conceptualization of action acknowledges that contextuality, path-dependency, and contingency fundamentally structure economic processes and shape their outcomes over time (Bathelt and Glückler 2003a). As emphasized in Chapter 2, this view rests on the assumption that economic action is deeply embedded in structures of social and institutional relations. Second, economic decision-making is path-dependent in that it is strongly influenced by past actions and resulting structures. Third, economic action is, nevertheless, contingent, as economic agents can follow new technological development paths and establish new technology linkages.

This conceptualization forces policymakers to assess regions in direct relation to the agents and organizations that operate both within and across them. Indeed, physical co-location does not automatically support the generation of local networks (Amin and Cohendet 2004; Clark and Tracey 2004), as fundamental interdependencies exist with economic, technological, social, and cultural dynamics in and between other places. Regional economic processes are closely linked to other economic and social processes through, for example, complex cross-regional networks that enable systematic knowledge exchange between different places in order to benefit from complementary assets (Bathelt and Glückler 2003a). Although policymakers may use spatial proximity to initiate collective learning and relational capital formation (Gertler 2004; Capello and Faggian 2005), there is no guarantee that local interaction will become a viable option for local firms and decision-makers.

The relational approach puts the actions and interactions of economic agents at the centre of policy initiatives. Such initiatives involve close interaction among economic agents, regional planners, and policymakers, which encourages a revised understanding of regional policy that is based not on hierarchical planning and supervision but on collective action and the negotiation of new ideas (e.g. Raines 2000). From this perspective, policies cannot be viewed as fail-proof recipes that simply depend on obtaining the necessary ingredients. A relational regional policy is based on an evolutionary and contextual understanding of economic action, which denies the possibility of deterministic planning.

The relational approach, consequently, uses existing regional structures and strengths as a starting point to trigger collective action. While a top-down policy approach might include the provision of land for industrial development or subsidies for individual investments, a relational view suggests that effective policy initiatives cannot simply be superimposed on regional agents (Amin 1999). Bottom-up initiatives that recruit the most important and dynamic local agents are more likely to be successful (Bathelt 2005a). Facilitating such initiatives is, of course, a time-consuming process that depends on participants incorporating collective matters of interest into their strategies. From this perspective, policymakers serve as mediators and boundary-spanners, rather than creators and dominators, in developing policy programmes and negotiating action plans between regional agents.

From a knowledge-based perspective, the goal of a relational policy is to strengthen the localized capabilities of agents (Maskell and Malmberg 1999a) by activating existing assets and combining them with new knowledge. Among other things, this involves processes of institution building, network generation, firm formation, interactive learning, and enrolment in joint

actions. Without denying the continued utility of conventional policy programmes, this perspective emphasizes the importance of combining different
policies to stimulate a wide range of opportunities for regional development
paths (Amin 1999; Boschma and Lamboy 2001; Grabher 2001).

The combination of global and local forces is central to a relational policy
framework. While regional policy traditionally draws on regional assets to
produce competitiveness, the value of this approach has been called into
question in an era defined by the increasing integration of economic linkages
on a global scale. As Amin (2004) observes, spatial configurations are not
necessarily territorial in character (Allen et al. 1998). Indeed, local economic
agents often travel to develop international business networks; local labour
markets are influenced by transnational migration; and local knowledge bases
are constantly shaped by news reports and experiences from other parts of the
world. A relational view of place, thus, requires that we abandon the idea of an
encapsulated local; the global exists and develops inside the local (Amin 2004;
Massey 2004). The way in which power is established and exercised across
nation-states, and between different cultural and institutional contexts, must,
therefore, be addressed from a somewhat different angle (Allen 1997, 2003).

As the above discussion indicates, a relational perspective has a number of
important policy implications. First, international flows, connectivities, and
multiple geographical expressions become the focal point of regional policy,
rather than static regional characteristics. Second, regions can no longer be
viewed as autonomous entities that determine their own futures as a result of
their internal strengths. Clearly, production and knowledge networks are not
limited to the local, and, at the same time, regional policies cannot fully
control these new transient spaces (see also Bathelt 2003). Third, instead of
protecting seemingly cohesive localities from unpredictable global forces,
regional policy must become a policy of active local engagement with the
global. As suggested by Bathelt and Boggs (2005), agents can be encouraged to
re-bundle local and non-local resources to systematically connect the local
and global spheres (Bathelt 2009). This is not to suggest that there is no room
for local agency. What it means, however, is that the development of regional
policy must include policy arenas and negotiations that extend beyond the
territorial level.

A relational approach, thus, sheds new light on the interdependencies
between global and local processes. While '[t]here is no definable regional
territory to rule over' (Amin 2004: 36), a policy that focuses on trans-local
connections instead of territorial structures has yet to be realized. In practice,
policy initiatives must involve both the creation of local networks in order to
provide opportunities for local synergies and recombinations, and the formation of trans-local 'pipelines' to secure knowledge inputs and provide access
to longer term growth potentials. In the context of industrial clusters, the
relational perspective discourages isolated, regionally focussed policy

approaches; rather, it encourages a cluster policy that follows a multilevel governance scheme aiming to overcome conventional regional fixes (e.g. Hooghe and Marks 2003; Benz 2004). In so doing, it becomes possible to simultaneously address processes of re-territorialization (Brenner 1999) and 'glocalization' (Hess 1998; Swyngedouw 1997) – two concepts that underscore recent trends towards new subnational and supranational forms of economic organization. Multilevel governance conceptions argue for coordinated policy efforts across discrete scales in order to generate greater synergies (Wolfe and Gertler 2004; Hudson 2007). Such conceptions also reposition the national state as a part of a broader collective of different policy scales, rather than the main authority on policy programmes. This perspective necessarily encourages a decentralized approach to policy processes.

11.3 **Theory versus Policy: Cluster Policies and Regional Economy**

From a regional policy standpoint, few concepts have been more intensively discussed in the social sciences than the cluster concept. Indeed, since its development in the early 1990s, the cluster concept has become increasingly widespread, and is now applied in many different contexts worldwide (OECD 1999, 2001; Europäische Kommission 2002; Sölvell et al. 2003; Kiese and Schätzl 2008). Lagendijk and Cornford (2000) describe two ways in which Michael Porter has promoted this diffusion: first as an innovative academic who established the cluster conception (Porter 1990b), and second as an influential policy consultant involved in the activities of the consulting firm Monitor. According to Lagendijk and Cornford (2000), the cluster concept's appeal as a regional policy instrument has less to do with its conceptual strength than its adaptability to different contexts and its ability to persuade political and economic agents to participate in joint economic goals. The cluster concept is, indeed, very broad and can be applied to various contexts, including industrial restructuring, stimulation of foreign direct investments, and endogenous regional development. Although some academics criticize the ambiguity surrounding the concept (Martin and Sunley 2003), others view this as an opportunity to generate support for a broader regional development agenda (Henry et al. 2006).

This conceptual ambiguity has led to a diverse array of economic policies that may be viewed as part of a cluster policy (OECD 1999, 2001). At least four types of cluster policies with different foci can be distinguished: (*a*) the approach of national competitive advantage, (*b*) the regional clustering approach, (*c*) policy approaches that focus on small- and medium-sized enterprises and their linkages, and (*d*) policies that support wider industry–university research networks. While such policies often focus on regional or urban clusters, they can also include national and international clusters (Raines 2001; Europäische Kommission 2002; Sölvell et al. 2003). Cluster policies can reflect a comprehensive regional development strategy, as well as a more narrow focus. With respect to the mode of implementation, bottom-up policies can be distinguished from top-down approaches.

This chapter uses a *regional* definition of clusters to explore the implications of a relational policy framework. To understand why existing cluster policies often differ, it is useful to look at the processes by which cluster policies are designed and implemented. From a relational perspective, clusters exist in different contexts, include different resource bases and strategic potentials, and involve different agent groups with deviating goals. This ultimately causes spatial differences in policy formulation. The process that leads to the design and execution of cluster policies has been described as a cluster policy cycle (Lagendijk 1999; Raines 2000; Benneworth and Charles 2001). A brief description of the six stages associated with this cycle is offered as follows:

1. *Initiation of cluster programmes.* The starting point of every cluster initiative is the decision to select cluster policies as instruments to improve or stabilize the economic conditions of a region. This decision is often based on interregional rivalry between neighbouring administrations regarding access to federal funding, rather than specific regional economic conditions (Lagendijk 1999). As a result, cluster initiatives are sometimes established in contexts that do not necessarily provide a sound basis for such policies (Enright 2003) due, for instance, to a lack of economic coherence.

2. *Identification of cluster industries.* The identification of industries that become part of a cluster programme is often based on quantitative studies, such as input–output, SWOT, or statistical indicator analyses (e.g. Feser and Bergman 2000; Sternberg and Litzenberger 2004). While qualitative studies provide important insights into the nature of social and economic relations that are difficult to compare across territories, quantitative studies have other distinct disadvantages. According to Martin and Sunley (2003), such methods only provide a partial understanding of clusters as they fail to capture the socio-economic processes in a region or its underlying institutional conditions. These are, however, important aspects of the multidimensional cluster conceptualization developed in Chapter 5 that need to be addressed (see also Chapters 6 and 7).

3. *Practices of industry selection.* The final selection of industries to be included in a cluster policy is often determined by strategic considerations and political power constellations (e.g. Benneworth and Charles 2001). In addition to lobby groups, which directly influence policy design, the actors

involved in this process are often under pressure to produce a selection that represents a large segment of the regional economy (Enright 2003) in order to achieve broad regional support. The selected industries are, thus, often too diversified. The strategic focus on industries with large future growth potential leads to a selection bias, as regions tend to identify similar industries for their cluster policies. Such policies initiate developments that will eventually compete against one another, and not all will be successful. As Enright (2003) explains, not all regions can, for instance, be leaders in information and communication technologies, although many cluster initiatives specifically focus on these industries.

4. *Governing the political process.* In terms of the design and implementation of a cluster programme, it is important to look at who initiates and drives the process and how strong administrative hurdles are. Conventional approaches (Lagendijk 1999) to public policy designs are characterized by a standardized sequence of stages (i.e. analysis – selection of industries – design and implementation of political programmes). These approaches can, however, suffer from a lack of flexibility if they undermine other initiatives and remain fixated on particular goals. In so doing, they may not leave room for spontaneous – but possibly important – alternative corporate initiatives.

5. *Role of mediators.* Mediators often play a key role in the implementation and acceptance of a cluster policy. They have to organize cooperation between local firms and with public organizations, and convince principal agents of the importance of the cluster initiative. This often occurs in an environment characterized by a high degree of scepticism regarding cooperation and collective action. In response to such challenges, some studies point to the role of external consultants (e.g. Raines 2000; Sölvell et al. 2003). There is, however, a tendency to ignore the fact that external specialists rarely receive as much support as locals. Indeed, local entrepreneurs with outstanding reputations – if they can be found – may be much more influential in securing support for cluster initiatives. The integration of local industries is particularly important in the context of bottom-up initiatives (Lagendijk 1999).

6. *Cluster policy as a reflexive learning process.* Despite its widespread use, cluster policy is still an experimental concept. This is largely due to the lack of clarity surrounding the precise conditions under which this policy achieves its best results. In this context, it is important that agents involved in the design and implementation stages display a high learning potential. The ongoing evaluation of policy tools is, for instance, an important basis for the adaptation of existing policies (Lagendijk 1999; Raines 2000; OECD 2001). Transparency also helps to improve the legitimacy of a specific cluster policy in a region. In reality, however, evaluation mechanisms are often not very well developed (Sölvell et al. 2003; Fromhold-Eisebith and Eisebith 2005).

In many cluster initiatives, there is little evidence of a strong connection between theory and regional policy implementation – that is, policy instruments are not systematically developed from theoretical considerations (see also Benner 2009). In order to achieve regional support, cluster initiatives often incorporate broad regional policy goals that are difficult to achieve. Over time, such policies tend to shift from their original cluster focus to broader regional development strategies. While cluster initiatives may eventually be integrated into such strategies, they should neither compete with nor replace such policies.

Another issue that creates problems between cluster theory and policy implementation relates to the time lag between expectations and actual outcomes. While cluster policies must adopt a long-term focus, given the time it takes to develop cohesive industry settings with a sound mix of local cooperation and international networking, individuals often expect successful outcomes within the short- or medium term. The length of election cycles at the local and regional level encourages policymakers to focus on policy measures that are likely to result in some short-term success, even if this fails to connect with long-term cluster development goals. In this context, regional policymakers often concentrate on existing clusters or cluster-like industry structures that are economically viable, rather than less mature clusters that have development potential. The emphasis on immediate successes encourages the development of short-term policy rationales, the long-term success of which remains unclear.

Before developing a relational cluster policy that works towards integrating theory and policy in a consistent way, it is important to clarify the general utility of cluster policies in light of recent and ongoing criticisms.

11.4 **Do we need a Cluster Policy?**

From a regional perspective, the above discussion suggests that clusters cannot always be successfully applied in every region regardless of its industry structure and context (Martin and Sunley 2003; Asheim et al. 2006). Given that the requirements for cluster development are not met by all regions, we must acknowledge that clusters cannot be usefully employed as a 'one-model-fits-all' strategy. Indeed, a key issue in designing cluster policies is to develop a regional industry structure that is sufficiently specialized to benefit from traded and untraded interdependencies, yet diversified enough to avoid the danger of lock-in (Chapter 5). It is highly unlikely that such trade-offs can be resolved following a simple optimization logic, as countervailing forces, power asymmetries, and the divergent interests of actors are always at work in a cluster. As such, there is no single equilibrium that resolves the inherent tensions; there is only the temporary stabilization of unequal power relations (Bathelt and Taylor 2002). Cluster policies may, thus, be affected by the development of new tensions within a seemingly stable industry network, which could ultimately lead to a new set of political actions.

Arguments in favour of a cluster strategy do not automatically imply that policy initiatives can easily create new clusters. Studies have shown that there are plenty of 'normal regions' or 'noncore regions' that do not exhibit economic specializations (Storper 1997c; Hellmer et al. 1999). Such regions do not have the potential to stimulate self-sustaining growth processes or develop into clusters. Furthermore, dynamic urban areas can be found with a diversified industry structure that does not have much in common with a cluster (Newlands 2003; Bramwell et al. 2004). In large metropolitan areas, several clusters may overlap (Crevoisier 2001; Bathelt and Boggs 2003; Porter 2003; Schamp 2005) in a way that creates synergies and strengthens the regional economy. In this context, a single cluster policy would clearly be too selective to achieve broad regional support. Similarly, smaller metropolitan economies might not have the sort of value-chain focus that would classify them as clusters.

It is unclear whether a standard cluster policy constitutes the most appropriate regional policy approach in each of these settings. In broad diversified metropolitan areas, for instance, the regional growth path might benefit from a large variety of urbanization instead of localization economies. The Kitchener-Waterloo region in Ontario, also known as Canada's Technology Triangle – one of the most dynamic city-regions in Canada with high productivity levels and low unemployment – falls into this category as it does not host a true cluster of interrelated firms tied to a particular value chain. Co-location is seemingly not the driving force behind the regional growth process (Parker 2001; Bathelt et al. 2010). Here, and in other regions, the processes underlying dynamic growth might, indeed, be quite different from those in clusters (Crevoisier 2001; Simmie 2003), making these regions particularly robust against economic shocks. As Wolfe and Gertler (2004) point out, the success of a regional cluster policy also depends on the institutions operating at the national and supranational level, in addition to the regional level. Some scholars even suggest that a particular regional policy is not required to stimulate cluster development (Newlands 2003). Scholars such as Porter (1990b) and Krugman (1991) are also sceptical about the benefits of universally applying cluster policies. From this perspective, the danger of allocating scarce resources in suboptimal ways, or strengthening inefficient industry structures, is extremely high.

Bresnahan et al.'s study (2001) of information and telecommunication technology clusters in different parts of the world demonstrates that the factors underlying the establishment of new clusters differ from those which support the growth of existing ones. While state policies, according to this study, have not had a notable influence on early-stage cluster formation, the degree of openness in regional economic relations and access to large external markets are identified as critical factors determining the success of emergent clusters. Although the studies find little evidence of clusters being jump-started through regional policy initiatives alone, cluster policies have been successful in strengthening and securing existing clusters (e.g. Rosenfeld 2007). Many examples indicate that policies can significantly influence the development of clusters, in both developed and less developed economies, as well as in early and later stages (Bathelt and Depner 2005; Depner 2006; Feldman 2001; Lundequist and Power 2002; Fromhold-Eisebith and Eisebith 2005). There is, however, little empirical evidence of the performance of policy programmes upon which to base wider claims regarding the effectiveness of cluster policies (Enright 2003).

Overall, it appears misleading to argue that policy initiatives do not at all strengthen cluster development. In the context of coordinated market economies such as Japan, and in liberal market economies such as the United States (Hall and Soskice 2001b), there is evidence of the impact of technology policies on the growth of industry clusters. Examples include the development of high-technology clusters in the Greater Boston and Silicon Valley regions, which would have been impossible without the US federal government's massive defence spending during the global and regional conflicts of the twentieth century (Bathelt 1991; Markusen et al. 1991). In almost every country, there are national and regional policies that influence the development and spatial dynamics of new technologies. At the very least, these policies reconfigure the institutional context and economic environment of existing and potential clusters by shaping regional labour markets, new firm formation, and financial conditions. Since most countries try to initiate new technological developments through specific research and technology policies, and many countries have had some success in implementing such policies, a no-policy choice is not a realistic option for a country. The fact that the cluster effects of national and regional policies are often a function of the unintended consequences of these policies is not decisive when choosing an appropriate technology policy.

In our view, cluster policies are, or can be, useful if applied in a way that is consistent with an overarching conceptual framework. It is necessary to develop contextualized cluster policies that leave room for alternative policies if local growth does not follow a cluster trajectory, or if clusters do not significantly enhance the competitiveness of regional firms. Cluster policies are more likely to be successful if they are multidimensional in character and sensitive to the specificities of the local economy and industry structure. Instead of focussing on the question of whether national policies can help initiate cluster developments in new industries, such as biotechnology and nanotechnology (see e.g. Feldman and Francis 2004; Henn 2006), the remainder of this book looks at how a relational cluster policy can be developed from a conceptual framework, drawing on the multidimensional cluster conceptualization developed in Chapter 5.

11.5 **Towards Relational Cluster Policies?**

In light of the previous discussion, the development of a consistent regional cluster policy depends upon a thorough investigation of the context in which industries and firms are embedded, and how they are integrated into wider national and global value chains and production contexts. Many cluster policies seemingly either lack systematic analyses of such economic processes and structures or fail to base their policy programmes on the results of such analyses. To avoid this, we suggest a detailed regional economic inventory according to the multidimensional cluster perspective developed in Chapter 5, and a combination of both quantitative and qualitative methods. This allows for a detailed analysis of the strengths and weaknesses of a regional economy and its clusters (Bathelt and Taylor 2002; Bathelt and Glückler 2003a). To the extent that we can identify the complementary firms of a regional value chain, connected through a combination of traded and untraded interdependencies, a policy programme can be developed to support and strengthen this cluster structure (Bathelt and Dewald 2008). This might involve some of the following components of the different cluster dimensions, depending on the previous regional analysis (see Table 11.1):[2]

1. *Vertical cluster dimension.* The vertical cluster dimension consists of firms that are connected as suppliers, producers, and users (Porter 1990b; Malmberg and Maskell 2002). Along this dimension, the focus of a cluster policy is on supporting regional networks in production or research, which allow agents to benefit from interactive learning and regional synergies. Such collaboration can be triggered by various mechanisms, including financial aid for joint development projects, and the formation of cross-corporate teams for problem-solving. In the long term, ongoing information exchange and dialogue between the regional firms become critical. Thus, policymakers might focus on establishing a detailed supplier database to be used by regional firms. They might also create incentives to deepen the social division of labour within the region. To accomplish this, one might establish a platform that systematically lists offers of and requests for specific economic services in the region, and connects supply and demand. A cluster policy would also identify gaps in the regional value chain, mediate discussions, and develop a policy to close these gaps.

Table 11.1. Aspects of relational multidimensional cluster policies

Cluster dimension/level	Selection of tasks/measures to be implemented	Important aspects to be considered/included
Vertical dimension Identification of regional potentials through vertical cooperation	Quantitative and qualitative analysis of industry, supplier, value-chain structures Ongoing updates of cluster inventory Continuous contact with/consulting through regional organizations, such as industry associations Interviews, meetings of entrepreneurs, presentations in work groups	Analyses should be conducted on an ongoing basis Realistic evaluations of local potentials should be carried out, instead of setting unreasonable goals Expectations regarding agglomeration/growth should not be too high
Horizontal dimension Identification of occasions/ topics for information exchange between competing firms	Identification of topics of mutual interest, such as funding, labour market shortages, educational programmes, environmental protection, and land use planning, etc.Organization of joint regional educational fairs, student/talent competitions, evaluations of regional industries/services/research facilities 'Entrepreneurial breakfasts', evening events with discussion opportunities	Cooperation should be treated as a sensitive topic that needs to be approached in a piecemeal fashion
Institutional dimension Analysis of the formal and informal institutional environment in the region	Evaluation of institutions/organizations and their local linkages, and emphasis of regional strengths Identification of regional weaknesses/ problems, such as insufficient communication and a lack of embedded research capabilities Establishment of platforms for ongoing interaction/exchange to support the generation of shared values/views	Avoiding an overestimation of regional interaction potentials Scheduling regular evaluations/ adaptations of institutional conditions, such as support policies and training programmes Focus on reduction of lock-in risks
Power dimension/relations Consideration of existing firm hierarchies and adjustment of political goals to the firms' needs	Creation of transparency in regional decision-making Respecting/mobilizing local 'power reservoirs' by enrolling agents in joint action Reliance on mediators that are independent from party/lobby interests Support of the development of regional coherence/identity	Avoiding to communicate cluster policy as a hegemonial project; emphasis of individual competencies within broader collective synergies Employing transparency in the creation of regional identity/trust
External dimension Recognition of the importance of external linkages	Integration of small-/medium-sized firms into cross-regional/international processes, such as support of joint trade fair exhibits Consideration of linkages of cluster firms in neighbouring regions/ employing openness to enrol external agents Assisting in the preparation/ implementation of globalization strategies	Avoiding 'hollowing-out' of cluster structures

Source: Adapted from Bathelt and Dewald (2008: 84).

The goal of such activities would be to extend vertical cooperation and knowledge transfers without employing a top-down policy approach.

2. *Horizontal cluster dimension.* This dimension consists of firms that produce similar products and are, at least in part, competing against one another (Porter 1990*b*; Maskell and Lorenzen 2004). These firms have few incentives to form close regional transaction networks or engage in regular knowledge exchange. They benefit, however, from increased competition and knowledge about one another and about the latest developments in their related specialty areas. Along this dimension, the focus of a cluster policy is to initiate some collaborative research in areas that are of mutual interest for these firms, without building too closely upon individual technological competences that could get lost through collaboration. Such a policy may involve joint activities in identifying international market and technology developments, or collaboration in basic research. Incentives might include funds that require the development of partnerships with other regional firms, universities, and public research institutes. If the horizontal dimension is not well developed, a regional cluster policy could actively advertise the location to attract new investors from outside or help stimulate new firm formation in related areas (see also Frenken et al. 2007). As part of this initiative, spin-off processes from local universities could be sponsored to increase regional knowledge spillovers and enable processes of renewal and modernization in existing industries (Bathelt et al. 2008). It is, however, unlikely that such initiatives would automatically generate horizontal cooperation. A piecemeal policy approach that focuses on generic topics to create a consciousness for joint interests, support the development of trust, and initiate the exchange of experiences might thus be required. Topics could include aspects of the local labour market, education and training institutions, professional services, as well as environmental protection. The improvement of regional skill levels, which benefit from a strong horizontal dimension, is an area in which firms might find it especially valuable to collaborate (for instance by developing new vocational training programmes). A suitable forum for such collaborative initiatives could be provided by regional industry associations or local chambers of commerce, which have close linkages to municipal and regional economic development offices.

3. *Power relations.* The above-mentioned initiatives also depend on the region's structure of power relations and on the institutional cluster dimension. In terms of power relations, the ability of regional firms to coherently respond to changes in markets and technologies, and engage other agents in collective responses, is of particular importance. A regional cluster may be successful if firms share similar expectations regarding future developments and react in a consistent way to external challenges. In this respect, it

is also important to recruit other regional firms to joint initiatives, instead of making atomistic decisions that drive the cluster context apart. Firms must be able to mobilize power within the cluster (e.g. Allen 2004), and find other agents that are willing to follow their lead in the development of joint strategies, or in the sharing of information about future plans. Such power relations would encourage the external recognition of clusters, and potentially enhance the region's attractiveness to new firms and specialized workers from outside. To accomplish this requires regular personal meetings and interactions of regional decision-makers (Raines 2000; Enright 2003). Support policies could include the involvement of prominent local personalities in the process of creating a shared identity, and joint engagement in charities, festivities, and recreational activities that serve to test initial interaction. It is also important to inform agents about the potentially destabilizing forces operating in the local economy and call for a permanent effort, on all sides, to ensure the cluster's stability for a certain time period (Taylor 2000*b*; Bathelt and Taylor 2002).

4. *Institutional cluster dimension.* This dimension defines the conditions under which interaction takes place between regional firms. As such, it has an important impact on the cluster's reproductivity. Local cluster firms benefit, for instance, from established education and training programmes, support for firm formation processes, and policies that encourage technological innovation and attract cluster-specific service and research facilities. Not only do such policies help to improve the competitiveness of cluster firms, they also provide a basis upon which local agents develop a common understanding, speak the 'same language', and share coherent views and visions. This, in turn, creates conditions that are conducive to economic interaction, joint problem-solving, a continuous exchange of experiences, and ongoing discussions about technology and market trends. From a policy standpoint, the institutional dimension relates to interaction that is based on both formal and informal structures. Whereas formal structures are often directly affected by new policies, such as in the establishment of incubator facilities for start-up firms, informal structures, like coherent technological visions, are only indirectly affected, such as in the emergence of routines that enable ongoing updates about training practices. A dense network of cluster-related institutions, or 'institutional thickness' (Amin and Thrift 1995), can provide the preconditions for 'local buzz' (Chapter 7), which, in turn, creates constant flows of information, supports ongoing learning processes and the renewal of technological competences, assists in the discovery of opportunities for innovation, and eases decision-making processes (Bathelt et al. 2004; Storper and Venables 2004).

5. *External cluster dimension.* The external cluster dimension, related to the technology and market environment outside the cluster region (Bathelt and Jentsch 2002; Wolfe and Gertler 2004), has traditionally received little attention in cluster studies. This dimension is important because local production linkages are not like self-sufficient systems. Regional institutional conditions also heavily depend on supra-regional policies (Bathelt 2003). The external dimension, which is, in itself, characterized by structures of horizontal, vertical, institutional, cultural, and power relations, is decisive in reducing the danger of negative lock-in processes. These can occur in closed clusters if firms collectively rely on inefficient technological structures that are not competitive at a national and international level. Furthermore, the regional market is usually too small as a basis for substantial growth processes. Cluster policies must, therefore, initiate the formation of international networks, provide access to foreign markets, and contact centres of technological innovation in other parts of the world, rather than simply concentrate on regional linkages and competencies. This can be supported in a number of ways, such as helping small- and medium-sized firms make contact with international customers, or providing advice in the internationalization process. A local coalition between government, financial organizations, and experienced consulting firms could, for instance, be established to support firms in finding appropriate international partners and access to outside markets. Efforts can also be made to enrol globally successful cluster firms as lead or anchor organizations in this process, assigning them as role models. A detailed understanding of the capabilities and needs of regional firms as well as systematic knowledge about cluster-related technology and market trends are important preconditions for such a policy. This could be provided through the combined efforts of industry associations, chambers of commerce, and local governments. It is also important to support firms to actively participate in leading international trade fairs through, for instance, joint exhibits (Chapter 9). This can be achieved by offering training on the importance of trade fairs in acquiring outside partners, gaining market access, and creating new knowledge (Bathelt and Schuldt 2008a).

Our purpose in developing a comprehensive relational cluster programme is not to suggest that clusters may be characterized as a one-size-fits-all policy instrument; nor is it to design a general policy that can be easily transferred to other regions like a recipe for success. Our objective is to demonstrate the need for a policy programme that responds to the contextual specificities of the respective firms. While such an agenda aims to modify or renew structures of socio-economic relations and practices at the regional level, it is not limited to this scale. Such a policy programme involves multiple dimensions of economic organization in space, their embeddedness in regional institutional structures and industry traditions, and the necessity to engage in systematic trans-local or global production, market, and technology linkages. Chapter 12 develops this perspective further by discussing potential future challenges to the geographies of knowledge creation, and their policy implications.

12 Outlook: Frontiers of Relational Thinking

12.1 Foundations of a Relational Perspective

In this book, we have aimed to develop a comprehensive and consistent relational perspective of the knowledge economy and its different geographies. Within the social sciences – and in economic geography in particular – the term 'relational' has been used quite widely, and sometimes only loosely, in different contexts over the last decade. It is now applied in so many intellectual projects that in concluding this book, it is helpful to consolidate the fundamental assumptions and elements of the 'relational approach' developed here and compare this with other approaches. Our conceptualization contributes to the debates about relational thinking that have gained so much momentum in recent years. This chapter summarizes the particular utility of this perspective in analysing the global knowledge economy and its different geographies. It also discusses the future conceptual and empirical challenges facing a relational perspective.

We view economic processes as 'relational' because economic action is social action. Individual preferences, norms, values, ethics, tastes, styles, needs, and objectives emerge from and are co-constituted through the social embedding of economic action and interaction. Economic actors are not isolated beings who carry out atomistic behavioural scripts. They are embedded in a social environment that constitutes meaning through interaction and institutions (Granovetter 1985). Therefore, economic action is social and not atomistic. It is relational because meaning, ambition, value, and fundamentally all social categories emerge from processes of social relations. Using this as a starting point in Chapter 2, we conceptualize three implications of a relational understanding of economic action: contextuality, path-dependence, and contingency. Since individual preferences, objectives, and strategies are shaped by experiences and relations with other agents, as well as material structures, economic action becomes contextual. It does not necessarily follow perceived universal social or spatial laws. Instead, economic processes require a contextual and situated understanding before conclusions regarding possible regularities can be drawn. From a dynamic perspective, contextuality leads to path-dependent developments because past economic actions and interactions both enable and constrain current actions. At the same time, since no social action is fully determined a priori, economic processes are contingent with respect to unforeseen changes or discretionary social action. As such, agents may break out of existing or expected development paths. Economic action in open systems thus cannot be predicted through universal spatial laws. A contextual, path-dependent, and contingent perspective of economic action and interaction is quite different from research programmes that view the economy in terms of universal laws, linear developments, and closed systems. The relational approach focuses on the actions and relations of individual and collective actors in evolving contexts of contingent economic exchanges. A relational framework views economic action as being embedded in structures of ongoing social relations, yet also related to the relevant institutional structures and material realities. This perspective pays particular attention to economic action as a social process, the structure of relations between agents, and the recursive reproduction of formal and informal institutions.

12.2 **The Relational Character of the Knowledge Economy**

Since the 1980s, the global economy has undergone fundamental changes that have been discussed and theorized in different ways in the context of the reflexive (Storper 1997c), associational (Cooke and Morgan 1998), or learning (Lundvall and Johnson 1994; Hodgson 1999) economy. All of these conceptions put human resources and collective social interplay at the centre of the analysis and view knowledge as the key driver of the economy. This work also views innovation increasingly as a collective process, in which economic agents move back and forth between competitive and collaborative configurations of knowledge development and exchange. In this context, interactive learning and learning by imitation have become opposing, yet complimentary strategies to connect, break up, and reconnect with other agents in the process of generating new knowledge. Due to the growing importance of knowledge generation and learning, innovation and productivity measures can vary widely across corporate organizations and between spatially distributed locations within the same organization – a situation that is sometimes referred to as the best-practice puzzle (Szulanski 2003).

Related to these insights, we develop a conceptualization of knowledge as a relational resource (Chapter 4). Accordingly, resources are relational to the extent that they are produced through collective efforts, and constituted within situated contexts and pre-existing uses. We demonstrate in the book that knowledge is highly specific, shaped by socio-institutional relations, and that these relationships may establish economic resources on their own – through their functioning as social capital. As a consequence, knowledge that is applied to a specific context becomes unique and can form the basis of competitive advantage. In turn, such knowledge may be almost worthless in other contexts and other locations. Further, situated knowledge is difficult to imitate or relocate to other places where its value is uncertain. To conceive economic knowledge as 'relational' leads to a more complex and appropriate understanding of the production, distribution, and use of knowledge.

There are multiple challenges illustrating the relational character of knowledge: (*a*) Knowledge is difficult to *produce* in isolation. Since knowledge is 'not given to anyone in its totality' (Hayek 1945), its generation usually depends on a collective effort requiring that different sources of knowledge and agents be brought together. (*b*) Knowledge is difficult to *protect* because the marginal costs of production are – at least for many forms of codifiable knowledge – close to zero. It may thus spill over in a specific context (e.g. high-density proximate interaction in an urban setting). (*c*) Paradoxically, some forms of knowledge are, at the same time, difficult to *copy* because they result from cognitive interpretations that depend on experience, skills, and information among many other contextual factors. (*d*) Knowledge is difficult to *move* because it is difficult to reproduce identical cognitive interpretations. Although codified knowledge can be transferred relatively easily, the comprehension of such knowledge requires additional knowledge, such as scientific knowledge and experience, which are not necessarily available in codified form. As such, it always consists of tacit and explicit elements. (*e*) Knowledge is difficult to *reuse* in other contexts because the underlying understanding may prove to be inappropriate. (*f*) Finally, knowledge is difficult to *store* because it is embodied in agents and thus cannot easily be detached from them.

We demonstrate the ways in which these relational resources are important for economic innovation, competitiveness, and growth, and describe their geographical expressions. Because of its characteristics, knowledge is a resource that cannot easily be reproduced or relocated. Nor can it be properly modelled in traditional economic growth theory. Whereas physical resources are often subject to depletion, knowledge is a resource that accumulates rather than exhausts. Romer (1994) was the first to systematically endogenize the cumulative effects of knowledge in a model of recursive open-ended economic growth. Based on conceptualizations in economics, sociology, and the geography of knowledge, we develop this further towards a relational approach that emphasizes the need to integrate the economic and social sphere, rather than viewing them as separate worlds. We view economic action as social action and focus on the relational characteristics of economic exchanges. This has been emphasized in various empirical case studies in different chapters. In contrast to this, however, other work exists in economic geography, economics, and political economy that does not apply such an integrated analysis. Even more so than during the 1990s, it appears that studies either propagate strict economic rigour, supported by quantitative methodology while underestimating the importance of social processes, or they use broader social and cultural theories with qualitative interpretative methods while ignoring economic rationales. In our view, it will be a major challenge to reintegrate these perspectives at a broad level to become part of a more holistic trans-disciplinary conceptualization of economic processes and their spatiality. After all, regional economic policies are bound to fail if they are based on partial explanations of the economic reality. In the future, therefore, the contextual character of economic processes needs to be more strongly emphasized.

12.3 The Relational Character of Geographies of Knowledge Circulation

A central part of our agenda has been to systematically sketch out different geographies of the knowledge economy, in both conceptual and empirical terms. In Chapter 2, we elaborate a concept of space as a perspective, rather than as a primary object of knowledge. Instead of seeking geometric or spatial laws of the economy, we adopt a spatial perspective as a way of looking at economic processes and structures, and as a lens that leads us to ask specific questions about localized phenomena. Conceptualizing space as a perspective is useful in unravelling the emerging geographies of the global knowledge economy. Knowledge emerges differently in different places, and knowledge generation involves individual and collective actors from different places in diverse patterns of temporary or more permanent interactions. As a consequence, knowledge flows and practices are distributed unevenly in space. Within the context of an existing industry agglomeration, agents watch each other's actions and do not even have to be in close contact with one another or engage in direct transactions to learn from each other. We discuss the relationship patterns of geographical and organized proximity to explore the range of social contexts in which knowledge is produced, shared, and used. Knowledge processes occur both locally through spillovers or interactive learning, and globally through organized exchange or global buzz in temporary clusters.

Parts II and III of this book provide in-depth analyses of numerous different geographies of the knowledge economy. The analyses move beyond traditional location studies in developing knowledge-based explanations for different spatial configurations: regional industry and service clusters, international relocations, global intra-firm networks, as well as inter-firm knowledge exchange in virtual contexts or temporary physical gatherings. As part of this, we demonstrate how technological know-how localizes and spreads through localized spillovers and buzz (Chapter 5). In Chapter 6, we discuss the geography of know-who and show that urban service clusters result from search processes for non-local business opportunities. Firms cluster locally not because they benefit from traded interdependencies but because they aim to draw from reputational spillovers that create business opportunities in other world regions. In these cases, new knowledge is often acquired through organized proximity over distance, while absorptive capacity is best developed in local clusters where firms appropriate and use this knowledge (Chapter 7). Social relations of trust and referrals become key mechanisms in bridging distances, either to establish permanent co-presence and physical locations in other regions of the world (Chapter 8) or to exchange expertise between these distant and sometimes remote places (Chapter 10). However, these structures of social relations also require places of immediate personal exchange and temporary clusters – be it in physical form, such as trade fairs, or virtually through electronic forums and user communities (Chapter 9). Physical space is no longer a morphological mirror of the economy where local clusters reflect unity and integration while spatial separation would be associated with division. The empirical cases illustrate that firms may be locked out of knowledge processes despite being co-located. In turn, firms may be tightly connected despite their distant locations. They may cluster in one place without any tangible contact or be scattered across the globe while collaborating closely thanks to recurrent temporary get-togethers. All these new geographies emerge from practices associated with the relational production, distribution, and use of knowledge in the globalizing economy.

12.4 **Frontiers and Challenges of Relational Thinking**

The 1990s and 2000s have experienced a rapid growth of inter-organizational relationships in the knowledge economy: Vertical disintegration of corporate production, flexible specialization in local production systems, loose couplings, strategic alliances, research and development collaborations, venture capital syndicates, temporary project coalitions in cultural industries, and many other collaborative arrangements exemplify the diverse empirical expressions of an economy that is social in nature. Related to this, research on inter-organizational relations emphasizes the importance of networks as a methodology to analyse global interactions (Dicken et al. 2001). Often, the term 'relational' simply points to the importance of inter-firm relations and stresses the need to study such relations in empirical research. Our conceptualization of relational thinking, however, is not limited to an empirical analysis of inter-firm or intra-firm relations. Instead, the relational approach presented in this book provides a broader bottom-up conceptualization of economic action as social action. It views the construction of institutions, values, and meanings as fundamentally anti-categorical.

When we adopted this notion of relationality and developed this relational conceptualization in the late 1990s, we drew from theoretical achievements in new economic sociology, institutional economics, evolutionary theory, and diverse streams of research in economic geography, especially the California School. All of these intellectual fields now appear to converge on the idea that individual economic action is constituted in concrete contexts of meaningful interaction, and that this relationality of action plays an increasingly important role in the knowledge economy in the form of relational capital (Capello and Faggian 2005), social capital (Coleman 1988; Putnam 1995; Burt 1997), or relational assets (Storper 1997*b*). The 1990s and 2000s have witnessed a terminological convergence towards 'relational thinking' (Fourcade 2007) in the social sciences in different streams of theories such as network analysis (e.g. White 2008), actor network theory (e.g. Latour 2005), and field theory (e.g. Bourdieu 2005). Although Emirbayer (1997) proposed a well-developed perspective for a relational sociology – with deep roots in philosophy and social theory – in an early 'manifesto', his plea has been echoed more actively in recent years (Fuhse and Mützel 2010; Pachucki and Breiger 2010; Mische 2011). A shared belief in these approaches is the 'anti-categorical imperative' (Emirbayer and Goodwin 1994) against substantialist thinking of social phenomena, such as power, social capital, or knowledge (Chapter 4). One of the major challenges in current relational social theory focuses on the theoretical relation of culture and connectivity (Pachucki and Breiger 2010). This debate is an effort to overcome deficiencies in prior approaches, and integrate structural sociology, which is interested in relationship patterns of social networks, with cultural theories that focus on the construction of meaning in these relations (Mische 2011). Relational thinking has become an overarching perspective in social theory that shifts the analytical focus from attributes and categories to context, process, and emergence.

In this book, we wish to contribute to this trend towards relational perspectives by disentangling the geographies of the knowledge economy in conceptual and empirical ways. Studies in the social sciences often focus on either a local/regional or a global perspective of economic processes. Although it has become increasingly clear that local and global developments are not separated (or not even separable), academic work has only begun to employ wider perspectives and integrate reflexive linkages between different spatial scales. One finding of this book is that local and global economic processes are intimately interwoven, especially through diverse processes of knowledge circulation. The local is part of the global and is influenced by the global, yet the global is driven by the local. As such, it cannot be viewed as some given external constraint. Problems of cohesion in the European Union are, for instance, related to economic and social policies that are separated and national in character. Policy configurations and programmes in the future will have to develop new forms of multi-tiered arrangements that link different spatial scales, instead of establishing fierce competition between territorial policy settings.

In the medium-term development of the knowledge economy and its geographies, we do not foresee a general substitution of global production and innovation linkages by local ties or the rise of a new era of localism. Under circumstances that do not favour global relationships, it might still be an important competitive advantage to maintain trans-local knowledge pipelines with agents in other parts of the world to continuously introduce innovations in domestic markets. This will require efficient interaction and communication patterns over distance without permanent or frequent face-to-face contact and with fewer material linkages. To maintain such interaction, it will be necessary to establish and develop personal relationships in different ways, drawing on new geographies of knowledge circulation – such as temporary face-to-face interaction through business travel and participation in international flagship fairs, virtual interaction through the use of Internet platforms, and interaction in knowing communities and pre-existing personal networks. To support this may require new economic policies and the provision of new public infrastructure.

In the future, global geographies of production and knowledge creation will be challenged by a number of important issues and trends. Global climate change and pollution problems will require new environmental protection strategies and pollution restrictions that have a strong impact on the nature of production and the flows of goods and people around the globe. In addition, anticipated shortages of raw materials and the effects of 'peak oil' will have a substantial impact on production, transportation, and transaction costs. Mobility costs will increase substantially and challenge current patterns of global transactions and exchanges. This might give rise to new social and spatial divisions of labour. While we assume that this will not weaken existing clusters per se, it might shape and redirect material linkages. The role of transportation costs in economic decision-making will likely increase (again), and input–output relations within regional or national systems will become interesting alternatives to long-distance relationships. Although it might be premature to speculate about decreases in global material linkages, this will have a distinct effect on existing economic geographies and stimulate the development of new ones. As such, it will change socio-economic relations, practices, and motivations – and open up important new avenues for future research.

To provide a better foundation for the formulation of economic policies at different spatial scales, economic analyses must improve our understanding of the foundations of economic decisions and practices. This requires investigating the very nature of socio-economic actions and interactions, instead of simply relying on macro-interpretations of structural regularities. As part of this, we need to develop a better understanding of how shifts in production and consumption are linked with global financial markets, pension funds, and real-estate markets. There is still relatively little work that systematically explores these interfaces, providing an integrated view of the material and immaterial economy. To understand global ruptures, such as the Asian financial crises in the late 1990s or the global financial crisis a decade later, and develop appropriate policy responses to overcome or even prevent them, it is necessary to develop perspectives that extend beyond the local scale. This will pose new empirical challenges.

As a consequence of changing global divisions of labour and systems of production, knowledge will become even more important in gaining and maintaining competitiveness. Knowledge might become the key object of trans-local linkages, and knowledge circulation the motor of global dynamics. Trans-local relationships on a global scale will increasingly be based on flows of information and knowledge, rather than transactions of products and technologies. Knowledge flows will connect decentralized production centres, potentially giving rise to global networks that are based on distributed rather than centralized competencies and control. Through this, personal relationships and processes of relationship-building will become a focus in international business organization. Economic policies that aim to support competitiveness at smaller spatial scales will have to shift their focus to support wide-ranging knowledge exchanges and ongoing circulation. A relational understanding of economic action and interaction and a geographical perspective of economic processes as outlined in this book may help in tackling these challenges and open alternative perspectives of the current knowledge economy.

■ NOTES

Chapter 1

1. In his speech at the Meeting of the Association of American Geographers in 2010, Krugman (2010) admitted that his original modelling of geographic space was imperfect and incomplete, yet that it opened up new research perspectives within the discipline of economics. He admitted that he would understand that geographers prefer the term 'geographical economics' over 'new economic geography', yet that the notion 'new economic geography' was the term used to refer to his work in economics.

2. Alternatively, Boschma and Frenken (2005) have suggested a turn towards evolutionary economic geography.

3. Barnes (2001) describes this as a shift from a narrow quantitative approach towards a reflexive and interpretative understanding in economic geography.

4. Others, such as Nancy Ettlinger, have gone similar routes in a different context (e.g. Ettlinger 2003, 2004).

5. In the case of Spanish economic geography, Sánchez Hernández (2003) has developed a re-conceptualization in a similarly unsatisfactory academic context, referred to as the structural–contextual project, which draws upon similar ideas and propositions. See also the interesting approach of Celata (2009) in the Italian context.

6. This is also supported by the views of other economic, social, cultural, and political geographers in Germany (Werlen 1995, 2003; Schamp 2000a; Reuber 2002; Berndt 2003).

7. This development has largely been dominated by a Euro-Anglo-American-centric perspective. References to African contexts or Asian views have been relatively rare (Lee 2001; Murphy 2003; Yeung and Lin 2003).

8. Other related approaches include conceptualizations of cultural economies (Lee and Wills 1997; Berndt and Boeckler 2009). In an approach that complements the relational approach, Berndt and Boeckler (2009), for instance, argue for the need to develop new cultural geographies of the economy by emphasizing the cultural construction of economic realities and practices using actor–network approaches. This conceptualization builds upon the work of Callon (2007) to understand why markets are performative, or socially constructed entities (Lee 2006).

9. While we build on the metaphor of local versus global relationships throughout the book, our research does not suggest a simple dualism. In fact, our empirical work emphasizes the multi-scalar nature of economic processes involving local, regional, national, and international structures, as well as the processes between all of these levels.

Chapter 2

1. This shift in causality between space and human action has also been emphasized in human geography (Werlen 1993, 1995, 2000).

2. One could argue that the economy, like space, is also a social construct and yet we have economic theories. Why then should there not also be spatial theories? The key to this question lies within the very nature of relational action. There are economic agents that develop strategies and act according to economic and non-economic goals. Their action and interaction have intended and unintended spatial outcomes. There are, however, no spatial agents that act according to spatial goals. Intentions for actions derive from the actors, not from spatial representations.

3. Maskell (2001*a*) criticizes traditional economic geography for often treating firms like a 'black box'. To overcome this, he suggests the use of a resource-based or competence-based view of the firm (Wernerfelt 1984; Prahalad and Hamel 1990). Nonaka et al. (2000) explicitly include the particular role of knowledge and develop this further into a knowledge-creation view of the firm. These views correspond nicely with a relational perspective of economic action.

4. Even further, such approaches need to consider aspects of cultural context and difference to explain different production patterns more carefully (e.g. Saxenian 1994; Schoenberger 1997; Thrift 2000*b*).

5. Particularly during the 1980s and early 1990s when 'new' regional configurations of industrial districts and industrial spaces were discovered and discussed, this encouraged researchers and policymakers, at least implicitly, to seek for general models of regional development. In a way, this was like searching for universal forms and general laws of spatial economic development and, thus, created similar problems to those of some earlier regional science work.

6. Interestingly, recent studies by Crevoisier (2001, 2004) and Hayter (2004) share remarkable parallels with this conceptualization.

7. This relational perspective suggests that the research questions asked are themselves contextual, depending on the context of a particular disciplinary focus. In this book, the organization of production and geography of the firm (Dicken 1990) serve as examples to demonstrate the consequences of a relational approach. This also means that a modified pattern of dimensions could result from a different disciplinary focus. Different contexts might, for instance, be derived from feminist, labour market, or political-economy literatures (e.g. Harvey 1982, 1996; Peck 1996; McDowell 2000).

8. The inclusion of this dimension does not, of course, imply that we prioritize time over space. Even though both are treated in a similar way, the spatial perspective serves as a key concept for our analysis of economic action to relate all four dimensions to one another. Despite its importance, the evolutionary dimension has often been neglected in neoclassical economics and regional science (see, however, Myrdal 1957; Hirschman 1958; Kaldor 1970).

Chapter 3

1. In fact, rigid interpretations of the theory of social systems and actor–network theory do not need to conceptualize individual agents and institutions, because they completely focus on the linkages and communication between them.

2. The argument here is that it is important to include both the individual motivations of economic agents *and* the socio-institutional contexts of their actor–networks, instead of primarily focusing on the latter relationships as suggested, for instance, by Yeung (2005).

3. Gertler (2004) provides a rich set of empirical illustrations of how institutions provide the basis for and how they shape economic interaction, albeit that this primarily builds upon a view of institutions as rules (Gertler 2010).

4. See also Jessop's structural–relational approach (2001).

5. We do not intend to review the critical debates about different research designs in detail. For an elaborate discussion and comparative analysis of qualitative and quantitative methodologies, see Sayer (1992, 2000).

6. For a review of the effects of social network structure on economic outcomes, see, for instance, Granovetter (2005).

7. There is no space here to introduce social network analysis in detail. There are several comprehensive introductions and reviews of this methodology and its applications in the social sciences (e.g. Marsden and Lin 1982; Wasserman and Faust 1994; J. Scott 2000; Knoke 2001; Kilduff and Tsai 2003; Jansen 2006).

Chapter 4

1. Scholars such as Asheim and Gertler (2005) have criticized this binary view of knowledge and propose a different classification of analytic, synthetic, and symbolic categories of knowledge. In our argument, however, we are more interested in knowledge practices than in knowledge categories.

2. These different sorts of knowledge lead our investigation in Parts II and III of this book. While Chapter 5, for instance, focuses on the know-how character of knowledge, Chapters 6 and 10 address the know-who aspect of it.

3. This draws on the work of Arrow (1962) who developed a similar argument with respect to market transactions of information.

4. Based on these considerations, Cowling and Sugden (1998) suggest a different relational understanding of firms that goes beyond an ownership-based classification. In defining a firm according to its existing network of power relations, they emphasize the nexus of strategic decision-making structures originating from the centre of the firm. As a consequence, long-term supplier contracts are viewed as internal instead of inter-firm transactions. Although this understanding of firms is attractive, problems regarding its operationalization have discouraged us from applying it here. Due to the high fluidity of power relations, this definition could hardly form a stable basis for an empirical study of firms.

5. This example demonstrates how different types of resources support one another. In this case, the inclusion of resources serves to stabilize social relations and strengthen power relations, which, in turn, affect the exploitation of the other resource types.

6. Spencer (2010) argues that challenges of extending control over larger distances in traditional societies required the mobilization of resources and the delegation of power. Drawing on an historical analysis of six regional cultures, he showed that the expansion of territories over more than a day's round-trip from the capital went along with the introduction of institutions that led to the establishment of primary state functions.

Chapter 5

1. The related-variety approach (Boschma and Frenken 2010) provides a quantitative methodology to measure complex cluster linkages that extend beyond a single industry branch, encompassing value-chain-based relationships similar to those described here (see also Porter 2003).

Chapter 6

1. The compound annual growth rate (CAGR) indicates the annual rate of change for an absolute growth difference over a period of several years. It is calculated as a geometric mean: $\text{CAGR}_x = (x_{t1}/x_{t0})^{1/t} - 1$, where x denotes the variable of interest, t_0 denotes the beginning value, t_1 the ending value of x, and T signifies the time passed in years. Since only 63.4 per cent of the firms were founded before 1997, absolute growth comparisons along these six years could not be made for the entire sample. However, the CAGR measurement technique permits relative comparisons between firms with different (but overlapping) time periods. Consequently, it is assumed to be acceptable to compare average annual growth rates with those firms that were established even after 1997. The time period between 1997 and 2002 is particularly suitable for the study, because the growth boom in German management consulting accelerated in the mid-1990s until a sudden economic downturn occurred in 2002. This period was characterized by continuous and relatively stable growth conditions for management consulting, in which most firms either increased their headcount or were newly founded. Earlier research on multinational consulting firms showed that employment is also a good proxy for revenues. Both measures were highly correlated with $r = 0.90$ ($p < 0.01$), and even their growth rates were correlated with $r = 0.60$ ($p < 0.01$) (Glückler 2004a). For this research, it was impossible to acquire financial performance data since most firms are organized as partnerships with no obligation to publish financial results.

2. Firms were asked to provide anonymous but individual information about their clients. These data were collected through a network questionnaire, which contained two elements: First, in a name generator, consulting firms were invited to list all their clients up to a maximum of ten. Second, in a name interpreter, consultants were asked to qualify each individual relationship along a number of criteria. Overall, 186 consulting firms provided detailed information on 982 individual client relationships where each company provided information about 5.28 clients on average.

3. With respect to methodological rigour and validity of the relational data, two potential sources of distortion need to be addressed. First, there is a problem of incomplete recalling of client relations. Interviewees usually do not remember all contacts that are relevant for a certain issue (Marsden 2003). In this context, however, the problem is of limited relevance as it is unlikely that a consultant would forget his most important clients. Moreover, the data collection was assessed in relation to a measure of revenue coverage. Revenue coverage is the cumulated percentage of revenues that each client contributes to the overall annual revenues of a consulting firm. In two-thirds of the cases, the set of clients accounted for at least 80 per cent of the revenues, and in over 40 per cent of the cases, all clients were listed, that is, they accounted for 100 per cent of the revenues. The data are, thus, relatively exhaustive. Second, there is a problem of information adequacy. Do respondents always learn about recommendations whenever they enter a new client relationship? Consultants were asked to indicate whether a client was acquired through referral, and whether this client, in turn, referred new clients to the company. Qualitative interviews suggest that successful recommendations always become overt to the consultant, as one interviewee explained: 'When somebody contacts us, we do, of course, ask him how he came to approach us. "Well, this person has recommended me to turn to you". Then we know it.' This is owed to the motivations of all three parties to disclose the recommendation: (*a*) the recommender is an existing client who invests in the relationship with the consultant by making an additional commitment; (*b*) the consultant, in turn, owes gratitude and reciprocation of commitment, thus reinforcing the position of the existing client; and (*c*) the recommended new client is also motivated to

disclose the referral in order to ensure a higher commitment by the consultant. If the consultant would fail to commit enough effort into the new client project, the firm would know that this would also be known by the existing client, and would damage its credibility. The consultant's reputation would erode due to the sanctions of both clients. Hence, following the incentive argument and the evidence from interviews, client referrals will always be reported to the consultant.

4. Test statistics: $N = 975$; $t = 2.252$; $p < 0.05$.

5. Test statistics: $N = 966$; $t = 1.999$; $p < 0.05$.

Chapter 7

1. Clearly, the categories 'local' and 'global' must be understood as metaphors that point towards a more complex reality of different nested scales, including the local, regional, national, and international scales (Bunnell and Coe 2001), as well as the linkages between these levels.

2. Local communication also involves contract-based cooperation or formalized networks, and firms look for partners within their environment to establish close 'pipelines' (Figure 7.1). At the same time, local buzz can easily extend beyond regional boundaries (Bathelt 2004, 2007) and expand through relational ties (Chapters 9 and 10). The point to emphasize here is twofold: On the one hand, we can observe that trade relationships and networks inside industrial agglomerations are often less prominent than expected. On the other hand, it is particularly the less planned, dense, automatic nature of internal knowledge flows that may distinguish many local from trans-local linkages.

3. From a relational perspective, the degree of local buzz and trans-local pipelines is contingent upon the context within which the firms operate. Especially in industries that are formed around epistemic communities (such as nanotechnology and biotechnology), local buzz may play a limited role or be replaced by buzz-like linkages through relational ties that span across distance (see Powell et al. 2002; Giuliani 2007; Moodysson 2008). Similar tendencies might prevail in some knowledge-intensive services. Furthermore, it is likely that industry agglomerations, such as software, which are linked to different value chains, would experience little local buzz (Trippl et al. 2009).

4. Using the case of diamond manufacturing and trade, Henn (2010) shows how such differences and related uncertainties can be minimized through strong family and community structures around the Indian Palanpuris and the Jewish communities.

5. The identification of non-local pipeline partners, which are located in different countries with specific institutional, cultural, and political circumstances, can be complicated and follow different patterns and logics. These may include reputational effects, leads through existing pipeline partners, former experience in different types of interaction, or initial communication during international trade fairs, and subsequent stepwise interaction (Chapter 9). Of course, there is no reason to assume that pipelines could not also be created with local partners as well (Figure 7.1).

6. There are many studies on industrial districts, clusters, or regional innovation systems that provide empirical evidence of the importance of buzz and/or pipelines.

7. The conception of buzz and pipelines has meanwhile been applied in different contexts, such as knowledge flows and innovation policy in Canadian city–regions (Wolfe and Gertler 2004; Gertler and Wolfe 2006), the role of universities in supporting economic development in the Netherlands (Benneworth and Hospers 2007), a Japanese research park (Edgington 2008),

spatial cooperation patterns in knowledge-intensive industries in Canada (Doloreux and Mattsson 2008), the development of new global production patterns in diamond manufacturing (Henn 2010), the spatiality of patent citations in Canada (Kogler 2010), and knowledge-creation capabilities of clusters (Arikan 2009). It has also been used in contexts that are not characterized by value-chain-based cluster structures, such as studies of biotechnology and software industries in Sweden and Austria, respectively (Moodysson 2008; Trippl et al. 2009), as well as the genesis of nanotechnology clusters in Germany (Henn 2006). Such contexts without a clear value-chain focus are not envisioned in the original formulation of the buzz-and-pipeline logic (Bathelt et al. 2004).

8. In a similar way, Moodysson (2008) shows how firms in the Swedish part of the so-called 'Medicon Valley' develop ties to members of their community in other regions and nations, and thus provide access to a similar type of buzz over distance. Jones et al. (2010) even provide evidence of the possibility of virtual buzz without face-to-face interaction (Chapter 9) that takes place through theatre blogs in New York, which are characterized by dense networks of interlinkages.

9. The challenge of such global corporate networks is, of course, to stimulate ongoing intra-firm knowledge exchange over distance – a task for which there is no routine solution (Chapter 10).

10. Some studies have taken the buzz-and-pipelines conception too far, and interpreted it as a meta-theory of industrial clustering. These studies seem to expect that local buzz and global pipelines would have the same importance across all sectors, or that local buzz would be a dominant phenomenon in clusters (e.g. Asheim et al. 2007; Moodysson 2008; Trippl et al. 2009). However, the approach does not claim the superiority of one component of knowledge circulation over another. The main argument, in fact, points to a different aspect: namely, the question of why clusters may exist despite the absence of strong material linkages.

Chapter 8

1. In fact, Johanson and Vahlne (1990) acknowledge this limitation of stage theory themselves and open their account towards network approaches to internationalization.

2. Since the relevant variables and their values (i.e. choice of market-entry form and context of market entry) result from observations which can be clearly codified, it is possible to integrate qualitative data into a quantitative analysis. Other research has adopted similar research designs and methodological operations (e.g. Gersick et al. 2000).

3. This case illustrates the value of qualitative research: Interviewees were first asked to reconstruct the business case through an organizational lens. Only when asked to contextualize the international venture, they began to reveal the deeper social context of the decision-making situation and the opportunities that drive their market-entry attempts. The analysis of socio-structural processes behind business decisions can benefit greatly from qualitative or mixed-method approaches.

4. Logistic regression is a subset of linear modelling usually employed to test the impact of a set of independent variables on a categorical dependent variable (Rese 2000). There are two basic applications of logistic regression in the social and management sciences: (a) to predict group membership as the dependent variable or (b) to measure the instantaneous rate of change in the probability of occurrence of an event with change in a given predictor (Tansey et al. 1996). This procedure has been increasingly used in economic geography (Wrigley

1985; Sternberg and Arndt 2001) and especially in the context of internationalization research (Agarwal and Ramaswami 1992; Li and Guisinger 1992; Hildebrandt and Weiss 1997). Independent variables can be scaled at the categorical, ordinal, or interval level. Despite the limited number of observations, the methodological assumptions for a logistic regression model are fulfilled in our analysis: There are more than twenty-five observations for each possible value of the dependent variable (Rese 2000: 137) and, since only two dependent variables are used, the size of the sample satisfies the conditions for the model estimations.

5. It is here where this research has limitations as it only focuses on the quality of external linkages between firms and not on international firm-specific competitive advantages.

Chapter 9

1. Of course, clusters are not permanent by definition. They can only exist as long as their internal workings can satisfy the final demand for the cluster's output in a competitive way, or as long as agents are willing to accept existing power asymmetries. For further on this, see Chapter 5.

2. It is important to note, however, that not all of the exhibitors interviewed expressed an interest in meeting customers after trade fair hours. Some were glad to have time off after a hard work day. The exhibitors that did not place much value on informal meetings with customers did not seem to recognize such meetings as an opportunity to develop stronger ties for joint future endeavours.

3. Firms can, of course, remain anonymous when they approach their competitors' exhibits in search of additional information (Maskell et al. 2004). Although the business literature suggests ways in which to deal with supposed colleagues from other firms who have not identified themselves as such (e.g. Clausen and Schreiber 2000), the extent to which such behaviour actually occurs and the significance of such behaviour remain unclear.

4. In contrast, other leading firms seem to prefer introducing innovations during their own special events in order to receive full attention by the customers and relevant media.

Chapter 10

1. MILECS is a pseudonym for a medium-sized German engineering firm dedicated to engineering, planning, and consulting services in client strategy and technology development.

2. Under conditions of imperfect network data, it has been shown that the correlation between real and observed measures of most centrality measures converges to one with increasing size of the sample. When the sample covers 70 per cent or more of the nodes of the complete network, as in this case, the correlation coefficients for almost all measures are 0.8 or higher (Costenbader and Valente 2003). Overall, network measures of centrality are relatively robust against random network disruptions and imperfect data (Borgatti et al. 2006).

3. Following a relational view of knowledge transfer, all variables included in the procedure are measured as dyadic relations between the corporate employees. The analytical approach aims to identify barriers to knowledge transfer at the level of the individual relationships. The dependent variable is represented by the set of exchange relations between all pairs of employees within the corporation. For each pair of colleagues that reported knowledge exchange, the value in the dependent variable is 1, and for each unconnected pair, the value is 0. The independent variables are based on attribute-specific dyadic relations. These

variables are obtained by converting individual attributes over a number of actors into relational information between these actors, for example, as expressions of similarity or dissimilarity between actors with respect to a particular characteristic (Borgatti and Everett 1997). The MRQAP methodology is an appropriate technique because it makes it possible to compare networks of the same members, but across different relations. It uses random matrix permutations to generate a reference distribution against which the correlation coefficients of the observed matrices are compared (for details of the procedure, cf. Krackhardt 1987; Kilduff and Krackhardt 1994; Snijders and Borgatti 1999).

4. The E-I Index is calculated as follows: E-I Index = $(EL - IL)/(EL + IL)$, where EL represents the external linkage and IL the internal linkage (Krackhardt and Stern 1988).

5. It is important to note, however, that the next generation of employees that grow up and are socialized with intensive use of the Internet and virtual social-network platforms might use document-to-people systems differently in the future than the present generation of employees.

Chapter 11

1. Since its introduction in the early 2000s, related approaches have been applied in many different contexts, including decision-making in financial markets (Strauss 2008; Clark 2009; Knox-Hayes 2009; Torrance 2009); the influence of location factors in real estate markets (Harmsen 2008); the organization of global value chains (Bormann 2008; Yeung 2009); economic transformation and social relations in Eastern Europe (Buzar 2007); and the analysis of social practices in the knowledge economy (Faulconbridge 2007; Huber 2009).

2. The proposed policy programme is intended as an example of a consistent policy framework, rather than a description of an optimal regional cluster policy.

■ REFERENCES

Agarwal, S. and Ramaswami, S. (1992), Choice of foreign entry mode: Impact of ownership, location and internationalization factors, *Journal of International Business Studies*, 23, 1–27.

Aharoni, Y. (1996), The organization of global service MNE's, *International Studies of Management and Organization*, 26 (2), 6–23.

Akerlof, G. (1970), The market for 'lemons': Quality uncertainty and the market mechanism, *Quarterly Journal of Economics*, 84, 488–500.

Akrich, M., Callon, M., Latour, B., and Monaghan, A. (2002), The key to success in innovation part I: The art of interessment, *International Journal of Innovation Management*, 6 (2), 187–206.

Allen, J. (1997), Economies of power and space, in R. Lee and J. Wills (eds.), *Geographies of Economies* (London, New York, Sydney: Arnold), 59–70.

——(2003), *Lost Geographies of Power* (Malden, MA, Oxford: Blackwell).

——(2004), The whereabouts of power: Politics, government and space, *Geografiska Annaler*, 86 B, 19–32.

——Massey, D., and Cochrane, A. (1998), *Rethinking the Region* (London, New York: Routledge).

Almeida, P. and Kogut, B. (1999), Localization of knowledge and the mobility of engineers in regional networks, *Management Science*, 45, 905–17.

Alpha Publications (1996), *The Market for Management Consultancy Services in Western Europe* (London: Alpha Publications Ltd).

Alvesson, M. and Kärreman, D. (2001), Odd couple: Making sense of the curious concept of knowledge management, *Journal of Management Studies*, 38, 995–1018.

Amin, A. (1994), *Post-Fordism* (Oxford, Cambridge, MA: Blackwell).

——(1999), An institutionalist perspective on regional economic development, *International Journal of Urban and Regional Research*, 23, 365–78.

——(2002), Moving on: Institutionalism in economic geography, *Environment and Planning A*, 33, 1237–42.

——(2004), Regions unbound: Towards a new politics of place, *Geografiska Annaler*, 86 B, 33–44.

——Cohendet, P. (1999), Learning and adaptation in decentralized business networks, *Environment and Planning A*, 17, 87–104.

————(2004), *Architectures of Knowledge: Firms, Capabilities, and Communities* (Oxford, New York: Oxford University Press).

——Thrift, N. (1992), Neo-Marshallian nodes in global networks, *International Journal of Urban and Regional Research*, 16, 571–87.

————(1995), Living in the global, in A. Amin and N. Thrift (eds.), *Globalization, Institutions, and Regional Development in Europe* (2nd edn.; Oxford, New York: Oxford University Press), 1–22.

————(2000), What kind of economic theory for what kind of economic geography, *Antipode*, 32, 4–9.

Amin, A. and Cohendet, P. (2003), *The Blackwell Cultural Economy Reader* (Oxford: Blackwell).

Antonelli, C. (2003), Knowledge complementarity and fungeability: Implications for regional strategy, *Regional Studies*, 37, 595–606.

Archer, M., Bhaskar, R., Collier, A., Lawson, T., and Norrie, A. (1998), *Critical Realism. Essential Readings* (London, New York: Routledge).

Argote, L., McEvily, B., and Reagans, R. (2003), Managing knowledge in organizations: An integrative framework and review of emerging themes, *Management Science*, 49 (4), 571–82.

Arikan, A. T. (2009), Inter-firm knowledge exchanges and the knowledge creation capabilities of clusters, *The Academy of Management Review*, 34 (4), 658–76.

Armbrüster, T. (2006), *The Economics and Sociology of Management Consulting* (Cambridge: Cambridge University Press).

——Glückler, J. (2007), Organizational change and the economics of management consulting, *Organization Studies*, 28, 1873–85.

Arrow, K. J. (1962), Economic welfare and the allocation of resources for invention, in R. Nelson (ed.), *The Rate and Direction of Inventive Activity: Economic and Social Factors* (Princeton, NJ: Princeton University Press), 609–25.

——(1974), *The Limits of Organization* (New York: W. W. Norton).

Arthur, W. B. (1988), Competing technologies: An overview, in G. Dosi, C. Freeman, R. R. Nelson, G. Silverberg, and L. Soete (eds.), *Technical Change and Economic Theory* (London, New York: Pinter Publishers), 590–607.

Asheim, B. T. (1999), Interactive learning and localised knowledge in globalising learning economies, *GeoJournal*, 49, 345–52.

——Gertler, M. S. (2005), The geography of innovation: Regional innovation systems, in J. Fagerberg, D. C. Mowery, and R. R. Nelson (eds.), *The Oxford Handbook of Innovation* (Oxford: Oxford University Press), 291–317.

——Herstad, S. J. (2003), Regional innovation systems and the globalising world economy, *SPACES, Vol. 1, 2003–12* (Marburg: Faculty of Geography, Philipps – University of Marburg).

——Isaksen, A. (2002), Regional innovation systems: The integration of local 'sticky' and global 'ubiquitous' knowledge, *Journal of Technology Transfer*, 27, 77–86.

——Coenen, L., and Vang, J. (2007), Face-to-face, buzz, and knowledge-bases: Sociospatial implications for learning, innovation, and innovation policy, *Environment and Planning C: Government and Policy*, 25, 665–70.

——Cooke, P., and Martin, R. (2006), The rise of the cluster concept in regional analysis and policy: A critical assessment, in B. T. Asheim, P. Cooke, and R. Martin (eds.), *Clusters an Regional Development: Critical Reflections and Explorations* (London, New York: Routledge), 1–29.

Atherton, A. and Johnston, A. (2008), Clusters formation from the 'bottom-up': A process perspective, in C. Karlsson (ed.), *Handbook of Research on Cluster Theory* (Cheltenham, Northampton, MA: Edward, Elgar), 93–113.

Audretsch, D. B. and Feldman, M. P. (2004), Knowledge spillovers and the geography of innovation, in V. Henderson and J.-F. Thisse (eds.), *Handbook of Urban and Regional Economics. Cities and Geography* (Vol. 4; Oxford: Elsevier Science).

Ausstellungs- und Messe-Ausschuss der Deutschen Wirtschaft (1996), *Ziele und Nutzen von Messebeteiligungen (Goals and Uses of Trade Fair Participation)*, AUMA edition no. 4 (Berlin: AUMA).

——(1999), *Messefunktions- und Potentialanalyse (Goals and Potentials of Trade and Fair Participation)*, AUMA edition no. 9 (Berlin: AUMA).

Backhaus, H. (1992), *Investitionsgütermarketing (Investment Goods Marketing)* (München: Vahlen).

——Zydorek, C. (1997), Von der Mustermesse zur ubiquitären Messe, in H. Meffert, T. Necker, and H. Sihler (eds.), *Märkte im Dialog – Die Messen der dritten Generation* (Leipzig: Leipziger Verlag).

Bahrenberg, G. (1987), Über die Unmöglichkeit von Geographie als 'Raumwissenschaft'. Gemeinsamkeiten in der Konstituierung von Geographie bei A. Hettner und D. Bartels, in G. Bahrenberg, J. Deiters, M. Fischer, W. Gaebe, G. Hard, and G. Löffler (eds.), *Geographie des Menschen. Dietrich Bartels zum Gedenken* (Bremer Beiträge zur Geographie und Raumplanung – Heft 11; Bremen), 225–39.

——(2002), Globalisierung und Regionalisierung: Die 'Enträumlichung' der Region, *Geographische Zeitschrift*, 90 (1), 52–63.

——Giese, E., and Nipper, J. (1985), *Statistische Methoden in der Geographie. Band 1: Univariate und bivariate Statistik* (2nd edn.; Stuttgart: Teubner).

Baker, W. E. and Faulkner, R. R. (2004), Social networks and loss of capital, *Social Networks*, 26, 91–111.

Baltes, B. B., Dickson, M. W., Sherman, M. P., Bauer, C. C., and LaGanke, J. S. (2002), Computer-mediated communication and group decision making: A meta analysis, *Organizational Behavior and Human Decision Process*, 87 (1), 156–79.

Barber, B. (1983), *The Logic and Limits of Trust* (New Brunswick, NJ: Rutgers University Press).

Barnes, T. J. (2001), Retheorizing economic geography: From the quantitative revolution to the 'cultural turn', *Annals of the Association of American Geographers*, 91 (3), 546–65.

——Gertler, M. S. (1999), *The New Industrial Geography: Regions, Regulation and Institutions* (London, New York: Routledge).

Bartels, D. (1988), Wirtschafts- und Sozialgeographie, *Handwörterbuch der Wirtschaftswissenschaft* (Band 9; Stuttgart, New York: Fischer), 44–54.

Bathelt, H. (1991), *Schlüsseltechnologie-Industrien: Standortverhalten und Einfluss auf den regionalen Strukturwandel in den USA und in Kanada* (Berlin, Heidelberg, New York: Springer).

——(1997), *Chemiestandort Deutschland: Technologischer Wandel, Arbeitsteilung und geographische Strukturen in der Chemischen Industrie* (Berlin: Edition Sigma – Bohn).

——(2000), Räumliche Produktions- und Marktbeziehungen zwischen Globalisierung und Regionalisierung. Konzeptioneller Überblick und ausgewählte Beispiele, *Berichte zur deutschen Landeskunde*, 74, 97–124.

——(2001a), Regional competence and economic recovery: Divergent growth paths in Boston's high technology economy, *Entrepreneurship & Regional Development*, 13, 287–314.

——(2001b), Warum Paul Krugmans Geographical Economics keine neue Wirtschaftsgeographie ist! Eine Replik zu Armin Osmanovic, *Die Erde*, 132, 107–18.

——(2002), The re-emergence of a media industry cluster in Leipzig, *European Planning Studies*, 10, 583–611.

——(2003), Geographies of production: Growth regimes in spatial perspective 1 – Innovation, institutions and social systems, *Progress in Human Geography*, 27, 763–78.

——(2004), Vom 'Rauschen' und 'Pfeifen' in Clustern: Reflexive Informations- und Kommunikationsstrukturen im Unternehmensumfeld, *Geographica Helvetica*, 59, 93–105.

Bathelt, H. (2005*a*), Geographies of production: Growth regimes in spatial perspective 2 – Knowledge creation and growth in clusters, *Progress in Human Geography*, 29 (2), 204–16.

——(2005*b*), Cluster relations in the media industry: Exploring the 'distanced neighbour' paradox in Leipzig, *Regional Studies*, 39, 105–27.

——(2005*c*), Chanye jiqunyanjiu de xin shijiao (Toward a reconceptualization of clusters), *World Regional Studies*, 14 (1), 1–8.

——(2007), Buzz-and-pipeline dynamics: Toward a knowledge-based multiplier model of clusters, *Geography Compass*, 1, 1282–98.

——(2009), Re-bundling and the development of hollow clusters in the East German chemical industry, *European Urban and Regional Studies*, 16, 363–81.

——Boggs, J. S. (2003), Towards a reconceptualization of regional development paths: Is Leipzig's media cluster a continuation of or a rupture with the past?, *Economic Geography*, 79, 265–93.

————(2005), Continuities, ruptures and re-bundling of regional development paths: Leipzig's metamorphosis, in G. Fuchs and P. Shapira (eds.), *Rethinking Regional Innovation and Change Path: Path Dependency or Regional Breakthrough?* (New York: Springer), 147–70.

——Depner, H. (2003), Innovation, institution and region: Zur Diskussion über nationale und regionale Innovationssysteme, *Erdkunde*, 57, 126–43.

————(2005), Exporting the German model: The establishment of a new automobile industry cluster in Shanghai, *Economic Geography*, 81 (1), 53–81.

——Dewald, U. (2008), Ansatzpunkte einer relationalen Regionalpolitik und Clusterförderung (Relational aspects of regional economic support and cluster policy), *Zeitschrift für Wirtschaftsgeographie*, 52, 163–79.

——Glückler, J. (2000), Netzwerke, Lernen und evolutionäre Regionalentwicklung, *Zeitschrift für Wirtschaftsgeographie*, 44, 167–82.

————(2002), Wirtschaftsgeographie in relationaler Perspektive. Das Argument der zweiten Transition, *Geographische Zeitschrift*, 90, 20–39.

————(2003*a*), Wirtschaftsgeographie. Ökonomische Beziehungen in räumlicher Perspektive (2nd edn.; Stuttgart: Ulmer, UTB).

————(2003*b*), Toward a relational economic geography, *Journal of Economic Geography*, 3, 117–44.

————(2003*c*), Plädoyer für eine relationale Wirtschaftsgeographie, *Geographische Revue*, 5, 66–71.

————(2005), Resources in economic geography: From substantive concepts towards a relational perspective, *Environment and Planning A*, 37 (9), 1545–63.

——Gräf, P. (2008), Internal and external dynamics of the Munich film and TV industry cluster, and limitations to future growth, *Environment and Planning A*, 40, 1944–65.

——Jentsch, C. (2002), Die Entstehung eines Medienclusters in Leipzig: Neue Netzwerke und alte Strukturen, in P. Gräf and J. Rauh (eds.), *Networks and Flows: Telekommunikation zwischen Raumstruktur, Verflechtung und Informationsgesellschaft* (Geographie der Kommunikation – Band 3; Hamburg, Münster: Lit), 31–74.

——Kappes, K. (2009), Necessary restructuring or globalization failure? Shifts in regional supplier relations after the merger of the former German Hoechst and French Rhône-Poulenc groups, *Geoforum*, 40, 158–70.

——Schuldt, N. (2005), Between luminaries and meat grinders: International trade fairs as temporary clusters, *SPACES, Vol. 3, 2005–06* (Marburg: Faculty of Geography, Philipps – University of Marburg).

————(2008*a*), Temporary face-to-face contact and the ecologies of global and virtual buzz, *SPACES online, Vol. 6, 2008–04* (Toronto, Heidelberg: www.spaces-online.com).

————(2008*b*), Between luminaries and meat grinders: International trade fairs as temporary clusters, *Regional Studies*, 42 (6), 853–68.

——Taylor, M. (2002), Clusters, power and place: Inequality and local growth in time-space, *Geografiska Annaler*, 84 B, 93–109.

——Turi, P. (2011), Knowledge creation and the geographies of local, global and virtual buzz, in P. Meusburger, M. Ries, and J. Glückler (eds.), *Knowledge and Economy* (Knowledge and Space, 5; Berlin, Heidelberg: Springer).

——Zakrzewski, G. (2007), Messeveranstaltungen als fokale Schnittstellen der globalen Ökonomie, *Zeitschrift für Wirtschaftsgeographie*, 51, 14–30.

——Zeng, G. (2005), Von ressourcenabhängigen, unvernetzen Industrien zu Industrieclustern? Das Beispiel der südchinesischen Großstadt Nanning, *Zeitschrift für Wirtschaftsgeographie*, 49, 1–22.

——Kogler, D., and Munro, A. (2008), *Social Foundations of Regional Innovation and the Role of University Spin-offs*, ISRN Publications – National Meeting Presentations Montreal 2008. Innovation Systems Research Network (Toronto: University of Toronto).

————————(2010), A knowledge-based typology of university spin-offs in the context of regional economic development, *Technovation*, 30, forthcoming.

——Malmberg, A., and Maskell, P. (2004), Clusters and knowledge: Local buzz, global pipelines and the process of knowledge creation, *Progress in Human Geography*, 28, 31–56.

Baum, J. A. and Oliver, C. (1992), Institutional embeddedness and the dynamics of organizational populations, *American Sociological Review*, 57, 540–59.

Baxter, J. and Eyles, J. (1997), Evaluating qualitative research in social geography: Establishing 'rigour' in interview analysis, *Transactions of the Institute of British Geographers*, 22, 505–25.

Beckert, J. (1996), What is sociological about economic sociology? Uncertainty and the embeddedness of economic action, *Theory and Society*, 25, 803–40.

——(2009), The social order of markets, *Theory and Society*, 38 (3), 245–69.

Bell, J. (1995), The internationalisation of small computer software firms – A further challenge to 'stage' theories, *European Journal of Marketing*, 29, 60–75.

Belussi, F. and Pilotti, L. (2001), *Learning and Innovation by Networking Within the Italian Industrial Districts. The Development of an Explorative Analytical Model*, Annual Residential Conference of the IGU Commission on the Dynamics of Economic Spaces (Turin).

Benner, M. (2009), What do we know about clusters? In search of effective cluster policies, *SPACES online, Vol. 7, 2009-04* (Toronto, Heidelberg: www.spaces-online.com).

Bennett, R. J., Bratton, W., and Robson, P. (2000), Business advice: The influence of distance, *Regional Studies*, 34, 813–28.

——Graham, D. J., and Bratton, W. (1999), The location and concentration of business in Britain: Business clusters, business services, market coverage and local economic development, *Transactions of the Institute of British Geographers*, 24, 393–420.

Benneworth, P. and Charles, D. (2001), Bridging cluster theories and practice: Learning from the cluster policy cycle, *Innovative Clusters: Drivers of National Innovation Systems* (Paris: OECD), 389–404.

——Hospers, G.-J. (2007), The new economic geography of old industrial regions: Universities as global–local pipelines, *Environment and Planning C: Government and Policy*, 25 (6), 779–809.

Benz, A. (2004), *Governance – Regieren in komplexen Reglesystemen: Eine Einführung* (Wiesbaden: VS Verlag).

Berndt, C. (1999), Institutionen, Regulation und Geographie, *Erdkunde*, 53, 302–16.

——(2003), El Paso del Norte . . . Modernization utopias, othering and management practices in Mexico's maquiladora industry, *Antipode*, 35, 264–85.

——Boeckler, M. (2007), Kulturelle Geographien der Ökonomie: Zur Performativität von Märkten, in C. Berndt and R. Pütz (eds.), *Kulturelle Geographien* (Bielefeld: Transcript), 193–238.

————(2009), Geographies of circulation and exchange: Constructions of markets, *Progress in Human Geography*, 33 (4), 535–51.

Bhaskar, R. (1975), *A Realist Theory of Science* (London, New York: Verso).

Biehler, H., Genosko, J., Sargl, M., and Sträter, D. (2003), *Standort München – Medienwirtschaft und Fahrzeugbau: Regionale Netzwerke und regionaler Arbeitsmarkt als Erfolgsfaktoren* (Marburg: Schüren).

Blanc, H. and Sierra, C. (1999), The internationalisation of R&D by multinationals: A trade-off between external and internal proximity, *Cambridge Journal of Economics*, 23, 187–206.

Blankenburg Holm, D., Eriksson, K., and Johanson, J. (1996), Business networks and cooperation in international business relationships, *Journal of International Business Studies*, 5, 1033–53.

Blythe, J. (2002), Using trade fairs in key account management, *Industrial Marketing Management*, 31, 627–35.

Boddewyn, J., Halbrich, M., and Perry, A. C. (1986), Service multinationals: Conceptualization, measurement and theory, *Journal of International Business Studies*, 17 (3), 41–57.

Boekema, F., Morgan, K., Bakkers, S., and Rutten, R. (2000), Introduction to learning regions: A new issue for analysis, in Boekema, K. Morgan, S. Bakkers, and R. Rutten (eds.), *Knowledge, Innovation and Economic Growth: The Theory and Practice of Learning Regions* (Cheltenham, Northampton, MA: Edward Elgar), 3–16.

Boggs, J. S. and Rantisi, N. M. (2003), The 'relational turn' in economic geography, *Journal of Economic Geography*, 3, 109–16.

Borgatti, S. P. and Cross, R. (2003), A relational view of information seeking and learning in social networks, *Management Science*, 49 (4), 432–45.

——Everett, M. G. (1997), Network analysis of 2-mode data, *Social Networks*, 19, 243–69.

——Foster, P. C. (2003), The network paradigm in organizational research: A review and typology, *Journal of Management*, 29 (6), 991–1013.

——Carley, K. M., and Krackhardt, D. (2006), On the robustness of centrality measures under conditions of imperfect data, *Social Networks*, 28, 124–36.

Borghini, S., Golfetto, F., and Rinallo, D. (2004), *Using Anthropological Methods to Study Industrial Marketing and Purchasing: An Exploration of Professional Trade Shows*, Industrial Marketing Purchasing Conference (Copenhagen).

—————————(2006), Ongoing search among industrial buyers, *Journal of Business Research*, 59, 1151–9.

Bormann, N. (2008), Akteurszentrierte Analyse einer nachhaltigen Gestaltung der globalen Warenkette von Schokolade, in D. M. Schlesinger (ed.), *Branchenspezifische Standortforschung aus relationaler Perspektive* (Müchen: Universität München, Wirtschaftsgeographie), 11–76.

Boschma, R. A. and Frenken, K. H. (2005), Why is economic geography not an evolutionary science? Towards an evolutionary economic geography, *Papers in Evolutionary Economic Geography (PEEG) 05–01* (Utrecht: U. U. Urban and Regional Research Centre).

—————————(2010), Technological relatedness and regional branching, in H. Bathelt, M. P. Feldman, and D. Kogler (eds.), *Dynamic Geographies of Knowledge Creation and Innovation* (London, New York: Routledge).

——Lamboy, J. G. (2001), Evolutionary economics and regional policy, *The Annals of Regional Science*, 35, 113–31.

Bouba-Olga, O. and Grossetti, M. (2008), Socio-économie de proximité, *Revue d'Economie Régionale et Urbaine*, 3/2008, 311–28.

Bourdieu, P. (1977), *Outline of a Theory of Practice* (Cambridge: Cambridge University Press).

——(1986), The forms of capital, in J. G. Richardson (ed.), *Handbook of Theory and Research for the Sociology of Education* (New York: Greenwood), 241–58.

——(2005), *The Social Structures of the Economy* (Cambridge: Polity).

Böventer, E. v. (1962), *Theorie des räumlichen Gleichgewichts* (Tübingen: Mohr Siebeck).

Boyer, R. (1997), The variety and unequal performance of really existing markets: Farewell to Doctor Pangloss?, in J. R. Hollingsworth and R. Boyer (eds.), *Contemporary Capitalism. The Embeddedness of Institutions* (Cambridge, New York: Cambridge University Press), 55–93.

Bradach, J. L. and Eccles, R. G. (1989), Price, authority and trust: From ideal types to plural forms, *Annual Review of Sociology*, 15, 97–118.

Bramanti, A. and Ratti, R. (1997), The multi-faced dimensions of local development, in R. Ratti, A. Bramanti, and R. Gordon (eds.), *The Dynamics of Innovative Regions: The GREMI Approach* (Aldershot, Brookfield: Ashgate), 3–44.

Bramwell, A., Nelles, J., and Wolfe, D. A. (2004), *Knowledge, Innovation and Regional Culture in Waterloo's ICT Cluster*, Innovation Systems Research Network (ISRN) National Meeting (Vancouver).

Brenner, N. (1999), Globalization and reterritorialisation: The re-scaling of urban governance in the European Union, *Urban Studies*, 36, 431–51.

Bresnahan, T., Gambardella, A., and Saxenian, A. (2001), 'Old economy' inputs for 'new economy' outcomes: Cluster formation in the new Silicon Valleys, *Industrial and Corporate Change*, 10, 835–60.

Brouthers, K. D. and Brouthers, L. E. (2000), Acquisition or greenfield start-up? Institutional, cultural and transaction cost influences, *Strategic Management Journal*, 21, 89–97.

Brown, J. S. and Duguid, P. (1991), Organizational learning and communities-of-practice: Toward a unified view of working, learning, and innovating, *Organization Science*, 2, 40–57.

Bryman, A. (1984), The debate about quantitative and qualitative research: A question of method or epistemology?, *The British Journal of Sociology*, 35 (1), 75–92.

Bryson, J. (1997), Business service firms, service space and the management of change, *Entrepreneurship & Regional Development*, 9, 93–111.

——Daniels, P. (1998), Business link, strong ties and the wall of silence: Small and medium sized enterprises and external business service expertise, *Environment and Planning C: Government and Policy*, 16, 265–80.

——Keeble, D., and Wood, P. (1993), The creation, location and growth of small business service firms in the United Kingdom, *Service Industries Journal*, 13, 118–31.

——————(1997), The creation and growth of small business service firms in post-industrial Britain, *Small Business Economics*, 9, 345–60.

——Henry, N., Keeble, D., and Marin, R. (1999), *The Economic Geography Reader. Producing and Consuming Global Capitalism* (Chichester, New York: Wiley).

Buckley, P. J. (1993), Foreign direct investment by small- and medium-sized enterprises: The theoretical background, in P. J. Buckley and P. N. Ghauri (eds.), *The Internationalization of the Firm: A Reader* (London: Academic Press), 91–105.

——Casson, M. C. (1998), Analyzing foreign market entry strategies: Extending the internalization approach, *Journal of International Business Studies*, 29, 539–61.

——Newbould, G. D., and Turwell, J. (1988), *Foreign Direct Investment by Smaller UK Firms* (London: Macmillan).

——Pass, C. L., and Prescott, K. (1992), Internationalization of service firms: A comparison with the manufacturing sector, *Scandinavian International Business Review*, 1, 39–56.

Bunge, W. (1973), Ethics and logic in geography, in R. J. Chorley (ed.), *Directions in Geography* (London: Methuen), 317–31.

Bunnell, T. G. and Coe, N. M. (2001), Spaces and scales of innovation, *Progress in Human Geography*, 25, 569–89.

Burt, R. (1992), *Structural Holes: The Social Structure of Competition* (Cambridge, MA, London: Harvard University Press).

——(1997), The contingent value of social capital, *Administrative Science Quarterly*, 42, 339–65.

Buzar, S. (2007), When homes become prisons: The relational spaces of postsocialist energy poverty, *Environment and Planning A*, 39, 1908–25.

Callon, M. (1998*a*), Introduction: The embeddedness of economic markets in economics, in M. Callon (ed.), *The Laws of the Markets* (Oxford: Blackwell), 1–57.

——(ed.) (1998*b*), *The Laws of the Markets* (Oxford: Blackwell).

——(2007), What does it mean to say that economics is performative?, in D. MacKenzie, F. Muniesa, and L. Siu (eds.), *Do Economists Make Markets?* (Princeton, Oxford: Princeton University Press), 311–57.

Camagni, R. (1991*a*), Local 'milieu', uncertainty and innovation networks: Towards a new dynamic theory of economic space, in R. Camagni (ed.), *Innovation Networks: Spatial Perspectives* (London, New York: Belhaven Press), 121–44.

——(ed.) (1991*b*), *Innovation Networks: Spatial Perspectives* (London, New York: Belhaven Press).

Cannon, T. and Willis, M. (1981), The smaller firm in overseas trade, *European Small Business Journal*, 1, 45–55.

Capello, R. (2000), The city network paradigm: Measuring urban network externalities, *Urban Studies*, 37, 1925–45.

——Faggian, A. (2005), Collective learning and relational capital in local innovation process, *Regional Studies*, 39, 75–87.

Carroll, G. R. and Stanfield, J. R. (2003), Social capital, Karl Polanyi, and American social and institutional economics, *Journal of Economic Issues*, 37, 397–404.

Caspers, R. and Kreis-Hoyer, P. (2004), Konzeptionelle Grundlagen der Produktion, Verbreitung und Nutzung von Wissen in Wirtschaft und Gesellschaft, in R. Caspers, N. Bickhoff, and T. Bieger (eds.), *Interorganisatorische Wissensnetzwerke. Mit Kooperation zum Erfolg* (Berlin, Heidelberg: Springer), 17–58.

Celata, F. (2009), *Spazi di produzione: Una prospettiva relazionale* (Torino: Giappichelli Editore).

Cheng, J. and Bennett, D. (2007), Success strategies in the Chinese chemical industry: A survey and case study investigations, *Journal of Chinese Economic and Business Studies*, 5 (2), 91–112.

Chesbrough, H. (2003), Managing your false negatives, *Harvard Management Update*, 8 (8), 3–4.

Chetty, S. and Blankenburg Holm, D. (2000), Internationalisation of small to medium-sized manufacturing firms: A network approach, *International Business Review*, 9, 77–93.

——Campbell-Hunt, C. (2004), A strategic approach to internationalization: A traditional versus a 'born-global' approach, *Journal of International Marketing*, 12, 57–81.

Chiang, L. (2007), Building links to prosperity, *Toronto Star*, B7.

China Petroleum and Chemical Industry Association (2007), *China Chemical Industry Yearbook* (Beijing: China National Chemical Information Center).

Christaller, W. (1933), *Die zentralen Orte in Süddeutschland: Eine ökonomisch-geographische Untersuchung über die Gesetzmäßigkeit der Verbreitung und Entwicklung der Siedlungen mit städtischen Funktionen* (Jena: Gustav Fischer).

Clark, G., Feldman, M., and Gertler, M. (eds.) (2000), *The Oxford Handbook of Economic Geography* (Oxford: Oxford University Press).

Clark, G. L. (1983), Fluctuations and rigidities in local labor markets. Part 2: Reinterpreting relational contracts, *Environment and Planning A*, 15, 365–77.

——(1998), *Stylized Facts and Close Dialogue: Methodology in Economic Geography*, Annals of the Association of American Geographers, 88, 73–87.

——(2005), Beyond close dialogue: Economic geography as if it matters, *Economic Geography Research Group Working Papers WPG 05–04* (2005; Oxford: School of Geography and the Environment, Oxford University).

——(2009), Human nature, the environment, and behaviour: Explaining the scope and geographical scale of financial decision-making, *SPACES online, Vol. 7, 2009–01* (Toronto, Heidelberg: www.spaces-online.com).

——Thrift, N. (2003), FX risk in time and space: Managing dispersed knowledge in global finance, *SPACES, Vol. 1, 2003–05* (Marburg: Faculty of Geography, Philipps – University of Marburg).

——Tracey, P. (2004), *Global Competitiveness and Innovation: An Agent-Centred Perspective* (Houndsmill, Basingstoke, New York: Palgrave Macmillan).

——Wrigley, N. (1995), Sunk costs: A framework for economic geography, *Transactions of the Institute of British Geographers*, 20, 204–23.

——Tracey, P., and Lawton Smith, H. (2001), Agents, endowments, and path-dependence: A model of multi-jurisdictional regional development, *Geographische Zeitschrift*, 89, 166–81.

Clark, G. L., Palaskas, T., Tracey, P., and Tsampra, M. (2004), Market revenue and the scope and scale of SME networks in Europe's vulnerable regions, *Environment and Planning A*, 36, 1305–26.

Clark, T. (1993), The market provision of management services, information, asymmetries and service quality. Some market solutions: An empirical example, *British Journal of Management*, 4, 235–51.

——(1995), *Managing Consultants: Consultancy as the Management of Impressions* (Buckingham: Open University Press).

Clausen, E. and Schreiber, P. (2000), *Messen optimal nutzen: Ziele definieren und Erfolge programmieren (How to Optimise the Use of Trade Fairs: Defining Goals and Planning Success)* (Würzburg: Schimmel).

Clegg, S. (1989), *Frameworks of Power* (London: Sage).

Coase, R. (1937), The nature of the firm, *Economica*, 4, 386–405.

Cochrane, A. (1998), Illusions of power: Interviewing local élites, *Environment and Planning A*, 30, 2121–32.

Cockburn, I. M. and Henderson, R. M. (1998), Absorptive capacity, coauthoring behavior, and the organization of research in drug discovery, *Journal of Industrial Economics*, 46 (2), 157–82.

Coe, N. and Bunnell, T. G. (2003), Spatializing knowledge communities: Towards a conceptualization of transnational innovation networks, *Global Networks*, 3 (4), 437–56.

——Townsend, A. R. (1998), Debunking the myth of localized agglomerations: The development of a regionalized service economy in South-East England, *Transactions of the Institute of British Geographers*, 23, 385–404.

——Kelly, P. F., and Yeung, H. W.-c. (2007), *Economic Geography: A Contemporary Introduction* (Malden, MA, Oxford: Blackwell).

——Hess, M., Yeung, H. W.-c., Dicken, P., and Henderson, J. (2003), *'Globalizing' Regional Development: A Global Production Networks Perspective*, GPN Working Paper 3 (Manchester).

Cohen, W. M. and Levinthal, D. A. (1990), Absorptive capacity: A new perspective on learning and innovation, *Administrative Science Quarterly*, 35, 128–52.

Cohendet, P., Héraud, J.-A., and Llerena, P. (2011), A microeconomic approach of the dynamics of creation, in P. Meusburger, M. Ries, and J. Glückler (eds.), *Knowledge and Space – Vol. 5: Knowledge and Economy* (Berlin, Heidelberg: Springer).

Cole, A. (2008), Distant neighbours: The new geography of animated film production in Europe, *Regional Studies*, 42, 891–904.

Coleman, J. S. (1988), Social capital in the creation of human capital, *American Journal of Sociology*, 94, 95–120.

Collier, P. (1998), *Social Capital and Poverty*, Social Capital Initiative Working Paper No. 4 (New York: The World Bank).

Cooke, P. and Morgan, K. (1998), *The Associational Economy. Firms, Regions, and Innovation* (Oxford, New York: Oxford University Press).

Costenbader, E. and Valente, T. (2003), The stability of centrality measures when networks are sampled, *Social Networks*, 25, 283–307.

Coviello, N. E. and Martin, K. A. M. (1999), Internationalization of service SME's: An integrated perspective from the engineering consulting sector, *Journal of International Marketing*, 7, 42–66.

——Munro, H. (1997), Network relationships and the internationalisation process of small software firms, *International Business Review*, 6, 361–86.

Cowling, K. and Sugden, R. (1998), The essence of the modern corporation: Markets, strategic decision-making and the theory of the firm, *The Manchester School*, 66 (1), 59–86.

Crang, M. (2002), Qualitative methods: The new orthodoxy?, *Progress in Human Geography*, 26, 647–55.

——(2003), Qualitative methods: Touchy, feely, look-see?, *Progress in Human Geography*, 27, 494–504.

Crang, P. (1994), It's showtime: On the workplace geographies of display in a restaurant in southeast England, *Environment and Planning D – Society and Space*, 12, 675–704.

——(1997), Cultural turns and the (re)constitution of economic geography, in R. Lee and J. Wills (eds.), *Geographies of Economies* (London, New York: Arnold), 3–15.

Crevoisier, O. (2001), Der Ansatz des kreativen Milieus. Bestandsaufnahme und Forschungsperspektiven am Beispiel urbaner Milieus, *Zeitschrift für Wirtschaftsgeographie*, 45, 246–56.

——(2004), The innovative milieus approach: Toward a territorialized understanding of the economy?, *Economic Geography*, 80, 367–79.

——Maillat, D. (1991), Milieu, industrial organization and territorial production system: Towards a new theory of spatial development, in R. Camagni (ed.), *Innovation Networks: Spatial Perspectives* (London, New York: Belhaven Press), 13–34.

Cross, R. and Baird, L. (2000), Technology is not enough: Improving performance by building organizational memory, *Sloan Management Review*, 41 (3), 69–78.

——Liedtka, J., and Weiss, L. (2005), A practical guide to social networks, *Harvard Business Review*, 83 (3), 124–32.

Dahl, M. S. and Pedersen, S. O. R. (2003), *Knowledge Flows Through Informal Contacts in Industrial Clusters: Myths or Realities?*, DRUID Working Paper 03–01 (Copenhagen).

Daniels, P. W. (1991), Producer services and the development of the space economy, in P. W. Daniels and F. Moulaert (eds.), *The Changing Geography of Advanced Producer Services* (London, New York: Belhaven Press), 135–50.

——(1995), Internationalisation of advertising services in a changing regulatory environment, *The Service Industries Journal*, 16, 276–94.

——Bryson, J. (2005), Sustaining business and professional services in a second city region, *Services Industries Journal*, 25 (4), 505–24.

——van Dinteren, J. J., and Monnoyer, M. C. (1992), Consultancy services and the urban hierarchy in Western Europe, *Environment and Planning A*, 24, 1731–48.

Das, T. K. and Teng, B. S. (2001), Trust, control, and risk in strategic alliances: An integrated framework, *Organization Studies*, 22, 251–83.

David, P. A. (1985), Clio and the economics of QWERTY, *American Economic Review, Papers and Proceedings*, 75, 332–7.

Dawes, P., Dowling, G. R., and Patterson, P. G. (1992), Criteria used to select management consultants, *Industrial Marketing Management*, 21, 187–93.

DeFillippi, R. J. and Arthur, M. B. (1998), Paradox in project-based enterprise: The case of film making, *California Management Review*, 40, 125–39.

de Lange, N. (1993), Standorte unternehmensbezogener Dienstleistungsfunktionen in Deutschland. Das Beispiel der Wirtschaftsprüfer, *Geographische Zeitschrift*, 81, 18–34.

De Laurentis, C., Cooke, P., and Williams, G. (2003), *Barriers to the Knowledge Economy – New Media Cluster in the Periphery*, Regional Studies Association International Conference on 'Reinventing Regions in the Global Economy' (Pisa).

Denzin, N. K. (1978), *The Research Act* (2nd edn.; New York: McGraw-Hill).

——(1989), *The Research Act* (3rd edn.; Englewood Cliffs: Prentice Hall).

Depner, H. (2006), *Transnationale Direktinvestitionen und kulturelle Unterschiede. Lieferanten und Joint Ventures deutscher Automobilzulieferer in China* (Global Studies; Bielefeld: transcript).

——Bathelt, H. (2003*a*), Cluster growth and institutional barriers: The development of the automobile industry cluster in Shanghai, P. R. China, *SPACES 2003–09* (Marburg: Faculty of Geography, Philipps – University of Marburg).

————(2003*b*), Cluster growth and institutional barriers: The development of the automobile industry cluster in Shangahai, P. R. China, *SPACES, Vol. 1, 2003–09* (Marburg: Faculty of Geography, Philipps – University of Marburg).

————(2005), Exporting the German model: The establishment of a new automobile industry cluster in Shanghai, *Economic Geography*, 81, 53–81.

Dicken, P. (1990), The geography of enterprise. Elements of a research agenda, in M. de Smidt and E. Wever (eds.), *The Corporate Firm in a Changing World Economy. Case Studies in the Geography of Enterprise* (London, New York: Routledge), 234–44.

——(1994), The Roepke Lecture in economic geography: Global-local tensions: Firms and states in the global space-economy, *Economic Geography*, 70, 101–28.

——(2003), *Global Shift: Reshaping the Global Economic Map in the 21st Century* (4th edn.; New York: Guilford Press).

——(2005), Tangled webs: Transnational production networks and regional integration, *SPACES, Vol. 3, 2005–04* (Marburg: Faculty of Geography, Philipps – University of Marburg).

——Malmberg, A. (2001), Firms in territories: A relational perspective, *Economic Geography*, 77, 345–63.

——Forsgren, M., and Malmberg, A. (1994), The local embeddedness of transnational corporations, in A. Amin and N. Thrift (eds.), *Globalization, Institutions, and Regional Development in Europe* (Oxford: Oxford University Press), 23–45.

——Kelly, P. F., Olds, K., and Yeung, H. W.-c. (2001), Chains and networks, territories and scales: Towards a relational framework for analysing the global economy, *Global Networks*, 1, 89–112.

DiMaggio, P. J. (1997), Culture and cognition, *Annual Review of Sociology*, 23, 263–89.

Doloreux, D. and Mattsson, H. (2008), To what extent do sectors 'socialize' innovation differently? Mapping cooperative linkages in knowledge-intensive industries in the Ottawa region, *Industry and Innovation*, 15, 351–70.

Dong, K. (2007), *Jingji quanqiuhua Beijing xia zhongguo shihua gingye quwei ji jizhi yanjiu (Research on the Spatial Structure and Evolution of the Petrochemical Industry in China under Globalization)* (Shanghai: East China Normal University).

Dopfer, K. (1991), Toward a theory of economic institutions: Synergy and path dependency, *Journal of Economic Issues*, 25, 535–50.

Dörry, S. (2008), *Globale Wertschöpfungsketten im Tourismus. Ohnmächtige Unternehmen in mächtiger Position? Relationale Governance bei der Organisation deutscher Pauschalreisen nach Jordanien* (Münster: LIT).

Dosi, G. (1982), Technological paradigms and technological trajectories: A suggested reinterpretation of the determinants and directions of technical change, *Research Policy*, 2, 147–62.

——(1988), The nature of the innovative process, in G. Dosi, C. Freeman, R. R. Nelson, G. Silverberg, and L. L. G. Soete (eds.), *Technical Change and Economic Theory* (London, New York: Pinter), 221–38.

——Marengo, L., Bassanini, A., and Valente, M. (1999), Norms as emergent properties of adaptive learning: The case of economic routines, *Journal of Evolutionary Economics*, 9, 5–26.

Downward, P., Finch, J. H., and Ramsay, J. (2002), Critical realism, empirical methods and inference: A critical discussion, *Cambridge Journal of Economics*, 26 (4), 481–500.

Dubrovsky, V. J., Kiesler, S., and Sethna, B. N. (1991), The equalization phenomenon: Status effects in computer-mediated and face-to-face decision making groups, *Human-Computer Interaction*, 6, 119–46.

Dunning, J. H. (1977), Trade, location of economic activity and the MNE: A search for an eclectic approach, in B. Ohlin, P. O. Hesselborn, and P. M. Wijkman (eds.), *The International Allocation of Economic Activity* (London: Macmillan), 395–418.

——(1988), The eclectic paradigm of international production: A restatement and some possible extensions, *Journal of International Business Studies*, 18, 1–31.

——(2000), The eclectic paradigm as an envelope for economic and business theories of MNE activity, *International Business Review*, 9, 163–90.

Duranton, G. (2007), Urban evolutions: The fast, the slow, and the still, *American Economic Review*, 97 (1), 197–221.

——Puga, D. (2001), Nursery cities: Urban diversity, process innovation, and the life cycle of products, *American Economic Review* 91 (5), 1454–77.

Edgington, D. W. (2008), The Kyoto Research Park in Japan, *Urban Geography*, 29 (5), 411–54.

Edquist, C. (1997), *Systems of Innovation: Technologies, Institutions and Organizations* (London: Pinter).

Eisenhardt, K. M. (1989), Building theories from case study research, *Academy of Management Review*, 14, 532–50.

Ellison, G. and Glaeser, E. L. (1999), The geographic concentration of industry: Does natural advantage explain agglomeration?, *The American Economic Review*, 89 (2), 311–16.

Emirbayer, M. (1997), Manifesto for a relational sociology, *The American Journal of Sociology*, 103 (2), 281–317.

——Goodwin, J. (1994), Network analysis, culture, and the problem of agency, *American Journal of Sociology*, 99 (6), 1411–54.

Enright, M. J. (2003), Regional clusters: What we know and what should we know, in J. Bröcker, D. Dohse, and R. Soltwedel (eds.), *Innovation Clusters and Interregional Competition* (Berlin, Heidelberg: Springer), 99–129.

Entwistle, J. and Rocamora, A. (2006), The field of fashion materialized: A study of London Fashion Week, *Sociology*, 40, 735–51.

Ernst & Young (2006), *Doing Business 2006 in Hungary* (Budapest: Ernst & Young Hungary).

Erramilli, M. K. (1990), Entry mode choice in service industries, *International Marketing Review*, 7 (5), 50–62.

——(1991), The experience factor in foreign market entry behavior of service firms, *Journal of International Business Studies*, 22, 479–501.

Erramilli, M. K. and D'Souza, D. E. (1995), Uncertainty and foreign direct investment: The role of moderators, *International Marketing Review*, 12, 47–60.

Ettlinger, N. (2001), A relational perspective in economic geography: Connecting competitiveness with diversity and difference, *Antipode*, 33, 216–27.

——(2003), Cultural economic geography and a relational and microspace approach to trusts, rationalities, networks, and change in collaborative workplaces, *Journal of Economic Geography*, 3, 145–72.

——(2004), Toward a critical theory of untidy geographies: The spatiality of emotions in consumption and production, *Feminist Economies*, 10 (3), 21–54.

Europäische Kommission (2002), Regionale Cluster in Europa, *Beobachtungsnetzwerk der europäischen KMU, Nr. 3* (Luxemburg: European Commission).

Farole, T., Rodríguez-Pose, A., and Storper, M. (2010), Human geography and the institutions that underline economic growth. Progress in Human Geography. DOI: 10.1177/0309132510372005.

Faulconbridge, J. (2006), Stretching tacit knowledge beyond a local fix? Global spaces of learning in advertising professional service firms, *Journal of Economic Geography*, 6 (4), 517–40.

——(2007), Relational networks of knowledge production in transnational law firms, *Geoforum*, 38, 925–40.

——(2008), Managing the transnational law firm: A relational analysis of professional systems, embedded actors, and time-space-sensitive governance, *Economic Geography*, 84, 185–210.

Feldman, M. P. (2001), The entrepreneurial event revisited: Firm formation in a regional context, *Industrial and Corporate Change*, 10, 861–91.

——Francis, J. L. (2004), Homegrown solutions: Fostering cluster information, *Economic Development Quarterly*, 18, 127–37.

Felsenstein, D., Schamp, E. W., and Shachar, A. (eds.) (2002), *Emerging Nodes in the Global Economy: Frankfurt and Tel Aviv Compared* (Dordrecht: Kluwer).

Feser, E. J. and Bergman, E. M. (2000), National industry cluster templates: A framework for applied regional cluster analysis, *Regional Studies*, 34, 1–20.

Festel, G. and Geng, Y. (2005), Chemical industry parks in China, in G. Festel, A. Kreimeyer, U. Oels, and M. v. Zedtwitz (eds.), *The Chemical and Pharmaceutical Industry in China: Opportunities and Threats to Foreign Companies* (Heidelberg: Springer), 53–62.

Fleetwood, S. (2002), Boylan and O'Gorman's causal holism: A critical realist evaluation, *Cambridge Journal of Economics*, 26, 27–45.

Florida, R., Cushing, R., and Gates, G. (2002), When social capital stifles innovation, *Harvard Business Review*, 80 (8), 20.

Fombrun, C. (1996), *Reputation* (Boston, MA: Harvard Business School Press).

Fourcade, M. (2007), Theories of markets and theories of society, *American Behavioral Scientist*, 50 (8), 1015–34.

Frankel, M. (1955), Obsolescence and technological change in a maturing economy, *American Economic Review*, 45, 296–319.

Frankfurter Allgemeine Zeitung (2002), Lange Schatten auf dem Medienstandort München (Dark shadows on the Munich media center), *Frankfurter Allgemeine Zeitung*, 9. April.

——(2003*a*), Kirch Media stößt Unternehmen ab (Kirch Media gets rid of former branches), *Frankfurter Allgemeine Zeitung*, 4. October.

——(2003*b*), Sparprogramm in Saban-Sebderb (Cost-cutting measures of the Saban broadcasters), *Frankfurter Allgemeine Zeitung*, 29. October.

Frankfurter Rundschau (2002*a*), Auffanggesellschaft soll den Kern des Kirch-Konzerns retten (Rescue company established to save the core of the Kirch Group), *Frankfurter Rundschau*, 9. April.

——(2002*b*), Aufstieg und Fall im Zeitraffer (Rise and decline at fast motion), *Frankfurter Rundschau*, 9. April.

Frenken, K., van Oort, F. G., and Verburg, T. (2007), Related variety, unrelated variety and regional economic growth, *Regional Studies*, 41, 685–97.

Friedman, T. L. (2005), *The World is Flat: A Brief History of the Twenty-First Century* (New York: Farrar, Straus, and Giroux).

Friedmann, J. (1986), The world city hypothesis, *Development and Change*, 4, 12–50.

Fromhold-Eisebith, E. and Eisebith, G. (2005), How to institutionalize innovative clusters? Comparing explicit top-down and implicit bottom-up approaches, *Research Policy*, 34, 1250–68.

Fromhold-Eisebith, M. (1995), Das 'kreative Milieu' als Motor regionalwirtschaftlicher Entwicklung: Forschungstrends und Erfassungsmöglichkeiten, *Geographische Zeitschrift*, 83, 30–47.

Fuchslocher, H. and Hochheimer, H. (2000), *Messen im Wandel: Messemarketing im 21. Jahrhundert (Trade Fair Marketing in the 21st Century)* (Wiesbaden: Gabler).

Fuhse, J. and Mützel, S. (eds.) (2010), *Relationale Soziologie* (Wiesbaden: Verlag für Sozialwissenschaften).

Fujita, K., Krugman, P., and Venables, A. J. (1999), *The Spatial Economy: Cities, Regions, and International Trade* (Cambridge, MA: MIT Press).

————————(2001), *The Spatial Economy: Cities, Regions, and International Trade* (2nd edn.; Cambridge, MA: MIT Press).

Gereffi, G. (1994), The organization of buyer-driven global commodity chains: How US retailers shape overseas production networks, in G. Gereffi and M. Korzeniewicz (eds.), *Commodity Chains and Global Capitalism* (Wesport, CT: Praeger), 95–122.

——(1999), International trade and industrial upgrading in the apparel commodity chain, *Journal of International Economics*, 48, 37–70.

——Humphrey, J., and Sturgeon, T. (2005), The governance of global value chains, *Review of International Political Economy*, 12 (1), 78–104.

Gersick, C. J. G., Bartunek, J. M., and Dutton, J. E. (2000), Learning from academia: The importance of relationships in professional life, *Academy of Management Journal*, 43 (6), 1026–44.

Gertler, M. S. (1993), Implementing advanced manufacturing technologies in mature industrial regions: Towards a social model of technology production, *Regional Studies*, 27, 665–80.

——(1995), 'Being there': Proximity, organization, and culture in the development and adoption of advanced manufacturing technologies, *Economic Geography*, 71 (1), 1–26.

——(1997), The invention of regional culture, in R. Lee and J. Wills (eds.), *Geographies of Economies* (London: Arnold), 47–58.

——(2001), Best practice? Geography, learning and the institutional limits to strong convergence, *Journal of Economic Geography*, 1 (1), 5–26.

——(2003), Tacit knowledge and the economic geography of context, or the undefinable tacitness of being (there), *Journal of Economic Geography*, 3, 75–99.

Gertler, M. S. (2004), *Manufacturing Culture: The Institutional Geography of Industrial Practice* (Oxford, New York: Oxford University Press).

——(2010), Rules of the game: The place of institutions in regional economic change, *Regional Studies*, 44, 1–15.

——Vinodrai, T. (2005), Learning from America? Knowledge flows and industrial practices of German firms in North America, *Economic Geography*, 81 (1), 31–52.

——Wolfe, D. A. (2006), Spaces of knowledge flows: Clusters in a global context, in B. Asheim, P. Cooke, and R. Martin (eds.), *Clusters and Regional Development: Critical Reflections and Explorations* (London: Routledge), 218–35.

Giaccaria, P. (2009), The 'magic and loss' of social capital and local development, in J. Häkli (ed.), *Social Capital and Urban Networks of Trust* (Aldershot, Brookfield: Ashgate), 67–90.

Giddens, A. (1984), *The Constitution of Society. Outline of the Theory of Structuration* (Cambridge: Polity Press).

——(1990), *Consequences of Modernity* (Stanford: Stanford University Press).

Giuliani, E. (2005), Cluster absorptive capacity: Why some clusters forge ahead and others lag behind?, *European Urban and Regional Studies*, 12, 269–88.

——(2007), The selective nature of knowledge networks in clusters: Evidence from the wine industry, *Journal of Economic Geography*, 7 (2), 139–68.

Glaeser, E. L. (2005), Reinventing Boston: 1630–2003, *Journal of Economic Geography*, 5 (2), 119–53.

——Kallal, H. D., Scheinkman, J. A., and Shleifer, A. (1992), Growth in cities, *The Journal of Political Economy*, 100 (6), 1126–52.

Glaser, B. G. and Strauss, A. L. (1967), *The Discovery of Grounded Theory: Strategies for Qualitative Research* (Hawthorne, NY: Aldine de Gruyter).

Glasmeier, A. K. (2000), *Manufacturing Time: The Global Competition in the Watch Industry, 1795–2000* (New York: Guilford).

Glückler, J. (1999), *Neue Wege geographischen Denkens? Eine Kritik gegenwärtiger Raumkonzepte und ihrer Programme in der Geographie* (Frankfurt am Main: Verlag Neue Wissenschaft).

——(2001a), Handeln in Netzen. Zur Bedeutung von Struktur für ökonomisches Handeln, in P. Reuber and G. Wolkersdorfer (eds.), *Politische Geographie* (Heidelberger Geographische Arbeiten, 112; Heidelberg), 257–68.

——(2001b), Zur Bedeutung von Embeddedness in der Wirtschaftsgeographie, *Geographische Zeitschrift*, 89, 211–26.

——(2004a), *Unternehmensberatung: Reputation, Netzwerke, Honorare und Unternehmenserfolg* (Frankfurt am Main: Goethe-Universität Frankfurt a.M.: Institut für Humangeographie).

——(2004b), *Reputationsnetze. Zur Internationalisierung von Unternehmensberatern. Eine relationale Theorie* (Sozialtheorie; Bielefeld: transcript).

——(2005), Making embeddedness work: Social practice institutions in foreign consulting markets, *Environment and Planning A*, 37 (10), 1727–50.

——(2006), A relational assessment of international market entry in management consulting, *Journal of Economic Geography*, 6, 369–93.

——(2007a), Economic geography and the evolution of networks, *Journal of Economic Geography*, 7 (5), 619–34.

——(2007b), Geography of reputation: The city as the locus of business opportunity, *Regional Studies*, 41 (7), 949–62.

——(2008), Die Chancen der Standortspaltung: Wissensnetze im globalen Unternehmen, *Geographische Zeitschrift*, 96, 125–39.

——(2010*a*), The evolution of a strategic alliance network: Exploring the case of stock photography, in R. Boschma and R. Martin (eds.), *Handbook of Evolutionary Economic Geography* (Cheltenham: Edward Elgar), 298–315.

——(2010*b*), Islands of expertise – Global knowledge transfer in a technology service firm, in D.-F. Kogler, M. P. Feldman, and H. Bathelt (eds.), *Beyond Territory – Dynamic Geographies of Innovation and Knowledge Creation* (London: Routledge).

——(2011), The problem of mobilizing knowledge at a distance, in P. Meusburger, M. Ries, and J. Glückler (eds.), *Knowledge and Economy* (Berlin: Springer).

——Armbrüster, T. (2003), Bridging uncertainty in management consulting: The mechanisms of trust and networked reputation, *Organization Studies*, 24 (2), 269–97.

——Bathelt, H. (2003*a*), Relationale Wirtschaftsgeographie: Grundperspektiven und Schlüsselkonzepte, in H. Gebhardt, P. Reuber, and G. Wolkersdorfer (eds.), *Kulturgeographie* (Stuttgart: Spektrum), 171–90.

————(2003*b*), Zur Bedeutung von Ressourcen in der relationalen Wirtschaftsgeographie. Vom Substanzkonzept zur relationalen Perspektive, *Zeitschrift für Wirtschaftsgeographie*, 47, 249–67.

——Hammer (2010), A pragmatic service typology: Capturing the distinctive dynamics of services in time and space, *Service Industry Journal* 31: DOI: 10.1080/02642060903078743.

Goehrmann, K. E. (2003*a*), *Die Nutzung der IT auf der Messe steht erst am Anfang (The Application of IT During Trade Fairs is Only Just Beginning)*, 24.

——(2003*b*), Messen als Instrument des Regionen- und Politmarketings (Trade fairs as an instrument of regional and political marketing), in M. Kirchgeorg, W. M. Dornscheidt, W. Giese, and N. Stoeck (eds.), *Handbuch Messemanagement: Planung, Durchführung und Kontrolle von Messen, Kongressen und Events (Handbook of Trade Fair Management: Planning, Execution and Control of Trade Fairs, Conventions and Events)* (Wiesbaden: Gabler), 87–96.

Gordon, I. R. and McCann, P. (2000), Industrial clusters: Complexes, agglomeration and/or social networks?, *Urban Studies*, 37, 513–32.

Grabher, G. (1993*a*), Rediscovering the social in the economies of interfirm relations, in G. Grabher (ed.), *The Embedded Firm. On the Socioeconomics of Industrial Networks* (London, New York: Routledge), 1–31.

——(1993*b*), The weakness of strong ties: The lock-in of regional development in the Ruhr area, in G. Grabher (ed.), *The Embedded Firm: On the Socioeconomics of Industrial Networks* (London: Routledge), 255–77.

——(1994), *Lob der Verschwendung. Redundanz in der Regionalentwicklung: Ein sozioökonomisches Plädoyer* (Berlin: Edition Sigma – Bohn).

——(2001), Ecologies of creativity: The village, the group, and the heterarchic organisation of the British advertising industry, *Environment and Planning A*, 33, 351–74.

——(2002*a*), Cool projects, boring institutions: Temporary collaboration in social context, *Regional Studies*, 36, 205–14.

——(2002*b*), The project ecology of advertising: Talents, tasks, and teams, *Regional Studies*, 36, 245–62.

——(2006), Trading routes, bypasses, and risky intersections: Mapping the travels of 'networks' between economic sociology and economic geography, *Progress in Human Geography*, 30 (2), 163–89.

Grabher, G. and Powell, W. W. (2004), Introduction, in G. Grabher and W. W. Powell (eds.), *Networks* (Critical Studies Economic Institutions Series; Cheltenham: Edward Elgar), xi–xxxi.

——Ibert, O., and Flohr, S. (2008), The neglected king: The customer in the new knowledge ecology of innovation, *Economic Geography*, 84, 253–80.

Gräf, P. (2005), München in der Krise? Projektorganisation und Wachstumsprobleme in der Film- und Fernsehproduktion – eine mehrdimensionale Clusterstudie (Munich in a state of crisis? Project organization and growth problems in Film and TV production – A multidimensional cluster study), *SPACES, Vol. 3, 2005–08* (Marburg: Faculty of Geography, Philipps – University of Marburg).

Granovetter, M. (1973), The strength of weak ties, *American Journal of Sociology*, 78, 1360–80.

——(1985), Economic action and economic structure: The problem of embeddedness, *American Journal of Sociology*, 91, 481–510.

——(1992*a*), Economic institutions as social constructions: A framework for analysis, *Acta Sociologica*, 35, 3–11.

——(1992*b*), Problems of explanation in economic sociology, in N. Nohria and R. G. Eccles (eds.), *Networks and Organisations: Structure, Form, and Action* (Cambridge, MA: Harvard Business School), 25–56.

——(1993), The nature of economic relationships, in R. Swedberg (ed.), *Explorations in Economic Sociology* (New York: Russell Sage), 3–41.

——(2005), The impact of social structure on economic outcomes, *Journal of Economic Perspectives*, 19 (1), 33–50.

Grönroos, C. (1999), Internationalization strategies for services, *Journal of Services Marketing*, 13, 290–97.

Grootaert, C. and Bastelaer, T. v. (2001), Understanding and measuring social capital, *Social Capital Initiative Working Paper No. 24* (New York: The World Bank).

Gulati, R. (1995), Does familiarity breed trust? The implications of repeated ties for contractual choice in alliances, *Academy of Management Journal*, 38, 85–112.

Haas, H. D. and Lindemann, S. (2003), Wissensintensive unternehmensorientierte Dienstleistungen als regionale Innovationssysteme, *Zeitschrift für Wirtschaftsgeographie*, 47, 1–14.

Hall, P. A. and Soskice, D. (2001*a*), An introduction to varieties of capitalism, in P. A. Hall and D. Soskice (eds.), *Varieties of Capitalism: The Institutional Foundations of Comparative Advantage* (Oxford, New York: Oxford University Press), 1–68.

————(2001*b*), *Varieties of Capitalism: The Institutional Foundations of Comparative Advantage* (Oxford, New York: Oxford University Press).

——Thelen, K. (2009), Institutional change in varieties of capitalism, *Socio-Economic Review*, 7 (1), 7–34.

Hall, S. (2008), Geographies of business education: MBA programmes, reflexive business schools and the cultural circuit of capital, *Transactions of the Institute of British Geographers*, 33, 27–41.

Hansen, M. T. (1999), The search-transfer problem: The role of weak ties in sharing knowledge across organizations subunits, *Administrative Science Quarterly*, 44, 82–111.

——(2002), Knowledge networks: Explaining effective knowledge sharing in multiunit companies, *Organization Science*, 13 (3), 232–48.

——Nohria, N., and Tierney, T. (1999), What's your strategy for managing knowledge?, *Harvard Business Review*, 77 (2), 106–16.

Hard, G. (1993), Über Räume reden. Zum Gebrauch des Wortes 'Raum' in sozialwissenschaftlichem Zusammenhang, in J. Mayer (ed.), *Die aufgeräumte Welt. Raumbilder und Raumkonzepte im Zeitalter globaler Marktwirtschaft* (Loccumer Protokolle 74/92; Loccum: Evangelische Akademie Loccum), 53–78.

Hargadon, A. B. and Douglas, J. Y. (2001), When innovations meet institutions: Edison and the design of electric light, *Administrative Science Quarterly*, 46, 476–501.

Harmsen, C. (2008), Standortfaktoren von Gewerbeimmobilien – eine Methode zu deren Bewertung, untersucht am Beispiel eines deutschen offenen Immobilienfonds (Impact of location factors on real estate values using the example of an open German real estate investment fund), in D. M. Schlesinger (ed.), *Branchenspezifische Standortforschung aus relationaler Perspektive (Industry-specific Location Research from Relational Perspective)* (München: Wirtschaftsgeographie, Universität München), 77–154.

Harrigan, K. R. (1983), Research methodologies for contingency approaches to business strategy, *The Academy of Management Review*, 8 (3), 398–405.

Harrison, B. (1992), Industrial districts: Old wine in new bottles?, *Regional Studies*, 26, 469–83.

Hartfiel, G. and Hillmann, K.-H. (1982), *Wörterbuch der Soziologie* (Stuttgart: Kröner).

Harvey, D. (1982), *The Limits of Capital* (Oxford: Blackwell).

——(1996), *Justice, Nature and the Geography of Differences* (Oxford: Blackwell).

Hassink, R. and Shin, D.-H. (2005), Guest editorial: The restructuring of old industrial areas in Europe and Asia, *Environment and Planning A*, 37, 571–80.

Hayek, F. A. v. (1945), The use of knowledge in society, *American Economic Review*, 35, 519–30.

Hayter, R. (2004), Economic geography as dissenting institutionalism: The embeddedness, evolution and differentiation of regions, *Geografiska Annaler*, 86 B, 95–115.

He, S. (2006), *Clusters, Structural Embeddedness, and Knowledge: A Structural Embeddedness Model of Clusters*, DRUID-DIME Winter PhD Conference (Skoerping).

Hellmer, F., Friese, C., Kollros, H., and Krumbein, W. (1999), *Mythos Netzwerke: Regionale Innovationsprozesse zwischen Kontinuität und Wandel* (Berlin: Edition Sigma – Bohn).

Henderson, J., Dicken, P., Hess, M., Coe, N., and Yeung, H. W. C. (2002), Global production networks and the analysis of economic development, *Review of International Political Economy*, 9, 436–64.

Henn, S. (2006), *Regionale Cluster in der Nanotechnologie: Entstehung, Eigenschaften, Handlungsempfehlungen (Regional Clusters of Nanotechnology: Genesis, Characteristics, Policy Implications)* (Frankfurt/Main: Lang).

——(2010), *Clusters, Transnational Entrepreneurs and the Emergence of New Global Production Patterns: The Palanpuris and the Reorganization of Diamond Manufacturing* (Cologne: Paper presented at the IGU Conference on 'Industrial Transition – New Patterns of Production, Work, and Innovativeness in Global Local Spaces').

Hennart, J. F. and Park, Y. R. (1993), Greenfield vs. acquisition: The strategy of Japanese investors in the United States, *Management Science*, 39, 1054–70.

Henry, N., Pollard, J., and Benneworth, P. (2006), Putting clusters in their place, in B. Asheim, P. Cooke, and R. Martin (eds.), *Clusters and Regional Development: Critical Reflections and Explorations* (London, New York: Routledge), 272–91.

Hermelin, B. (1998), Location of professional business services. Conceptual discussion and Swedish case-study, *European Urban and Regional Studies*, 5, 263–75.

Hess, M. (1998), *Glokalisierung, industrieller Wandel und Standortstruktur. Das Beispiel der EU-Schienenfahrzeugindustrie* (Wirtschaft und Raum – Band 2; München: VVF).

Hildebrandt, L. and Weiss, C. (1997), Internationale Markteintrittsstrategien und der Transfer von Marketing-Know-How, *Zeitschrift für die Betriebswirtschaftliche Forschung*, 49, 3–25.

Hirschman, A. O. (1958), *The Strategy of Economic Development* (New Haven: Yale University Press).

Hislop, D. (2002), Mission impossible? Communicating and sharing knowledge via information technology, *Journal of Information Technology*, 17 (3), 165–77.

Hodgson, G. M. (1988), *Economics and Institutions: A Manifesto for a Modern Institutional Economics* (Cambridge: Polity).

——(1998), The approach of institutional economics, *Journal of Economic Literature*, 36, 166–92.

——(1999), *Economics & Utopia. Why the Learning Economy is not the End of History* (London, New York: Routledge).

——(2003), The hidden persuaders: Institutions and individuals in economic theory, *Cambridge Journal of Economics*, 27, 159–75.

Hofmann, H. and Vogler-Ludwig, K. (1991), *The Impact of 1992 on Services Activities: Management Consultancy* (Munich: IFO Research Group Labour Market and Social Policies Final Report).

Hollingshead, A. B. and McGrath, J. E. (1995), Computer-assisted groups: A critical review of the empirical research, in R. A. Guzzo and E. Salas (eds.), *Team Effectiveness and Decision Making in Organizations* (Francisco: Jossey-Bass/Pfeiffer), 46–78.

Hooghe, L. and Marks, G. (2003), Unraveling the central state, but how? Types of multi-level governance, *American Political Science Review*, 97, 233–43.

Horak, J. C. (1996), Munich's first fiction feature: Die Wahrheit, in T. Elsaesser (ed.), *A Second Life: German Cinema's First Decade* (Amsterdam: Amsterdam University Press), 86–92.

Hsu, J. and Saxenian, A. L. (2000), The limits of guanxi capitalism: Transnational collaboration between Taiwan and the USA, *Environmental Planning A*, Vol. 32, 1991–2005.

Huber, F. (2009), Social capital of economic clusters: Towards a network-based conception of social resources, *Tijdschrift voor Economische en Sociale Geografie*, 100, 160–70.

Hudson, R. (2004), Conceptualizing economies and their geographies: Spaces, flows and circuits, *Progress in Human Geography*, 28, 447–71.

——(2007), Regions and regional uneven development forever? Some reflective comments upon theory and practice, *Regional Studies*, 41, 1149–60.

Hughes, A. (1999), Constructing economic geographies from corporate interviews: Insights from a crosscountry comparison of retailer-supplier relationships, *Geoforum*, 30, 363–74.

Hume, D. (1900), *An Enquiry Concerning Human Understanding* (Chicago: The Open Court Publishing Co).

Humphrey, J. and Schmitz, H. (2002), How does insertion in global value chains affect upgrading in industrial clusters?, *Regional Studies*, 36, 1017–27.

Ibert, O. (2003), Projects and firms as discordant complements: Organisational learning in the Munich software ecology, *Research Policy*, 33, 1529–46.

——(2007), Towards a geography of knowledge creation: The ambivalences between 'knowledge as an object' and 'knowing in practice', *Regional Studies*, 41, 103–14.

Illeris, S. (1994), Proximity between service producers and service users, *Tijdschrift voor Economische en Sociale Geografie*, 85, 294–302.

Industrie- und Handelskammer für München und Oberbayern and Landeshauptstadt München (2003), *Der Medienstandort München (Munich as a Media Location)* (München: Industrie- und Handelskammer für München und Oberbayern and Landeshauptstadt München).

Isard, W. (1956), *Location and Space-Economy. A General Theory Relating to Industrial Location, Market Areas, Land Use, Trade, and Urban Structure* (Regional science studies series, 1; Cambridge: Published jointly by the Technology Press of Massachusetts Institute of Technology and Wiley).

——(1960), *Methods of Regional Analysis; An Introduction to Regional Science* (Regional Science Studies; Cambridge: Published jointly by the Technology Press of the Massachusetts Institute of Technology and Wiley).

Jacobs, J. (1969), *The Economy of Cities* (New York: Random House).

Jaffe, A. B., Trajtenberg, M., and Henderson, R. (1993), Geographic localization of knowledge spillovers as evidenced by patent citations, *Quarterly Journal of Economics*, 108, 577–98.

Jansen, D. (2006), *Einführung in die Netzwerkanalyse: Grundlagen, Methoden, Forschungsbeispiele* (3rd edn.; Wiesbaden: VS-Verlag).

Jentsch, C. (2004), Projektorganisation in der Frankfurter Werbeindustrie (Project Organization in the Frankfurt Advertising Industry). *SPACES, Vol. 2, 2004–03* (Marburg: Faculty of Geography, Philipps-University of Marburg).

Jeppesen, L. B. and Frederiksen, L. (2006), Why do users contribute to firm-hosted user communities? The case of computer-controlled music instruments, *Organization Science*, 17 (1), 45–63.

——Molin, J. M. (2003), Consumers as co-developers: Learning and innovation outside the firm, *Technology Analysis & Strategic Management*, 15, 363–83.

Jessop, B. (1992), Fordism and post-fordism: A critical reformulation, in M. Storper and A. J. Scott (eds.), *Pathways to Industrialization and Regional Development* (London, New York: Routledge), 46–69.

——(2001), Institutional re(turns) and the strategic-relational approach, *Environment and Planning A*, 33, 1213–35.

Jick, T. D. (1979), Mixing qualitative and quantitative methods: Triangulation in action, *Administrative Science Quarterly*, 24, 602–11.

Johannisson, B. (1990), Economies of overview: Guiding the external growth of small firms, *International Small Business Journal*, 9 (1), 32–44.

Johanson, J. and Mattsson, L. G. (1987), Interorganizational relations in industrial systems: A network approach compared with the transaction-cost approach, *International Studies of Management and Organization*, 17, 34–48.

————(1993), Internationalization in industrial systems – A network approach, in P. J. Buckley and P. N. Ghauri (eds.), *The Internationalization of the Firm: A Reader* (London: Academic Press), 303–21.

——Vahlne, J. E. (1977), The internationalization process of the firm – A model of knowledge development and increasing foreign market commitment, *Journal of International Business Studies*, 8 (1), 23–32.

Johanson, J. and Mattsson, L. G. (1990), The mechanism of internationalization, *International Marketing Review*, 7, 11–24.

————(1992), Management of foreign market entry, *Scandinavian International Business Review*, 1, 9–27.

——Wiedersheim-Paul, F. (1975), The internationalization of the firm – Four Swedish case studies, *Journal of Management Studies*, 12, 305–22.

Johnson, B., Lorenz, E., and Lundvall, B. Å. (2002), Why all this fuss about codified and tacit knowledge?, *Industrial and Corporate Change*, 11 (2), 245–62.

Jones, A. M. (2003), *Management Consultancy and Banking in an Era of Globalization* (Basingstoke: Palgrave).

——(2007), More than managing across borders? The complex role of face-to-face interaction in globalizing law firms, *Journal of Economic Geography*, 7, 223–46.

——(2008), Beyond embeddedness: Economic practices and the invisible dimensions to transnational business activity, *Progress in Human Geography*, 32, 71–81.

Jones, M. (2009), Phase space: Geography, relational thinking, and beyond, *Progress in Human Geography*, 33, 487–506.

Jones, B. W., Spigel, B., and Malecki, E. J. (2010), Blog links as pipelines to buzz elsewhere: The case of New York theatre blogs, *Environment and Planning B – Planning and Design*, 37.

Jöns, H. (2003), Von Menschen und Dingen: Konstruktivistisch-kritische Anmerkungen zum (a)symmetrischen Akteurskonzept der Akteursnetzwerktheorie (Humans and non-humans: Critical comments on the (a)symmetrical actor concept in actor-network theory), in J. Hasse and I. Helbrecht (eds.), *Menschenbilder in der Humangeographie (Human Images in Human Geography)* (Oldenburg: Bibliotheks- und Informationssystem), 109–42.

——(2006), Dynamic hybrids and the geographies of technoscience: Discussing conceptual resources beyond the human/non-human binary, *Social and Cultural Geography*, 7 (4), 559–80.

Kaas, K. P. and Schade, C. (1995), Unternehmensberater im Wettbewerb. Eine empirische Untersuchung aus der Perspektive der Neuen Institutionenlehre, *Zeitschrift für Betriebswirtschaft*, 65, 1067–89.

Kaldor, N. (1970), The case for regional policies, *Scottish Journal of Political Economy*, 17, 337–47.

Katz, M. L. and Shapiro, C. (1985), Network externalities, competition, and compatibility, *American Economic Review*, 75, 424–40.

Keeble, D. and Nachum, L. (2002), Why do business service firms cluster? Small consultancies, clustering and decentralization in London and Southern England, *Transactions of the Institute of British Geographers*, 27, 67–90.

——Bryson, J., and Wood, P. (1992), Entrepreneurship and flexibility in business services: The rise of small management consultancy and market research firms in the United Kingdom, in K. Caley, F. Chittenden, E. Chell, and C. Mason (eds.), *Small Enterprise Development: Policy and Practice in Action* (London: Chapman), 43–58.

Kern, H. (1996), Vertrauensverlust und blindes Vertrauen: Integrationsprobleme im ökonomischen Handeln, *SOFI-Mitteilungen*, Nr. 24/1996, 7–14.

Kiese, M. and Schätzl, L. (2008), *Cluster und Regionalentwicklung: Theorie, Beratung und praktische Umsetzung* (Dortmund: Verlag).

Kilduff, M. and Krackhardt, D. (1994), Bringing the individual back in: A structural analysis of the internal market for reputation in organizations, *Academy of Management Journal*, 37, 87–108.

——Tsai, W. (2003), *Social Networks and Organizations* (London: Sage).

Kirchgeorg, M. (2003), Funktionen und Erscheinungsformen von Messen (Functions and types of trade fairs), in M. Kirchgeorg, W. M. Dornscheidt, W. Giese, and N. Stoeck (eds.), *Messemanagement: Planung, Durchführung und Kontrolle von Messen, Kongressen und Events (Handbook of Trade Fair Management: Planning, Execution and Control of Trade Fairs, Conventions and Events)* (Wiesbaden: Gabler), 51–72.

Knack, S. (1999), Social capital, growth and poverty: A survey of cross-country evidence, *Social Capital Initiative Working Papers 7* (Washington, DC: World Bank).

——Keefer, P. (1997), Does social capital have an economic payoff? A cross-country investigation, *The Quarterly Journal of Economics*, 112, 1251–88.

Knoke, D. (2001), *Changing Organizations: Business Networks in the New Political Economy* (Foundations of social inquiry; Boulder, CO: Westview Press).

——Kuklinski, J. H. (1991), Network analysis: Basic concepts, in G. Thompson, J. Frances, R. Levacic, and J. Mitchell (eds.), *Markets, Hierarchies and Networks* (London: Sage), 173–82.

Knorr Cetina, K. (1999), *Epistemic Cultures: How the Sciences Make Sense* (Chicago: Chicago University Press).

Knox-Hayes, J. (2009), The developing carbon financial service industry: Expertise, adaptation and complementarity in London and New York, *Journal of Economic Geography*, 9 (6), 749–77.

Kogler, D. (2010), *The Geography of Knowledge Formation: Spatial and Sectoral Aspects of Patents and Patent Citations in the Canadian Economy, 1983–2007* (Toronto: University of Toronto).

Kollock, P. (1994), The emergence of exchange structures: An experimental study of uncertainty, commitment, and trust, *American Journal of Sociology*, 100, 313–45.

Kostiainen, J. (2002), Learning and the 'ba' in the development network of an urban region, *European Planning Studies*, 10 (5), 613–31.

Krackhardt, D. (1987), QAP partialling as a test of spuriousness, *Social Networks*, 9, 171–86.

——Hanson, J. (1993), Informal networks: The company behind the chart, *Harvard Business Review*, 71 (4), 104–11.

——Stern, R. N. (1988), Informal networks and organizational crises: An experimental simulation, *Social Psychology Quarterly*, 51 (2), 123–40.

Krätke, S. (2002), *Medienstadt. Urbane Cluster und globale Zentren der Kulturproduktion* (Opladen: Leske + Budrich).

Kreimeyer, A. (2005), Swimming ahead of the shoal – The history of BASF in greater China, in G. Festel, A. Kreimeyer, U. Oels, and M. v. Zedtwitz (eds.), *The Chemical and Pharmaceutical Industry in China: Opportunities and Threats to Foreign Companies* (Heidelberg: Springer), 159–70.

Kreps, D. and Wilson, R. (1982), Reputation and imperfect information, *Journal of Economic Theory*, 27, 253–79.

Krugman, P. (1991), *Geography and Trade* (Gaston Eyskens Lecture Series; Leuven, Cambridge, MA: Leuven University Press; MIT Press).

Krugman, P. (2000), Where in the world is the 'New Economic Geography'?, in G. Clark, M. Feldman, and M. Gertler (eds.), *The Oxford Handbook of Economic Geography* (Oxford: Oxford University Press), 49–60.

——(2010), *The New Geography, Now Middle Aged* (Washington, DC: Annual Meeting of the Association of American Geographers).

Krumberger, O. (2005), Establishing a competitive production network in Asia, in G. Festel, A. Kreimeyer, U. Oels, and M. v. Zedtwitz (eds.), *The Chemical and Pharmaceutical Industry in China: Opportunities and Threats to Foreign Companies* (Heidelberg: Springer), 171–9.

Kurp, M. (2004), Medienfonds als ,Stupid German Money'. Steuersparmodell unterstützt Hollywood statt deutsche Filmmakers (Mediafonds as ,Stupid German Money'. Tax Saving Models Support Hollywood Rather Than German Filmmakers).

——(2005), *Die größten deutschen Medienkonzerne 2000 (The Largest German Media Firms 2000).*

Kurz, S. and Schmidkonz, C. (2005), *The Impact of Direct Investment of BASF in Nanjing, China on the Sustainable Development of the Region* (Study of the Deutsche Gesellschaft für Technische Zusammenarbeit (GTZ); Nanjing), Summer.

Lagendijk, A. (1999), *Good Practices in SME Cluster Initiatives. Lessons from the 'Core' Regions and Beyond* (Newcastle: CURDS).

——Cornford, J. (2000), Regional institutions and knowledge – Tracking new forms of regional development policy, *Geoforum*, 31, 209–18.

Lane, P. J. and Lubatkin, M. (1998), Relative absorptive capacity and interorganizational learning, *Strategic Management Journal*, 19 (5), 461–77.

La Porta, R., Lopez-de-Salinas, F., Shleifer, A., and Vishny, R. W. (1997), Trust in large organizations, *American Economic Review*, 87, 333–8.

Latour, B. (1986), The powers of association, in J. Law (ed.), *Power, Action and Belief: A New Sociology of Knowledge?* (London: Routledge & Kegan Paul), 264–80.

——(2005), *Reassembling the Social: An Introduction to Actor-Network-Theory* (Oxford: Oxford University Press).

Lave, J. and Wenger, E. (1991), *Situated Learning: Legitimate Peripheral Participation* (Cambridge: Cambridge University Press).

Lawrence, J., Payne, T. R., and De Roure, D. (2006), *Co-Presence Communities: Using Pervasive Computing to Support Weak Social Networks* (Manchester: Paper presented at the 15th IEEE International Workshops on 'Enabling Technologies: Infrastructure for Collaborative Enterprises').

Lawson, C. (1999), Towards a competence theory of the region, *Cambridge Journal of Economics*, 23, 151–66.

——Lorenz, E. (1999), Collective learning, tacit knowledge and regional innovative capacity, *Regional Studies*, 33, 305–17.

Lazer, D. and Friedman, A. (2007), The network structure of exploration and exploitation, *Administrative Science Quarterly*, 52 (4), 667–94.

Leamer, E. and Storper, M. (2001), The economic geography of the internet age, *Journal of International Business Studies*, 32 (4), 641–65.

Leborgne, D. and Lipietz, A. (1991), Two social strategies in the production of new industrial spaces, in G. Benko and M. Dunford (eds.), *Industrial Change and Regional Development: The Transformation of New Industrial Spaces* (London, New York: Belhaven), 27–50.

Lee, J. H. (2001), Geographies of learning and proximity reconsidered: A relational/ organizational perspective, *Journal of the Korean Geographical Society*, 36, 539–60.

Lee, R. (2002), 'Nice maps, shame about the theory'? Thinking geographically about the economic, *Progress in Human Geography*, 26, 333–55.

——(2006), The ordinary economy: Tangled up in values and geography, *Transactions of the Institute of British Geographers*, 31, 413–32.

——Wills, J. (1997), *Geographies of Economies* (London, New York, Sydney: Arnold).

Li, J. and Guisinger, S. (1992), The globalization of service multinationals in the 'Triad' regions: Japan, Western Europe and North America, *Journal of International Business Studies*, 23, 675–96.

Lilja, K. and Poulfelt, F. (2001), The anatomy of network building in management consulting firms, in A. F. Buono (ed.), *Current Trends in Management Consulting* (Greenwich, CT: Information Age Publications), 3–21.

Lindahl, D. P. and Beyers, W. B. (1999), The creation of competitive advantage by producer service establishments, *Economic Geography*, 75, 1–20.

Lindkvist, K. and Sánchez Hernández, J. L. (2008), Conventions and innovation: A comparison of two natural resource-based industries, *Regional Studies*, 42 (3), 343–54.

Lindner, P. (2008), *Der Kolchoz-Archipel im Privatisierungsprozess: Wege und Umwege der russischen Landwirtschaft in die globale Marktgesellschaft* (Bielefeld: Transcript).

Lippman, S. A. and Rumelt, R. P. (1982), Uncertain imitability: An analysis of interfirm differences in efficiency under competition, *The Bell Journal of Economics*, 13 (2), 418–38.

Lissoni, F. (2001), Knowledge codification and the geography of innovation: The case of Brescia mechanical cluster, *Research Policy*, 30 (9), 1479–500.

Lloyd, P. E. and Dicken, P. (1972), *Location in Space: A Theoretical Approach to Economic Geography* (London, New York: Harper & Row).

Loasby, B. J. (2000), Market institutions and economic evolution, *Journal of Evolutionary Economics*, 10, 297–309.

Lorenz, E. (1999), Trust, contract and economic cooperation, *Cambridge Journal of Economics*, 23, 301–15.

Lovering, J. (1989), The restructuring debate, in R. Peet and N. Thrift (eds.), *New Models in Geography* (London: Hyman), 159–74.

Løwendahl, B. (2000), The globalization of professional business service firms. Fad or genuine source of competitive advantage, in Y. Aharoni and L. Nachum (eds.), *Globalization of Services. Some Implications for Theory and Practice* (London, New York: Routledge), 125–41.

Lowey, S. (1999), *Organisation und regionale Wirkungen von Unternehmenskooperationen: Eine empirische Untersuchung im Maschinenbau Unter- und Mittelfrankens (Organization and Regional Impact of Inter-firm Co-operation: An Investigation of the Machinery Industry in Lower/Middle Frankonia, Germany)* (Wirtschaftsgeographie, 16; Münster, Hamburg: LIT).

Luhmann, N. (1984), *Soziale Systeme: Grundriss einer allgemeinen Theorie (Social Systems: Foundations of a General Theory)* (Frankfurt/Main: Suhrkamp).

——(2000), *Organisation und Entscheidung* (Opladen: Westdeutscher Verlag).

Lundequist, P. and Power, D. (2002), Putting Porter into practice? Practices of regional cluster building: Evidence from Sweden, *European Planning Studies*, 10, 685–704.

Lundin, R. A. (1995), Editorial: Temporary organizations and projects management, *Scandinavian Journal of Management*, 11, 315–18.

Lundvall, B.-Å. (1988), Innovation as an interactive process: From producer-user interaction to the national system of innovation, in G. Dosi, C. Freeman, R. R. Nelson, G. Silverberg, and L. L. G. Soete (eds.), *Technical Change and Economic Theory* (London, New York: Pinter), 349–69.

——(1992), *National Systems of Innovation: Towards a Theory of Innovation and Interactive Learning* (London: Pinter).

——Johnson, B. (1994), The learning economy, *Journal of Industry Studies*, 1, 23–42.

——Maskell, P. (2000), Nation states and economic development: From national systems of production to national systems of knowledge creation and learning, in G. L. Clark, M. P. Feldman, and M. S. Gertler (eds.), *The Oxford Handbook of Economic Geography* (Oxford: Oxford University Press), 353–72.

——Johnson, B., Andersen, E. S., and Dalum, B. (2002), National systems of production, innovation and competence building, *Research Policy*, 31, 213–31.

Mahoney, J. and Pandian, J. R. (1992), The resource-based view within the conversation of strategic management, *Strategic Management Journal*, 13, 363–80.

Maillat, D. (1998), Vom 'Industrial District' zum innovativen Milieu: Ein Beitrag zur Analyse der lokalen Produktionssysteme, *Geographische Zeitschrift*, 86, 1–15.

——Léchot, G., Lecoq, B., and Pfister, M. (1997), Comparative analysis of the structural development of milieux: The watch industry in the Swiss and French Jura arc, in R. Ratti, A. Bramanti, and R. Gordon (eds.), *The Dynamics of Innovative Regions: The GREMI Approach* (Adlershot, Brookfield: Ashgate), 109–37.

Malecki, E. J. (2000), Knowledge and regional competitiveness, *Erdkunde*, 54, 334–51.

Malmberg, A. and Maskell, P. (1997), Towards an explanation of industry agglomeration and regional specialization, *Environment Planning Studies*, 5, 25–41.

————(2002), The elusive concept of localization economies: Towards a knowledge-based theory of spatial clustering, *Environment and Planning A*, 34, 429–49.

——Power, D. (2003), (How) do (firms in) clusters create knowledge? *Paper presented at the Danish Research Unit on Industrial Dynamics summer conference 'Creating, sharing and transferring knowledge. The role of geography, institutions and organizations* (Copenhagen).

March, J. G. (1991), Exploration and exploitation in organizational learning, *Organization Science*, 2 (1), 71–87.

Markusen, A., Hall, P., Dampbell, S., and Deitrick, S. (1991), *The Rise of the Gunbelt: The Military Remapping of Industrial America* (New York, Oxford: Oxford University Press).

Marquis, C. (2003), The pressure of the past: Network imprinting in intercorporate communities, *Administrative Science Quarterly*, 48 (4), 655–89.

Marsden, P. V. (2003), Interviewer effects in measuring network size using a single name generator, *Social Networks*, 25, 1–16.

——Lin, N. (eds.) (1982), *Social Structure and Network Analysis* (Beverly Hills: Sage).

Marshall, A. (1920), *Principles of Economics* (8th edn.; Philadelphia: Porcupine Press).

——(1927), *Industry and Trade. A Study of Industrial Technique and Business Organization; And Their Influences on the Conditions of Various Classes and Nations* (reprint of the 3rd edn., Nachdruck der 3. Auflage; London: Macmillan).

——(1956 [1890]), *Principles of Economics* (reprinted 8th edn.; London: Macmillan).

Marshall, J. N. and Wood, P. A. (1992), The role of services in urban and regional development: Recent debates and new directory, *Environment and Planning A*, 24, 1255–70.

Martin, R. (1994), Economic theory and human geography, in D. Gregory, R. Martin, and D. Smith (eds.), *Human Geography. Society, Space and Social Science* (Houndmills: Macmillan), 21–53.

——Sunley, P. (1996), Paul Krugman's geographical economics and its implications for regional development theory: A critical assessment, *Economic Geography*, 74, 259–92.

————(2001), Rethinking the 'economic' in economic geography: Broadening our vision or losing our focus?, *Antipode*, 33, 148–61.

————(2003), Deconstructing clusters: Chaotic concept or policy panacea, *Journal of Economic Geography*, 3, 5–35.

————(2006), Path dependence and regional economic evolution, *Journal of Economic Geography*, 6 (4), 395–437.

Martinelli, F. and Moulaert, F. (1993), The location of advanced producer services firms: Theory and illustrations, *Geographische Zeitschrift*, 81, 1–17.

Maskell, P. (2001*a*), The firm in economic geography, *Economic Geography*, 77, 329–44.

——(2001*b*), Towards a knowledge-based theory of the geographical cluster, *Industrial and Corporate Change*, 10, 921–43.

——Lorenzen, M. (2004), The cluster as market organization, *Urban Studies*, 41 (5/6), 991–1009.

——Malmberg, A. (1999*a*), Localised learning and industrial competitiveness, *Cambridge Journal of Economics*, 23, 167–85.

————(1999*b*), The competitiveness of firms and regions: Ubiquitification and the importance of localised learning, *European Urban and Regional Studies*, 6 (9), 26.

——Bathelt, H., and Malmberg, A. (2004), Temporary clusters and knowledge creation: The effects of international trade fairs, conventions and other professional gatherings, *SPACES*, Vol. 2, 2004–04 (Marburg: Faculty of Geography, Philipps – University of Marburg).

——————(2006), Building global knowledge pipelines: The role of temporary clusters, *European Planning Studies*, 14, 997–1013.

Massey, D. (1985), New directions in space, in D. Gregory and J. Urry (eds.), *Social Relations and Spatial Structures* (Basingstoke: Macmillan), 9–19.

——(2004), Geographies of responsibility, *Geografiska Annaler*, 86 B, 5–18.

McCann, P. (2008), Agglomeration economies, in C. Karlsson (ed.), *Handbook of Research on Cluster Theory* (Cheltenham, Northampton, MA: Edward Elgar), 23–38.

McDermott, R. (1999), Why information technology inspired but cannot deliver knowledge management, *California Management Review*, 41 (4), 103–17.

McDougall, P. P., Shane, P., and Oviatt, B. M. (1994), Explaining the formation of international new ventures: The limits of theories from international business research, *Journal of Business Venturing*, 9, 469–87.

McDowell, L. (2000), Feminists rethink the economic: The economics of gender/the gender of economics, in G. L. Clark, M. P. Feldman, and M. S. Gertler (eds.), *The Oxford Handbook of Economic Geography* (Oxford: Oxford University Press), 497–517.

McGuire, T. W., Kiesler, S., and Siegel, J. (1987), Group and computer-mediated discussion, *Personality and Social Psychology*, 52 (5), 917–30.

Meffert, H. (1993), Messen und Ausstellungen als Marketinginstrument (Trade fairs and exhibitions as a marketing tool), in K. E. Goehrmann (ed.), *Polit-Marketing auf Messen (Marketing Policy on Trade Fairs)* (Düsseldorf: Wirtschaft und Finanzen), 74–96.

Meffert, H. (1997), Neuere Entwicklungen in Kommunikation und Vertrieb (New developments in communication and distribution), in H. Meffert, T. Necker, and H. Sihler (eds.), *Märkte im Dialog: Die Messen der dritten Generation (Markets in Dialogue: Trade Fairs of the Third Generation)* (Wiesbaden: Gabler), 134–58.

——(2003), Ziel und Nutzen der Messebeteiligung von ausstellenden Unternehmen und Besuchern (Goals and Effects of Trade Fair Participation), in M. Kirchgeorg, W. M. Dornscheidt, W. Giese, and N. Stoeck (eds.), *Handbuch Messemanagement: Planung, Durchführung und Kontrolle von Messen, Kongressen und Events (Handbook of Trade Fair Management: Planning, Execution and Control of Trade Fairs, Conventions and Events)* (Wiesbaden: Gabler), 1145–63.

Ménard, C. (1995), Markets as institutions vs. organizations as markets? Disentangling some fundamental concepts, *Journal of Economic Behavior and Organization*, 28, 161–82.

Meusburger, P. (1998), *Bildungsgeographie. Wissen und Ausbildung in der räumlichen Dimension* (Heidelberg: Spektrum Akademischer Verlag).

——(2008), The nexus between knowledge and space, in P. Meusburger, M. Welker, and E. Wunder (eds.), *Clashes of Knowledge. Knowledge and Space, Vol. 1* (Dordrecht: Springer), 35–90.

Miao, C.-H., Wei, D. Y., and Ma, H. (2007), Technological learning and innovation in China in the context of globalization, *Eurasian Geography and Economics*, 48, 1–20.

Miles, M. B. and Huberman, A. M. (1994), *Qualitative Data Analysis* (2nd edn.; Thousand Oaks, London: Sage).

Mische, A. (2011), Relational sociology, culture, and agency, in J. Scott and P. Carrington (eds.), *Sage Handbook of Social Network Analysis* (London: Sage).

Mitchell, J. C. (1969), The concept and use of social networks, in J. C. Mitchell (ed.), *Social Networks in Urban Situations. Analyses of Personal Relationships in Central African Towns* (Manchester: Manchester University Press), 1–50.

Mizruchi, M. S. (1994), Social network analysis: Recent achievements and current controversies, *Acta Sociologica*, 37, 329–43.

Moodysson, J. (2008), Principles and practices of knowledge creation: On the organization of 'buzz' and 'pipelines' in life science communities, *Economic Geography*, 84, 449–69.

Morgan, K. (1997), The learning region: Institutions, innovation and regional renewal, *Regional Studies*, 31, 491–503.

Mossig, I. (2006), *Netzwerke der Kulturökonomie. Lokale Knoten und globale Verflechtungen der Film- und Fernsehindustrie in Deutschland und den USA* (Bielefeld: Transcript).

Moulaert, F. and Djellal, F. (1995), Information technology consultancy firms: Economics of agglomeration from a wide-area perspective, *Urban Studies*, 32, 105–22.

Mu, J. (2006), *Changjiang sanjiaozhou shihua gongye kongjian jiegou yanhua yanjiu (Research on the Spatial Structure of the Petrochemical Industry in the Yangtze delta region)* (Shanghai: East China Normal University).

Mullings, B. (1999), Insider or outsider, both or neither: Some dilemmas of interviewing in a crosscultural setting, *Geoforum*, 30, 337–50.

Murdoch, J. (1995), Actor-networks and the evolution of economic forms: Combining description and explanation in theories of regulation, flexible specialization, and networks, *Environment and Planning A*, 27, 731–57.

Murphy, J. T. (2003), Social space and industrial development in East Africa: Deconstructing the logics of industry networks in Mwanza, Tanzania, *Journal of Economic Geography*, 3, 173–98.

Myrdal, G. (1957), *Economic Theory and Underdeveloped Regions* (London: Duckworth).

Nachum, L. and Keeble, D. (2001), *External Networks and Geographic Clustering as Sources of MNE Advantages: Foreign and Indigenous Professional Service Firms in Central London* (Working Paper No. 195; Cambridge: ESRC Centre for Business Research University of Cambridge).

————(2003), Neo-Marshallian clusters and global networks: The linkages of media firms in Central London, *Long Range Planning*, 36, 459–80.

Nanjing Chemical Industry Park Corp. (2005), *Investment Guide 2005 – Brochure* (Nanjing: Nanjing Chemical Industry Park Corp.).

Nelson, R. R. (1993), *National Innovation Systems: A Comparative Analysis* (Oxford: Oxford University Press).

——(1995*a*), Evolutionary theorizing about economic change, *Journal of Economic Literature*, 23, 48–90.

——(1995*b*), Recent evolutionary theorizing about economic change, *Journal of Economic Literature*, 33, 48–90.

——Winter, S. G. (1982), *An Evolutionary Theory of Economic Change* (Cambridge, MA: Harvard University Press).

Newlands, D. (2003), Competition and cooperation in industrial clusters: The implications for public policy, *European Planning Studies*, 11, 521–32.

Ningbo Chemical Industry Zone Corp. (2007*a*), *Investment Guide – Brochure* (Ningbo: Ningbo Chemical Industry Zone Corp.).

——(2007*b*), *Ningbo Chemical Industry Zone* (Ningbo: Ningbo Chemical Industry Zone Corp.).

Nonaka, I. (1994), A dynamic theory of organizational knowledge creation, *Organization Science*, 5, 14–37.

——Takeuchi, H. (1995), *The Knowledge-Creating Company* (New York: Oxford University Press).

——Toyama, R., and Nagata, A. (2000), A firm as a knowledge-creating entity: A new perspective on the theory of the firm, *Industrial and Corporate Change*, 9, 1–20.

Nooteboom, B. (1996), Trust, opportunism and governance: A process and control model, *Organization Studies*, 17, 985–1010.

——(2000), *Learning and Innovation in Organizations and Economies* (Oxford: Oxford University Press).

——(2002), *Trust. Forms, Foundations, Functions, Failures and Figures* (Cheltenham, Northampton, MA: Edgar Elgar).

North, D. C. (1990), *Institutions, Institutional Change and Economic Performance* (Cambridge: Cambridge University Press).

——(1991), Institutions, *The Journal of Economic Perspectives*, 5, 97–112.

OECD (1999), *Boosting Innovation: The Cluster Approach* (Paris: OECD).

——(2001), *Innovative Clusters: Drivers of National Innovation Systems* (Paris: OECD).

O'Farrell, P. N. and Wood, P. (1998), Internationalisation by business service firms: Towards a new regionally based conceptual framework, *Environment and Planning A*, 30, 109–28.

O'Farrell, P. N. and Wood, P. (1999), Formation of strategic alliances in business services: Towards a new client-oriented conceptual framework, *Services Industries Journal*, 19, 133–51.

——Moffat, L., and Wood, P. (1995), Internationalisation by business service firms: A methodological critique of foreign-market entry-mode choice, *Environment and Planning A*, 27, 683–97.

——Wood, P., and Zheng, J. (1996), Internationalization of business services: An interregional analysis, *Regional Studies*, 30, 101–18.

Ofek, E. and Sarvary, M. (2001), Leveraging the customer base: Creating competitive advantage through knowledge management, *Management Science*, 47, 1441–56.

Oinas, P. (1997), On the socio-spatial embeddedness of business firms, *Erdkunde*, 51, 23–32.

——(1999), Voices and silences: The problem of access to embeddedness, *Geoforum*, 30, 351–61.

——(2005), The firm and its many boundaries, in M. Taylor and P. Oinas (eds.), *Conceptualising the Firm: Capabilities, Cultures, and Conditions* (Oxford: Oxford University Press).

Olson, C. and Olson, J. (2003), Mitigating the effects of distance on collaborative intellectual work, *Economics of Innovation and New Technology*, 12 (1), 27–42.

Ong, L. H. (2007), Between developmental and clientelist states: Explaining rural industrialization in China, *Department of Political Science Series 'Politics at Noon'* (Toronto: University of Toronto).

Overman, H. G. (2004), Can we learn anything from economic geography proper?, *Journal of Economic Geography*, 4 (5), 501–16.

Owen-Smith, J. and Powell, W. W. (2002), *Knowledge Networks in the Boston Biotechnology Community*, conference on 'Science as an Institution and the Institutions of Science' (Siena).

——————(2004), Knowledge networks as channels and conduits: The effects of spillovers in the Boston biotechnology community, *Organization Science*, 15 (1), 5–21.

Pachucki, M. A. and Breiger, R. L. (2010), Cultural holes: Beyond relationality in social networks and culture, *Annual Review of Sociology*, 36 (1), 205–24.

Parker, P. (2001), Local-global partnerships for high-tech development: Integrating top-down and bottom-up models, *Economic Development Quarterly*, 15, 149–67.

Peck, J. (1996), *Workplace: The Social Regulation of Labour Markets* (New York: Guilford).

Penrose, E. T. (1959), *The Theory of the Growth of the Firm* (Oxford: Blackwell).

——(1997), The theory of the growth of the firm, in N. J. Foss (ed.), *Resources, Firms and Strategies: A Reader in the Resource-based Perspective* (Oxford, New York: Oxford University Press), 27–39.

Perlitz, U. (2005), Chemieindustrie in China: International auf der Überholspur (Chemical industry in China: Overtaking internationally), *Deutsche Bank Research: Aktuelle Themen 333: China Spezial* (Frankfurt/Main: Deutsche Bank).

Perrons, D. (2001), Towards a more holistic framework for economic geography, *Antipode*, 33, 208–15.

Peteraf, M. A. (1993), The cornerstones of competitive advantage: A resource-based view, *Strategic Management Journal*, 14, 179–88.

Pfeffer, J. and Salancik, G. R. (1978), *The External Control of Organizations* (New York: Harper and Row).

Philo, C. (1989), Contextuality, in A. Bullock, O. Stally-Brass, and S. Trombly (eds.), *The Fontana Dictionary of Modern Thought* (London: Fontana Press), 173.

Podolny, J. M. (2001), Networks as the pipes and prisms of the market, *American Journal of Sociology*, 107 (1), 33–60.

——Page, K. L. (1998), Network forms of organization, *Annual Review of Sociology*, 24, 57–76.

Polanyi, M. (1967), *The Tacit Dimension* (London: Routledge & Kegan Paul).

Porter, M. E. (1986), Competition in global industries: A conceptual framework, in M. Porter (ed.), *Competition in Global Industries* (Cambridge, MA: Harvard Business School Press), 15–60.

——(1990a), The competitive advantage of nations, *Harvard Business Review*, 68 (Mar/Apr), 73–93.

——(1990b), *The Competitive Advantage of Nations* (New York: Free Press).

——(1998), Clusters and the new economics of competition, *Harvard Business Review* (Nov–Dec), 77–90.

——(2000), Locations, cluster, and company strategy, in G. L. Clark, M. P. Feldman, and M. S. Gertler (eds.), *The Oxford Handbook of Economic Geography* (Oxford: Oxford University Press), 253–74.

——(2003), The economic performance of regions, *Regional Studies*, 37 (6/7), 549–78.

Portes, A. (1998), Social capital: Its origins and applications in modern sociology, *Annual Review of Sociology*, 24, 1–24.

——Sensenbrenner, J. (1993), Embeddedness and immigration: Notes on the social determinants of economic action, *American Journal of Sociology*, 98, 1320–50.

——Haller, W. J., and Eduardo Guarnizo, L. (2002), Transnational entrepreneurs: An alternative form of immigrant economic adaptation, *American Sociological Review*, 67, 278–98.

Powell, W. W., Koput, K. W., Bowie, J. I., and Smith-Doerr, L. (2002), The spatial clustering of science and capital: Accounting for biotech firm-venture capital relationships, *Regional Studies*, 36 (3), 291–306.

Power, D. and Jansson, J. (2008), Cyclical clusters in global circuits: Overlapping spaces in furniture trade fairs, *Economic Geography*, 84, 423–48.

Prahalad, C. and Bettis, R. (1986), The dominant logic: A new linkage between diversity and performance, *Strategic Management Journal*, 7, 485–501.

——Hamel, G. (1990), The core competence of the corporation, *Harvard Business Review*, 68 (May/Jun), 79–91.

Prüser, S. (1997), *Messemarketing: Ein netzwerkorientierter Ansatz (Trade Fair Marketing: A Network Approach)* (Wiesbaden: Deutscher Universitäts-Verlag).

——(2003), Die Messe als Networking-Plattform (Trade fairs as a platform for networking), in M. Kirchgeorg, W. M. Dornscheidt, W. Giese, and N. Stoeck (eds.), *Handbuch Messemanagement: Planung, Durchführung und Kontrolle von Messen, Kongressen und Events (Handbook of Trade Fair Management: Planning, Execution and Control of Trade Fairs, Conventions and Events)* (Wiesbaden: Gabler), 1181–95.

Putnam, R. D. (1993), *Making Democracy Work: Civic Traditions in Modern Italy* (Princeton: Princeton University Press).

——(1995), Bowling alone: America's declining social capital, *Journal of Democracy*, 6 (1), 65–78.

Raines, P. (2000), Developing cluster policies in seven European regions, *Regional and Industrial Policy Research Paper* (42; Glasgow: European Policies Research Center).

——(2001), Local or national competitive advantage? The tensions in cluster development policy, *Regional and Industrial Policy Research Paper* (43; Glasgow: European Policies Research Center).

Rallet, A. and Torre, A. (1999), Is geographical proximity necessary in the innovation networks in the era of global economy?, *Geojournal*, 49, 373–80.

——————(2009), Temporary geographical proximity for business and work coordination: When, how and where?, *SPACES online, Vol. 7, 2009–02* (Toronto, Heidelberg: www.spaces-online.com).

Ratti, R., Bramanti, A., and Gordon, R. (eds.) (1997), *The Dynamics of Innovative Regions: The GREMI Approach* (Aldershot, Brookfield: Ashgate).

Reid, D. (1983), Firm internationalization, transaction costs and strategic choice, *International Marketing Review*, 1, 45–55.

Reid, F. J. M., Ball, L., Morley, A., and Evans, J. (1997), Styles of group discussion in computer-mediated decision making, *British Journal of Social Psychology*, 36 (3), 241–62.

Reihlen, M. and Ringberg, T. (2006), Computer-mediated knowledge systems in consultancy firms: Do they work?, *Research in the Sociology of Organizations*, 24, 317–47.

Rese, M. (2000), Logistische regression, in K. Backhaus, B. Erichson, W. Plinke, and R. Weiber (eds.), *Multivariate Analysemethoden* (Berlin: Springer), 104–44.

Reuber, P. (2002), Die Politische Geographie nach dem Ende des Kalten Krieges – Neue Ansätze und aktuelle Forschungsfelder (New approaches and research fields in political geography after the Cold War), *Geographische Rundschau*, 54 (7–8), 4–9.

Rice, R. E. (1984), Mediated group communication, in R. E. Rice & Associates (ed.), *The New Media: Communication, Research and Technology* (Beverly Hills: Sage), 129–56.

Richardson, H. W. (1978), *Regional Economics* (Urbana, Chicago, London: University of Illinois Press).

Rinallo, D. and Golfetto, F. (2006), Representing markets: The shaping of fashion trends by French and Italian fabric companies, *Industrial Marketing Management*, 35, 856–69.

Roberts, J. (2000), From know-how to show-how? Questioning the role of information and communication technologies in knowledge transfer, *Technology Analysis & Strategic Management*, 12 (4), 429–43.

Roberts, P. and Dowling, G. (2002), Corporate reputation and sustained superior financial performance, *Strategic Management Journal*, 23, 1077–93.

Robinson, W. S. (1950), Ecological correlation and the behaviour of individuals, *American Sociological Review*, 15, 351–7.

Rodríguez-Pose, A. (2001), Killing economic geography by a 'cultural turn' overdose. A reply to Amin and Thrift, *Antipode*, 33 (2), 176–82.

——Storper, M. (2006), Better rules or stronger communities? On the social foundations of institutional change and its economic effects, *Economic Geography*, 82 (1), 1–25.

Romer, P. (1994), The origins of endogenous growth, *Journal of Economic Perspectives*, 8 (1), 3–22.

Romo, F. P. and Schwartz, M. (1995), The structural embeddedness of business decisions: The migration of manufacturing plants in New York State, 1960–1985, *American Sociological Review*, 60, 874–907.

Roos, M. W. M. (2005), How important is geography for agglomeration?, *Journal of Economic Geography*, 5 (5), 605–20.

Rosenfeld, S. (2007), *Cluster-Based Strategies for Growing State Economies* (Washington, DC: National Governors Association and Council on Competitiveness).

Rosson, P. J. and Seringhaus, F. H. R. (1995), Visitor and exhibitor interaction at industrial trade fairs, *Journal of Business Research*, 32, 81–90.

Rowley, T., Behrens, D., and Krackhardt, D. (2000), Redundant governance structures: An analysis of relational and structural embeddedness in the steel and semiconductor industries, *Strategic Management Journal*, 21, 369–86.

Rubalcaba, L. (1999), *Business Services in European Industry: Growth, Employment and Competitiveness* (Brussels: European Commission).

Rugman, A. M. (1980), Internalization as a general theory of foreign direct investment: A reappraisal of the literature, *Weltwirtschaftliches Archiv*, 116, 365–79.

Samie, S. (1999), The internationalization of services: Trends, obstacles and issues, *Journal of Services Marketing*, 13, 319–28.

Sampson, G. P. and Snape, R. H. (1985), Identifying the issues of trade in services, *World Economy*, 8, 171–82.

Sánchez Hernández, J. L. (2003), *Naturaleza, localización y sociedad: Tres enfoques para la geografía económica* (Salamanca: Ediciones Universidad de Salamanca).

——Aparicio Amador, J., and Alonso Santos, J. L. (2010), The shift between worlds of production as an innovative process in the wine industry in Castile and Leon (Spain), *Geoforum*, 41 (3), 469–78.

Sandefur, R. L. and Laumann, E. O. (1998), A paradigm for social capital, *Rationality and Society*, 10, 481–501.

Sandmüller, M. (2008), Globale Netzwerke und regionale Einbettung: Das Fallbeispiel der Behringwerke Marburg (Global networks and regional embeddedness: The case of the Behring Works in Marburg), *SPACES online, Vol. 6, 2008–02* (Toronto, Heidelberg: www.spaces-online.com).

Sassen, S. (1994), *Cities in a World Economy* (Sociology for a New Century; Thousand Oaks, CA: Pine Forge Press).

Saunders, P. (1989), Space, urbanism and the created environment, in D. Held and J. B. Thompson (eds.), *Social Theory of Modern Societies: Anthony Giddens and his Critics* (Cambridge: Cambridge University Press), 215–34.

Saxenian, A. L. (1994), *Regional Advantage: Culture and Competition in Silicon Valley and Route 128* (Cambridge, MA, London: Harvard University Press).

Sayer, A. (1985), The difference that space makes, in D. Gregory and J. Urry (eds.), *Social Relations and Spatial Structures* (Basingstoke: Macmillan), 49–66.

——(1992), *Method in Social Science* (London: Routledge).

——(1995), *Radical Political Economy* (London, New York: Sage).

——(2000), *Realism and Social Science* (London: Sage).

——(2001), For a critical cultural political economy, *Antipode*, 33, 687–708.

Sayer, R. A. and Walker, R. (1992), *The New Social Economy: Reworking the Division of Labor* (Cambridge, MA: Blackwell).

Schamp, E. W. (1986), Industriestandort und Wirtschaftsdienste im ländlichen Raum. Zum Reichweitenmuster der Dienstleistungsnachfrage von Industrieunternehmen in Niedersachsen, *Berichte zur deutschen Landeskunde*, 60, 201–26.

Schamp, E. W. (2000a), *Vernetzte Produktion. Industriegeographie aus institutioneller Perspektive* (Darmstadt: Wissenschaftliche Buchgesellschaft).

——(2000b), Decline and renewal in industrial districts: Exit strategies of SMEs in consumer goods industrial districts of Germany, in E. Vatne and M. Taylor (eds.), *The Networked Firm in a Global World: Small Firms in New Environments* (Aldershot: Ashgate), 257–81.

——(2002), Evolution und Institution als Grundlage einer dynamischen Wirtschaftsgeographie. Die Bedeutung von externen Skalenerträgen für geographische Konzentration, *Geographische Zeitschrift*, 90 (1), 40–51.

——(2003), Raum, Interaktion und Institution. Anmerkungen zu drei Grundperspektiven der deutschen Wirtschaftsgeographie, *Zeitschrift für Wirtschaftsgeographie*, 47, 145–58.

——(2005), Cluster und Netzwerke als Werkzeuge der regionalen Entwicklungspolitik, in O. Cernavin, M. Führ, M. Kaltenbach, and F. Thießen (eds.), *Cluster und Wettbewerbsfähigkeit von Regionen. Erfolgsfaktoren regionaler Wirtschaftsentwicklung* (Berlin: Duncker & Humblodt), 91–110.

Scharrer, J. (2000), *Internationalisierung und Länderselektion. Eine empirische Analyse mittelständischer Unternehmen in Bayern. Wirtschaft und Raum, Band 7* (München: V. Florentz).

Schätzl, L. (1978), *Wirtschaftsgeographie 1: Theorie* (Paderborn: Schöningh).

——(1998), *Wirtschaftsgeographie 1: Theorie* (7th edn.; Paderborn, München, Wien: UTB Schöningh).

Schickhoff, I. (1985), Dienstleistungen für Industrieunternehmen: Einflüsse von Unternehmens- und Standorteigenschaften auf die Reichweite ausgewählter industrieller Dienstleistungsverflechtungen, *Erdkunde*, 39, 73–84.

Schoenberger, E. (1997), *The Cultural Crisis of the Firm* (Cambridge, MA; Oxford: Blackwell).

Schuldt, N. and Bathelt, H. (2008), *Practices of Global Buzz*, Annual meeting of the Association of American Geographers (Boston).

Scitovsky, T. (1954), Two concepts of external economies, *The Journal of Political Economy*, 62 (2), 143–51.

Scott, A. J. (1988), *New Industrial Spaces: Flexible Production Organization and Regional Development in North America and Western Europe* (Studies in Society and Space 3; London: Pion).

——(1998), *Regions and the World Economy: The Coming Shape of Global Production, Competition, and Political Order* (Oxford, New York: Oxford University Press).

——(2000a), *The Cultural Economy of Cities* (London: Sage).

——(2000b), Economic geography: The great half-century, *Cambridge Journal of Economics*, 24, 483–504.

——(2002), A new map of Hollywood: The production and distribution of American motion pictures, *Regional Studies*, 36, 957–76.

——(2004), A perspective of economic geography, *Journal of Economic Geography*, 4 (5), 479–99.

——(2006), Entrepreneurship, innovation and industrial development: Geography and the creative field revisited, *Small Business Economics*, 26 (1), 1–24.

Scott, J. (2000), *Social Network Analysis. A Handbook* (2nd edn.; London: Sage).

——(2001), *Power* (Cambridge, Oxford: Polity Press).

Setterfield, M. (1993), A model of institutional hysteresis, *Journal of Economic Issues*, 27, 755–74.

Shanghai Chemical Industry Park Development Corp. (2005), *Shanghai Chemical Industry Park – Brochure* (Shanghai: Shanghai Chemical Industry Park Development Corp.).

——(2007), *Shanghai Chemical Industry Park* (Shanghai: Shanghai Chemical Industry Park Development Corp.).

Shanghai Economic Commission (2004), *Shanghai Municipal Statistics Bureau, and Shanghai Development Park Association (2004), 2004 Shanghai Development Park Annual (in Chinese)* (Shanghai).

——(2007), *2007 Shanghai Development Park Statistical Manual* (in Chinese) (Shanghai).

Shapiro, C. (1982), Consumer information, product quality, and seller reputation, *Bell Journal of Economics*, 13 (1), 20–35.

——(1983), Premiums for high quality products as return to reputation, *Quarterly Journal of Economics*, 98, 659–79.

Shapiro, P. P. (1987), The social control of impersonal trust, *American Journal of Sociology*, 93, 623–58.

Sharland, A. and Balogh, P. (1996), The value of nonselling activities at international trade shows, *Industrial Marketing Management*, 25, 59–66.

Sharma, D. D. and Johanson, J. (1987), Technical consultancy in internationalisation, *International Marketing Review*, 4 (Winter), 20–9.

Sheppard, E. and Barnes, T. J. (2000), *A Companion to Economic Geography* (Oxford, Malden: Blackwell).

Short, J., Williams, E., and Christie, B. (1976), *The Social Psychology of Telecommunications* (New York: Wiley).

Simmie, J. (2003), Innovation and urban regions as national and international nodes for the transfer and sharing of knowledge, *Regional Studies*, 37, 607–20.

——(2006), Do clusters or innovation systems drive competitiveness?, in B. Asheim, P. Cooke, and R. Martin (eds.), *Clusters and Regional Development: Critical Reflections and Explorations* (London, New York: Routledge), 164–87.

Skocpol, T. (1979), *States and Social Revolutions: A Comparative Analysis of France, Russia and China* (Cambridge: Cambridge University Press).

Skov, L. (2006), The role of trade fairs in the global fashion business, *Current Sociology*, 54, 764–83.

Smith, A. (2003), Power relations, industrial clusters, and regional transformations: Pan-European integration and outward processing in the Slovak clothing industry, *Economic Geography*, 79, 17–40.

Smith, D. A. and Timberlake, M. (1995), Conceptualising and mapping the structure of the world system's city system, *Urban Studies*, 32, 287–302.

——White, D. (1992), Structure and dynamics of the global economy: Network analysis of international trade 1965–1980, *Social Forces*, 70, 857–93.

Snijders, T. A. and Borgatti, S. P. (1999), Non-parametric standard errors and tests for network statistics, *Connections*, 22 (2), 61–70.

Sofer, M. and Schnell, I. (2002), Over- and under-embeddedness: Failures in developing mixed embeddedness among Israeli Arab entrepreneurs, in M. Taylor and S. Leonard (eds.), *Embedded Enterprise and Social Capital: International Perspectives* (Aldershot: Ashgate), 207–24.

Sölvell, Ö., Lindquist, G., and Ketels, C. (2003), *The Cluster Initiative Greenbook* (Stockholm: Ivory Tower).

Song, M., Berends, H., van der Bij, H., and Weggeman, M. (2007), The effects of IT and co-location on knowledge dissemination, *The Journal of Product Innovation Management*, 24 (1), 52–68.

Sorenson, O. (2005), Social networks, informational complexity and industrial geography, in D. B. Audretsch, D. Fornahl, and C. Zellner (eds.), *The Role of Labour Mobility and Informal Networks for Knowledge Transfer* (New York: Springer), 79–95.

Spencer, C. S. (2010), Territorial expansion and primary state formation, *PNAS*, 107, 7119–26.

Sproull, L. and Kiesler, S. (1991), *Connections: New Ways of Working in the Networked Organization* (Cambridge, MA: MIT Press).

Stabell, C. and Fjeldstad, Ø. (1998), Configuring value for competitive advantage: On chains, shops, and networks, *Strategic Management Journal*, 19, 413–37.

Staber, U. (1996), The social embeddedness of industrial district networks, in U. Staber, N. Schaefer, and B. Sharma (eds.), *Business Networks. Prospects for Regional Development* (Berlin, New York: De Gruyter), 148–74.

Stachels, E. (2005), Bayer – A multinational committed to China, in G. Festel, A. Kreimeyer, U. Oels, and M. v. Zedtwitz (eds.), *The Chemical and Pharmaceutical Industry in China: Opportunities and Threats to Foreign Companies* (Heidelberg: Springer), 181–8.

Stark, D. (2000), *For a Sociology of Worth*, conference on economic sociology at the edge of the third millennium (Moscow).

Sternberg, R. and Arndt, O. (2001), The firm or the region: What determines the innovation behavior of European firms?, *Economic Geography*, 77, 364–82.

——Litzenberger, T. (2004), Regional clusters in Germany – Their geography and their relevance for entrepreneurial activities, *European Planning Studies*, 6, 767–91.

Stigler, G. J. (1951), The division of labor is limited by the extent of the market, *The Journal of Political Economy*, 59, 185–93.

Stiglitz, J. (2006), *Making Globalization Work* (New York: W. W. Norton and Company).

Stinchcombe, A. L. (1965), Social structure and organization, in J. G. March (ed.), *Handbook of Organizations* (Chicago: Rad McNelly), 142–93.

Storper, M. (1993), Regional 'worlds' of production: Learning and innovation in the technology districts of France, Italy and the USA, *Regional Studies*, 27, 433–55.

——(1995), The resurgence of regional economics, ten years later, *European Urban and Regional Studies*, 2, 191–221.

——(1997a), Territories, flows, and hierarchies in the global economy, in K. R. Cox (ed.), *Spaces of Globalization. Reasserting the Power of the Local* (New York, London: Guilford), 19–44.

——(1997b), Regional economies as relational assets, in R. Lee and J. Wills (eds.), *Geographies of Economies* (London, New York, Sydney: Arnold), 248–58.

——(1997c), *The Regional World: Territorial Development in a Global Economy* (New York: Guilford Press).

——(2004), *Institutions, Incentives and Communication in Economic Geography* (Hettner-Lectures 2003; Wiesbaden: Franz Steiner Verlag).

——(2009), *Regional Context and Global Trade Paper*, presented in the seminar on 'Innovation and Governance' at the University of Toronto (Toronto).

——Venables, A. J. (2002), Buzz: The economic force of the city, *DRUID summer conference on 'Industrial Dynamics of the New and Old Economy – Who is Embracing Whom?'* (Copenhagen, Elsinore).

————(2004), Buzz: face-to-face contact and the urban economy, *Journal of Economic Geography*, 4 (4), 351–70.

————Walker, R. (1989), *The Capitalist Imperative: Territory, Technology, and Industrial Growth* (New York: Blackwell).

Strambach, S. (1994), Knowledge intensive business services in the Rhine-Neckar area, *Tijdschrift voor Economische en Sociale Geografie*, 85, 354–65.

————(1995), *Wissensintensive unternehmensorientierte Dienstleistungen: Netzwerke und Interaktion* (Münster: Lit).

————(2004), Wissensökonomie, organisatorischer Wandel und wissensbasierte Regionalentwicklung – Herausforderungen für die Wirtschaftsgeographie, *Zeitschrift für Wirtschaftsgeographie*, 1–18.

Strandskov, J. (1993), Towards a new approach for studying the internationalization process of firms, in P. J. Buckley and P. N. Ghauri (eds.), *The Internationalization of the Firm: A Reader* (London: Academic Press), 201–16.

Strauss, K. (2008), Re-engaging with rationality in economic geography: Behavioural approaches and the importance of context in decision-making, *Journal of Economic Geography*, 8, 137–56.

Streeck, W. and Thelen, K. (2005), Introduction, in W. Streeck and K. Thelen (eds.), *Beyond Continuity: Institutional Change in Advanced Political Economies* (Oxford: Oxford University Press), 1–39.

Strothamm, K.-H. (1992), Segmentorientierte Messepolitik (Segmented trade fair policy), in K.-H. Strothmann and M. Busche (eds.), *Handbuch Messemarketing (Handbook of Trade Fair Marketing)* (Wiesbaden: Gabler), 99–115.

Sun, Y. and Wen, K. (2007), Uncertainties, imitating behaviors and foreign R&D locations: Explaining the over-concentration of foreign R&D in Beijing and Shanghai within China, *Asia Pacific Business Review*, 13, 405–24.

Sunley, P. (1996), Context in economic geography: The relevance of pragmatism, *Progress in Human Geography*, 20, 338–55.

————(2008), Relational economic geography: A practical understanding or a new paradigm? *Economic Geography*, 84, 1–26.

Swain, A. (2006), Soft capitalism and a hard industry: Virtualism, the 'transition industry' and the restructuring of the Ukrainian coal industry, *Transactions of the Institute of British Geographers*, NS 31, 208–23.

Swedberg, R. and Granovetter, M. (1992), Introduction, in M. Granovetter and R. Swedberg (eds.), *The Sociology of Economic Life* (Oxford: Westview Press), 1–26.

Swyngedouw, E. (1997), Neither global nor local: 'Glocalization' and the politics of scale, in K. R. Cox (ed.), *Spaces of Globalization: Reasserting the Power of the Local* (New York, London: Guilford), 137–66.

Szulanski, G. (1996), Exploring internal stickiness: Impediments to the transfer of best practice within the firm, *Strategic Management Journal*, 17, 27–43.

————(2003), *Sticky Knowledge. Barriers to Knowing in the Firm* (London: Sage).

————Jensen, R. J. (2004), Overcoming stickiness: An empirical investigation of the role of the template in the replication of organizational routines, *Managerial and Decision Economics*, 25 (6/7), 347–63.

Tansey, R., White, M., Long, R. G., and Smith, M. (1996), A comparison of loglinear modelling and logistic regression in management research, *Journal of Management*, 22, 339–58.

Taylor, M. J. (1995), The business enterprise, power and patterns of geographical industrialisation, in S. Conti, E. J. Malecki, and P. Oinas (eds.), *The Industrial Enterprise and its Environment: Spatial Perspectives* (Aldershot: Ashgate), 99–122.

——(1999), The small firm as a temporary coalition, *Entrepreneurship and Regional Development*, 11, 1–19.

——(2000a), Industrialisation, enterprise power, and environmental change: An exploration of concepts, *Environment and Planning A*, 28, 1035–51.

——(2000b), Enterprise, power and embeddedness: An empirical exploration, in E. Vatne and M. Taylor (eds.), *The Networked Firm in a Global World: Small Firms in New Environments* (Aldershot, Burlington: Ashgate), 199–233.

——(2004), The firm as a connected, temporary coalition, *SPACES, Vol. 2, 2004–05* (Marburg: Faculty of Geography, Philipps-University of Marburg).

Taylor, P. J. (2004), *World City Network: A Global Urban Analysis* (London, New York: Routledge).

——Hoyler, M. (2000), The spatial order of European cities under conditions of contemporary globalisation, *Tijdschrift voor Economische en Sociale Geografie*, 91, 176–89.

——Catalano, G., and Walker, D. R. F. (2002), Measurement of the world city network, *Urban Studies*, 39, 2367–76.

Terpstra, V. and Yu, C.-M. (1990), Piggybacking: A quick road to internationalism, *International Marketing Review*, 7 (4), 52–63.

Ter Wal, A. L. J. and Boschma, R. A. (2009), Applying social network analysis in economic geography: Framing some key analytic issues, *The Annals of Regional Science*, 43 (3), 739–56.

Thelen, K. (2003), How institutions evolve: Insights from comparative historical analyses, in J. Mahoney and D. Rueschemeyer (eds.), *Comparative Historical Analyses in the Social Sciences* (Cambridge: Cambridge University Press), 208–40.

Thompson, J. B. (1989), The theory of structuration, in D. Held and J. B. Thompson (eds.), *Social Theory of Modern Societies: Anthony Giddens and his Critics* (Cambridge: Cambridge University Press), 56–76.

Thrift, N. (1990), For a new regional geography 1, *Progress in Human Geography*, 14, 272–7.

——(1996), *Spatial Formations* (London: Sage).

——(2000a), Performing cultures in the new economy, *Annals of the Association of American Geographers*, 90, 674–92.

——(2000b), Pandora's box? Cultural geographies of economies, in G. Clark, M. Feldman, and M. Gertler (eds.), *The Oxford Handbook of Economic Geography* (Oxford: Oxford University Press), 689–704.

Tichauer, P. (2005), Chemie für die Turnschuhgeneration: Das Joint Venture von BASF und Sinopec wird zum drittgrößten Chemiestandort der Welt (Chemistry for the sports shoes generation: The joint venture between BASF and Sinopec becomes the third largest in the world), *Asia Bridge*, 1/2005, 23.

Tordoir, P. P. (1994), Transactions of professional business services and spatial systems, *Tijdschrift voor Economische en Sociale Geografie*, 85, 322–32.

Torrance, M. (2009), The rise of a global infrastructure market through relational investing, *Economic Geography*, 85, 75–97.

Torre, A. and Rallet, A. (2005), Proximity and localization, *Regional Studies*, 39 (1), 47–59.

Toulmin, S. (1972), *Human Understanding: The Collective Use and Evolution of Concepts* (Princeton: Princeton University Press).

Tracey, P. and Clark, G. L. (2002), Cognition, learning and European regional growth: An agent-centred perspective on the 'new' economy, in School of Geography and the Environment (ed.), *School of Geography Working Paper 02–10* (Oxford: University of Oxford).

——— (2003), Alliances, networks and competitive strategy: Rethinking clusters of innovation, *Growth and Change*, 34, 1–16.

Trippl, M., Tödtling, F., and Lengauer, L. (2009), Knowledge sourcing beyond buzz and pipelines: Evidence from the Vienna software sector, *Economic Geography*, 85, 443–62.

Tsai, K. S. (2007), *Capitalism Without Democracy: The Private Sector in Contemporary China* (Ithaca: Cornell University Press).

——— (2010), *The Great Socialist Transformation: Capitalism Without Democracy in China* (University of Toronto, Toronto: Munk Centre for International Studies).

Tsai, W. (2001), Knowledge transfer in intra-organizational networks: Effects of network position and absorptive capacity on business unit innovation and performance, *Academy of Management Journal*, 44, 996–1004.

Turnbull, P. W. (1993), A challenge to the stages theory of the internationalization process, in P. J. Buckley and P. N. Ghauri (eds.), *The Internationalization of the Firm: A Reader* (London: Academic Press), 172–85.

Uzzi, B. (1996), The sources and consequences of embeddedness for the economic performance of organizations: The network effect, *American Sociological Review*, 61, 674–98.

——— (1997), Social structure and competition in interfirm networks: The paradox of embeddedness, *Administrative Science Quarterly*, 42, 35–67.

——— Gillespie, J. J. (2002), Knowledge spillover in corporate financing networks: Embeddedness and the firms's debt performance, *Strategic Management Journal*, 23, 595–618.

——— Lancaster, R. (2003), Relational embeddedness and learning: The case of bank loan managers and their clients, *Management Science*, 49 (4), 383–99.

van den Berg, L., Braun, E., and van Winden, W. (2001), *Growth Clusters in European Metropolitan Cities. A Comparative Analysis of Cluster Dynamics in the Cities of Amsterdam, Eindhoven, Helsinki, Leipzig, Lyons, Manchester, Munich, Rotterdam and Vienna* (Aldershot, Burlington, VT: Ashgate).

van den Bosch, F. A. J., Volberda, H. W., and de Boer, M. (1999), Coevolution of firm absorptive capacity and knowledge environment: Organizational forms and combinative capabilities, *Organizational Science*, 10, 551–68.

van Wezemael, J. (2004), Erkenntnis und Interesse: Zur handlungstheoretischen Wirtschaftsgeographie am Beispiel der Sanierung genossenschaftlicher Wohnbauten (Towards an agency-based conceptualisation of economic geography: The case of housing co-operatives), *Geographica Helvetica*, 59, 81–92.

Vandermerwe, S. and Chadwick, M. (1989), The internationalization of services, *Service Industries Journal*, 9, 79–93.

von Hippel, E. (1994), 'Sticky information' and the locus of problem solving: Implications for innovation, *Management Science*, 40 (4), 429–39.

——— (2001), Innovation by user communities: Learning from open-source software, *MIT Sloan Management Review*, 42 (2), 82–6.

von Weizsäcker, C. C. (1984), The costs of substitution, *Econometrica*, 52, 1085–116.

Wainfan, L. and Davis, P. K. (2004), *Challenges in Virtual Collaboration: Videoconferencing, Audioconferencing, and Computer-Mediated Communications* (Santa Monica: RAND Corporation).

Walker, R. and Storper, M. (1981), Capital and industrial location, *Progress in Human Geography*, 5, 473–509.

Walther, J. B., Loh, T., and Granka, L. (2005), Let me count the ways: The interchange of verbal and nonverbal cues in computer-mediated and face-to-face affinity, *Journal of Language and Social Psychology*, 24 (1), 36–65.

Wang, X. (1996), Pudong kaifa moshi ying cong 'tudi gundong' zhuanxiang 'shuishou gundong' (The basis of the Pudong model of development: From land to tax reference), *Tansuo Yu Zhengming (Explorations and Free Views)*, 1996 (1), 45–6.

Wang, J. H. and Lee, C. K. (2007), Global production networks and local institution building: The development of the information-technology industry in Suzhou, China, *Environment and Planning A*, 39, 1873–88.

Wasserman, S. and Faust, K. (1994), *Social Network Analysis. Methods and Applications* (Cambridge: Cambridge University Press).

Watzlawick, P., Beavin, J. H., and Jackson, D. D. (2000), *Menschliche Kommunikation – Formen, Störungen, Paradoxien (Human Communication – Forms, Interferences, Contradictions)* (10th edn.; Bern: Huber).

Webb, E. J., Campbell, D. T., Schwartz, R. D., and Sechrest, L. (1965), *Unobtrusive Measures* (Chicago: Rand McNally).

Webber, M. J. and Rigby, D. (1996), *The Golden Age Illusion: Rethinking Postwar Capitalism* (New York: Guilford).

Weber, A. (1909), *Über den Standort der Industrien. Erster Teil: Reine Theorie des Standorts* (Tübingen: Mohr Siebeck).

Wei, Y. D., Li, W., and Wang, C. (2007), Restructuring industrial districts, scaling up regional development: A study of the Wenzhou model, China, *Economic Geography*, 83, 421–44.

Weick, K. E. (1985), Cosmos vs. chaos: Sense and nonsense in electronic contexts, *Organizational Dynamics*, 14 (2), 50–64.

Weigelt, K. and Camerer, C. (1988), Reputation and corporate strategy: A review of recent theory and applications, *Strategic Management Journal*, 9, 443–54.

Wenger, E. C. (1998), *Communities of Practice: Learning, Meaning, and Identity* (Cambridge: Cambridge University Press).

——Snyder, W. M. (2000), Communities of practice: The organizational frontier, *Harvard Business Review*, 78 (1), 139–45.

Wengraf, T. (2001), *Qualitative Research Interviewing: Biographic Narrative and Semi-Structured Methods* (London and Thousand Oaks: Sage).

Werlen, B. (1993), *Society, Action and Space. An Alternative Human Geography* (London: Routledge).

——(1995), *Sozialgeographie alltäglicher Regionalisierungen. Band 1: Zur Ontologie von Gesellschaft und Raum* (Erdkundliches Wissen, Heft 119; Stuttgart: Steiner).

——(2000), *Sozialgeographie: Eine Einführung* (Bern, Stuttgart: UTB – Haupt).

——(2003), Kulturgeographie und kulturtheoretische Wende (Cultural geography and cultural turn), in H. Gebhardt, P. Reuber, and G. Wolkersdorfer (eds.), *Kulturgeographie: Aktuelle Ansätze und Entwicklungen (New Approaches and Developments in Cultural Geography)* (Heidelberg, Berlin: Spektrum), 251–68.

Wernerfelt, B. (1984), A resource-based view of the firm, *Strategic Management Journal*, 5, 171–80.

Westhead, P., Wright, M., Ucbasaran, D., and Martin, F. (2001), International market selection strategies of manufacturing and services firms, *Entrepreneurship & Regional Development*, 13, 17–46.

White, H. C. (2008), *Identity & Control. How Social Formations Emerge* (2nd edn.; Oxford, Princeton: Princeton University Press).

Whitley, R. (1999), *Divergent Capitalisms: The Social Structuring and Change of Business Systems* (Oxford: Oxford University Press).

Wickham, J. and Vecchi, A. (2008), Local firms and global reach: Business air travel and the Irish software cluster, *European Planning Studies*, 16, 693–710.

Williamson, O. E. (1975), *Markets and Hierarchies: Analysis and Anti-Trust Implications* (New York: Free Press).

——(1979), Transaction-cost economics: The governance of contractual relations, *Journal of Law and Economics*, 22, 233–61.

——(1981), The economics of organizations: The transaction cost approach, *American Journal of Sociology*, 87, 548–77.

——(1985), *The Economic Institutions of Capitalism. Firms, Markets, Relational Contracting* (New York: Free Press).

Winchester, H. (1999), Interviews and questionnaires as mixed methods in population geography: The case of lone fathers in Newcastle, Australia, *Professional Geographer*, 51, 60–7.

Wolfe, D. A. and Gertler, M. S. (2004), Clusters from the inside and out: Local dynamics and global linkages, *Urban Studies*, 41, 1071–93.

Wood, P. (1996), Business services, the management of change and regional development in the UK: A corporate client perspective, *Transactions of the Institute of British Geographers*, 21, 644–65.

——(2002*a*), European consultancy growth: Nature, causes and consequences, in P. Wood (ed.), *Consultancy and Innovation: The Business Service Revolution in Europe* (London, New York: Routledge), 35–71.

——(ed.) (2002*b*), *Consultancy and Innovation: The Business Service Revolution in Europe* (London, New York: Routledge).

Wrigley, N. (1985), *Categorical Data Analysis for Geographers and Environmental Scientists* (London: Longman).

Yeung, H. W.-c. (1994), Critical reviews of geographical perspectives on business organizations and the organization of production: Towards a network approach, *Progress in Human Geography*, 18, 460–90.

——(1997), Critical realism and realist research in human geography: A method or a philosophy in search of a method, *Progress in Human Geography*, 21, 51–74.

——(1998), The socio-spatial constitution of business organizations: A geographical perspective, *Organization*, 5, 101–28.

——(2003), Practicing new economic geographies: A methodological examination, *Annals of the Association of American Geographers*, 93, 442–62.

——(2005), Rethinking relational economic geography, *Transactions of the Institute of British Geographers*, 30 (1), 37–51.

Yeung, H. W.-c. (2009), Transnational corporations, global production networks, and urban and regional development: A geographer's perspective on multinational enterprises and the global economy, *Growth and Change*, 40, 197–226.

——Lin, G. C. S. (2003), Theorizing economic geographies of Asia, *Economic Geography*, 79, 107–28.

Young, S. (1987), Business strategy and the internationalization of business: Recent approaches, *Managerial and Decision Economics*, 8, 31–40.

Zademach, H.-M. and Haas, H.-D. (2008), Außenwirtschaftliche Verflechtungen Bayerns – von vollen Tönen und dem Echo ferner Klänge, *Geographische Rundschau*, 60 (10).

Zahra, S. A. and George, G. (2002), Absorptive capacity: A review, reconceptualization, and extension, *Academy of Management Review*, 27, 185–203.

Zeller, C. (2001), *Globalisierungsstrategien – Der Weg von Novartis* (Berlin, Heidelberg, New York: Springer).

——Messerli, P. (2004), Transition zur relationalen Wirtschaftsgeographie (Transition toward relational economic geography), *Geographische Zeitschrift*, 91, 57–60.

Zeng, G. (2000), The financial crisis in Asia and the modification of economic structure in Shanghai (in Chinese), *Asian Geographer*, 19, 37–48.

——(2001), Shi gongye buju tiaozhen chu Tan (Research on the modification of industrial spatial distribution in Shanghai), *Geographical Research*, 20 (3), 330–7.

——Bathelt, H. (2010), Divergent growth trajectories in China's chemical industry: The case of the newly developed industrial parks in Shanghai, Nanjing and Ningbo, *GeoJournal*, 60.

Zhong, H. (2007), Shiyiwu kaiju de Jiangsu huaxue gongye (The development of the chemical industry in the Jiangsu province in the eleventh five-year period), *Jiangsu Huagong (Jiangsu Chemical Industry)*, 35 (3), 20–4.

Ziegler, R. (1992), Messen – ein makroökonomisches Subsystem (Trade fairs as a macroeconomic subsystem), in K.-H. Strothmann and M. Busche (eds.), *Handbuch Messemarketing (Handbook of Trade Fair Marketing)* (Wiesbaden: Gabler), 115–26.

Zucker, L. G. (1986), Production of trust: Institutional sources of economic structure, 1840–1920, *Research in Organizational Behavior*, 8, 53–111.

Zukin, S. and DiMaggio, P. (1990), Introduction, in S. Zukin and P. DiMaggio (eds.), *Structures of Capital: The Social Organization of the Economy* (Cambridge: Cambridge University Press), 1–36.

Zundler, A. W. and Tesche, M. (2003), Maßnahmen zur effizienten Vor- und Nachbereitung von Messeauftritten (Efficient ways to prepare and analyze trade fair participation), in M. Kirchgeorg, W. M. Dornscheidt, W. Giese, and N. Stoeck (eds.), *Handbuch Messemanagement: Planung, Durchführung und Kontrolle von Messen, Kongressen und Events (Handbook of Trade Fair Management: Planning, Execution and Control of Trade Fairs, Conventions and Events)* (Wiesbaden: Gabler), 1163–80.

■ INDEX

Figures and tables indexed in bold.